The Changing Role of
Women in Bengal,
1849-1905

The
Changing Role of
Women in Bengal
1849-1905

BY MEREDITH BORTHWICK

PRINCETON UNIVERSITY PRESS

PRINCETON, N.J.

All Rights Reserved
Library of Congress Cataloging in Publication Data will be
found on the last printed page of this book
ISBN 0-691-05409-6

Publication of this book has been aided by a grant from
The Whitney Darrow Fund of
Princeton University Press

This book has been composed in Linotron Sabon

Clothbound editions of Princeton University Press books
are printed on acid-free paper, and binding materials are
chosen for strength and durability. Paperbacks,
while satisfactory for personal collections, are not
usually suitable for library rebinding.

Printed in the United States of America by
Princeton University Press
Princeton, New Jersey

History scarcely mentions her. . . . Occasionally an individual woman is mentioned, an Elizabeth, or a Mary; a queen or a great lady. But by no possible means could middle-class women with nothing but brains and character at their command have taken part in any one of the great movements which, brought together, constitute the historian's view of the past. Nor shall we find her in any collection of anecdotes. . . . She never writes her own life and scarcely keeps a diary; there are only a handful of her letters in existence. She left no plays or poems by which we can judge her. What one wants, I thought—and why does not some brilliant student at Newnham or Girton supply it?—is a mass of information; at what age did she marry; how many children had she as a rule; what was her house like; had she a room to herself; did she do the cooking; would she be likely to have a servant? . . . It would be ambitious beyond my daring, . . . to suggest to the students of those famous colleges that they should rewrite history, though I own that it often seems a little queer as it is, unreal, lopsided; but why should they not add a supplement to history? calling it, of course, by some inconspicuous name so that women might figure there without impropriety?

Virginia Woolf, *A Room of One's Own*, 1928

Contents

List of Illustrations

List of Tables

Preface

The nineteenth century in Bengal was a time of great intellectual excitement. Accepted values were closely questioned as part of the reaction to changes brought about by the imposition of colonial rule. There was heated debate among men on matters such as widow burning, child marriage, the status of women, and the merits and demerits of female education. The intensity and volume of this debate has diverted inquiry from the extent to which the ultimate objects of the debate, women, participated in the process of change, or whether their lives were significantly affected by it. This book is part of the slow process of "redressing the balance" in historical writing on India, an attempt to reassess the much-vaunted "emancipation of women" in the nineteenth century from the perspective of women themselves, and thus illumine our understanding of the process of social change under colonial rule.

The *bhadramahilā*, the subject of this book, were, in broad terms, the mothers, wives, and daughters of the many schoolmasters, lawyers, doctors, and government servants who made up the English-educated professional Bengali "middle class" or *bhadralok*. The impact of change in the lives of these women was not always dramatic—education broadened their horizons; developments in such areas of health care as childbirth ameliorated some of the hardships of their lives—but a necessary process of adaptation was taking place between the framework of ideals imposed by the colonizing power and the more resistant of indigenous cultural values. Inevitably, such progress was accompanied by losses as well as gains.

Conventional historical sources, concerned with public life, are of only marginal use in research in this uncharted area. A series of journals for and by women, beginning with the *Māsik Patrikā* in 1854 and leading up to *Antahpur* in 1898, which was "edited and conducted by the ladies only," formed the core of my source material. Many of these ran for a few years at a stretch, and often only a few scattered issues are extant. However, the *Bāmābodhinī Patrikā*, started in 1863, continued uninterrupted for the next forty-two years. Fortunately, I was able to piece together a complete set through the combined resources of the British Museum, the National Library in Calcutta, and the Ramakrishna Mission Library. The journals covered a vast range of subjects concerning women, or of interest to them. They set up ideals of behavior and attempted to mold attitudes; published women's writings, literary and otherwise; and carried informative articles on history, travel, science, news, household duties, medicine, and cookery. Admittedly, the purpose of the journals was to instruct, and therefore they do not necessarily reflect social reality; but they were certainly crucial in propagating the *bhadramahilā* ideal. Circulation figures indicate that they were widely read, and women's keenness to participate in the journals as subscribers or contributors demonstrates that they also provided an important means of communication among women, and performed a mediating function with the outside world.

Biographies and autobiographies were fruitful sources of information. Although many displayed a tendency to idealize, they also provided a wealth of detail about lifestyle, feelings, and emotions. Instructive literature was examined for information on sexual relations, pregnancy, child rearing, medical treatment, and allied domestic subjects. Again, this was largely prescriptive material, but corroborative evidence was found to show that advice given in manuals was often followed. Moreover, these manuals also gave some insight into the values of the authors and their vision of an ideal society.

I had hoped to be able to locate more collections of private papers, but found that very few have been preserved. The type of materials by women that had been kept by their families were assorted memorabilia—books, scrapbooks, and songbooks—that I made some use of. I also conducted a number of interviews with women who were born either before 1905 or shortly after, in order to gain an immediate sense of the changes that had taken place and how women perceived them.

Although I provided a list of questions, the interviews were conducted informally, following leads given by interviewees. In this way, I was privileged to share memories that often illuminated in a very personal way the issues I was dealing with.

My choice of the dates 1849 to 1905 may need a word of explanation. The first government school for girls was founded in 1849, and 1905 was the year of the partition of Bengal and the beginning of the *swadeshi* movement. As domestic history is a process of gradual change, not clearly marked by public events, these dates have to be regarded as convenient cut-off points rather than definite limits. Only a handful of women were directly affected by the opening of the Bethune School in 1849, but in the long term, literacy and education had a profound effect on the position of women. 1905 was not a crucial year for most *bhadramahilā*, but it represented the beginning of a significant interest among women in political activities.

It is hoped that this study will provide some insight into the position of women in India today. During the latter part of the nineteenth century, there was a gradual growth in awareness of outside activities, which made it possible for women to become prominent in public life in this century. Traditional domestic roles were modified to enable women to engage in public activity, without a radical redefinition of female roles. The progressive model of public participation for women that has generally been followed had its roots in the period of this study.

I am aware of many gaps and limitations in the book that, for reasons of time and space, have been unavoidable. The Bengali Muslim *bhadramahilā* has not been mentioned, and deserves a separate study. The importance of religion in a woman's life has only been touched upon. The fertile field of literary works by and for women should be analyzed in order to extend our understanding of their consciousness and "inner life." I hope that the present work will help to generate interest in women's history among scholars of South Asia, and that they will proceed with further research into other aspects of women's lives.

The experience of working on the lives of women cross-culturally has been a rich and rewarding one, forcing me continually to reexamine my own values and assumptions. I am grateful to the *bhadramahilā* for providing me with that opportunity.

Acknowledgments

This book is based on my doctoral thesis, for which I was awarded a degree in Asian Studies from the Australian National University in April 1981. Research was carried out in Calcutta, London, Canberra, and Melbourne from 1977 to 1980. It would not have been possible without the help and attention given by librarians and library assistants in these places. Eight months were spent working in Calcutta, where the bulk of my research was carried out in the pleasant surroundings of the National Library. I was fortunate in that the library of the Ramakrishna Mission, where I was staying, held an almost complete set of the *Bāmābodhinī Patrikā*, the main women's journal used, and that the librarian gave me permission to microfilm some of their holdings. I am grateful to Sri Dilip Biswas for letting me have access to the S. D. Collet collection of books and manuscripts held in the Sadharan Brahmo Samaj Library. I obtained some material at the Bangiya Sahitya Parisad Library in north Calcutta, and also found a few useful items in the Jaykrishna Mukherjee Library at Utterpara. Dr. Manashi Dasgupta arranged for me to see private papers belonging to some members of the Tagore family at Rabindra Bhavan Library at Visvabharati University, Santiniketan. During three weeks in London I worked in the Oriental Manuscripts Reading Room of the British Museum, and in the India Office Library.

In Australia, there was a great deal of relevant official government material at the Victorian State Library, and a diverse assortment of literature from nineteenth-century Bengal in the Benoy Ghose Collection in the Baillieu Library, University of Melbourne. Census reports and reports of native newspapers were consulted at the National Library of Australia. All other material was obtained from the Menzies Library, Australian National University. I am grateful to staff there for arranging interlibrary loans and for ordering microfilm.

ACKNOWLEDGMENTS

I was financially assisted in carrying out my research through a Commonwealth Post-graduate Research Award. This was supplemented by a travel grant from the Faculty of Asian Studies that enabled me to travel to Calcutta and London. The manuscript was completed during my term as Third Secretary in the Australian Embassy, Bangkok.

Many people have contributed to the progress of the book by commenting on early drafts. I am indebted to the two supervisors of my doctoral thesis, Dr. S. N. Mukherjee and Dr. J.T.F. Jordens, for their encouragement, help, and intellectual inspiration throughout. In addition, I would especially like to thank Professor Barun De, Professor J. H. Broomfield, Dr. Stephen Henningham, Dr. Tapan Raychaudhuri, Dr. Hiren Chakrabarti, Dr. John McGuire, Dr. Gail Minault, and Dr. Dipesh Chakrabarty, for their patience in reading through part or all of my material and for their comments and criticism. Dr. Margaret Case, of Princeton University Press, gave helpful editorial comments. I would like to take this opportunity to acknowledge my debt to S. N. Ray, former head of the Department of Indian Studies, University of Melbourne, for arousing my interest in Indian history generally and Bengal studies in particular. Professor A. L. Basham, former head of the Department of Asian Civilizations, Australian National University, was unfailingly kind and encouraging.

A number of people gave me access to references or material that I would not otherwise have come across. I extend my thanks for this to Pauline Rule, Mr. and Mrs. A. K. Moitra, Sati Kumar Chatterjee, Dr. Gholam Murshid, Santa Deb, Dr. Manashi Dasgupta, Sanjay Sircar, Dr. Gail Pearson, and Arundhati Mukherjee. Apart from this, I am grateful to many others in Calcutta who arranged for me to interview members of their families, and to those who granted me interviews. I enjoyed listening to their reminiscences, and would like to extend my special thanks to them for helping to bring the subject to life, providing me with a sense of continuity between the *bhadramahilā* of the nineteenth century and of the present day.

Many Bengali speakers helped me in my attempts to capture

ACKNOWLEDGMENTS

the nuances of the language in translation. Their advice was invaluable. I am grateful to Margaret Tie, Faculty of Asian Studies, and Lyn Hayes, Australian Embassy, Bangkok, for typing an often confusing manuscript so ably.

Finally I would like to thank my parents, Alex and Rosemary Borthwick, for fostering my spirit of enquiry into the world in general and Asia especially; my husband, John Hannoush, for his help in proofreading and constant encouragement; and our son Theo, for providing diversion from academic pursuits.

Note on Transliteration

As there are numerous Bengali references throughout the book, an explanation of the transliteration system I used is required. All Bengali words are italicized in the text, except for those that have been accepted into the English language (such as pandit, purdah). Whereas in some cases the common Anglicized spelling has been used (*mofussil, zamindar, zenana*), in all other instances I have attempted to give a literal transliteration. However, for reasons of convenience I have omitted all diacritical marks except to distinguish between long and short vowels. Diacritics have only been employed for Bengali words and phrases, and for titles of books, journals, and newspapers. I have not used diacritics for any proper nouns—names of persons, places, or associations—as in many cases a variety of Anglicized spellings, more familiar to the reader, were adopted in the nineteenth century. In the footnotes and bibliography, the full name and surname of authors writing in Bengali have been given, but initials have been substituted for the first names of authors writing in English.

List of Abbreviations

BP	*Bāmābodhinī Patrikā*
CR	*Calcutta Review*
GRPI	*General Report on Public Instruction in the Lower Provinces of the Bengal Presidency*
IMS	*Indian Mirror, Sunday edition*
RNNB	*Report on Native Newspapers, Bengal*

The Changing Role of
Women in Bengal,
1849-1905

ONE

Traditional Roles of Women
in Bengali Society

By the middle of the eighteenth century, the British had already acquired almost monopoly control over the foreign trade of Bengal, and were subsequently to extend their control to include the system of land tenure. Changes in the socioeconomic structure that came in the wake of the British presence unsettled the earlier indigenous balance of power.[1] The old aristocratic elite, both Hindu and Muslim, continued to perform a useful function for the new British rulers, but it was not large enough to fulfil all the needs of the rapidly expanding colonial administration. A new social group emerged out of the upheaval to serve the needs of the rulers, dependent on their patronage for its rise to power. Although this "middle class" owed its rise to prominence entirely to opportunities for gaining wealth and status provided by the British, the relationship with the conquerors was one of interdependence. This class was vital to the maintenance of British rule. Its members functioned as intermediaries between the rulers and the bulk of the ruled, serving as clerks and junior administrators in the expanding colonial bureaucracy, and as brokers, financiers and agents in trade with the East India Company. These were advantageous positions that allowed them to build up their own fortunes. Wealth gained was invested in the joint stock market and in the expansion of building in Calcutta, as well as in rural property.[2]

[1] S. N. Mukherjee, "The Social Implications of the Political Thought of Raja Rammohun Roy," in R. S. Sharma and V. Jha, eds., *Indian Society: Historical Probings. In Memory of D. D. Kosambi* (New Delhi, 1974), p. 361.
[2] S. N. Mukherjee, "Class, Caste and Politics in Calcutta, 1815-1838," in his *Calcutta: Myths and History* (Calcutta, 1977).

The new social group was known collectively as the *bha-dralok*, meaning literally "respectable men" or "gentlemen." The term is imprecise, and has been the subject of scholarly debate. In its broadest sense it includes all those who are not *chotolok*, or the *hoi polloi*. However, in the context of nineteenth-century Bengal, it is generally used to refer to a group sharing certain characteristics—"a *de facto* social group, which held a common position along some continuum of the economy, enjoyed a style of life in common and was conscious of its existence as a class organized to further its ends."[3] The *bhadralok* represented a highly significant social phenomenon, using the authority conferred by recently acquired wealth to gain status according to traditional caste categories.

The term *bhadralok* encompassed two main groups: the *abhijāt bhadralok* and the *grihastha bhadralok*. The *abhijāt bhadralok* became permanent residents of Calcutta in the second half of the eighteenth century. They rapidly acquired fortunes, and consequently social status and influence, by working as junior partners for the British. In the first half of the nineteenth century, and even later, they exercised undisputed social leadership in Calcutta through gaining control of the *dals*, multicaste social factions formed under the leadership of rich men who had the authority to arbitrate disputes over caste rules and customary law. The *grihastha bhadralok*, also known as the *madhyabitta srenī*, were a middle-income group including small landholders, government employees, members of the professions, teachers, and journalists.[4]

[3] S. N. Mukherjee, "Bhadralok in Bengali Language and Literature: An Essay on the Language of Class and Status," *Bengal Past and Present*, 95:2 (July-December 1976), 225-237. J. H. Broomfield, *Elite Conflict in a Plural Society: Twentieth-Century Bengal* (Berkeley and Los Angeles, 1968), pp. 1-20, "Bengal and the Bhadralok," gives a succinct account of the *bhadralok* at the beginning of the twentieth century. J. McGuire, *The Making of a Colonial Mind: A Quantitative Study of the Bhadralok in Calcutta, 1857-1885* (Canberra, 1982), is a detailed quantitative study of the composition of the *bhadralok* in the second half of the nineteenth century.

[4] S. N. Mukherjee, "Class, Caste," parts III, IV.

Women in the *bhadralok* household

The pace of change in the early nineteenth century makes it extremely difficult to pinpoint a distinctly "typical" *bhadralok* lifestyle. However, it is possible to draw out certain common features of social organization and their effect on the position of women. The nucleus of the new middle class was in Calcutta, the center of British economic and political activity, although through the colonial administrative system in rural towns it had a solid *mofussil* base as well. When men came to Calcutta seeking their fortunes in the late eighteenth and early nineteenth centuries, they came alone, leaving their families in the village home. There was a high preponderance of males over females in the urban population of Calcutta.[5] As they became established, they brought their families to Calcutta. The presence of women played an important part in consolidating the social identity of the *bhadralok*.

In Calcutta, control over women's behavior according to orthodox practice was adhered to with greater rigidity than ever before. In the fluid and uncertain social atmosphere of the new colonial metropolis, the position of women was an additional means of determining social status. The practice of purdah was a well-established feature of social organization governing women's behavior in Bengali society. Under strictest purdah, women were confined to the *antahpur*, or to the "invisibility" of closed carriages when moving around outside the home. These rules applied to women of the *bhadralok* in Calcutta, but social commentators noted that women in the *mofussil* were able to move about with greater freedom:

> Even in Bengal, if you are travelling through an unfrequented part of the country, you will sometimes meet women of the more respectable classes walking out of doors. As soon as they observe you, they try to get out of the way; or if this cannot be done, they will veil their

[5] *Ibid.*, pp. 6-7.

faces by drawing their white cotton scarf over their heads. The women of the most respectable classes are also allowed to leave their apartments to bathe in the Ganges. They rise early for this purpose, and return home before daybreak. I have often heard their shrill voices very early in the morning, about three or four o'clock, when passing on their way to the river.[6]

The rigid observance of purdah in Calcutta is encapsulated in the image of the women of the Tagore family being taken to the Ganges in a closed palanquin and lowered into the water to bathe, in order to ensure complete invisibility in a public place.[7] In Hindu society the position of women had always been a symbol of male honor, to be maintained by careful control over female sexuality.[8] The move from the *mofussil* to Calcutta brought women's behavior under much closer scrutiny because of the need to enforce rules of behavior in order to determine and maintain social status in a loose and dynamic social situation.[9] In the *mofussil*, respectable

[6] J. Kerr, *The Domestic Life, Character, and Customs of the Natives of India* (London, 1865), p. 84.

[7] Reminiscences of Swarnakumari Debi, cited in Pulinbihari Sen, "Satyendranāth Thākur Bānglāi strīswādhīnatār anyatam pathikrith," in Indira Debi Caudhurani, ed., *Purātanī* (Calcutta, 1957), p. 197.

[8] For a full discussion of the implications and rationale of purdah, see H. Papanek, "Purdah: Separate Worlds and Symbolic Shelter," *Comparative Studies in Society and History*, 15 (1973). This has since been included in a useful collection devoted to purdah among both Hindus and Muslims; see H. Papanek and G. Minault, eds., *Separate Worlds: Studies of Purdah in South Asia* (Delhi, 1982). Another excellent study of purdah has recently been published: P. Jeffery, *Frogs in a Well. Indian Women in Purdah* (London, 1979).

[9] C. Pastner, "Accommodations to Purdah: The Female Perspective," *Journal of Marriage and the Family*, 36:2 (May 1974), notes that "full purdah" is only likely to happen where there is a change in factors governing the traditional maintenance of social stratification. L. Davidoff, *The Best Circles. Society, Etiquette and the Season* (London, 1973), shows a similar process taking place in Victorian England. The rise of the middle classes after the industrial revolution upset the traditional class hierarchy, and the strict application of rules of etiquette was used as a way of determining and consol-

women were to be seen bathing publicly alongside men, smoking, and even walking in groups through the streets, but these "liberties" were not possible in Calcutta.[10] A practical reason for circumscribing women's freedom of movement in the city was a fear of the real dangers of the unfamiliar urban environment.

In Calcutta and the *mofussil* alike, the *antahpur* was the center of the female world. It represented a separate community of women, subject to male control through confinement to an enclosed space without access to the world outside it. The *bhadralok* themselves moved freely between the public world of streets and offices and the private world of household affairs. The houses they built gave architectural expression to the division between public and private space. Women carried out the daily domestic routine within the *antahpur*, an inner courtyard surrounded by a kitchen and living apartments. The male recreation and reception area was located beyond this, around an outer courtyard from which there was access to the public street (Fig. 1). The inner courtyard was smaller, darker and less airy than the outer (Figs. 2, 3). According to one missionary visitor to a Calcutta *zenana*, it was "a collection of dirty courtyards, dark corners, break-neck staircases, filthy outhouses and entries, overlaid with rubbish, or occupied by half-clad native servants, stretched about on charpoys, or on the ground indifferently—narrow verandahs, and unfurnished, or semi-furnished, and very small rooms.[11]" A Bengali observer gave a more favorable impression:

> Making allowances for a queer taste, the women's apartments are always prettily ornamented. The furniture is

---

idating rank, as well as a means of maintaining position in the new social hierarchy.

[10] "Strīlokdiger snān pranālī," *BP*, 5, 72 (August 1869); "Bhadra strīlokdiger madhye tāmāk byābahār," *BP*, 6, 81 (May 1870); Kerr, *Domestic Life*, p. 84.

[11] Mrs. Weitbrecht, *The Women of India, and Christian Work in the Zenana* (London, 1875), p. 105.

7

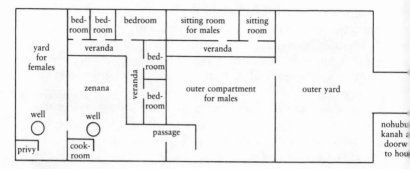

Houses of the Very Rich

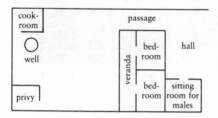

Houses of the Middle Class

1. Internal layout of houses of the very rich and of the middle class.

not very rich or expensive; but everything is neat and orderly, from the door-mat and the spitting-vessel to the daubs pasted on the walls, representing the countless millions of gods and goddesses of the Hindu pantheon. One of the most prominent articles of furniture, almost in every room, is the cot or *tuktposh* to sleep upon. The beds are almost all of them well-made and very commodious, for the Bengali loves to roll in bed. There is first the *tuktposh*, which is a very wide bench, or rather a number of wide benches put together; then a mat or carpet on it; then a mattress, commonly of cotton, which makes the bed somewhat too warm; then a cotton *lape*, which is a light and soft mattress, over it; and then the

8

2. Outer quadrangle (*sadarmahal*) and shrine (*chandīmandap*) of the house of a rural *zamindar*.

bed-sheet, and an infinite number of pillows. Carpeting the room is not in fashion in the *zenānā*, but there are small carpets for the ladies to sit upon, which have the advantage of being moveable at pleasure.[12]

In wealthy houses one would pass through court after court to reach the *zenana*. In a less wealthy family, sometimes it would be just "one small room, no windows for ventilation."[13] The only exposure women had to sun and light was the time spent in recreation on the rooftop, if it was not too publicly visible, where they played games and tended potted plants.[14]

[12] S. C. Dutt, "Home-Life in Bengal," in *India: Past and Present* (London, 1880), p. 221.
[13] Weitbrecht, *Women of India*, pp. 98, 100.
[14] *Ibid.*, p. 98; M. M. Urquhart, *Women of Bengal. A Study of the Hindu Pardanasins of Calcutta* (Calcutta, 1927) p. 18; Kerr, *Domestic Life*, p. 76.

3. Inner quadrangle (*antahpur* or *andarmahal*) of the house of a rural *zamindar*. Note the "unreformed" dress of the women.

Women were not allowed to cross the threshold of the *antahpur* into the outer apartments of the public male world.

The typical *bhadralok* house would have been occupied by a joint family. This was the basic unit of social organization in Bengal, and would usually have spanned three generations of the paternal line. Within the joint family authority was vested in the oldest male member, the *kartā*, and the oldest female, the *ginnī*, except in cases where the most senior person had abdicated his or her authority in favor of someone younger. The *kartā* was responsible for the financial support and general welfare of the whole family. The *ginnī* looked after the household stores, made arrangements for meals, and supervised the behavior of family members.[15] The average number of females in a joint family would be hard to determine in the absence of reliable statistics, but the Reverend Krishna Mohan

[15] S. C. Bose, *The Hindoos as They Are* (Calcutta, 1881), pp. 2-3.

Banerjea estimated in 1840 that "the number of females in each family is on the average about six or eight, including grown-up and elderly women."[16] The women in the joint family household were usually the *ginnī*, her prepubertal unmarried daughters (if she was not herself very old), her daughters-in-law, younger granddaughters, and often a widowed aunt or sister.

The smooth functioning of the joint family depended on the degree of harmony among its womenfolk, who were responsible for maintaining the daily domestic routine. Whereas males in the family were related by ties of blood, women were "strangers" brought in from outside. Daughters left their natal home between the ages of ten and twelve to live with their husband's family, only returning home for occasional short visits. Their place would be taken by other girls of the same age who joined the household as daughters-in-law. If there were a number of sons in a family, there would be a continuing procession of young brides, or *bou*. A woman was culturally bonded into her husband's family on marriage, and in the subsequent socialization process of the young *bou*. This bond was always regarded as more tenuous than the blood tie between males, however, and women were often treated with suspicion and accused of attempting to disrupt filial and fraternal solidarity. A well-defined set of prescriptive roles provided guidelines for harmonious living and for avoiding conflict that would upset the solidarity of the joint family, but at times personality clashes between individuals undermined the authority of the ideal.[17]

[16] Questions proposed to the Reverend Krishna Mohan Banerjea, with his answers, in the *Calcutta Christian Observer*, March 1840, cited in [T. Smith], "Native Female Education," *CR*, 25:49 (1855), 97-99. In the same article, Mrs. Wilson (formerly Miss Cook, the first lady teacher sent from London to Calcutta by the British and Foreign School Society in 1821), estimated that there would be ten to twenty women in a large household. The editor added a footnote here to say that an even larger number of women could be collected to form a class if there was a desire for education.

[17] See M. Roy, *Bengali Women* (Chicago, 1975), chapter one, section on "Family Roles," and chapter three, "Marriage."

When a young *bou* was taken into a family on marriage, her relationship with other members was governed by intricate rules of conduct. The "intruding" *bou* avoided becoming a source of tension by strict observance of the rules governing familial relationships. A husband's relation to his wife was subordinate to that with his mother. In order that men could maintain the mother-son link as the primary relationship even after marriage, wives were not allowed to speak with their husbands in the daytime, or in the presence of others, and were only permitted to attend to his most private needs. On occasions when a meeting was unavoidable, symbolic distance was maintained by the woman covering her head with her sari border as a sign of invisibility. A *bou* had to observe purdah with all senior males in her husband's family, and defer to their wives. She could only relax in a nonhierarchical relationship with her husband's younger unmarried brothers (*debar*) and sisters. She was expected to wait on her father-in-law, and to obey the orders of her mother-in-law. The latter was often the most forceful presence in her early married life. The authority structure was strictly hierarchical, with the old *ginnī* at the top and the youngest *bou* at the bottom.

The young *bou* was generally made well aware of the lowliness of her position, and her life was fraught with the hardships of being a newcomer. Her training "commences under the superintendence of a mother-in-law somewhat advanced in life, and not unoften of a tyrannical disposition. She is a stern disciplinarian, keen observer, and eloquent admonisher. The elderly lady is sometimes seconded by one or two of her grown up daughters, to whom the youthful daughter-in-law is an intruder and rival. And between the mother and the daughters they make the life of the poor novice, during the first years of her tutelage, sometimes very uncomfortable indeed."[18]

A woman would move up in the household hierarchy when

[18] P. C. Mozoomdar, "Hindu Women," *Theistic Quarterly Review*, 3 (October 1879). See also S. C. Dutt, "Hindu Women; Their Condition and Character," part one, *India*, p. 185.

a younger bride came, but a surer means of ensuring her status was by becoming the mother of a son, the progenitor of a link in the patriarchal system. In a large household not all women could ever expect to rise to the elevated position of *ginnī*. They would have authority only over their own immediate family, particularly over their sons, who remained with them after marriage.[19]

The young *bou* would be taught to perform the domestic tasks and religious rituals that constituted the daily routine of the *antahpur*. The sacred and the mundane were intertwined in her life, giving it greater significance and satisfaction than purely routine housework would have done. The day began with sweeping the floors and washing utensils. Then she would bathe and carry out the morning's religious duties. Next came cooking—a communal activity participated in by all the women in the house. Older women served the meal to the men of the house. Women ate afterwards, and would then wash at the tank. The main period of leisure was the afternoon. In the evening the *bou* performed the worship of the family deity again, and then cooked the last meal of the day.[20] Apart from this routine, there were children to attend and sick patients to care for. An important feature of her work was that it was all communal. Although there was often inequity in the distribution of the workload, causing resentment, domestic life constituted social life and was not something separate from it.

Whether a woman did most of this household work herself or supervised servants depended on the family's economic

[19] Weitbrecht, *Women of India*, p. 48; E. Storrow, *The Eastern Lily Gathered: A Memoir of Bala Shoondaree Tagore with Observations on the Position and Prospects of Hindu Female Society* (London, 1852), p. 18; Girish Chunder Ghose, "Social Reformation. The Condition of Women in India," reprinted from the *Hindoo Patriot*, 10 August 1854, in M. N. Ghosh, ed., *Selections from the Writings of Grish Chunder Ghose* (Calcutta, 1912), p. 185.

[20] J. C. Gangooly, *Life and Religion of the Hindoos, with a Sketch of My Life and Experience* (London, 1860), pp. 74ff; S. C. Dutt, "Home-Life in Bengal," *India*, pp. 222-223. For a similar though much more recent description, see M. Cattell, *Behind the Purdah* (Calcutta, 1916), pp. 28-75.

position. Born in 1809, Rassundari Debi was the first Bengali woman to write an autobiography, in which she gave a full description of her domestic life. She had a relatively easy life for the first few years of marriage, but suddenly, at the age of eighteen, found herself responsible for about twenty-five servants, after her mother-in-law became blind. None of these servants was internal to the household, so that she also had to do all the housework. She mentioned that she had to attend to food offerings for the family deity, give hospitality to guests and travelers, cook twice a day for the family and all the servants, and wait on her blind mother-in-law. The amount of work was so great that she worked ceaselessly from dawn till late at night.[21]

A woman was initiated into her role by specific rituals from childhood. At the age of five a girl was initiated into the various *bratas*, or vows, that gave religious authority and sanctity to the priorities and values in a woman's life. The *bratas* initiated her into the observance of religion in her daily life and instructed her in the method of performing the rituals at the same time.

One *brata* was the Siva Puja. Before performing it the girl had to fast, bathe, and change into clean clothes. After this she conducted the worship, the aim of which was to pray for a husband like Siva. The Hari or Krishna *brata* consisted of painting the feet of the god in white sandal paste on a brass plate, and then asking boons of him. In another *brata* the girl painted ten images of deified men on the floor with *ālpanā* or rice paste. She then asked for certain qualities represented by these figures. In the Sajuti *brata*, the girl again painted various pictures on the floor, then an elderly lady dictated "a volley of abuses and curses" against any potential *satīn*, or rival wife, which the girl would repeat.[22]

There was a wide range of *bratas*, of which a girl would generally be proficient in only a few. Some *bratas* were sea-

[21] Rassundari Debi, *Āmār jīban* (Calcutta, 1898?), pp. 28, 31.
[22] S. C. Bose, *The Hindoos*, pp. 35-40.

sonal, others regional. In East Bengal, girls aged between six and ten would often perform the Maghmandal *brata*. Throughout the cold month of Magh, the young girl would have to rise at dawn and carry the clay *stūpa* representing the sun to the side of the tank, where she would recite *mantras* and worship it with flowers.[23] *Bratas* were also performed for the sake of correcting temperamental faults. For example, one girl was made to perform the *madhu-sankranti brata*, giving a small bell metal bowl of honey and a silver coin to a holy man for two successive years, to curb her bad temper and sharp tongue.[24] A girl would be taught how to perform each *pūjā* ritual in full detail, with the natural result that "her mind being filled with germinal susceptibilities, she imbibes almost instinctively an increasing predilection for the performance of religious ceremonies."[25] When a girl married, she would then perform the *bratas* designated for married women.

The performance of *bratas* undoubtedly played an important part in conditioning a woman to her ideal role in society and the family. Though in the context of the purdah system these rituals conditioned women into acceptance of a fairly rigid role, they also provided a liberating diversion. Rituals and ceremonies were a relief from daily routine, and released the imagination and deeper feelings from the immediate confines of the environment.

Purdah women were well versed in the art of relaxation during their leisure hours. Their favorite occupations were said to be "cards and gossip, in which friends, foes, relatives and neighbours, and servants thump and bump against every point of the scandal compass."[26] Some were more industrious

---

[23] Sudaksina Sen, *Jīban smriti* (Calcutta, 1933), pp. 13-15.

[24] S. Mazumdar, *A Pattern of Life. The Memoirs of an Indian Woman* (New Delhi, 1977), pp. 29-36.

[25] S. C. Bose, *The Hindoos*, p. 35. See also the section on *brata* rites in A. Kayal, "Women in Folk-sayings of West Bengal" in S. Sen Gupta, *A Study of Women of Bengal* (Calcutta, 1970), Appendix II, pp. xxi-xxv.

[26] Girish Chunder Ghose, "Female Occupations in Bengal," paper read to the Bengal Social Science Association on 30 January 1868. Reprinted in B. Dutt Gupta, *Sociology in India* (Calcutta, 1972), Appendix V, p. 53.

and prepared pickles or sweets for their husbands and children.[27] Most descriptions of leisure time by nineteenth-century commentators carried an element of disapproval. For instance one missionary, Reverend Storrow, saw purdah women as languid and licentious, lounging on couches, listening to gossip, fanned by servants, or having their arms and limbs rubbed.[28] Male commentators tended to see women's leisure pastimes as indicative of the barrenness of *zenana* life. Their judgments tended more to reflect the influence of nineteenth-century puritanism on their thinking than present accurate descriptions.

Performance of the daily household tasks may have been monotonous, but it was usually a shared social activity rather than a solitary burden. In any case, the routine was continually interrupted by festivals and special occasions, on which women from different families would have the opportunity to meet and talk. A wedding was celebrated by days and nights of festivities. Female guests were conveyed to the host's house in closed palanquins. Unseen, they were able to peep out at the street life, which provided them with "abundant material" for talk in their leisure hours.[29]

The various *pūjās* performed during the course of the year— the Saraswati Puja, the Laksmi Puja, the Jaggadhatri Puja, and the grandest of all, the Durga Puja—also provided a chance to participate in activities that had meaning beyond the immediate surroundings. In wealthy families, nautch parties were watched by women through thin bamboo screens around the upper stories.[30] In describing such an occasion in 1826, Fanny Parkes gave a glimpse of the wholeness of the two seemingly separate worlds of the inner and outer apartments: "from the interior we could look down upon the guests in the hall below,

[27] *Ibid.*, p. 59; K. M. Banerjea, *Native Female Education* (Calcutta, 1858), p. 43.

[28] E. Storrow, *The Eastern Lily Gathered*, p. 25.

[29] G. W. Johnson, *The Stranger in India; or, Three Years in Calcutta* (London, 1843), I, 240.

[30] [H. Ashmore], *Narrative of a Three Months' March in India; and a Residence in the Doab* (London, 1841), pp. 96-98; R. Heber, *Narrative of a Journey through the Upper Provinces of India, from Calcutta to Bombay, 1824-25* (London, 1861), I, 37.

and distinguish perfectly all that passed. The ladies of the *zenāna* appeared to know all the gentlemen by sight, and told me their names." Mrs. Parkes was disappointed that the women were inquisitive about personal matters, and "not ladylike," but her account showed the vitality of these women in contrast to the meekness and submissive passivity of the ideal.[31]

Wealthy women could arrange for readings of the epics and *purānas* to be held in their own homes, "an act of religion fully equal in expense as well as its devotional effects to a poojah." The family deity was ritually installed in the compound, then a Brahmin would proceed to expound the stories of the *Rāmāyana* and *Mahābhārata* in colloquial Bengali:

> A good reader must be an inimitable actor. The voice, the gesture, the proud or piteous look of the characters whom he brings forward, must be represented with the truthfulness and reality of nature. At times his audience is convulsed with laughter—in another moment audible sobs proceed from the listeners who press closer and closer around him. When he describes the scene in which the five sons of Pandoo after having lost every inch of land at the gaming table, lose also their common wife—and the beautiful Drapodi is dragged into the divan of the ruthless Doorjadhon, an attempt being here made to forcibly reduce her to nudity and the Gods come to her rescue supplying her with endless garments as fast as those worn by her are taken away—the commotion in that female audience, the outbursts of indignation and grief, the flash of a chaste shame, may be better imagined than described.

The wife of the *abhijāt bhadralok* millionaire, Ramdoolal Dey, organized such a reading. It lasted ninety days, during which time "thousands" of women came to listen to it.[32]

---

[31] F. Parkes, *Wanderings of a Pilgrim in Search of the Picturesque, during Four-and-Twenty Years in the East; with Revelations of Life in the Zenana* (London, 1850), I, 59-60.

[32] Girish Chunder Ghose, "Ramdoolal Dey, the Bengalee Millionaire," from M. N. Ghosh, ed., *Selections*, pp. 23-24. See also his reply to a lecture

Women were given wide scope for the exercise of their imagination by these semi-theatrical events. Readings from the epics formed a part of women's social conditioning in ideal female roles. However, women also delighted in less pious literature such as the *Bidyāsundar*, a highly erotic masterpiece composed by the court poet Bharatcandra around the middle of the eighteenth century.[33] In this tale of triumphant love between a prince of Kanci and a princess of Burdwan, one of the most entertaining sections describes the women of the city indulging in *pati-nindā*, or "husband revilement," with great wit and sarcasm.[34]

Women also found relief from the repressive strictures of the ideal stereotype of pure, chaste Hindu womanhood in their interaction with each other. Much of their leisure was spent in gossip—about their husbands, families, food, surroundings, or ornaments. Gossip could in itself be creative, and was a natural outlet for tension and avoidance of escalated conflict. It was an enjoyable and functional pastime for women.

In contrast with the prescribed ideal, a large part of women's conversation was frankly sexual. In 1839, one English missionary lady had noted that women "will sit for hours in circles wiling away the time in silly obscene conversation, to which none but an experienced Christian female can safely hazard exposure."[35] A Bengali woman, writing in 1848, confirmed her impression: "The only colloquy of which we are capable is of the following sort: 'What was cooked in your house today? How many curries? How many persons dined? How is your he? I hope he comes to you daily at night.' "[36] Most *bhadralok* commentators on female behavior were equally

---

by Mr. Justice Phear at the Canning Institute, Howrah, on 25 March 1868. M. N. Ghosh, *The Life of Grish Chunder Ghose* (Calcutta, 1911), p. 127.

[33] E. Dimock, tr., *The Thief of Love* (Chicago, 1963).

[34] For a good discussion of the development of this literary convention, see W. Smith, "The *Pati-nindā* in Medieval Bengali Literature," *Journal of the American Oriental Society*, 99:1 (1979), 105-109.

[35] P. Chapman, *Hindoo Female Education* (London, 1839), p. 28.

[36] Letter in *Sadhu Ranjan*, 17 Sraban 1255 (1848). Reprinted in K. M. Banerjea, *Native Female Education*, p. 130.

censorious. One such observer, S. C. Bose, listed women's amusements as needlework, cards, and listening to puerile stories. He commented sanctimoniously that "their social tone is neither so pure nor so elevated as becomes a polished, refined community."[37]

Comments of this type are indicative of the influence of nineteenth-century puritanism on the mind of the *bhadralok*. In practice, sexual gossip and innuendo served an important function. In a society where free expression of women's sexuality in relation to men was heavily repressed, other outlets for such a powerful force were inevitable. Extreme repression seemed to result in a heightened consciousness of sex among Hindu women, rather than the culturally approved sexless opposite. For instance, at weddings the female customs of *strī ācār*, with their profusion of sexual rites, allusions, and teasing, provided an opportunity for the repressed sexuality of women to find release in a socially sanctioned way.[38] The "double standard" of conduct accepted by *bhadralok* society, where it was not uncommon for a man to have more than one wife, or at least to have extramarital relations with prostitutes and nautch girls, would have contributed to women's preoccupation with sexuality. Women's anxiety and insecurity in these matters was evident from the abundance of charms and *bratas* that they could use in attempting to stabilize their husbands' affections.[39] The release of sexual tension through female conversation was a psychological outlet for women who were obliged to maintain extremely strict propriety in front of males.[40]

[37] S. C. Bose, *The Hindoos*, p. 8.

[38] *Ibid.* Chapter V, "Marriage Ceremonies," mentions some "obscene" rites that the author terms "relics of unmitigated barbarism" (p. 87). However, he felt that to describe any of these fully "would be an outrage on common decency" (p. 86).

[39] T. Raychaudhuri, *Bengal under Akbar and Jahangir* (Delhi, 1969), pp. 9-11, notes this preoccupation with sexuality in medieval Bengali society.

[40] C. Pastner, "Accommodations to Purdah," explains the predominance of sexual themes in female language and behavior in contemporary village society in these terms.

Nondomestic activities

Although for the most part women were physically confined within the narrow boundaries of the *antahpur*, opportunities for venturing beyond it were occasionally available. Pilgrimages provided an exceptional chance for exploring wider horizons, especially for older women and widows. Women could travel all over India to places of pilgrimage. Respectable Bengali women attempted to maintain purdah by traveling in closed carriages, but inevitably in a public place such as a *ghāt* or temple strict segregation of the sexes broke down. A party of women often traveled with a few male relatives for added protection.[41] Even greater mobility was permitted to older women who devoted themselves to a religious life and went to live in holy cities such as Gaya, Benares, or Brindaban.[42]

There were always exceptions to the commonly accepted depiction of the *zenana* women as illiterate, uneducated, and "the sure victims of ennui."[43] Although the lot of most women was undoubtedly domestic, some were involved in pursuits that had more connection with the outside world of male activity. For instance, there was scope for exercising some authority in the religious sphere. Some women even managed to obtain an independent income. Instances are recorded of women who set up small money-lending enterprises. Reformer Iswarcandra Vidyasagar's grandmother and *zamindar* Jaykrishna Mukherjee's mother are both known to have done this.[44]

Women were theoretically unable to inherit property. Their only economic asset was their jewelry, brought with them to

[41] Nalinikanta Cattopadhyay, *Nabakānta Cattopādhyāy (jībanī o bangsa brittānta)* (Calcutta, 1922), pp. 11, 27.

[42] Niranjan Niyogi, *Sādhan o sebā. Nababidhān pracārak sradheya bhāi Brajagopāl Niyogī Mahāsayer jibanālekhya* (Calcutta, 1963), p. 2; Sibnath Sastri, appendix to *Ātmacarit* (Calcutta, 1918), in *Sibnāth Racanāsangraha* (Calcutta, 1975), II, p. 219.

[43] E. Storrow, *The Eastern Lily Gathered*, p. v.

[44] N. Mukherjee, *A Bengal Zamindar: Jaykrishna Mukherjee of Uttarpara and His Times 1808-1888* (Calcutta, 1975), pp. 7-8.

the marriage as *strīdhan*, or dowry. This could often amount to a substantial sum. A *zamindari* could even be purchased for a woman as part of her *strīdhan*.[45] Women were supposed to have absolute rights in their *strīdhan*, which was passed down in the female line. In exceptional circumstances, women were able to inherit. Widows without heirs had a life interest in their husbands' property.[46] Possession of property gave them not only financial independence and power, but also a chance to prove that they were capable of competently managing the property they had inherited. As they remained in purdah, their estates were managed by appointed male agents, who could become quite influential,[47] but even so, women property owners had to have a thorough understanding of the public functioning of the legal and administrative structure of the larger society in order to retain their control.

In 1836, more than half the principal *zamindars* in Rajshahi were women.[48] Janhabi Chaudhurani was a famous landowner in Mymensingh in the nineteenth century, feared for her power, strength, and tyranny but loved for her benevolence. She established the Janhabi High School, a charitable dispensary, and a guesthouse in her area.[49] Kamalkamini Debi, a *zamindar* of the Hughly district, spent one *lakh* of rupees on a village resthouse.[50] Daughters of some *zamindars* were among the very few women who were educated, to enable them to deal with the outside world and not be cheated of their inheritance on becoming widows.[51] Maharani Swarnamayi, a prominent *zamindar*, was recognized by Sir Richard

[45] P. C. Ray, *Life and Experiences of a Bengali Chemist* (Calcutta, 1932), p. 46.

[46] C. Sorabji, *India Calling* (London, 1935). Cornelia Sorabji, the first Indian woman to graduate in and practice law, was of the opinion that "till the English Married Women's Property Act, indeed, Hindu women might be said to have had greater rights than English married women" (pp. 84-85).

[47] *IMS*, 16 October 1881.

[48] W. Adam, *Reports on the State of Education in Bengal 1835 and 1838*, edited by A. M. Basu (Calcutta, 1941), p. 189.

[49] Krishna Kumar Mitra, *Ātmacarit* (Calcutta, 1974), pp. 59-61.

[50] *BP*, 4:2, 287 (December 1888).

[51] W. Adam, *Reports*, p. 187.

Temple as a "leader of Native Society." She was no less powerful for having to communicate with him from behind the barrier of a curtain.[52] An exceptional woman, she was active in the management of her estates and an even-handed benefactor of numerous good causes throughout the nineteenth century. The title Maharani and the insignia of the Order of the Crown of India were conferred on her by the British government.[53]

There were also other women of exceptional talent who shone in traditionally male realms. Their cases cannot be put forward as options available to any ordinary women, but are nevertheless interesting. One such woman was Hati Vidyalankar, daughter of a *kulīn* Brahmin pandit of Burdwan. She opened her own *tol*, or traditional school, in Benares to teach the *nabanyāya* school of philosophy. She died in 1810.[54] Another woman pandit was Rupamanjari, called Hatu, who did not marry but studied under pandits in Gaya and Benares until she was welcomed home with the title Vidyalankar.[55] Drabamayi was educated in her father's *tol*, and later helped to instruct students there, to the amazement and admiration of the Brahmin pandits.[56] Evidently these women were curiosities even in their own time, but their achievements show that women were occasionally recognized by men as being competent in the same sphere as themselves.

Undeniably, purdah was a system by which men exercised ultimate control over women's behavior, albeit unconsciously. However, it cannot simply be assumed that such a system was repressive and unbearable for those who lived under it. It is

[52] *Liberal and New Dispensation*, 23 April 1882.

[53] U. Chakraborty, *Condition of Bengali Women around the 2nd Half of the 19th Century* (Calcutta, 1963), pp. 113-116; "Mahārānī Swarnamayī C. I.," *BP*, 6:2, 392 (September 1897).

[54] Brajendranath Bandopadhyay, *Catuspātīr juge bidusī bangamahilā* (Calcutta, 1964), pp. 7-8; [Gourmohan Vidyalankar], *Strīsiksā bidhāyak* (Calcutta, 1822), p. 16.

[55] She died in 1875. B. Bandopadhyay, *Catuspātīr juge bidusī bangamahilā*, pp. 9-12.

[56] *Ibid.*, pp. 13-14.

not particularly meaningful to use a standard of judgment based on the concept of individual freedom to analyze the social structure of nineteenth-century Bengal, in which group identification was preeminent. In a society where neither men nor women were socialized as individuals, but as members of a group, to "judge this socialization by our standards of coercion and oppression is misleading."[57]

One can only fully understand the lives of women by viewing them from the perspective of their own experience. Over time, Bengali women had devised numerous ways of adjusting and accommodating to the strictures of purdah. Some of these ways have already been mentioned, such as the sexual frankness permissible in female conversation, and the sociability accompanying women's performance of household tasks. Women could also exercise power over men from within purdah in a number of subtle ways, alluded to by Bankim Chandra Chatterjee as "the indirect agency of *sari* Government."[58] They could use "feminine" emotional power over men's affections to win concessions for themselves, or try to achieve the same ends by persistent nagging. One English resident of Calcutta in the nineteenth century observed that a Hindu wife was a lot more independent than was generally supposed: "In cases not a few she disputes his authority and domineers over him."[59] There were other means of protesting against male decisions that were often more effective than straightforward confrontation. These included the withdrawal of sexual favors, the disruption of the household through a refusal to perform domestic tasks, feigning illness, or threatening to return to the natal home. Women could also play male relatives off against each other, using their skills of diplomacy to co-

[57] L. A. Tilly, "The Social Sciences and the Study of Women: A Review Article," *Comparative Studies in Society and History*, 20:1 (January 1978), 166-173, criticizes the Rosaldo and Lamphere collection of essays (*Woman, Culture, and Society* [Stanford, 1978]) on these grounds.

[58] Bankim Chandra Chatterjee, *Rajmohan's Wife* (1864) in J. C. Bagal, ed., *Bankim Rachanavali* (Calcutta, 1969), III, 14.

[59] Kerr, *Domestic Life*, p. 81. The author was a principal of the Hindu College.

ordinate the desired result according to their own needs. In all of these situations, the tactics used by women relied on "a male awareness of their dependence on women for the successful maintenance of the domestic arena of society."[60]

For those women who did not fall into the special and unfortunate categories of widows or *kulīn* brides, who were seen to be ill-treated and deprived within the terms of their own society, the social system prevailing in Bengal in the early nineteenth century would have been valued for its positive aspects. The world of purdah represented a separate culture, with its own complex rituals and behavioral codes, generating a confidence in group identity and a sense of communality among women. Separateness enhanced male dependence on women's activities, placing a higher value on women's work.[61] Women's activities were important for the functioning of society as a whole. Their actions were crucial to status areas connected with the male, public world. Women's role in the "politics of status maintenance" would have included such work as "the formal and informal gift exchanges between families that accompany ceremonies; conveying information—'gossip'—that establishes or injures family status or that is crucial to economic affairs; preparation and management of feasts that validate family status in the community and discharge obligations to others." Other important status-maintenance activities relying on women's involvement were marriage negotiations and the observance of public religious rituals.[62] An exceptionally devout woman, or devoted wife, would bring honor to the whole family. Women would have

[60] C. Pastner, "Accommodations to Purdah," p. 411. Although Pastner's study is based on recent fieldwork, the analysis of how a theoretical system functions in reality is useful for understanding purdah in nineteenth-century Bengal. P. Jeffery's study, *Frogs in a Well*, is similarly useful.

[61] H. Papanek, "Purdah"; C. Pastner, "Accommodations to Purdah," noted that social stratification was less evident among women than among men.

[62] H. Papanek, "Family Status Production: The 'Work' and 'Non-Work' of Women," *Signs*, 4:4 (1979), 778. The article is about women generally, but seems particularly applicable to nineteenth-century Bengal.

perceived the importance of their function and accepted their role as being of value to the community.[63]

The thoroughness of their socialization, and their lack of access to any knowledge of alternative modes of social organization, would have been factors contributing to women's adjustment to prescribed roles. The system held its own socially sanctioned outlets for those who felt themselves unable to make this adjustment, the most widely adopted being that of withdrawal to a life of exclusive religious activity or contemplation.[64] Admittedly, illiterate women were a "muted group," unable to express their feelings about their position in written form. A historian, therefore, has very little direct evidence of women's perceptions. It is also true that discontent did surface when a wider range of options was made available to women. However, indirect evidence would suggest that although the ideological inferiority of women was institutionalized in the purdah system, the evolution of ways of exerting female control and initiative within it led to the creation of a social system that most women accepted and some even appreciated.

[63] S. C. Rogers, "Woman's Place: A Critical Review of Anthropological Theory," in Rosaldo and Lamphere, eds., *Woman, Culture, and Society.*

[64] This was seen as an outlet for the "individuality" of both men and women in the rigidly hierarchical Hindu social system. See L. Dumont, *Homo Hierarchicus,* new ed. (London, 1972); M. Eliade, *Yoga: Immortality and Freedom* (London, 1958).

⇢⇢ TWO ⇠⇠

The "Condition of Women" Issue:
The Impetus for Reform

The conceptualization of "tradition" as a static model is incorrect and illusory. The period prior to British rule in Bengal had seen numerous changes in the position and status of women. However, the "condition of women" did not become a major social reform issue until the nineteenth century. The previous chapter sketched the broad outlines of Bengali *bhadralok* society in the early part of the century. This chapter will focus on the changes taking place in Bengal under British rule that directed attention to the status of women in society.

The shaping of *bhadralok* thought

The main impetus for social reform in nineteenth-century Bengal was a complex response to the presence of British colonial rule. British attitudes to Indian society in the early nineteenth century were not uniformly critical. Orientalist administrators were rediscovering, in their terms, the glory of India's ancient civilization. They did not attack contemporary social customs, but adopted a policy of noninterference. Contact between representatives of the two cultures was based on a footing of mutual respect. The zeal for Oriental learning shown by men such as Sir William Jones or Warren Hastings, the fruitful cooperation between pandits and administrators at Fort William College, and the close personal friendship between scholarly gentlemen such as H. H. Wilson and Ramkamal Sen, testify to the reciprocity of cultural interests between the British and the Bengalis. After 1818, when the British Empire in India came to rest on solid foundations and British rule became a reality, attitudes began to change. The previous tolerance was overwhelmed by a contempt for Indian customs shared by the Utilitarians, Liberals, and Evangelicals alike.[1] Although there were many important differences in their ideas, all shared a belief in the superiority of the British way of life, the pinnacle of "civilization."

The position of women was an integral part of their judgment of "civilization." The famous Utilitarian thinker James Mill, in his *History of British India*, made the connection thus:

> The condition of women is one of the most remarkable circumstances in the manners of nations. Among rude people, the women are generally degraded; among civilized people they are exalted. . . . As society refines upon its enjoyments, and advances into that state of civilization, . . . in which the qualities of the mind are ranked above the qualities of the body, the condition of the weaker sex is gradually improved, till they associate on equal terms with the men, and occupy the place of voluntary and useful coadjutors.

He went on to say that "a state of dependence more strict or humiliating than that which is ordained for the weaker sex among the Hindus cannot easily be conceived."[2] The enumeration of criteria for what constituted "civilization," based on perceptions of English society as it entered the industrial phase, naturally excluded by definition any Indian claims to have attained this enlightened state.

Christian missionaries were particularly vehement in their denunciation of Bengali society. The main targets of their attack were those customs most obviously alien to British practice, such as *sati* and polygamy, but they also strongly

---

[1] D. Kopf, "Macaulyism and the Defeat of the Orientalists" in *British Orientalism and the Bengal Renaissance* (Berkeley and Los Angeles, 1969); E. Stokes, *The English Utilitarians and India* (London, 1959); G. D. Bearce, *British Attitudes towards India 1784-1858* (London, 1961). Such views did exist before this, but they were not part of the dominant official philosophy.

[2] James Mill, *The History of British India*, 4th ed. (London, 1840), I, 445-447.

disapproved of purdah and the lack of education among women. Missionaries were especially concerned about the position of women because they saw them as playing a major role in conversion. As mothers, women were the formative influence on the next generation. If women could be converted, it was possible to visualize the gradual conversion of the whole of Bengal. As one missionary put it,

> Man requires a "Help Meet," and in every country the infant mind receives its earliest impressions from the female sex. Wherever, therefore, this sex is left in a state of ignorance and degradation, the endearing and important duties of Wife and Mother, cannot be duly discharged, and no great progress in general civilisation and morals can . . . be reasonably hoped for.[3]

To the missionaries, progress in civilization was directly equated with conversion to Christianity.

Although the secondary literature on early British attitudes to India barely mentions criticisms of the position of women, early commentators were preoccupied with this issue and devoted a significant portion of their writings to it. The Bengali *bhadralok* would have been aware of widespread British disapproval of their social customs through direct communication, literature, the press, and the education system.

One of the main avenues for "cultural colonialism," or the imposition of alien values by ideological means rather than by legislation or by force, was education. The *bhadralok* depended on English education for their advancement. They were only able to maintain their status as intermediaries as long as they were functionally useful to the British. As British rule developed, and the colonial administration expanded, the need for Bengali intermediaries increased. The *grihastha bhadralok* class enlarged to fill this function, with *mofussil* families sending their sons to Calcutta to gain an English edu-

[3] From "Native Female Education," Calcutta, 23 February 1822. Circular of Calcutta Corresponding Committee of the C.M.S. quoted in M. A. Laird, *Missionaries and Education in Bengal 1793-1837* (Oxford, 1972), p. 134.

cation and secure a foothold in the new bureaucracy. In 1835, the primacy of English education was enshrined in Lord Macaulay's *Minute on Education*. The content of the curriculum, as well as the medium of instruction, was to be wholly English. Macaulay explicitly outlined his aims for the cultural colonization of the *bhadralok*: "a class who may be interpreters between us and the millions whom we govern; a class of persons, Indian in blood and colour, but English in taste, in opinions, in morals, and in intellect."[4]

As the condition of women was only a subject for debate in certain progressive circles in contemporary England, it was unlikely that it would have formed part of the normal course of studies in educational institutions in Bengal.[5] However, general principles derived from topics debated in western philosophical writings, such as the rights of the individual or the merits of a society based on contract rather than status, were taken up and applied to issues more immediately relevant to Indian society. One such issue was the condition of women. It was commonly believed by the British that western education itself would lead to social transformation: "Thousands in the Presidencies, and hundreds in some of the large cities in the interior, have received and are receiving a liberal English education. It is inconceivable that the female members of the families to whom they belong can long remain with uncultivated minds."[6]

Forced into a defensive position by the persuasive rhetoric of British liberalism and the cultural intolerance of most representatives of the British Empire in India, many of the *bhadralok* would have been genuinely troubled by the failure of

[4] W. T. de Bary, ed., *Sources of Indian Tradition* (New York, 1966), II, 49.

[5] In England in the 1830s the condition of women was only a subject for debate in certain circles where there was an awareness of the ideas of the Saint-Simonians and followers of Fourier in France, and of the Owenites in Britain. See J. Kilham, *Tennyson and 'The Princess': Reflections of an Age* (London, 1958); chapters 4, 5, and 6 are on the feminist controversy.

[6] Preface by Rev. James Kennedy in E. Storrow, *The Eastern Lily Gathered*, p. ix.

their womenfolk to conform to British standards of ideal womanly conduct. Criticisms of the position of women hit at the crux of the personal life of the *bhadralok*. For some it precipitated a major crisis of identity; for most it caused at least some disquiet and forced them to revaluate their own society.[7] If they accepted the British definition of civilization, then that set the standard by which they judged themselves, and the present position of women became a stumbling block in their advancement toward the goal of a "civilized" society.

British ideas were undoubtedly influential, as well as being exciting and stimulating to those Bengalis who came into contact with them. Rammohun Roy, the first of the great nineteenth-century reformers, was fortunate enough to be steeped in the various strands that made up his own Indian tradition as well as being well-informed in the writings of western liberal thinkers such as Locke and Bentham. He shared with the latter the belief that humanity could only be free if it was in control of its individual reason and its economic wealth. He extended his analysis of Bengali society to the position of women within it, deducing that "modern expounders" of law had deprived them of their right to inheritance and thereby their freedom as well.[8] His theoretical position was suffused with a sympathetic understanding of the problems of women:

> Women are in general inferior to men in bodily strength and energy; consequently the male part of the community, taking advantage of their corporeal weakness, have denied to them those excellent merits that they are entitled to by nature, and afterwards they are apt to say that women are naturally incapable of acquiring those merits. . . . As to their inferiority in point of understanding, when did you ever afford them a fair opportunity of exhibiting their natural capacity?[9]

[7] See D. Kopf, "Macaulyism."

[8] See S. N. Mukherjee, "The Social Implications of the Political Thought of Raja Rammohun Roy."

[9] From "A Second Conference between an Advocate for, and an Opponent of the Practice of Burning Widows Alive," (Calcutta, 1813) in J. C. Ghose,

He showed acute perception of the root causes of female oppression, especially in his appreciation of the importance of property and economic independence to a woman's status.

Young Bengal, the group of students taught by the radical Derozio at the Hindu College in the 1820s, followed in Rammohun's wake as enthusiastic advocates of improving the position of Bengali women. They promulgated their ideas through the columns of their journals, the *Jnānānvesan* and the *Bengal Spectator*, and in their formal associations, the Academic Association and the Society for the Acquisition of General Knowledge.[10] A statement by the Reverend Krishna Mohan Banerjea, one of the "firebrands" of Young Bengal, that "it is impossible that a nation can take rapid strides to civilization while half the members that compose it are sunk in ignorance and degradation"[11] typified the extent to which the group had internalized British condemnations of their social structure. The Young Bengal group was passionately fervent in its pleas for the betterment of the condition of women. A contributor to the *Jnānānvesan* in 1837 wrote that

God having made men and women in this way would never have thought that one was to be the slave of another or that one was to be counted as inferior to the other; the Creator is so wise and merciful that it is not his wish that in his creation one is to be the slave of the other for

ed., *The English Works of Raja Rammohun Roy* (Calcutta, 1901), II, 177. For his ideas on property, see his "Brief Remarks Regarding Modern Encroachments on the Ancient Rights of Females," 1822, *ibid.*, pp. 195-208. For a critical assessment of Rammohun's views on women, see G. Pearson, "The Women Question in the Nineteenth Century—Four Social Reformers," in S. N. Mukherjee, ed., *A New History of Modern India*, I (forthcoming).

[10] M. Borthwick, "Young Bengal and the Waning of Its Radical Impact in the 1830s and 1840s," B. A. Honours thesis, Department of Indian Studies, University of Melbourne, 1972, is a study of the relationship between ideology and personal life, and the changes this relationship underwent.

[11] K. M. Banerjea, "Reform, Civil and Social," address to the Society for Acquisition of General Knowledge, in G. Chattopadhyay, ed., *Awakening in Bengal in Early Nineteenth Century (Selected Documents)*, I (Calcutta, 1965), 190.

her life's duration. But gradually man's cunning has replaced God's wishes with his own restrictive fetters.[12]

The youthful enthusiasm of these "junior" members of the
bhadralok was often the butt of satire and ridicule. One caricature attempted a composite portrait of the Young Bengal
"type"—Rajchunder Roy, the son of a China Bazar shop-
keeper, author of a prize essay "On The Best Means of Amel-
iorating the Condition of Hindoo Females," and a member
of the Society for the Acquisition of General Knowledge:

> It can hardly be expected that a youth so gifted as our
> young Baboo has been shown to be can be a very ortho-
> dox Hindoo. He is in truth considered by his relations
> as a lost non-conformist; and even the wife of his bosom
> holds him as little better than a heretic. . . . It is, however,
> more for sins of omission than of commission that he is
> condemned. He neglects the ceremonies enjoined on all
> pious Hindoos, it is true, but he still retains (slightly
> modified) their dress and manner of living. He does not
> horrify his family by indulging in forbidden meats or
> drinks and in all social and domestic relations he is, to
> the full, as irreproachable as the most orthodox member
> of the Dhurma Subha.[13]

This sketch, albeit rather patronizing, indicates the adaptive
strategy of the young *bhadralok* struggling with the impact
of new ideas on a coherent and well-developed social system.

Although the "emancipation of women" was a catchword
associated with social rebels, it was in fact an issue that drew
together sections of the *bhadralok* that otherwise held opposing views on fundamental social questions. For instance
Radhakanta Deb, staunch opponent of Rammohun Roy and
founder of the Dharma Sabha for the defense of Hindu tradition, was an ardent supporter of women's education. He

---

[12] *Jnānānvesan*, 16 December 1837, reprinted in Benoy Ghose, *Sāmayikpatre Bānglār samājcitra 1840-1905*, part 4 (Calcutta, 1966), p. 805.
[13] From Mawson, *A Few Local Sketches*, 1846. Quoted in P. Sinha, *Calcutta in Urban History* (Calcutta, 1978), p. 121.

was closely associated with the research that went into the first Bengali work to advocate the education of women, *Strī-sikṣā bidhāyak* by Pandit Gourmohan Vidyalankar. This attempted to establish a precedent for female education by citing examples of learned women in ancient and modern India and in the west.[14]

In the heyday of the "Orientalist" period, social contact between rulers and ruled encouraged a revaluation of social norms. The *bhadralok* were exposed to examples of British domesticity that embodied the idea of wife as "helpmeet," a partner to her husband in the social sphere. The presence of Englishwomen on public occasions gave the *bhadralok* direct experience of a social companionship with women that was not possible in their own circles. Krishna Mohan Banerjea used to attend "conversation parties" once a fortnight at the home of an Englishman, where the host's whole family were present. He recommended that all European gentlemen who desired the "amelioration of native society" should allow intelligent Hindus a sight of what female education had done in their own domestic circle, by occasionally introducing them to their families. He regretted that his countrymen had no personal experience of the superiority that education imparted to its female recipients.[15]

Bishop Heber gave an evening party to which he invited "several of the wealthy natives" in 1824. Hurree Mohun Thakoor, one of the guests, observed that the presence of females gave an added interest to the party. The bishop reminded him that the introduction of women into society was an ancient Hindu custom, only discontinued because of the Muslim conquest. Overhearing the conversation, Radhakanta Deb remarked that "it is very true that we did not use to shut up our women till the times of the Mussulmans. But before we could give them the same liberty as the Europeans they

---

[14] [Gourmohan Vidyalankar], *Strīsikṣā bidhāyak*. Printed at the Baptist Mission Press, for the Female Juvenile Society for the Establishment and Support of Bengalee Female Schools. Calcutta, 1822.

[15] K. M. Banerjea, *Native Female Education*, p. 104.

must be better educated." Mrs. Heber presented the guests with *pān*, rose water, and attar of roses, which also pleased them very much.[16] Through such social contacts with the British, Bengalis were seeing respectable women play the role of public hostess, performing a social function that was of obvious assistance to their menfolk. Another attraction was that they provided the pleasure of feminine company without any "uncivilized" overtones of sexuality, contrasting with *bhadralok* experience of prostitutes or nautch girls as the only women who had public social contact with men. They were impressed by the refined asexual tone of gatherings where purdah was not observed.

Although purdah as an institution was supposed to protect women from exposure to other males, segregation also heightened consciousness of sexuality. Not everyone could overcome the equation of a public social life for women with a lack of respectability, and this was a constant source of tension between those who acted on their theoretical principles and the rest of orthodox society. Most of the *bhadralok* did not come into social contact with the British, and associated freedom for women with seeing Englishwomen riding through the streets or hearing reports of Government House balls. They were repelled rather than impressed by the spectacle of western womanhood, and staunchly upheld the domestic status quo. One woman missionary spoke for them when she said, "I do not see how a waltz or polka could possibly be defended in the eyes of an Oriental."[17]

Cultural differences masked some of the underlying similarities between the condition of middle-class women in England and in Bengal. The absence of purdah conveyed an exaggerated image of female "emancipation" in the west. For instance, J. C. Gangooly, a convert to Unitarianism who had visited the United States in the 1850s, was impressed by the freedom of American women to read their "Adam Bede, Har-

[16] Heber, *Narrative of a Journey*, I, 59-60.
[17] C. Mackenzie, *Life in the Mission, the Camp, and the Zenáná; or, Six Years in India*, 2nd ed. (London, 1854), I, 51.

per's or Atlantic Monthlies," as well as letters from their "parents, friends and beaux." He contrasted that with the "terrible reality" of a woman's life in Bengal, where she would spend all her time in her room, speaking only to a few of her own sex, taking meals in a solitary corner of the kitchen, consuming time in telling or hearing nonsensical stories, and worshiping idols.[18] However, the latter description would also have been partly true of the household role of many middle-class women in America and England at that time.[19]

For all their exposure to western ideas through education, the *bhadralok* did not have access to internal criticism of the position of women in English society. The united front of self-righteousness adopted by the British in India at this stage did not provide the *bhadralok* with any material that may have challenged the superiority of British civilization. The outspoken British feminist Mary Wollstonecraft, on the other hand, had painted a very different picture of the effect of "civilization" on the lives of women: "yet such is the blessed effect of civilization! the most respectable women are the most oppressed; and, unless they have understandings far superior to the common run of understandings, taking in both sexes, they must, from being treated like contemptible beings, become contemptible."[20] Apart from sporadic contacts with English women, the Bengali *bhadralok* had very little acquaintance with the condition of women in England. Their view of English

[18] J. C. Gangooly, *Life and Religion of the Hindoos*, p. 79. In fact, English women of the period spent most of their time with other women, too. See L. Davidoff, J. L'Esperance, and H. Newby, "Landscape with Figures: Home and Community in English Society," in J. Mitchell and A. Oakley, eds., *The Rights and Wrongs of Women* (London, 1976), p. 166: "girls and women actually spent a good deal of their time only with other women. They were very often educated at home, or if at school only with other girls, and afternoon calls were almost entirely female affairs in the middle class. House parties, balls and dinners where the sexes mixed were highly ritualized."

[19] See P. Branca, *Silent Sisterhood: Middle-Class Women in the Victorian Home* (London, 1977); A. Douglas, *The Feminization of American Culture* (New York, 1978).

[20] Mary Wollstonecraft, *Vindication of the Rights of Women* (London, 1975), p. 262.

women, and of their influence on English society, was therefore highly idealized. Many had imbibed the belief that "much of the civilization of Europe is due to the high position of the fair sex in the social scale." This high position was characterized by "their education, their capacity for rearing their children in orderly and virtuous habits, their elevated conceptions of a Supreme Being, their social and domestic manners, the purity of their lives, their natural tenderness and affection, their freedom, and the moral influence of their actions on society," which together "give them a rank in no way inferior to that of the other sex."[21]

Some members of the *bhadralok* felt that their self-respect was threatened by the sustained attack on evils inherent in Hindu society. One of the more thoughtful critics of his own society, Peary Chand Mitra, a leading figure of the Young Bengal coterie, used examples from ancient India to refute James Mill's assertion that Indian civilization had always degraded women. He went even further, and pointed out that women in other civilizations, such as those of ancient Greece and Rome, had been badly treated, and that the condition of women in England itself left much room for improvement. As he said,

> If such be the lot of women in a country, where the immortal labours of Bentham and other eminent jurists have shed a flood of light on the science of legislation, where civilization has caused a refinement in the manners of men, and the practice of gallantry is in every social circle lauded with enthusiastic cheers, no great astonishment ought to be expressed at the defects that may be found in our institutions respecting the female sex; especially, if we consider the time when they were framed, and the fact, that the laws of no country suit the state of society equally in all ages.[22]

[21] S. C. Bose, *The Hindoos*, p. 227.
[22] Peary Chand Mitra, "A Few Desultory Remarks on the 'Cursory Review of the Institutions of Hindooism Affecting the Interest of the Female Sex'

Criticisms of the position of women in Bengali society by representatives of the colonial power forced the cultural intermediaries, the *bhadralok* reformers, to direct their attention to this issue. They found that the position of women in the traditional household did not fit in easily with the new set of values transmitted by the British in Bengal. They formulated their own critique of the condition of Bengali women, and argued for the need for reform.

There were also indigenous reasons prompting reform. Many of the advocates of reform were from high-caste *kulīn* Brahmin groups, whose numbers were declining. Their practice of *kulīn* polygamy, by which many women were widowed from childhood or only nominally married to men with whom they never cohabited, left a large number of women barren.[23] The custom of *satī* and the ban on widow remarriage contributed to this demographic change.

It would be an oversimplification to try to establish a direct causal connection between ideological developments and changes in social behavior. Ideological change does not immediately produce behavioral change, nor do changes in the economic and political system. Such explanations of change overlook the elements of continuity and evolution in the historical process. "Traditional" values persisted in "modernizing" environments; Anglicized behavior was modified to fit in with Bengali values. Gradual modifications of the social system were the most widespread means of adapting to and coping with changes in other areas.[24]

An autonomous process of changing values made some of

---

contained in the Reverend K. M. Banerjia's Prize Essay on Native Female Education," in G. Chattopadhyay, ed., *Awakening in Bengal*, p. 297.

[23] See S. N. Mukherjee, "Raja Rammohun Roy and the Status of Women in Bengal in the Nineteenth Century," in M. Allen and S. N. Mukherjee, eds., *Women in India and Nepal* (Canberra, 1982), for a full explanation of the complexity of this phenomenon.

[24] For a very lucid discussion of continuity in the process of historical change, see J. W. Scott and L. A. Tilly, "Women's Work and the Family in Nineteenth-Century Europe," in *Comparative Studies in Society and History*, 17 (1975), 36-64.

the *bhadralok* feel a repugnance for those customs which seemed to degrade women. However, the *bhadralok* also responded to sustained criticism by their colonial rulers, with mixed perceptions of responsibility and guilt, inferiority, and resentment. They had been made to feel that unless they initiated some changes in their domestic lives they would be regarded as inferiors in the scale of civilization. To retain their self-respect, they could not ignore the issue, but for them it was far more confusing and less clear-cut than their English critics assumed. Real reform would have meant a major reshaping of the entire social structure. For instance, the *bhadralok* had been used to thinking of purdah as a measure of high status, but with the gradual incursion of British values, the removal of purdah was to become an indication of advancement. Although English education may indirectly have shown an anomaly between their public and private lives, domestic change was not a necessary consequence of such a realization. The upheaval of ideas inherent in English education meant that many held even more dearly to the security of the traditional order in the home. To minimize conflict and retain continuity they could adapt to the new situation by "compartmentalizing" their domestic and working lives. These people coped with the stresses of their intermediary position by ensuring that their womenfolk remained in a "traditional" state, symbols of continuity in a time of rapid change.[25]

While rhetoric proliferated, practical schemes to change the position of women were scarce. Reform was readily taken up at a theoretical level. Within the set limits of the wife-mother

[25] See the section "Compartmentalization of Modern Industry and Tradition" in "Industrial Leadership, the Hindu Ethic, and the Spirit of Socialism" in M. Singer, *When a Great Tradition Modernizes* (London, 1972), pp. 320-325. Singer discusses the idea of separation of spheres, which become different in norms of behavior and belief as well as physically separate. He calls this "a *compartmentalization* of two spheres of conduct and belief that would otherwise collide," and says that "as such, it is an adaptive process working to reduce the conflict between tradition and modernity" (p. 321). For a discussion of women as symbols of continuity, see H. Papanek, "Toward Models of Development—Development Planning for Women" in *Signs*, 3:1 (Autumn 1977), 15.

role, the "improvement" of the position of women was a relatively safe issue that did not present a vision of imminent social chaos. It implied some changes in domestic arrangements, but not necessarily in social relationships. The *Strīsikṣā bidhāyak* stressed that women's education did not mean greater freedom of behavior, nor did it override a woman's primary duty to her husband. It was assumed that women would only be interested in education to enhance their wife-mother role. The possibility of women developing their own interests along different lines was not forseen. Many other suggested social reforms seemed to pose a threat to the supremacy of the *bhadralok*, but the emancipation of women implied no such dangers for them. Reform of the caste system would have entailed a total restructuring of society, but the improvement of the condition of women applied only within the *bhadralok* group and did not represent a threat from without. Women's emancipation gradually became a matter of self-interest, as the *bhadralok* internalized new social norms under the influence of British rule. The absence, or reduced observance, of purdah in any Bengali household was a matter for favorable comment by the British.

Bhadralok reformers, it should be remembered, were not hardened self-seekers, motivated solely by a desire for career advancement under British rule. For many, the condition of women was genuinely disturbing in an extremely personal way. Ram Gopal Ghose, another "firebrand" of Young Bengal, alluded to this in his diary:

> 4th April 1839. But our conversation did not take on a personal aspect till we touched the subject of women. We spoke of the peculiarities of each other's wives. Poor Ramtanu [Lahiri] appeared to be worried about his wife. But I should not indulge myself in writing the secrets of my friends in this book.[26]

---

[26] Sibnath Sastri, *A History of the Renaissance in Bengal. Ramtanu Lahiri: Brahman and Reformer*, translated by R. Lethbridge (1907), new ed. (Calcutta, 1972), p. 77.

Ramtanu Lahiri's orthodox Hindu father had prevented him from seeing his wife because he disapproved of Ramtanu's participation in the Young Bengal group. His case illustrates the frequent disjunction between belief and practice. Even when wholeheartedly committed to reform, the *bhadralok* were often powerless against the more widely accepted sanctity of traditional values. The comforts to be had from the security of a traditional environment, and the resistance to change within it, were stumbling blocks in the way of reform.

In 1849, the topic set by British examiners for the Bengali essay in the Senior Scholarship Examination was: "Describe the possible results of the education of Indian women." The winning essays all described the fruits of female education in glowing terms. For instance, in the opinion of Nilcomul Bhadoory, First class, Krishnagar College, female education would mean that women

> would no longer perform household tasks like slaves; that the flame of freedom would burn in their hearts; they would no longer be misled by priestly superstition; they would not receive stupid men as their husbands in compliance with their fathers' wishes; they would no longer have to veil themselves in the presence of their own relatives; they would dare to converse easily with their elders; husband and wife would not have to inhabit separate spaces; in the family they would live absolutely according to those customs prevalent in ancient times.[27]

It is unlikely that many of these schoolboys would have been able to initiate in their own domestic environments the kinds of changes that they depicted.

Women's responses

In Bengal, the fervor of ideological debate during the first half of the nineteenth century had little perceptible effect on the

[27] Senior Scholarship Examination 1849, Bengali Essay. *GRPI from 1st May 1848 to 1st October 1849* (Calcutta, 1850), Appendix E, p. ccxxvii.

condition of women. Discussion may have paved the way for later changes in behavior, but in general ideological debate was a rhetorical exercise, even a safety-valve, undertaken by men who were themselves experiencing a crisis of identity, with little reference to the practical details of social organization. While the reform issue was being debated by the *bhadralok* in public forums and in the press, women continued with their usual household routine. Their views were not consulted, and it is probable that few even knew that they were the subject of heated controversy. Traditionally, women did not concern themselves with the world outside the *antahpur*. In a few households women were included in men's discussions of general topics, but this was exceptional. The mother of J. C. Gangooly was able to rejoice with great pleasure over American independence, because in their family circle "every opportunity was availed of to speak of the United States."[28] In other circles women would have been barely conscious of the existence of such a place.

British rulers and *bhadralok* reformers alike saw women as passive objects of reform. J.E.D. Bethune, renowned as a benefactor of female education, exhibited this well-meaning but patronizing attitude in his speech to students of Krishnagar College in 1850:

> The education of your females is the next great step to be taken in the regeneration of the Hindu character, and it is a consolatory reflection that while many social reforms of which you stand greatly in need are thought to be opposed to the doctrines of your religion and customs, it is generally admitted by every learned native who has examined the question that there is no such obstacle in the way of your consenting to receive this great blessing. . . . Your modern ethical writers teach that the nature of women is so depraved that it is only by material restraints that they are kept from seeking out and following evil: our wiser belief is that in all the elements of virtue the

[28] J. C. Gangooly, *Life and Religion*, p. 271.

female character is far superior to the male; and that
whatever there is of evil common to all human nature,
is best combatted, not by the vain obstacles of bolts and
bars, but by laying the foundation of a virtuous life in
the early inculcation of sound morality, and by teaching
women to respect themselves by showing that by us also
they are also held in honour. Were it only for selfish
considerations, you ought to educate your women.[29]

Women were not to be given an opportunity to participate in
a male world, but to be released from representing traditional
values to become instead repositories of "modern" virtues, to
be of benefit to future generations.

Reformers seemed to assume that women's reactions to
proposed reforms would be favorable, and did not see the
need to consult them. They saw women as passively grateful
objects of reform. Yet women did have some influence in
accelerating reform—directly, through active encouragement,
and marginally, through acquiescence. Women's perceptions
of their own situation were frequently very different from
those of men. For men the "woman question" was separate
from their working lives, but for women questions such as
education or a public social life were connected with the whole
form of their existence. The usual stereotype with regard to
women and reform in the nineteenth century is of women as
traditional creatures, embodying the conservative influences
of home and family. In fact, women were frequently impatient
with men's lack of determination in introducing reforms, and
in many cases were the main pressure forcing reformers to
live up to their convictions. The meagerness of men's efforts
to introduce domestic reform was unintentionally highlighted
by the faint praise accorded to them by a female correspondent
to the newspaper *Sādhu Ranjan* in 1848. She wrote that

[29] J.E.D. Bethune's address to students of Krishnagar College, February
1850. *GRPI from 1st October 1850 to 30th September 1851* (Calcutta,
1852), pp. xiii-xiv.

I have heard from my dearest husband that many young men of the rising generation speak of instructing us, and that they occasionally show sufficient boldness in encouraging such attempts. But how great is our misfortune? This magnanimous intention on the part of our youth is not realized. . . . Shall we ever live in misery and distress? We can then have recourse to thee alone, O Death![30]

When Bala Shoondaree, the daughter-in-law of Prasanna Kumar Tagore, wanted to be baptized, her husband Gyanendra Mohun, although also a believer in Christianity, opposed the move on grounds of expediency. Under family pressure he even signed a statement explicitly renouncing Christian teachings, which she resolutely refused to do.[31] At a later date, Durga Mohan Das, well known as a "female emancipationist," wanted to have his daughters married at an early age because he could not afford to pay for their education. It was his wife's accusation that he was turning back the clock of progress that made him agree to educating them.[32]

Many women were quick to seize any opportunity that came to them for acquiring knowledge and acquainting themselves with a wider world. As some women from Chinsurah wrote to the editor of the *Samācār Darpan* in 1836,

If the dignity of any set of men is to consist in the degradation of women (which God be praised is not the case) we would say to these tantamount lords of creation that we care very little for such men and their dignity. . . .

---

[30] Letter from "A Muffusile Lady" in K. M. Banerjea, *Native Female Education*, p. 129. There is some debate as to whether letters purported to be written by women in this early period were actually written by them. In most cases, the internal evidence of language and style would indicate that women were the authors. Women's language in this period was more direct and colloquial, especially regarding sexual matters, than that of the *bhadralok*.

[31] E. Storrow, *The Eastern Lily Gathered*, pp. 65-66.

[32] [Dwarkanath Ganguly], *Jībanālekhya*, 2nd ed. (Calcutta, 1879), pp. 102-106.

Education is working its way rapidly in the families of enlightened Hindoos, and where it has already dispersed, the clouds of ignorance, the want of liberty, and independence is keenly felt.[33]

On the whole, the writings of women do not refer to the pursuit of knowledge in order to attain an ideal state of "civilization." Their thirst for knowledge itself was their driving motivation, and their writings had an immediacy and urgency seldom found in the writings of male reformers.

Among women, knowledge could not serve as a means for external advancement, because there was no place for them in the public domain. An educated wife may have enhanced her husband's status, but she did not necessarily boost her own standing in the household. In fact, she was often risking critical censure and ostracism from the people among whom she had to live. For a woman, a commitment to reform was of greater consequence than for a man. Her whole life was spent in a traditional setting, without the male option of spending at least half her time in circles where reform was lauded and even rewarded.

The case of Rassundari Debi, born in 1809, is an example of the intensity of effort some were prepared to put into the acquisition of literacy. In her autobiography she gave a detailed narrative of the arduous process of how she learned to read. She was overjoyed by a dream she had in which she found herself, an illiterate woman, suddenly able to read the whole of the *Caitanya Bhāgabat*. The next day, her husband fortuitously brought out that same book and left it on the table, instructing their eight-year-old son to bring it to him later. Rassundari was in the kitchen cooking, and chanced to overhear him. When he had gone, she came out and looked at the book, finding herself only able to respond to the pictures. She stole a page of the manuscript, and spent every spare moment trying to decipher it. She was extremely frus-

[33] *Samācār Darpan*, 17 December 1836. I am grateful to Vicky Worstead for bringing this to my notice.

trated to find that it meant nothing to her, but over a long period of time, with the help of her son's schoolbooks and from listening to other people, she managed to piece together a reading knowledge. In fulfilment of an intense yearning to extend her religious experience, she went on to read all the devotional literature she could find—the *Caitanya Bhāgabat, Caitanya Caritāmrita* (in eighteen parts), the *Jaiminībhārat, Gobindalīlāmrita, Bidagadhamādhab, Prembhakticandrikā,* and the *Bālmikīpurāna.* In most aspects of her life, Rassundari was a conventionally "traditional" woman, but she whole-heartedly approved of the prevalence and growth of women's education that had taken place by the time she was writing her memoirs.[34] The details of her case have been given because it shows how strongly motivated some women were to gain knowledge for its own sake. It also shows how the acquisition of literacy did not necessarily equate with concepts of "modernization" or "westernization," as Rassundari's only ambition was to widen her knowledge and to read devotional literature.

The only women to adopt Anglicized social habits openly were Christian converts. They alienated themselves from their own culture by doing so, and as a result were left to fraternize mainly with each other or with British missionaries. Their lack of contact with *bhadralok* society meant that they were not seen as models of emancipated womanhood that other women should emulate. Although one British gentleman said that the wife of Krishna Mohan Banerjea was "distinguished for her high propriety of conduct and superiority of attainments,"[35] a more astute female observer noted that "Mrs Banerjéa, as she calls herself on her visiting cards, imitates the European lady, and by adopting the European dress and customs, she is as much cut off from all influence over her countrywomen as if she were the wife of any other Pádre Sáhib."[36]

One of the main assumptions so far has been that most

[34] Rassundari Debi, *Āmār jīban,* pp. 40-44, 62.
[35] G. W. Johnson, *The Stranger in India,* II, 122.
[36] C. Mackenzie, *Life in the Mission,* p. 57.

social change affecting women in the nineteenth century was triggered by contact with an alien ruling culture. It is therefore interesting to note an important exception to this pattern, an increase in the power of women unconnected with the impact of British values and behavior. An examination of how female *ghatakīs*, professional genealogists or matchmakers attached to each caste, took over the field of marriage negotiations from male *ghataks* gives an insight into social change in an area of Bengali life that the British could not penetrate. This trend is first mentioned in 1843, and the process is referred to repeatedly by later authors.[37]

Apart from being one of the most significant events in a woman's life, marriage was an arrangement with political, economic, and social implications. Questions of property and inheritance, family influence and political power were all connected through marriage. Although women had always been indirectly influential in the settlement of marriages, the rise of the *ghatakī* was a direct acknowledgment of that influence. The easy access to the *antahpur* that *ghatakīs* possessed facilitated the direct exercise of female influence in marriage negotiations. *Ghatakīs* could use their powers of persuasion to gain the consent of the females of the family with faster results than a *ghatak* dealing with male family members, who could always be refuted by the *ginnī* and her associates in the final instance. It was said that the sharp wit and glib tongue

[37] G. W. Johnson, *The Stranger in India*, I, 228; Girish Chunder Ghose, "Female Occupations in Bengal," in B. Dutt Gupta, *Sociology in India* (Calcutta, 1972), p. 61; D. N. Das, *Sketches of Hindoo Life* (London, 1887), p. 89; S. C. Bose, *The Hindoos*, pp. 42-43. In 1843, G. W. Johnson noted that "of late" women had embraced the profession of *ghatak*. In 1881, S. C. Bose also noted that "of late" the solution of the marriage question had come to rest with females, and a "new class of female *Ghatucks (Ghatkees)*" had arisen. In 1911, it was noted that "the illiterate Ghataki (female negotiator of Hindu marriages) had fairly ousted her male rival (Ghatak) by taking advantage of the *purda* system at Calcutta. The Ghataki now brings about more Hindu matrimonial alliances at the Indian capital than the Ghatak, who, until twenty years ago, had held for centuries the monopoly as agent of Cupid." The Maharani of Baroda and S. M. Mitra, *The Position of Women in Indian Life* (London, 1911), p. 57.

of females enabled them to overcome difficulties in cases where
ghataks had failed.[38] Two popular *ghatakīs*, "Shibi Ghatkee"
and "Badnee's mother," reputedly made a fortune as their
recommendations were very influential with *zenana* women
who then persuaded their husbands to agree with the *ghatakī*'s
choice.[39]

In 1868 it was noted that *ghataks* had "been superseded
by the female members of the craft, and have almost passed
away from cities and large towns,"[40] and by 1885 most marriages in Calcutta were arranged by *ghatakīs*.[41] This suggests
that the rise of *ghatakīs* was a result of increased urbanization
in Bengal. As Calcutta and the *mofussil* towns developed during the nineteenth century, the *bhadralok* brought their womenfolk to the urban centers with them instead of leaving them
in the ancestral village home. When a member of the *bhadralok* felt that he had established a position for himself in
Calcutta, he set up a complete household in the city to reflect
the solidity of his claim to respectability. Hence a class of
leisured women, strictly confined to the *antahpur*, arose in
Calcutta and rapidly increased throughout the century. The
greater rigidity of social life for women in Calcutta, along
with the loose social composition and the size of the population, meant that information about other families was no
longer a matter of common knowledge, as it would have been
in a village situation. *Ghatakīs* arose in response to women's
need for essential information in a time of rapid urban development.

The practice of reform: the Brahmo Samaj after 1860

By 1860, social conditions had become more favorable to the
implementation of reforms. The *grihastha bhadralok* had in-

[38] D. N. Das, *Sketches*, p. 89.
[39] S. C. Bose, *The Hindoos*, p. 43.
[40] G. C. Ghose, "Female Occupations" in B. Dutt Gupta, *Sociology in India*, p. 61.
[41] "Strī dālāl," *BP*, 3:2, 245 (June 1885).

creased substantially, and were becoming the most important social group in Calcutta. The *dals*, groupings clustered around members of the *abhijāt bhadralok* that were influential in determining social ranking in the early phase of the establishment of the *bhadralok* in Calcutta, were losing their hold. Forms of social organization better suited to liaison with the British colonial power took their place—membership of social and political associations, and the establishment and development of vernacular and English-language newspapers.[42] The *grihastha bhadralok* shared a common experience of English education. Professionally, most of them served as functionaries in the wide network of the British administrative service. These common factors produced a homogeneity of attitude in many respects. There was a definite need to maintain an identity distinct from both the *chotolok* and the old aristocracy. Specific social changes affecting women, which were part of the consolidation of the *bhadralok* image, will be discussed in later chapters.

Reform within the domestic circle was fostered by certain concrete changes brought about by British rule. The growth of a bureaucratic class from among the *bhadralok*, and the British practice of appointing Bengalis to administrative positions all over India, precipitated a separation from the traditional society with its sanctions and mechanisms for enforcing convention. Mobility increased not only within government service; among the *bhadralok* the pressure on jobs in Calcutta and the *mofussil* towns often forced them to follow their fortunes elsewhere. Although it was most common for men in these situations to leave the women of the family behind in the ancestral home in the *mofussil*,[43] from the 1860s on it became increasingly the practice for the immediate family to accompany them. The geographical mobility engendered by the *bhadralok* search for employment outside their home environment led to a lessening of the hold of the joint family.

[42] J. McGuire has studied this transition in *The Making of a Colonial Mind*.
[43] *Bengal Census 1872*, part II, pp. 138-141; *Calcutta Census 1881, Town and Suburbs*, part II, p. 26.

Within the joint family, with its well-entrenched accepted codes of behavior, divisions of opinion were often on generational rather than sexual lines. Separation gave young members of the *bhadralok* the freedom to experiment with altered models of family life without fear of reprisals from their elders.

The ongoing influx of young men to Calcutta from the provinces of East Bengal gave rise to a group within the *bhadralok* that was searching for a means of establishing its separate identity. In cooperation with members of established Calcutta *grihastha bhadralok* families, they provided a nucleus of people ready to adopt reform as a means of establishing their distinctiveness as a social group. Apart from that, a genuine social concern and desire for thoroughgoing reform brought them together, providing a bulwark of support against opposition from conservative opinion. Reforms could only be successful in the context of group support and positive affirmation for those who attempted to live by their adopted principles.[44]

Although intense fervor for social reform had permeated the thinking of a small sector of the *bhadralok* in the first part of the nineteenth century, it was not until after 1860 that reforms began to be put into practice. Before then, in 1856, the passing of the Widow Remarriage Bill proposed by Vidyasagar had been considered a victory for the cause of social reformation. The triumph was more theoretical than practical. Enthusiasm for widow marriage diminished once legislation had been passed, when the possibility of more than nominal commitment became a reality. Very few widow marriages were performed, and in a number of cases the bridegrooms were not motivated by reformist zeal but by the prospect of pecuniary advantage. Vidyasagar put a substantial amount of

[44] It could be argued further here that reform can only be successful if there is also a sufficiently prosperous burgeoning capitalist economy to provide a material base for reform activities. See, for instance, Asok Sen's account of the failure of Vidyasagar's reform attempts: A. Sen, *Iswar Chandra Vidyasagar and His Elusive Milestones* (Calcutta, 1977).

his own income into providing rewards for men who agreed to marry widows.[45]

The widow remarriage movement had no formal organizational structure. It depended heavily on the efforts of a single individual, and thus had little chance of enduring success. But the Brahmo Samaj, founded as a religious association by Rammohun Roy in 1828, was large enough by 1860 to provide firm group support for social experimentation. Members of the Samaj were drawn from the *bhadralok* intelligentsia. Although older members were generally disinclined to undergo the ostracism from orthodox society that reform entailed, young recruits were prepared to take greater risks and to go to considerable lengths of self-sacrifice for the causes they espoused. Keshub Chunder Sen joined the Brahmo Samaj in 1857. By 1860 he had established himself as the charismatic leader of a group of young enthusiasts within the Samaj. Keshub was fervently committed to reform, and under his leadership a distinctive attempt was made to introduce changes in Bengali society that would markedly affect the position of women within it.

From 1860 to his death in 1884, Keshub experimented with implementing a variety of reforms. He had been profoundly influenced by Victorian ideas of social reform, which had reached him through correspondence with English Unitarians, contact with English administrators in India, and a visit to England. The improvement of the condition of women was a central feature of the young Brahmos' commitment to social reform, beginning with the foundation of the Sangat Sabha group within the Brahmo Samaj in 1860. Members of the Sabha pledged that they would promote female education in their own families. Their pledge endeavored to go beyond a verbal affirmation alone. Under Keshub, a distinction was created between *anusthānik*, or practicing, Brahmos and those

---

[45] See *ibid.* for a complex account of the way in which Vidyasagar was eventually financially ruined and demoralized by the failure of the Act to encourage men to remarry widows without the prospect of financial gain.

who were merely committed to Brahmoism as a religious faith.[46] In 1863, some of Keshub's followers established the Bama-bodhini Sabha. Its major achievement was to produce the journal *Bāmābodhinī Patrikā* for women. The *Bāmābodhinī Patrikā* continued up until the 1920s with only minor inter-ruptions, and had a wider circulation than any other women's journals of that time. Its readership was not confined to the Brahmo community. The Brahmika Samaj was created in 1865, to further the religious instruction and devotional activities of Brahmo women. "Female Improvement" was one of the five sections of the Indian Reform Association, set up by Ke-shub on his return from England in 1870. Other Brahmo women's organizations proliferated, and will be described in a later chapter. After a major split in the Brahmo Samaj in 1878, Keshub continued to redefine traditional Hindu ideals of womanhood in accordance with middle-class Victorian val-ues as one aspect of the conscious synthesis of "East" and "West," "tradition" and "modernity," carried out by his New Dispensation. The rival faction, the Sadharan Brahmo Samaj, was also zealous in encouraging the development of a new model of womanhood, although it allowed greater scope for independence through promotion of higher education and the limited pursuit of suitable womanly careers.

Brahmos took the lead in social experimentation during the 1860s and 1870s. They had considerable scope for departure from conventional behavior, as many of them had been dis-inherited and forcibly cut off from their Hindu families on embracing Brahmoism. Although this was a source of hard-ship, it also enabled them to flout the dictates of traditional society and yet remain beyond the reach of its sanctions. Brah-mos tended to set up their own communities, using this free-dom to create a society in accordance with their professed

[46] Details of the Brahmo Samaj under Keshub Chunder Sen are taken from my own work, *Keshub Chunder Sen. A Search for Cultural Synthesis* (Cal-cutta, 1977). D. Kopf, *The Brahmo Samaj and the Shaping of the Modern Indian Mind* (Princeton, 1979), also discusses the reform activities of the Brahmo Samaj.

ideals. Brahmo communities, or clusters of families, were set up for security and joint support in many of the *mofussil* towns. Families became involved in attempts to further female education, widow remarriage, the setting up of temperance organizations, night schools, and small charities, and the propagation of Brahmoism. This kind of reformed community was epitomized in the group set up around the household of Durga Mohan Das and his wife Brahmamayi in Barisal in the 1860s.[47] They bought a large piece of land and set it aside specifically for the creation of a Brahmo *pārā*, or neighborhood.

The most ambitious attempt to create an ideal community was Keshub Chunder Sen's Bharat Ashram, founded in 1870. Its aim was to demonstrate the possibilities of harmonious family living. The ashram was located in Calcutta, with a number of families communally sharing domestic arrangements although living in separate rooms. Their lives were strictly ordered, but on reformed rather than traditional lines. They rose at 6 a.m., had an hour for study, and spent the rest of the day in morning worship, housework, the women's meal followed by the men's meal (a reversal of the usual order), afternoon school, exercise, and evening worship before they finally retired at 11 p.m. Purdah was not observed, and apart from performing their household tasks, women went to the Indian Reform Association Girls' School or the Adult Female Normal School, read "improving works" in the reading room and attended meetings of a Brahmo women's discussion group, the Bama Hitaisini Sabha.[48] This ideal community disintegrated in 1875 under the pressure of internal tension over finance.

In all of these situations, the old hierarchical joint family was broken up, and the hold of the elders and of the traditions they embodied was consequently loosened. Increasingly, men and women lived among their peers rather than their elders, enabling them to make some departures from previously bind-

[47] Dwarkanath Ganguly, *Jībanālekhya, passim.*
[48] "Bhārat Āsram," *BP*, 8, 107 (July 1872).

ing social conventions. Not only Brahmos, but other sectors of the *bhadralok* as well, affected changes in their family living patterns. In 1881, one writer asserted that

> A European becomes a housekeeper as soon as he marries. The arrangement is an excellent one, no doubt, and as educated Hindoos are very much disposed to imitate English manners, the practice where feasible is gradually gaining ground, despite the prevalence of the old patriarchal system throughout the greater portion of the country.[49]

The break with the old style of life contained different implications for men and women. The *bhadralok* were able to enhance their sense of self-esteem by pursuing the goal of a "civilized" society in terms set up by the colonial power. Occasionally there were also material rewards in career advancement for those who emulated the social behavior of the rulers. The significance for women was twofold. There was indeed greater freedom for new pursuits and an expansion of their mental and physical horizons. At the same time, there were fewer links with traditional supports, and it was therefore difficult for them to cope with normal household duties. The discontinuity became a matter for constant lament by the end of the century. R. C. Dutt acknowledged this phenomenon in his Positivist social reform novel *Sangsār* in 1885:

> In the olden days we lived in community; ... and the family was one indissoluble unit under the regulation of the old parents. Now we are all seeking to have separate homes. ... This may be all for good; but in setting up separate houses, men have new responsibilities to undertake, and women have new lessons to learn, and this we do not often study. Hence we often find disorder where there should be affection, dissensions where there should be peace.[50]

[49] S. C. Bose, *The Hindoos*, p. 223.
[50] R. C. Dutt, *Sangsār* (Calcutta, 1885). Quotation is from the translation, *The Lake of Palms. A Story of Indian Domestic Life* (London, 1902), p. 92.

53

Dutt was commenting on *bhadralok* society generally, not merely the Brahmos. Many of the reforms initiated originally by Brahmos had become widely accepted among the English-educated class. As a result, by the end of the century there was an articulate group of women able to make their voices heard through public institutional channels hitherto confined to men. This type of modern woman became known as the *bhadramahilā*.

The *bhadramahilā*

Various terms had been used to describe the female kinsfolk of the *bhadralok: bhadrakulabālā* (girls of good family),[51] *bhadrabangsajabālā* (girls of good lineage),[52] and *madhyabitta grihastha kāminī* (middle-class housewives).[53] *Bhadramahilā* was originally only one of these words used to describe the female members of *bhadralok* families,[54] but it crystallized into the term for an ideal type, embodying a specific set of qualities and denoting a certain lifestyle.

The model of the *bhadramahilā* was created by Brahmo reformers, and initially was emulated mainly by Brahmo women. In the 1860s, the few women to break with orthodox custom in matters of education, dress, or discarding of purdah were Brahmos. They were consciously welded into a body with a progressive image, and seen as pioneers of a new way of life to be adopted by other non-Brahmo women. This was clear from as early as 1870:

[51] "Bāmāracanā," by 'kon bhadrakulabālā' of Dattapukur, *BP*, 2:1, 25 (September 1865); "Siksayitrī bidyālay," *BP*, 6, 82 (June 1870).

[52] *BP*, 2:1, 27 (November 1865).

[53] "Bāmāganer racanā—'Bidyā sikhile ki grihakarmma karite nāi?'" by Srimati Kundamala Debi of Billagram, eldest daughter of pandit Madan Mohan Tarkalankar, *BP*, 6, 86 (October 1870).

[54] See the usage in *BP*, 6, 92 (April 1871). Unfortunately I have not been able to do the same kind of research into early occurrences of the term *bhadramahilā* as S. N. Mukherjee has done for the word *bhadralok* in "Bhadralok in Bengali Language and Literature." Such a study would be very illuminating.

Our Brahmo sisters are demonstrators of the path of future progress for the women of Bengal. We extremely hope that they will give a good account of the purity of their progressive lives, untainted by such low qualities as laziness, disunity, subservience or selfishness, and that they will organize a society for Bengali women to carry out God's commands with care and attention. As you cannot learn to swim without plunging into the water, so you cannot gain strength if you are not appointed to a task. "God is your help in good works"—begin on your work with this great saying, and you will see that what now is beyond reach will become possible.[55]

The term *bhadramahilā* gained currency once it became identified with a distinct group. In the public mind, certain features of the Brahmo lifestyle became part of the composite image of the *bhadramahilā*. She wore a sari with blouse and petticoat, shoes, and little heavy jewelry. She appeared in mixed social gatherings, and was a member of various philanthropic and social women's organizations; she had received a basic education and read improving literature—domestic instruction manuals and "refined" fiction. A *bhadramahilā* was capable and competent in the running of a household, as well as able to provide support and understanding for her husband in his career. As a mother, she educated her children in "enlightened" ways.

Brahmo women identified with the image presented to them, and expanded it with moral dimensions. One Brahmo woman, in an essay on the subject, defined a *bhadramahilā* as one whose life was an ideal for other women to follow:

Just as modesty, humility, softness, patience, self-sacrifice, and the giving up of eating and sleeping to nurse sick relatives are all good qualities that can be found in Hindu women, one can also find ignorance, superstition and error among them. Educated modern women become

[55] "Bangīya strī-samāj," *BP*, 6, 86 (October 1870).

more civilized every day, by studying to gain knowledge and refine and enlarge their intellect, and learning to express their opinions after independent consideration of right and wrong like men do. If they can also show humility, patience, and self-sacrifice that knowledge will become graceful. ... Those who study only to follow their own pleasure and for their own adornment first without interest in their primary duty, and who through laziness show unwillingness in performing their family duties, can do society a great deal of harm. Thus it is the duty of the educated *bhadramahilā* to give up the defects of both old and new women, and to adopt their good qualities.[56]

The model was an attempt to synthesize the virtues of new and old, based on traditional Hindu womanly qualities mixed with modern features derived from the Victorian image of the "perfect lady."[57] The ideal Victorian lady embodied many of the characteristic virtues of a Hindu wife, combining moral goodness with a basic education and social presence. In 1864, Ruskin described the ideal in his lecture "Of Queens' Gardens":

This, the home then, I believe to be,—will you not admit it to be,—the woman's true place and power? But do not you see that, to fulfil this, she must—as far as one can use such terms of a human creature—be incapable of error? So far as she rules, all must be right, or nothing

[56] "Bhadramahilā," an essay written by Saraswati Sen between 1880 and 1889 when she was a teacher at Bethune School. Muralidhar Bandopadhyay, *Srimatī Saraswatī Sener sangksipta jībanī. Racanā o patra* (Calcutta, 1930), pp. 72-73. See also "Bhadra ebang abhadramahilā," *Paricārikā*, 1, 2 (June 1878).

[57] For a discussion of this stereotype, see M. Vicinus, "The Perfect Victorian Lady," in M. Vicinus, ed., *Suffer and Be Still. Women in the Victorian Age* (Bloomington, Indiana, 1972). P. Branca, *Silent Sisterhood*, points out that it was an ideal that did not correspond closely to the realities of life for middle-class women in nineteenth-century England. See also P. Branca, "Image and Reality: The Myth of the Idle Victorian Woman," in M. Hartman and L. W. Banner, eds., *Clio's Consciousness Raised* (New York, 1974).

is. She must be enduringly, incorruptibly good; instinctively, infallibly wise—wise, not for self-development, but for self-renunciation: wise, not that she may set herself above her husband, but that she may never fail from his side: wise, not with the narrowness of insolent and loveless pride, but with the passionate gentleness of an infinitely variable, because infinitely applicable, modesty of service—the true changefulness of woman.[58]

This image may not have borne much relation to the daily lives of most middle-class women in Victorian England, but it was an ideal that appealed to Bengali reformers anxious for social change but wary of too radical a disruption of woman's traditional role. The desirability of the "perfect lady" type was frequently and forcefully conveyed by "benevolent" British administrators like J. B. Phear, judge of the High Court. Phear mixed socially with the Bengali *bhadralok*, and liked to exchange ideas with them in forums such as the Bethune Society. In his speech on being elected president of the Society in 1866, he said:

Many among you must have learned in our drawing rooms that refinement, accomplishment, do but add lustre to all that is attractive and charming in the feminine character: and so many of you, at least, as have had this experience must be willing, nay must be anxious to accept any lending hand held out from us towards raising the intellectual culture of your ladies somewhat nearer than it now is to the European standard, if only that hand be tendered to you in a spirit of true modesty and brotherhood.[59]

[58] J. Ruskin, *Sesame and Lilies, Unto This Last, The Political Economy of Art* (London, 1907), p. 74. Ruskin's lecture "Of Queens' Gardens" was published in *Sesame and Lilies* in 1865. For an earlier glorification of this type, see Coventry Patmore's poem "The Angel in the House" (1854-1856). The Victorian idealization of the home as a place of peace is discussed in E. Trudgill, *Madonnas and Magdalens. The Origins and Development of Victorian Sexual Attitudes* (London, 1976), and C. Christ, "Victorian Masculinity and the Angel in the House" in M. Vicinus, *A Widening Sphere. Changing Roles of Victorian Women* (Bloomington, Indiana, 1977).

[59] J. B. Phear, in his speech on being elected president of the Bethune Society,

In another lecture he voiced the opinion that there must be many Bengalis who felt that the education of the women of their families did not correspond with the position they themselves had attained "in knowledge, in experience and in culture," and that they must be raised to that level.[60]

It is interesting to note that the closest English female friends and associates of Keshub Chunder Sen and the Brahmo reformers did not conform to the Victorian "angel in the house" ideal. Women such as S. D. Collet, Mary Carpenter, and Frances Power Cobbe were highly intelligent Unitarians who attempted to exert some influence on their society through the channels that were available to them, principally philanthropic activity. They managed to forge an independent path contrary to prevailing ideals of proper womanly roles. Lacking sufficient outlets for the exercise of their influence on their own society, they took up the religious and social reform of India as a worthy "cause." As women, they believed that they felt a particular "sisterly" empathy for the women of India, and worked to "improve" their condition.

Keshub Chunder Sen seems to have dealt with these women on an intellectual level by making exceptions of them and exempting them from his general conceptualization of womanhood. Despite his close association with them, he did not incorporate their "type" into the model of the *bhadramahilā* that he helped create. His lack of enthusiasm for the independent qualities of the philanthropic Victorian spinster was possibly encouraged by an open clash with one such Unitarian reformer, Annette Akroyd. In response to Keshub's appeal during his stay in England for Englishwomen to come out and teach their poor benighted Indian sisters, Miss Akroyd came

13 December 1866, in *Proceedings and Transactions of the Bethune Society, from November 10th 1859 to April 20th 1869* (Calcutta, 1870), pp. lxxxvii-viii.

[60] J. B. Phear on "Women Teachers for Women," 28 November 1867, *ibid.*, p. cxii. Phear saw himself as a middle-class Victorian, aware of the inequities of the position of "helpless dependence upon the other sex" of women of his own English upper classes. See his lecture on "The Hindoo Joint Family" on 18 March 1867, *ibid.*, p. 84.

to India in 1870, but shortly after her arrival she found that her plans for Indian women differed from his. She quarreled publicly with him, and thereafter the Brahmos exhibited a distinct mistrust of the type they termed "the strong-minded woman."[61]

The *bhadramahilā* ideal had taken shape according to the particular reform ideology of the Brahmos, at once puritanical and progressive, but the set of values it embodied was eventually adopted by a widening circle of women in *bhadralok* families. Once the extreme Anglicist and socially discordant aspects of Brahmo advocacy of reform had been tempered to suit the requirements of Hindu society, it was acceptable to all who belonged to the *bhadralok* class. As representatives of a successful westernizing elite, able to communicate in the same social idiom as their British rulers, the Brahmo *bhadramahilā* provided an attainable ideal for other women. The stereotype was created to suit the purposes of an elite under colonial rule, combining the self-sacrificing virtues of the ideal Hindu woman with the Victorian woman's ability to cooperate in the furtherance of her husband's career. The ideal was to gain wide currency throughout the later nineteenth century through dissemination in a growing number of journals and instruction manuals for and by women.[62]

[61] She even clashed with the "female emancipationists" in the Brahmo Samaj, and thus lost support from all quarters. The dispute was referred to repeatedly in her letters and diaries for the period. See the Akroyd-Beveridge Papers, India Office Library. *BP*, 9, 118 (June 1873), uses the term "strong-minded woman" in a report on her conduct in the English Supplement. More general use of the term followed. *BP*, 9, 120 (August 1873), English Supplement, reported that a Bengali lady gave a lecture saying that women must go as far on the road to knowledge and power as men, with the comment, "Are we going to have 'strong-minded women' and fighting ladies in our midst?" See also *BP*, 9, 121 (September 1873), and *BP*, 9, 119 (July 1873), "Strījātir aswābhābik unnati." At a later date Nababidhan Brahmos accused their Sadharan rivals of fostering the development of this type of woman; *Abalābāndhab*, I, 8 (June 1879).

[62] These will be referred to in subsequent chapters, and a list of those used will be given in the bibliography. They would make a fascinating study in themselves, but unfortunately there is no scope for doing so in this book.

THREE

Expanding Horizons: The Education
of the *Bhadramahilā*

Contact with a different culture in the colonial period directed
the attention of Bengalis to the condition of women in society.
Faith in modern education led *bhadralok* reformers to believe
that the education of women was necessary to achieve any
reform, not only in the condition of women but in the state
of society at large. It was the key that would open the door
to all other social progress. Their conviction ran counter to
existing taboos against female literacy and was thus slow to
gain wide adherence. Initially, discussion focused on whether
female education was permissible, but as the needs of society
changed, the fact of female education became accepted and
the debate shifted to the desirable nature and extent of education.

Overcoming the taboo

In the early nineteenth century, there were strong prejudices
against women's education. In his *Report on the State of
Education in Bengal* for 1836, William Adam recorded the
belief that female education not only produced widows, but
also facilitated romantic intrigue.[1] It was said that no man

---

[1] W. Adam, *Reports*. From the second report (Rajshahi, 1836), p. 187.
These beliefs were widely held. See also discussion "Grihakathā," *Māsik
Patrikā*, 1, 1 (August 1854) and "Strīlokdiger bidyār siksār ābasyaktā," *BP*,
1, 1 (September 1863). The latter points out the logical fallacy in the argument. If all educated women were widows, then a lot of English women
would be widows but no Hindus would. A list of these prejudices was also
given by Madan Mohan Tarkalankar in "Strīsiksā," *Sarbasubhakārī Patrikā*,
2 (Āswin 1772 [1850]) from B. Ghose, *Sāmayikpatre Bānglār samājcitra
1840-1905*, part 3 (Calcutta, 1964), pp. 542-554.

would marry an educated girl.[2] Male objections to female education seem to have been based on a fear of the unknown powers education could give a woman. Literacy supposedly gave women greater capacity for unfaithful liaisons through their ability to write letters of assignation. A husband's control over an educated woman was therefore less secure.

Saudamini Ray of Barisal personally experienced the effect of these beliefs. As a child, she was sometimes sent to the village *pāthsālā* along with her brothers. The teacher took no notice of her, but she was a quick learner, and absorbed his instructions as well as the other pupils did. One day he saw that she had written something very advanced. His amazement was quickly followed by an angry outburst: "For women to pursue education is a terrible sin. The education of women leads to destruction, if they are educated they will become widows, so from now on don't come to my *pāthsālā* again."[3]

Whereas education for males was directly related to the pursuit of employment, female education had no economic function. An educated girl would become a liability to her parents, as no man would marry her. The domestic role of women fostered a belief that education for girls was wasted because it could not be put to any financial use. In addition, literacy was suspected of diverting women's attentions from their domestic duties. The cost of female education, in terms of fees, materials, and so on, as well as the temporary loss of one helper in the household, and the lack of visible pecuniary return, were strong economic deterrents reinforcing the existing taboo. The education of female members of a family also involved the hidden cost of replacing their previously unpaid labor with that of hired servants.[4]

The first schemes for female education were established by missionary groups, whose main purpose was proselytization.

---

[2] W. Adam, *Reports.* First report (Rangpur, 1835), p. 110.

[3] Rakhal Chandra Ray, *Jīban bindu* (Calcutta, 1880), pp. 7-11.

[4] "Grihakathā," *Māsik Patrikā*, I, 1, and Krishna Mohan Banerjea's answers to questions on female education in the *Calcutta Christian Observer*, March 1840, reprinted in [T. Smith], "Native Female Education," *CR*, 25:49, pp. 97-99.

Thus the fear of conversion became an additional reason for opposition. Another objection was that the missionaries had been most successful in the education of lower-caste women. The availability of modern female education to the *chotolok* meant that the *bhadralok* were reluctant to adopt it as a part of their own distinctive lifestyle.[5]

The earliest advocates of female education furnished historical and scriptural examples of educated women in ancient India to show that female education was not prohibited by religion. They traced the decline in female education from the period of Muslim rule. The *Strīsiksā bidhāyak*, written in 1822, provided prototypes that were used as a touchstone to prove women's capacities throughout the century.[6] The argument was not, however, a compelling one, as scriptural prohibitions were not really the issue. The strong influence of taboo and the prospect of an economic loss were sanctions powerful enough to deter people from contravening accepted practice without any recourse to *sāstric* injunctions.

William Adam's survey of education in Bengal concluded that almost all Bengali women were illiterate. Daughters of *zamindars* were sometimes given an elementary education in reading, writing, and keeping accounts, so that they could retain and manage their estates on widowhood.[7] There were also occasional examples of women pandits.[8] It was said that the fact that they were so rare made them arrogant, and even opposed to an extension of education for other women.[9] In

[5] M. A. Laird, *Missionaries and Education*, p. 138; Tarasankar Sarma, *A Prize Essay on Hindu Female Education* (in Bengali) (Calcutta, 1851), p. 51.

[6] *Strīsiksā bidhāyak* was first published by the "Female Juvenile Society for the establishment and support of Bengalee female schools" in Calcutta in 1822. It was published anonymously, but is known to be by Gourmohan Vidyalankar. Radhakanta Deb helped supply some of the materials to the author. See J. C. Bagal, *Women's Education in Eastern India—The First Phase* (Calcutta, 1956), pp. 102-103, 127.

[7] W. Adam, *Reports*. Second report (Rajshahi, 1836), pp. 187, 188.

[8] See Chapter One, and also [Gourmohan Vidyalankar], *Strīsiksā*, pp. 16-17.

[9] Koilasbasini Debi, *Hindu Female Education and Its Progress* (Calcutta, 1865), pp. 13-15.

some exceptional *bhadralok* families, women were taught basic literacy at home. Debendranath Tagore's mother-in-law was able to read difficult religious texts, such as the *Tantra Purānas*, and works on *Sāmkhyan* philosophy. In the absence of anything else, she would read through the dictionary.[10] The women of Peary Chand Mitra's family were also literate.[11]

Despite the entrenched objections of the majority, the benefits of female education were enthusiastically put forward by a vocal reformist minority. Even a writer on the native theater in 1835 included a recommendation for female education because of its potential not only for improving the performance of actresses but also for the good of society as a whole:

> Had this girl, who made such a capital figure on the stage, been educated in the study of the vernacular language, I, as a Hindu, beg my countrymen to consider how her talents would have shown! . . . Was not this display sufficient to convince the Hindu visitors that a woman, as long as she is devoid of education is a perfect blank in society?[12]

The Reverend Krishna Mohan Banerjea was convinced that educated women would exert a humanizing influence on society and check its tendencies to indelicacy and "lax manners."[13] Others put forward more tangible benefits. The *Strīsiksā bidhāyak*, for instance, enumerated the advantages of education as including the ability to correspond with an absent husband, to instruct one's children, and to do household accounts.[14] With a knowledge of hygiene, women could raise

[10] Brajendranath Bandopadhyay, *Swarnakumārī Debī* (Calcutta, 1965), pp. 6-7.

[11] See the preface to his *Ādhyātmikā* (1880) in Asitkumar Bandopadhyay, ed., *Pyārīcād racanābalī* (Calcutta, 1971).

[12] Bhuban Mohun Mittra, "The Native Theatre," *Hindu Pioneer*, 1:2 (October 1835). Reprinted in *Nineteenth Century Studies*, 6 (1974), 190-196.

[13] Krishna Mohan Banerjea, *Native Female Education*, p. 66. See also Chapter Two for a discussion of the notion of the civilizing presence of women.

[14] [Gourmohan Vidyalankar], *Strīsiksā*, pp. 18-19.

healthier children. They could share in part in the new worlds of their husbands, and delight them by writing poetry or prose.[15] It was argued that an educated wife, rather than neglecting her duties, would make a much better housewife than her uneducated counterpart. In an imaginary dialogue between husband and wife in the earliest women's journal, *Māsik Patrikā*, the husband spoke in favor of education to his wife, who was against it. The benefits he perceived were that if a wife could do accounts, then she would understand the family's financial situation and avoid quarrels. She would also be able to manage the property if her husband was absent or dead. The latter point convinced his wife, because she could relate it to cases among her own relatives. In one case her cousin, an educated woman, had been widowed at thirty. Her husband's elder brother tried to deceive her, but she understood the accounts so well that he was unable to do so. Another cousin was uneducated, and was therefore financially ruined on widowhood. The husband went on with the other major arguments in favor of female education—the extent of female influence on the home and on the next generation. He said that whereas in Europe a mother is her child's first teacher, in Bengal "the blind led the blind."[16]

The argument that education was necessary for the creation of an enlightened mother, and thence of an enlightened race, continued to be advanced throughout the century and therefore deserves closer scrutiny. In all societies in which women are primarily responsible for child rearing, they have a formative influence on the child's mind and body. In Bengal the tie between mothers and sons was especially close. Although the importance of enlightened mothers was a universal argument in favor of female education,[17] it would have had even greater application in Bengal, where a son's obedience and

[15] Tarasankar Sarma, *A Prize Essay*, pp. 25-36.

[16] "Grihakathā," *Māsik Patrikā*, I, 1.

[17] The idea of motherhood was also used to prevent women from using their education to enter traditionally male preserves. See A. Davin, "Imperialism and the Cult of Motherhood," *History Workshop*, 1974.

closeness to his mother continued beyond childhood, throughout the mother's lifetime. Colonial administrators wanted to harness the direction of this influence so that new ideas would be reinforced in the home environment. It was said that in the absence of female education, "the evil influence of the zenana is, in very many instances, never eradicated; and much of the good learnt by a boy at school and college, is neutralized by the habits of his domestic circle, and the absence of educated companions for his hours of leisure and repose."[18]

Uneducated women began to be perceived as a potential danger to the healthy physical development of children, as an anonymous mother pointed out to her daughter:

> Look what dangerous and useless things ignorant women do if their children fall ill. Sometimes they put *saphārid* around the child's throat, sometimes they use *mantras* to drive the disease away, sometimes they perform their own religious rituals. None of these are proper treatments, and do so much harm besides! If they had had a proper education they would not do such ridiculous things.[19]

Women were also responsible for the mental outlook of their children. An "ignorant" woman perpetuated all "traditional" social practices, which were seen as harmful. It was said that if women studied physics they would no longer believe in ghosts, and that if they studied chemistry they would cease to believe in *mantras* and magic.[20]

One writer summarized it as follows: "the existence of intelligently educated mothers, and sisters, and wives, is essential to the training of a race of intelligent and high-spirited sons, and brothers, and husbands."[21] Here the presumption implicit in many other similar statements was made clear. Women were to be educated primarily for their role in grooming men.

---

[18] *GRPI from 1st October 1849 to 30th September 1850* (Calcutta, 1851), p. 4.
[19] "Kanyār prati mātār dvītiya upades," *BP*, 1:2, 10 (June 1864).
[20] "Desācār," *BP*, 1:2, 14 (October 1864).
[21] "Native Female Education," *CR*, 25:49, pp. 61-62.

Their own edification was secondary. A frequent way of illustrating the importance of the mother-function was to show how many great men attributed their success to their mothers. Among these were Napoleon, George Washington, and Theodore Parker.[22] In Bengal, a favorite example was the mother of Vidyasagar.[23] Women's task was to prepare a general climate of receptiveness to new ideas, in order to influence men, who were the initiators of specific schemes for social progress and advancement: "We cannot estimate the influence for good upon (for instance) the future landed proprietors of the country which a generation of educated and careful mothers might effect."[24]

Despite the utilitarian approach of male champions of female education, once women themselves were educated they were able to say feelingly that mothers should make sure their daughters were educated simply in order to make their lives much happier: "My humble prayer to all is that you give your own daughters an adequate education. What is the point of lamenting the fate that we had. Every mother should see that the same misery does not befall her daughters in future."[25]

It was also hoped that female education would help preserve harmony within the joint family. Many writers stated that uneducated women were the main cause of dissension.[26] Female education was seen, too, as a way of improving marital relations. The author of a didactic manual for women in 1862 described a situation in which an uneducated girl was taught by a group of educated girls to "appreciate" her husband, and to go back to his home. She was advised to apologize to him for her bad behavior, and to acquire an education herself.[27]

[22] Kumari Lahiri, "Strīloker abasya siksanīya ki?" *BP*, 11, 142 (June 1875).

[23] Pramilabala Debi, "Jananī," *Antahpur*, 7, 7 (November 1904).

[24] "Hindoo Women," *CR*, 40:79 (1864), 90-91.

[25] "Strīsiksā bisaye ardha siksitā hindu mahilādiger matāmat," *Antahpur*, 4, 4 (September 1901).

[26] Mohendracandra Gupta, *Strībodh* (Dacca, 1862), pp. 25-30; editorial in *Sangbād Prabhākar*, 7 August 1850, in Benoy Ghose, *Sāmayikpatre*, part 1 (Calcutta, 1962), p. 320.

[27] Mohendracandra Gupta, *Strībodh*, pp. 8-9.

In the initial stages of female education, opposition was rarely stated in public debate. It came not only from orthodox males, but also from older women within the household. According to Girish Chunder Ghose, editor of the *Hindoo Patriot*, older *zenana* women were privately obdurate in their objections:

> But if even every man of wealth could be induced to listen to reason, what would their sufferance avail in educating the majority of respectable Hindoo women who constitute the middle classes of Hindoo Society? . . . The hearts of the matronhood of Bengal are harder in this matter than stone walls.[28]

His testimony was corroborated by other writers who said that elderly women had a strong prejudice against female education, and a "despotic" power over the younger ladies in the *zenana*.[29] The most prevalent obstacle was apathy:

> Native ladies of the most respectable caste in society have both sent their daughters, and in some instances have themselves expressed anxiety to obtain instruction, [at the Church Missionary Society's Girls' School]. . . . The majority of the more respectable Natives, however, still continue to manifest great apathy concerning the education of their daughters.[30]

One quarter from which no objections were reported was that of the women—girls and young married women—who were most likely to be beneficiaries of female education.

Koilasbasini Debi was one of the first women to be educated and to publish her writings. In her book on *Hindu Female Education and Its Progress*, published in 1865, she expressed the opinion that most *madhyabitta grihastha* (middle-class

[28] "Hindoo Female Education," *Hindoo Patriot*, 28 August 1856, in M. N. Ghosh, ed., *Selections*, p. 225.

[29] Replies to the enquiries of the Bengal Social Science Association on the subject of Female Education, 1869. Reprinted in B. Dutt Gupta, *Sociology in India*, Appendix V, pp. 123-124. See also "Native Female Education," *CR*, 25:49, p. 91.

[30] W. Adam, *Reports*, First report (1835), p. 47.

householders) in the early part of the century saw no need for female education, but that the extension of British rule meant that this was no longer the case.[31]

The *bhadralok* intelligentsia were united in their support for female education. As was shown in the previous chapter, even the "conservatives" among them were in favor of it. The *Strīsiksā bidhāyak* outlined the reasons for this. The author believed that education would help women in leading a virtuous life, without necessarily upsetting the traditional fabric of Hindu society. This is evident in the final injunction:

> And whether the husband is a town-dweller or a forest-dweller, saint or sinner, prosperous or poor, virtuous or worthless, living in a mansion or in a hut, handsome or ugly, it is a wife's duty to obey him. It is said in the *sāstras* that there is no greater ornament for a husband than to have a virtuous wife. Hence, women, if you all use your leisure time to cultivate knowledge and morality you will certainly find supreme happiness in scholarship and morals.[32]

Progressives and conservatives alike believed that educated mothers would improve the physical health and mental vigor of future generations of Bengali *bhadralok*. While conservatives believed that educated women would uphold the values of traditional Hindu society, progressives hoped that they would use their influence to bring about social change.

Methods of education: home, *zenana*, and school

In the first half of the century, and even later, the debate among those in favor of female education centered on the method to be employed. The three broad types under consideration were informal home education, *zenana* education, and education in schools. Initially, more time was spent in discussing the merits of the various schemes than in executing any of them.

[31] Koilasbasini Debi, *Hindu Female Education*, pp. 12, 20.
[32] [Gourmohan Vidyalankar], *Strīsiksā*, p. 24.

Home education was probably most frequently adopted. Progressive husbands would educate their wives, brothers teach their sisters, or fathers and uncles instruct their daughters and nieces. There is a great deal of biographical evidence for this.[33] In spite of the frequency of home education, however, it was not often advocated in theory. The domestic duties of a *bhadramahilā* meant that she had a very long working day. Custom forbade her from speaking to her husband during that time; she could only see him late at night, after finishing all the household work. At such a time she was in no fit state to absorb new knowledge.[34] Household opinion did not look kindly on her education:

> While the other women in the family railed at every idea of education, the wife of an enlightened husband, could scarcely venture to act according to his better advice; . . . many are deterred from attempting to teach their wives privately from the little prospect of success that is before them.[35]

The second method was that of private tuition, known as *zenana* education. At the outset this was promoted by missionaries, and all teachers were European ladies. Although many favored the scheme in principle because it did not upset purdah arrangements or disturb domestic organization too greatly, its evangelical character tended to create obstacles that overwhelmed its obvious advantages.

The Reverend Krishna Mohan Banerjea felt that nothing could be expected from schemes for public education of the

[33] See, for instance, Swarnalata Debi, *Mātri-tarpan* (Calcutta, 1914); Candrakanta Sen, *Bāmāsundarī bā ādarsa-nārī* (Calcutta, 1909); Muralidhar Bandopadhyay, *Srīmatī Saraswatī Sener sangksipta jībanī; Bāmā-carit* (Dacca, 1893); Suniti Mallik, *Akāl-kusum* (Calcutta, 1896); Girish Chandra Sen, *Brahmamayī-carit* (Calcutta, 1869); Dwarkanath Ganguly, *Jībanālekhya*; Prakascandra Ray, *Aghor-prakās* (Calcutta, 1958). See also Chapter Four.

[34] Replies to the enquiries of the Bengal Social Science Association in B. Dutt Gupta, *Sociology in India*, Appendix V, p. 124.

[35] Krishna Mohan Banerjea, cited in "Native Female Education," *CR*, 25:49, p. 99.

"high and middling" classes, but that benefits would result if the government could sponsor a *zenana* education scheme whereby some "wealthy and influential native gentlemen can also be induced to give up rooms in their inner courts for the use of private schools, where none but ladies shall be admitted as tutoresses or visitors, nor any except girls from select families allowed to enter as pupils."[36]

The *zenana* education system presented a reasonable compromise, "combining as it does the advantages of tutorial instruction at home with those of a public education."[37] Even so, it was some time before it was accepted. The earliest case of *zenana* education was the instruction of the wife and daughters of Jay Narain Ghosal by the wife of Mr. Tracey of the Church Missionary Society. Jay Narain's aim was to enable the womenfolk to put their domestic grievances in writing instead of calling him home to settle disputes. The lessons worked well, but were discontinued because of social criticism. They were resumed two years later.[38] In 1840 Mrs. Wilson (formerly Miss Cooke, the first lady teacher sent to Calcutta by the British and Foreign School Society, in 1821) could only think of two cases of *zenana* education, in 1823 and 1829, neither of which lasted for very long.[39]

The fear of public ridicule and criticism, and of Christian influence, were the chief obstacles to success. Fears were fed by occasional conversions, as in the case of Bala Shoondaree, first wife of Gyanendra Mohun Tagore and daughter-in-law of Prasanna Kumar Tagore. When she had learned to read and write through her own efforts, her husband hired an English governess for her for one and a half years in the mid-1840s. She died shortly after she had made up her mind to

[36] Krishna Mohan Banerjea, *Native Female Education*, pp. 80-90.

[37] "Social Reformation: The Condition of Women in India," *Hindoo Patriot* (17 August 1854), from M. N. Ghosh, *Selections*, p. 188.

[38] Weitbrecht, *The Women of India*, pp. 66-69.

[39] One of which was probably to Kali Shunker Ghosal's family in Kidderpore, cited in Laird, *Missionaries and Education*, p. 136. This may even have been the same as the family of Jay Narain Ghosal.

be baptized. Prasanna Kumar Tagore's own daughter, Sura-sundari Debi, was also formally educated at home.[40]

Zenana education was not freely available to the *chotolok*, and therefore was compatible with the preservation of *bha-dralok* status. Antimissionary sentiment was not aggravated by the fear of mixing of castes, as it was in the *bhadralok* aversion to public missionary schools. Even strict caste Hindus engaged the services of female missionaries to instruct their daughters.[41] A *zenana* education scheme proposed in 1855 cost sixteen rupees per month for those in town, and twenty-five rupees for those in the suburbs.[42] Female education of this kind was a luxury, and only the wealthier *bhadralok* could afford it.

The content of *zenana* education by untrained missionary ladies placed heavy emphasis on Biblical instruction and wool-work. Though probably of limited educational value, the les-sons formed a bridge between the *zenana* and the world out-side. They were a point of cultural contact with British women, providing the *bhadramahilā* with the opportunity of learning

[40] For details of Bala Shoondaree's life, see E. Storrow, *The Eastern Lily Gathered*. The education of Prasanna Kumar Tagore's daughter was not as successful as had been hoped, because of the "defective system" of her ed-ucation and the "want of intercourse with European ladies." Letter from "an enlightened friend" to Krishna Mohan Banerjea, no date, appendix B of his *Native Female Education*, pp. 131-132. No names are mentioned, but it refers to the "splendid apparatus that my father had laid down for the ed-ucation of my late lamented sister," and Prasanna Kumar Tagore is the best known case at that time of a father making formal arrangements for his daughter's education. See also Koilasbasini Debi, *Hindu Female Education*, p. 30.

[41] Kumudini Ghose was born in Calcutta in 1855. Her father, Kalikumar Ghose, was a strict Hindu, yet he allowed his daughter to have lessons from an English missionary woman, along with the daughter of the neighboring Brahmin family. *Kumudinī-caritra. A Brief Sketch of the Life of Srimati Kumudinee the wife of R. C. Sinha of the New Dispensation Brahma Somaj of India* (Cooch Behar, 1890), pp. 1-2, 6.

[42] Review of "Zenana and Select School Scheme," pamphlet VI in the series "Fly Leaves for Indian Homes," 1855-56 in *CR*, 25:50 (1855), xxxiv. Not all fees could have been set that high, as Mrs. Weitbrecht, *The Women of India*, mentioned women whose husbands were clerks in government offices—although their fees may have been paid for by wealthier relatives (pp. 96-99).

the habits and even the language of Europeans, a kind of "improving" contact much desired by enlightened *bhadralok* husbands. *Zenana* education must have been a palliative for boredom and frustration for women in the *zenana*, who had little novelty, excitement, or stimulation in their daily lives. It was little wonder that the possibility of conversion existed. For many women, education and Christianity were linked through the missionaries' *zenana* education schemes, and conversion would have appeared to be one of the few ways of breaking out of an unsatisfactory pattern of life.

Some members of the *bhadralok* hoped for a more rapid and thorough extension of the benefits of education. As early as 1822, the *Strīsiksā bidhāyak* argued the case for the education of young girls of less wealthy families in public schools.[43] In 1828 Raja Baidyanath Roy of Jorasanko donated 20,000 rupees to the Central Female School, run by missionaries. However, his own wife was educated at home by Mrs. Wilson, and none of the *bhadralok* would send their daughters to the school.[44] A more direct attempt to found a school for the *bhadramahilā* was made in 1845, when Jaykrishna Mukherjee submitted a proposal to the government for a girls' school at Utterparah. Not only was he willing to match the government grant, but more importantly, he also indicated that he was willing to send his own daughters there. The government did not take up the offer, and the scheme lapsed until proposed again, in more specific detail, in 1849. The government again failed to respond, this time on the advice of the educationalist J.E.D. Bethune, who wanted to observe the progress of the girls' school he had established himself as a test case.[45] Despite theoretical advocacy of the benefits of female education, of-

[43] [Gourmohan Vidyalankar], *Strīsiksā*, p. 22. Wealthy families were advised to have private tuition.

[44] J. C. Bagal, *Women's Education*, pp. 29-31.

[45] J. A. Richey, *Selections from Educational Records, part II, 1840-59* (New Delhi, 1965). Extract from Report of the Council for Education, Bengal, 1848-49, pp. 47-49 and letter from J.E.D. Bethune to the Marquis of Dalhousie, Governor-General, Calcutta, 29 March 1850, pp. 53-54. See also N. Mukherjee, *A Bengal Zamindar*, pp. 82-83, 153-155.

ficial lack of enthusiasm may have been due to the absence of any possibility of future employment for girls. Female education did not correspond with the government's educational aim of providing clerks for the imperial bureaucracy.

The distinction of being the first school for the *bhadramahilā* in Bengal went to the Barasat Girls' School, established in 1847 by the educationalist Peary Charan Sircar and others.[46] The progressive local *bhadralok* who sent their daughters to the school were persecuted by the orthodox community both physically and through legal harassment. The opposition eventually subsided, and the remaining total of twenty pupils continued to be the average number of enrolments.[47] Although the school was not very well known, it did set a precedent for the public education of girls. It may have been the inspiration for the girls' school in the village of Nibadhai, which was founded in 1848 without any opposition.[48]

All other experiments were eclipsed by the foundation of the Bethune School in Calcutta in May 1849. In his opening speech the Honorable J.E.D. Bethune, president of the Council of Education, gave his reasons for founding the school. He reiterated the need for educated mothers, and the familiar belief in the "civilizing" mission of women:

> I believed that you, having felt in your own person that elevating influence of a good education, would before long begin to feel the want of companions, the cultivation of whose taste and intellect might correspond in some

[46] J. C. Bagal, *Women's Education*, p. 77; *BP*, 6:1, 384 (January 1897); *GRPI from 1st October 1849 to 30th September 1850*, pp. 4-5, lists the names of all *bhadralok* involved.

[47] "Native Female Education," *CR*, 25:49, pp. 77-78; J. A. Richey, *Selections*, p. 54. Bethune offered money for the building of the schoolhouse at Barasat, but the managers said that they hoped to raise sufficient funds from among themselves.

[48] "Nibādhai Bālikā Bidyālay," *BP*, 2:2, 34 (June 1864); "Nibādhai Grāmastha Bidyālay," *Tattwabodhinī Patrikā*, 116 (Chaitra 1774 [1852]), in B. Ghose, *Sāmayikpatre*, part 2 (Calcutta, 1963). J.E.D. Bethune mentioned the "Neebudhia" school as predating his school. J. A. Richey, *Selections*, p. 54. See also *GRPI from 1st October 1849 to 30th September 1850* (Calcutta, 1851), p. 5.

degree to your own; that you would gradually begin to understand how infinitely the happiness of domestic life may be enhanced by the charm which can be thrown over it by the graceful virtues and elegant accomplishments of well-educated woman; that you would be led to the reflection, in your study of the history of other nations, that in the degree of estimation in which females are held, the amount of mental culture to which they attain, and the extent of influence which they are permitted to exercise over the tastes and habits of society, the best and surest test may be found of the degree in which one nation surpasses another in civilization.[49]

To attain these goals, women were to be taught in Bengali, using English only for "subsidiary advantages" and when parental approval had been granted. Apart from more general subjects, girls were also going to learn "a thousand feminine works and accomplishments" in embroidery, fancy work, and drawing, to give them a "means of adorning their own homes, and of supplying themselves with harmless and elegant employment." In short, it was the same kind of education that was in vogue among their British middle-class contemporaries. An Englishwoman, Mrs. Risdale, presided over the institution.

The Bethune School was thus launched with all the advantages of a central location in Calcutta, government patronage, and adequate funding. Bethune had also realized that the school could only be successful if it had the support of the leaders of *bhadralok* society, not merely in an individual capacity but as the heads of the influential *dals*. He wrote to the governor-general, Lord Dalhousie, not long after the school had opened that he had "secured the promise from some of the 'Dhols' or 'clans' into which Calcutta is divided that if any are excommunicated and turned out of a Dhol for sending their

[49] J. C. Bagal, "History of the Bethune School and College," Appendix I, in K. Nag, ed., *Bethune School and College Centenary Volume 1849-1949* (Calcutta, 1949), p. 107. It was first known as the Calcutta Female School. It became known as the Bethune School after 1862 (pp. 12, 25).

daughters to my school they shall be taken into theirs."[50] Many eminent members of the *bhadralok* elite openly expressed their commitment by sending their own daughters to the school. The first pupils included the daughters of Brahmo Debendranath Tagore, of orthodox pandit Madan Mohan Tarkalankar, and of the former "firebrand" of Young Bengal, Ram Gopal Ghose.

Education at the school was emphatically secular, and the staff was not allowed to preach Christianity at any time.[51] The girls were taken to and from school in covered carriages, but because male pandits did most of the teaching, purdah could not be fully maintained. The initial enrolment of twenty-one rose to eighty within two years, but then numbers began to drop.[52] In spite of all its advantages, the Bethune School initially was not a success. There were both apathy and the opposition of the orthodox *bhadralok* to contend with. Even many who agreed on the necessity of female education saw public schooling as offending custom and religious propriety.[53] The school continued to disappoint the hopes of its founders for some time. In 1868 an article in the women's magazine *Bāmābodhinī Patrikā* lamented the failure of the educated middle classes in taking the lead in female education. The article claimed that the Bethune School was kept going solely by government assistance.[54] In 1863 there were ninety-three girls enrolled, and the annual expenditure of the school was 7,000 rupees. It was said that many of the girls were low-caste, and that the duration of their education was very brief. Attendance was irregular, and it was estimated that "only a quarter of the girls know how to read a simple tale and un-

[50] Bethune to Dalhousie, 9 June 1849, Dalhousie Papers. This letter was brought to my notice by J. McGuire.

[51] Weitbrecht, *The Women of India*, pp. 189-190.

[52] J. C. Bagal, *Women's Education*, pp. 81-95. J. A. Richey, *Selections*, p. 52; Bethune mentioned the initial enrolment as eleven.

[53] "Bhāskar pāthak hoite prāpta," *Sangbād Bhāskar*, 22 (13 May 1849), in B. Ghose, *Sāmayikpatre*, part 3, pp. 411-412.

[54] *BP*, 3, 55 (March 1868).

derstand its meaning."[55] In January 1868 there were only thirty girls left at the school. Miss Pigot, superintendent at the time, was accused of mismanagement and forced to resign.[56]

Miss Pigot's inefficiency was clearly not the main cause for the decline, since after her departure the school showed no rapid improvement. The introduction of a monthly fee of one rupee in 1866 was one reason for the reduction in enrolments. Middle-income *bhadralok* families, which supplied most of the pupils, were unable to afford the fee in addition to the other costs of female education.[57]

A survey conducted by divisional inspectors of schools for the Committee of Public Instruction in 1870 provides valuable insight into the social background of pupils at the school. It showed that they were all from what the British categorized as the "upper and middle ranks." Of the 76 pupils at Bethune School at that time, 51 were from the "Small Landholder, Higher Professional, and Lower Professional" groups. The composition of other schools was more mixed. Only 1,741 out of 3,331 girls attending schools receiving government grants-in-aid in Calcutta and Central district were classed as upper- and middle-ranking, and only 89 of the 150 girls at unaided, privately run schools were so classified. It was assumed that most of the 1,327 women receiving *zenana* education in Calcutta were from the upper and middle ranks, but substantiating evidence was unobtainable because of "alleged unwillingness on the part of the ladies receiving instruction to speak of the occupations of their husbands." The social classification

[55] "The Bethune Female School," *The Bengalee*, 13 January 1863, in M. N. Ghosh, *Selections*, pp. 445-447. See also a summary of Woodrow's Report on Public Instruction for 1863-1864 in J. C. Bagal, *Bethune School*, p. 26.

[56] The charge was that she had introduced Christianity into her teachings, but she claimed it was because she wished to go beyond needlework. D. Kopf, "The Brahmo Idea of Social Reform and the Problem of Female Emancipation in Bengal," in J. McLane, ed., *Bengal in the Nineteenth and Twentieth Centuries* (Ann Arbor, 1975), p. 46.

[57] See J. C. Bagal, *Bethune School*, pp. 23-29, for the school's history between 1857 and 1869.

TABLE I

SOCIAL CLASSIFICATION OF THE UPPER AND MIDDLE RANKS, AS
DEFINED BY THE COMMITTEE OF PUBLIC INSTRUCTION

1. Titled aristocracy
2. Large landholders
3. Small landholders
4. Higher professional (barristers, surgeons, engineers, pleaders, clergy, . . . mullas, . . . professors . . . , English teachers, university degree holders, editors . . .)
5. Lower professional (*muktear*, *amla*, writer, surveyor, overseer, native doctor, apothecary, pandit, English teacher, *munshi*, printer, *ghatak*, press proprietor . . .)
6. Higher commerce (bankers, brokers, gold merchants, *mahajan*, large traders, manufacturers of sugar . . .)
7. Lower commerce (large shopkeepers)
8. Art (musicians, photographers, portrait painters, engravers)
9. Government officers (200 rupees per month and above)
10. Government officers (50-200 rupees per month)
11. Government officers (20-50 rupees per month)
12. Government officers (less than 50 rupees per month—military officers, teachers, pandits, postmasters, *amlas*)

system used, and the results of the survey, were as shown in Tables I and II.[58]

The quality of education imparted did not appear to be a significant factor affecting enrolments. Even when the standard of education at the Bethune School was low, enrolments were still high. The school's failure to produce well-educated graduates of the same standard as male schools was not due solely to the particular problems involved in introducing female education in a society where post-adolescent purdah and child marriage drastically shortened the average time of schooling for women. Even in England, where these obstacles were not present, the Schools' Inquiry Commission of 1864-1867 found that in most British girls' schools, history, English,

[58] *GRPI for 1869-70* (Calcutta, 1870), pp. 16-22.

TABLE II

SOCIAL BACKGROUND OF PUPILS AT SCHOOLS IN CALCUTTA

Girls' Schools	Number	Pupils	1	2	3	4	5	6	7	8	9	10	11	12	Total
Government	1	76	2	2	9	14	28	3	7	—	6	5	—	—	76
Aided	90	3331	1	31	157	260	813	156	46	6	25	89	72	85	1741
Unaided*	4	150	—	—	10	21	51	5	—	—	—	—	—	2	89
Zenana	87	1327	—	8	22	27	63	49	13	7	20	16	6	—	231

* The unaided category encompassed schools as diverse as European and foreign girls' schools such as Loreto House and La Martiniere, and native girls' schools such as the Scotch Orphanage.

and general knowledge were learned entirely by rote and without an understanding of the meaning.[59]

One early pupil of the Bethune School reminisced that she had shown little interest in gaining an education while she was a pupil there. Her main pleasure was in racing to the carriage with a friend in the mornings, to try to win the coveted seating position on the side farthest from the open door.[60] Young unmarried girls, used to a large degree of freedom in their own homes, may not have liked the formality and restrictiveness imposed on them by school life. Lack of a tangible purpose for study meant that this group was not highly motivated.

The apparent failure of the Bethune School turned attention back to *zenana* education. In any case, the Bethune School had not catered for older married women, who were the group most conscious of the benefits of education and most anxious to take advantage of them. *Zenana* education was the most practical means of educating them, and their eagerness augured well for the success of this method. The Brahma Bandhu Sabha was started in 1863 by some younger members of the Brahmo Samaj, whose aims included sponsoring female education in the home.[61] The hope was expressed that a branch of the new association would be founded in every *mofussil* town where there was already a Brahmo Samaj.[62]

Zenana associations were a popular means of conducting female education. Many were operated by missionary agencies, but others were managed by "enlightened native gentlemen." They were mainly examining bodies that prescribed textbooks for home study at the beginning of the year and

[59] J. Kamm, *How Different From Us. A Biography of Miss Buss and Miss Beale* (London, 1958). They were pioneers of modern girls' education in Britain (pp. 84-87).

[60] Nabin-kali Dasi, *Kumārī siksā* (Calcutta, 1883), pp. 20-21.

[61] P. S. Basu, *Life and Works of Brahmananda Keshav* (Calcutta, 1940), p. 68.

[62] *Tattwabodhinī Patrikā*, 245 (Pous 1785 [1863]), in B. Ghose, *Sāmayikpatre*, part 2, p. 432.

awarded prizes after an annual examination.[63] There was some doubt as to the efficacy of *zenana* associations. In her report for 1877-1878, the inspectress of female schools found that mission schemes for *zenana* education were preoccupied with increasing numbers to the detriment of the standard of education. In most cases, mistresses only devoted two hours each week to a house, when they would answer general questions, conduct reading lessons, teach needlework, and read Bible stories. Native *zenana* agencies were equally deficient. Teaching was spasmodic, and examinations were often unsupervised, which invited dishonesty. Husbands were suspected of giving assistance, as the inspectress often found pupils able only to read books of a lower standard than those set for the examinations that they were supposed to have passed.[64]

The debate over curriculum content

The prevalence of *zenana* education caused a controversy over the content of the curriculum. The main issue was the extent to which female education should differ from that of men. A closer examination of this debate yields a great deal of information on the role of women in society. In England, there had been a battle to rescue women's education from the purely decorative function it had performed in the early nineteenth century, and to give girls a challenging and stimulating modern education. The content of the latter was never fully agreed upon. Educationalists tended to divide into two groups, the "uncompromising," who advocated exactly the same education as males in order to prove equality, and the "separatists," who favored a modified curriculum to train women for their future role.[65] Although there was extensive debate on the mode of education in the early stages of female education in Bengal,

[63] *GRPI for 1875-76*, p. 87.
[64] *GRPI for 1877-78*, pp. 79-80.
[65] See an interesting discussion of this in "The Contradictions in Ladies' Education" by Sara Delamont in S. Delamont and L. Duffin, eds., *The Nineteenth-Century Woman. Her Cultural and Physical World* (London, 1978).

there had been little discussion of its content. The curriculum followed in the Bethune School and other girls' schools was similar to that followed in a vernacular boys' school. Yet it should not be supposed that therefore the education of men and women was seen in the same way.

There was a continued lament over the lack of suitable textbooks for girls, indicating that female education was perceived differently from that of males. Madan Mohan Tarkalankar wrote *Sisusiksā* as a text for girls in 1849, after his two daughters had started going to the Bethune School.[66] However, much of the preoccupation with distinctively female subjects was a reflection of British preconceptions. Needlework was not traditionally associated with females in most parts of India, but it formed a large part of the curriculum in girls' schools and in the *zenana*, due largely to the English predilection for needlework as a feminine accomplishment. The education of the English ladies who were responsible for teaching Bengali women had fitted them only for instructing others in such accomplishments, and therefore the quality of education imparted by them was lower than that received by boys taught by better-educated male teachers.

The *Bāmābodhinī Patrikā* for January 1866 announced the Antahpur Stri Siksa scheme proposed by the Brahma Bandhu Sabha.[67] Husbands, or whoever had taken on the task of instruction, had to give a progress report to the Sabha every three months, and there would be annual examinations with prizes awarded. The curriculum included such general subjects as mathematics, geography, and grammar. It was noted that there had been objections that those subjects were too difficult and beyond women's capabilities, but the objections went unheeded because it was felt that these subjects were a necessary part of helping women to become more rational beings. In England at the same time opposition to such subjects was more entrenched. Arithmetic was seen as a dangerous addition

---

[66] *Kabibar Madanmohan Tarkālankārer jībancarit o tadgrantha samālocanā* (Calcutta, 1871), pp. 9-11.

[67] "Antahpure strīsiksā," *BP*, 2:1, 29 (January 1866).

to the curriculum, and science could only be safely admitted under the guise of physical geography.[68] A writer in the *Calcutta Review* in 1864 was eloquent about the need for a semiscientific education for Hindu women:

> With reference to purely intellectual education, let everything be taught a Hindu girl which forms and exercises the habit of attention and the power of judging by the eye. Popular Astronomy will expand the mind and carry it from nature up to nature's God. History and Geography will free the mind from the prejudices of the nursery and will inoculate it with correct ideas of the seats, the causes, and the progress of civilization. ... We would teach composition, but the themes must be drawn not from the abstractions of metaphysicians, but from the observations and actualities of life.[69]

Music and drawing were also recommended, but although the author stated that he did not want to create "a tribe of literary and scientific ladies" looking down on mundane affairs, it was also recognized that "the capacity to cook and to operate on Berlin wool are not the *summum bonum* of woman." An educated woman was declared to be better at everything, including household duties, than an uneducated one.

Although the course set for the Antahpur Stri Siksa scheme in 1866 may have been slightly less heavy than that studied by boys, it was not a noticeably "feminine" curriculum. The highest class had passed the double rule of three and decimals in arithmetic and the twelfth theorem in geometry; had studied the first part of Tarinicaran's *Bhāratbarser itihās* for history, and eight sections of a text on the science of matter, and was required to read Kalidasa's *Rāghuvamsa* and Michael Madhusudan's *Megnādbadh kābya* for literature.[70] Any girl who had

[68] J. Kamm, *How Different From Us*, pp. 55-56, 63.
[69] "Hindoo Women," *CR*, 40:79, pp. 93-94.
[70] *BP*, 2:2, 37 (September 1866). In 1865 there had been no pupils in the highest class (class 5). Of the two in class 4, Kamini Debi got 55 percent in the examination paper, but Saraswati Sen only got 25 percent, a result that elicited editorial disapproval and the expressed hope that she would be more attentive to her studies in future. *BP*, 2:3, 36 (August 1866).

reached this level would have had an advanced education by any standard.

As time went on, the number of special textbooks for females increased. Reliance on these meant that the content of female education became increasingly differentiated from that of men and probably suffered a decline in standard. One such text was the *Strī-siksā*, part one, published in 1861. This text was designed to follow on from the *Barnaparicay*, parts one and two, the basic reading primers written by Vidyasagar.[71] It was a book of short moral tales written in the simple colloquial style used in women's conversation. Many of the stories illustrated pious and good behavior. For instance, Susila was a clever girl who had won many prizes at school. She was now married and at home, but still read good books, and was able to draw a map with towns, mountains, and rivers marked on it. Another story was about Binodini's skill in sewing. Other essays proclaimed the advantages of female education, especially when continued after marriage, and the value of cleanliness. Another essay was about the earth, and undermined the old superstitions that the earth rested on a turtle's back and that men could not travel further north than the Himalayas. Such a text directed the education of women to fit them for their designated sphere. It touched on household matters, and dealt mainly with moral problems faced in daily life rather than with abstruse metaphysics.

In the 1860s there was already the beginning of a cleavage of opinion over the desirable content of female education, but it did not come to a head until the next decade. Even the most vehement British enthusiasts of female education seemed to agree on the need for some "feminine" content. After her visit in 1866, Mary Carpenter made suggestions for the education of Hindu girls. Although she was herself an exceptional case, having had the classical education of a boy,[72] her proposals included the cultivation of beautiful flowers to soften the girls' minds, music for their refinement, and drawing, as well as

[71] Ramtanu Gupta, *Strī-siksā pratham bhāg* (Calcutta, 1861).
[72] J. Manton, *Mary Carpenter and the Children of the Streets* (London, 1976).

calisthenic exercises and experiments in natural philosophy. She saw the aim of their education being to render them "fit and useful helpmates."[73] In 1876, the Committee of Public Instruction proposed to replace higher mathematics with the study of needlework and embroidery. A vernacular newspaper, the *Bhārat Mihir*, objected on the grounds that needlework and embroidery were merely of recreational benefit, whereas the study of mathematics "quickens and sharpens the intellect."[74] By the turn of the century, needlework and domestic science were a routine part of the curriculum in girls' schools.[75]

A writer in the *Bāmābodhinī Patrikā* for 1870 warned of the necessity for educated women to retain traditional Hindu womanly virtues. The article listed ten of these, including devotion to God, charity, self-sacrifice, faithfulness, and honesty.[76] Education was considered dangerous not because it made a woman manly, as was feared in England and America,[77] but because it drew her away from her traditional role. The concept of "femininity" in connection with a stereotyped image of physical and mental frailty was not as persistent in India as it was in the west. In India being female was defined more by role than by behavioral and personality traits.[78]

The growth of female education continued, uninterrupted by the debate over its content. Enthusiasm for female education was especially apparent in the *mofussil*, where girls' schools sprang up for the daughters of the resident *bhadralok*.

[73] Address to a meeting in Madras in 1867, cited in "Miss Carpenter's Six Months in India," *CR*, 47:94 (1868), pp. 7-8.

[74] *Bhārat Mihir*, 18 May 1876 in *RNNB* 27 May 1876.

[75] H. Sharp, ed., *Progress of Education in India 1907-1912. Sixth Quinquennial Review*, I (Calcutta, 1914), 222.

[76] "Strīlokdiger bidyāsikser sahit dharmma-siksār ābasyaktā," *BP*, 6, 82 (June 1870).

[77] S. Delamont, "The Contradictions in Ladies' Education."

[78] For a contemporary discussion of this, see M. Roy, "The Concepts of 'Femininity' and 'Liberation' in the Context of Changing Sex-Roles: Women in Modern India and America," in D. Raphael, ed., *Being Female* (The Hague, 1975).

They were rarely set up by government initiative. In 1859-1860 the government rejected a recommendation for a grant to establish girls' schools in Hughly, Burdwan, and the Twenty-Four Parganas on the grounds of "financial pressure."[79] The task was left to philanthropic individuals or to social reform associations. The Utterparah Hitakari Sabha was particularly active in sponsoring women's education. It set up a girls' school in Utterparah in 1863.[80] Regular examinations were held and scholarships awarded. Similar associations existed in other towns. Female education was one of the hallmarks of the Brahmo program for social reform. Wherever a Brahmo was posted, he would set up—often with the help of his wife—a Brahmo Samaj, a boys' school, a charitable dispensary, and a school for girls. Sasipada Banerjea was a perfect example of this type. The girls' school he established in Burranagore in 1865 began as a class for girls held in his own home.[81] Over the years the *Bāmābodhinī Patrikā* noted the rise of a number of schools for girls in the *mofussil*. In 1864 a small school was started by the Mallik family of Sindhuriapati, with twenty-two pupils and two lady superintendents.[82] When Mary Carpenter came to Bengal in 1866 she visited girls' schools in Konnegore and Krishnagar as well as in Utterparah, Ranaghat, and Burranagore.[83] The deputy magistrate in Ranaghat started a girls' school there in 1868, which grew from ten to forty pupils in five months.[84] The number of female pupils in schools in the Central Division rose from 999 in April 1863

[79] Government of India, *Selections from the Educational Records of the Government of India, v. I, Education Reports 1859-71* (Delhi, 1960), p. 86.
[80] N. Mukherjee, *A Bengal Zamindar*, p. 252; M. Carpenter, *Six Months in India*, I (London, 1868), 243-244. BP, 2:2, 35 (July 1866), said that it grew from an enrolment of eight to sixty in three years.
[81] M. Carpenter, *Six Months*, pp. 248-249; Albion Banerji, *An Indian Pathfinder* (Calcutta, 1971), p. 13; Srinath Canda, *Brāhmasamāje callis bathsar* (Calcutta, 1969); Shib Chunder Deb, "Autobiography," in M. N. Ghosh, ed., *The Life of Grish Chunder Ghose*.
[82] "Strī-bidyālay," *BP*, 5, 74 (October 1869).
[83] M. Carpenter, *Six Months*, pp. 232-269.
[84] "Rānāghāt Bālikā Bidyālay," *BP*, 5, 73 (September 1869).

to 3,307 in April 1866.[85] By 1878 there were 21,587 girls receiving instruction in the whole of Bengal.[86]

Differing philosophies: the expansion of female education in Calcutta

Keshub Chunder Sen, leader of the Brahmo Samaj of India, returned from a visit to England in 1870 fired with renewed enthusiasm for female education. The Bethune School had apparently stagnated,[87] so in February 1871 Keshub started the Native Ladies' Normal School under the auspices of the new philanthropic organization, the Indian Reform Association. The school's main aim was teacher training. A girls' primary school was added in September 1871 to give the trainees some experience.[88] The normal school was small, increasing from thirteen or fourteen pupils initially to twenty-four or twenty-five a year later.[89] Nearly all the pupils were Brahmos,[90] and the school was located for some time within the grounds of the Bharat Ashram. Pupils living outside were inconvenienced because their domestic duties left little time for study.[91]

Keshub's address on the first anniversary of the Bama Hi-taisini Sabha, a discussion group connected with the school, made his limited aims for the pupils quite clear. He said that women occupied a different sphere from men, and that there-

[85] Not all schools catered for the *bhadramahilā*, but they would account at least for the 125 pupils in the Bethune School and the 610 in the Zenana Associations, as well as part of the 1,877 in government-aided schools and the 103 in unaided schools under native managers. Taken from the report of Mr. Woodrow, inspector of the Central Division, in Government of India, *Selections*, p. 212.

[86] *GRPI from 1877-1878*, p. 77.

[87] The attempt to incorporate a normal school section in 1868 had failed. See J. C. Bagal, *Bethune School*, pp. 29-31.

[88] P. S. Basu, *Life and Works*, p. 276.

[89] "Bāmā hitoisini sabhār sāngbathsarik uthsab," *BP*, 8, 105 (May 1872).

[90] Only two or three pupils at the normal school were Hindus, but over twenty at the girls' school came from orthodox Hindu families. *Indian Mirror*, 28 May 1873.

[91] Letter from P.K.R. Chowdry, *Indian Mirror* (Calcutta), 16 October 1873.

fore their progress should be different. They should progress not only in general knowledge, but in their special duties of doing housework, serving their parents, raising children, and helping their menfolk. They should not aim at being great scholars, but at being good wives, mothers, daughters, and sisters.[92]

The running of the school embodied Brahmo principles of social reform by breaking the purdah system. Pupils were taken on excursions to public places such as the Asiatic Museum.[93] The school curriculum also demonstrated a shift in the perception of women's role by teaching English. Texts studied in the highest class included the English *Fifth Book of Reading*, and McCulloch's *Course of Reading and Grammar*. A basic knowledge of English was beginning to be seen as a mark of social accomplishment. General opinion, however, was still wary of English education for women, because of the fear that they would begin to speak English in the home and that this would lead to a gradual decline in the Bengali language.[94] By 1874 the senior girls had become very proficient in English, reading prose by Addison and Goldsmith, and such poems as Wordsworth's "Ode to Duty," Campbell's "The Mother" and Byron's "Farewell to England." A few of the girls read their English compositions in the presence of the lieutenant-governor at the prize-giving ceremony in 1875. Radharani Lahiri read an essay on "The Duties of an Unmarried Woman," replete with lofty sentiments about modesty and diligence. The ideal unmarried woman was not to be too attentive to dress, but to work hard to attain knowledge and to be modest and careful in her spiritual culture: "Such is the picture of a true virgin who is faithful to her God, and a flower of loveliness in the social circle." Mohini Khastagir

[92] "Bāmā hitoisini sabhār sāngbathsarik uthsab," *BP*, 105.
[93] A separate viewing time was, however, arranged for them. *BP*, 6, 92 (April 1871).
[94] *Bhārat Ranjan*, 21 January 1867 in *RNNB* 31 January 1867; *Bangabāsī*, 13 August 1898 in *RNNB* 20 August 1898.

read an essay on "The People Whom I Like, and Whom I Don't Like."[95]

Regular monthly, half-yearly, and yearly examinations were held. The senior classes also received lessons in vocal and instrumental music and drawing—though critics complained that the teaching of "European airs and tunes" by the European teacher was of no use to native ladies.[96] All classes were taught needlework. The school had a European head-mistress, who was aided by the Brahmo preachers Aghorenath Gupta, Gour Gobinda Roy, and Bijoy Krishna Goswami in the Vernacular Department. Older girls also helped teach the younger.[97] Although the prevailing tone of education was "feminine," Sibnath Sastri, who favored a fuller development of women's intellectual capacities, gave lectures there on "mental science."[98]

When Annette Akroyd announced her plans to come to Calcutta, Keshub had expected her to teach at the Native Ladies' Normal School, but she cancelled the arrangement before she arrived.[99] She presented a very clear alternative to Keshub's ideal, and hence her arrival sharpened the debate over female education. She had been educated at Bedford College, and trained as a governess by the Home and Colonial School Society in 1871-1872.[100] Aged thirty, unmarried, and

[95] P. K. Sen, *Biography of a New Faith*, II (Calcutta, 1954). Appendix II, Annual Report of Indian Reform Association 1870-71, pp. 276-284; Appendix V, Report of the Native Ladies' Normal School and Girls' School for 1875-76, pp. 411-423.

[96] Letter from P.K.R. Chowdry, *Indian Mirror*, 16 October 1873.

[97] P. K. Sen, *Biography*, Appendices II, V.

[98] "Manobijnān," *BP*, 11, 147-148 (November-December 1875).

[99] P. K. Sen, *Biography*, Appendix II, p. 349. She fell out with Keshub. There was a heated debate during 1873 in which she was accused of belonging to the "rationalistic school of theology," and of offering her services "uninvited" to the Indian Reform Association as lady superintendent of the Native Ladies' Normal School. See *Indian Mirror*, April-July 1873. All extracts relating to this matter are collected in Catalogue Item 173 in the S. D. Collet Collection, Sadharan Brahmo Samaj Library. For more information on Annette Akroyd, see W. H. Beveridge, *India Called Them* (London, 1947), and P. Barr, *The Memsahibs* (London, 1976).

[100] Akroyd-Beveridge Papers, India Office Library.

committed to a vocation, she represented the progressive trend in female education, and came to Bengal to put theory into practice. A determined and single-minded woman, she held her theories to be universal, making no concessions to the local environment. Visiting Keshub's school on 27 December 1872, she was horrified by its remoteness from her own concept of what a school should be. The general disorder shocked her, as she was led along dirty passages into a room with dirty paint, with a rough shelf and piles of pamphlets, the only "tolerable" thing being some of the girls and an orderly table and book that showed "traces of a woman's hand"—the British feminist still equated femininity with neatness. External objections apart, she was disappointed in the lack of any real teaching method. Radharani Lahiri read a paper and Keshub discussed it, with barely any participation from the other girls.[101]

This experience increased Annette Akroyd's determination to start a school of her own. It was to be a boarding school, so that she could have full control over the social habits of her charges. She founded the Hindu Mahila Bidyalaya in November 1873 with five boarders. All the girls were Brahmos, including Indumati, daughter of Ramtanu Lahiri; the daughters of Durga Mohan Das and Dwarkanath Ganguly; and Harasundari, the wife of Srinath Datta, who was studying in England.[102] Although her feminism made her a radical in the English context, with regard to India she firmly believed that the way to improvement was by following the English ideal of civilization. She supervised the teaching herself. At mealtimes girls sat at the table and ate with spoons and forks. Although her English teaching certificate had commented that her governing power and influence over children were very good, she had little success with Bengali girls. Probably partly

---

[101] *Ibid., Diary and Notebook in India 1872-1878,* entry for 27 December 1872.

[102] *Ibid., Pocket Diaries 1873-75;* Dwarkanath Ganguly, *Jībanālekhya,* pp. 51-52; Sarala Ray Centenary Committee, *Sarala Ray Centenary Volume* (Calcutta, 1961), p. 93; Prabhatcandra Gangopadhyay, *Bānglār nārī-jāgaran* (Calcutta, 1945), p. 64.

on account of cultural misunderstanding, she found them ca-
pricious about food, dishonest, and hysterical.[103] Apart from
the normal curriculum, her girls had their minds broadened
by frequent open-air excursions—to the Burranagore jute factory, the Botanical Gardens, the Bethune School prize-giving,
and the Fine Arts Exhibition. They were also taught to mix
with Englishwomen, being taken to dine with Mrs. Hobhouse,[104] wife of the legal member of the viceroy's Executive
Council.

Miss Akroyd had made the effort of learning Bengali even
before she came to India in order to be able to speak to Bengali
women, but her cultural rigidity prevented her from attaining
any real understanding of their situation. Although she had
come to Calcutta as a sympathizer with native complaints of
British arrogance and misrule, she herself lacked the patience
necessary for cooperating with Bengalis in their attempts at
reform. On 6 April 1875 she married Henry Beveridge, a
benefactor of the school[105] and a member of the I.C.S. sta-
tioned at Barasat, and relinquished control of the school. The
responsibility was taken over by the "female emancipationist"
Brahmos Durga Mohan Das, Dwarkanath Ganguly, and Ananda Mohan Bose, Miss Akroyd's former associates from whom
she had parted on bad terms. They had not given her the
support she had demanded, and she left the school convinced
that "it was as well to have as little to do with Bengalis as
possible."[106] The school ceased to operate for a short while,
then reopened as the Banga Mahila Bidyalaya in June 1876.[107]

The Banga Mahila Bidyalaya was small, with only fourteen
pupils in 1878, but its influence, and the controversy it provoked, were extensive. Instead of delineating a separate female
sphere, its educational policy was to further the scope of ed-

[103] Akroyd-Beveridge Papers. Letters to her sister, Fanny Mowatt, 1874.
[104] *Ibid., Pocket Diaries 1873-75.*
[105] *Ibid.*, list of donors to the Hindu Mahila Bidyalaya.
[106] *Ibid.*, letters to Fanny Mowatt, 14 May 1874, 17 May 1874. Her falling
out with Bengali reformers was accompanied by bitterness and disillusion-
ment on both sides. See the correspondence with Dwarkanath Ganguly in
August-September 1874.
[107] *Indian Mirror*, 9 April 1876; J. C. Bagal, *Bethune School*, p. 33.

ucation for women to include any area of knowledge that interested them. Along with this, the social training of girls was unmistakably western. The girls had to speak English during school hours, and were brought up almost as if they were English girls. Apart from their academic subjects they learned music, darning, sewing, and knitting, and took turns at being kitchen monitor and keeping school accounts.[108]

The unsatisfactory state of the Bethune School was a matter for grave concern to all connected with female education.[109] Through Miss Akroyd's connections, the education personnel in the government were familiar with the advanced state of the Banga Mahila Bidyalaya. A proposal to amalgamate the two, in a union of financial and intellectual resources, was agreed upon. The *Indian Mirror* led the protest against amalgamation, commenting on the inexpediency and undesirability of uniting a "notoriously un-Hindu" with a strictly Hindu school. Its main objection was not academic, but to the imposition of "heterodox eating" (of meat) and the use of spoons and forks on orthodox Hindus.[110] The cry of orthodox Hinduism in danger was a little disinguous, as not many of the girls already attending the Bethune School would have been from strictly orthodox Hindu families. The defenders of amalgamation argued that an essential part of being taught to be good wives, mothers, and housewives was to be taught manners enabling women to conduct themselves in civilized societies. They said that the accusation of "denationalization" had become a mania: "Is there any harm in introducing among us habits of regularity and punctuality which mark an Englishman? or the tidiness and neatness which mark an Englishwoman? Are such things to be rejected because they are European? What a sad logic!"[111]

An ambitious writer to the *Indian Mirror* in 1873 had wanted

[108] From Director of Public Instruction Report 1876-77, quoted in *Brahmo Year Book*, 1878.

[109] J. C. Bagal, *Bethune School*, pp. 31-36.

[110] *IMS*, 30 June 1878. The protest was echoed in many quarters, including the conservative *National Paper* and the *Christian Herald*. See *Brahmo Public Opinion*, 11 July 1878.

[111] "The Bungo Mohila Vidyaloya," *Brahmo Public Opinion*, 4 July 1878.

Miss Akroyd's curriculum to include arithmetic, algebra, astronomy, experimental physics, natural history, botany (creating a love of gardening and the cultivation of flowers), social and political economy "so far as to enable our ladies to show an intelligent appreciation of, and take an interest in, the topics of the day, so as to be agreeable in society," vernacular literature, English, drawing, painting and music—with native tunes adapted for the piano, harmonium, and flute—horse riding, and household management. In the latter girls were to be taught "to appreciate the beauty, ease, elegance and comfort of the European style of living, so as to be able to adopt the same in their houses when they become their own mistresses. False notions of *nationality* ought to have no place in moving in [sic] the matter."[112] Such a total Anglicization never occurred, but since the most advanced female school was also the most westernized, the issue of female education inevitably became confused with the issue of loss of national identity.

The reaction against western education for women gained in intensity with the rise of nationalist sentiment among the *bhadralok*. Hindu revivalism, with its idealization of a stereotyped all-virtuous Hindu woman, condemned the widening of opportunities for women as "westernizing." Nationalist ideology was used to preserve the status quo with regard to women's role. This was evident in the curriculum outlined by the *Naba Bibhākar Sādhāranī* as suitable for women:

The present system of female education is in no sense a "national" system. It does not enable its incipients [sic] to develop a well-balanced character, or to make themselves worthy and useful members of their homes. The best system of education for Hindu females will be that which will take note of their character, capabilities and lifework, and implant in their minds those priceless domestic virtues which it is necessary for Hindu wives to possess. Considered from this point of view, it is not desirable that the Hindu girl should be given the dena-

[112] *Indian Mirror*, 5 April 1873.

tionalising English education which is given to the Hindu boy. After the primers and easy readers, Hindu girls should be made to read easy books on domestic economy, the bringing up of children, cookery, artistic work suited to Hindu households, and the formation of character. Biographies of noble Aryan women, such as Sita, Sabitri, Damayanti, Gargi, Durgavati, etc., and domestic tales, like Pandit Sibanath Sastri's "Mejabau" and Babu Taraka Nath Ganguli's "Swarnalata" will be wholesome reading for native girls. Advanced girls may study the Ramayan, the Bhagavat, and the Gita with great advantage, because such study will impress them with the truth, beauty, purity and grandeur of the higher principles of the Hindu religion. In this connection the great importance of *bratas* (pious vows) should also be pointed out. . . .

. . . The art work which is taught to girls in the girls' schools can hardly be called "national." Instruction in wool and silk work is not objectionable, but it is desirable that, in addition to such work, Hindu girls should be taught the sort of fancy needle-work and tracing (*alipanā*) for which Hindu women have always been famous. Miniature gardens made of catechu, paper fishes and tortoises and fruits, artistic models made of thickened milk, miniature clay houses and similar toys evince considerable artistic skill, and native girls should be taught to make them.[113]

The controversy became even more heated when it became clear that the newly amalgamated Bethune School was going to train girls for university examinations. Qualified permission was given to Candramukhi Basu, a student of the Dehra Dun School for Native Christian girls, to sit for the Entrance Arts Examination in 1876.[114] The pressure of Dwarkanath Ganguly and others on the government for full recognition resulted

---

[113] *Naba Bibhākar Sādhāranī*, 8 April 1889 in *RNNB* 13 April 1889.
[114] Prabhatcandra Gangopadhyay, *Bānglār nārī-jāgaran*, p. 67.

in a set of rules governing the admission of women to examinations for the degree in Arts in 1878.[115] The requirements for the Entrance Arts (E.A.) examination were to be the same as for men. In the First Arts (F.A.) examination, the differences were that they could choose among French, German, Italian, or an Indian vernacular as a second language, or substitute botany for the second mathematics paper. In the Bachelor of Arts examination they again had freedom in the choice of a second language, and could substitute political economy for mathematics.[116] As the editor of the *Brahmo Public Opinion* remarked, the University of Calcutta had gone even further than the English universities, where women were not yet admitted to degrees.[117]

This remarkable position had been arrived at without the lengthy and tumultuous storm of opposition that had attended the broaching of the subject in England.[118] Apparently, at the meeting of the University Syndicate that decided the issue there had been a division of opinion on whether university education for women should be specifically feminine or not. The editor of the *Bāmābodhinī Patrikā* was of the opinion that there should be differences. It was suggested that English literature be made easier, that history be offered in Bengali, the amount of mathematics be lessened, and art, midwifery, and housework be included.[119] The proposed course of study at the new Bethune School was of a high academic order. Well-known male teachers taught mathematics, physical sciences and chemistry, literature, history, and mental and moral phi-

[115] Sarala Ray Centenary Committee, *Sarala Ray*, pp. 93-94.

[116] *Brahmo Public Opinion*, 23 May 1878.

[117] London University admitted women to degrees later in 1878. J. Kamm, *Hope Deferred—Girls' Education in English History* (London, 1965), p. 261.

[118] J. Kamm, *How Different From Us*; S. Delamont, "The Contradictions in Ladies' Education"; Emily Davies, "The Influence of University Degrees on the Education of Women," *Victoria Magazine*, 1863, in E. Davies, *Thoughts on Some Questions Relating to Women* (New York, 1971; Cambridge, 1910). The latter recounts that the question was first raised in 1856, when a lady applied for admission to the examinations of the University of London and was refused.

[119] "Biswabidyālaye strīlokdiger parīksā," *BP*, 13, 166 (June 1877). See also *Education Gazette*, 23 January 1885 in *RNNB* 31 January 1885.

losophy.[120] It was hoped by its well-wishers that it would become "the Girton College of the East."[121] In *Abalābāndhab*, a women's journal run by the progressive Brahmos who had managed the Banga Mahila Bidyalaya, Girton College was again held up as the model for the education to be given at Bethune School.[122]

Kadambini Basu sat for the Entrance Arts examination in 1878, and missed obtaining a first division pass by only one mark. It was noted that she obtained high marks in Bengali, tolerable marks in history, "and even in exact science—a subject which is not usually considered to be congenial to the female intellect—she acquitted herself creditably."[123] Accordingly she continued to study for the F.A., and the status of the school was raised to that standard.[124] The Free Church Normal School also opened college classes for Candramukhi Basu, the pioneer of the E.A. Both she and Kadambini passed the F.A. in 1880. In 1881 both were awarded government scholarships to read for their degrees at Bethune School, and both received their B.A. in 1883. Candramukhi went on with further study, to become the first woman M.A. in 1884, and Kadambini went on to medical college.[125] Vidyasagar noted this landmark in female achievement by presenting Candramukhi with a set of Shakespeare's works, inscribed "from her sincere well wisher Isvara Chandra Sarma."[126] By the end of the century, twenty-seven girls had B.A. degrees.[127] In 1904, thirty girls passed the E.A., and nine passed the F.A. There

[120] "The Bethune School," *Brahmo Public Opinion*, 6 March 1879.
[121] *Brahmo Public Opinion*, 24 April 1878. Girton College was the first women's college at Cambridge.
[122] *Abalābāndhab*, 1, 4 (February 1879).
[123] From the Minutes of Calcutta University for 1878-79, cited in Prabhatcandra Gangopadhyay, *Bānglār nārī-jāgaran*, p. 73.
[124] The school became a full-fledged college attached to Calcutta University in February 1888. From then on the school section was known as the Bethune Collegiate School. J. C. Bagal, *Bethune School*, pp. 46-47.
[125] *Ibid.*, pp. 40-45.
[126] Chabi Ray, *Bānglār nārī āndolan—sangkrāmī bhumikāy dersa' bachar* (Calcutta, 1955), p. 35.
[127] See the list of women graduates in U. Chakraborty, *Condition of Bengali Women*, Appendix IV.

were no B.A.s that year, however, suggesting a high dropout rate. Very few women continued with tertiary studies after marriage.[128]

Inevitably, the growth of higher education for women prompted some opposition. Much of this would have been from less-educated men who sensed competition and a loss of their authority in society. The "educated woman" became a figure of fun and the butt of numerous Bengali satires in prose and drama. The vituperativeness of some of these attacks indicated a deep feeling that educated women were a real threat to male dominance and social control. While praising the first women graduates, the vice chancellor of Calcutta University attempted to allay popular fears in his convocation address in 1883:

> I can readily understand that there may be many in India, perhaps some even among this assembly, who look upon this part of to-day's ceremonial with some measure of doubt and apprehension. St. Paul has told us that the path of safety for woman lies in the performance of the functions of wife-hood and mother-hood, that is to say, in the exercise of the domestic duties and virtues. . . . No one wishes, no one expects, that the extension of education to Indian women will lead them at once to throw aside the restraints of caste, the habits of seclusion which the practice of the country justifies, or even the timidity of temperament which characterises them today. Those who apprehend anything like a disorganization of the present social system of India may lay aside their fears. The customs of a nation are not so easily changed.[129]

[128] Sarala Ray Centenary Committee, *Sarala Ray*, p. 94; interview with Mrs. Sailaja Chakravarty, daughter of Hemantakumari Chaudhuri, in Calcutta, 13 February 1978. Both women dropped their plans for sitting the E.A. when they got married.

[129] University of Calcutta, *Convocation Addresses*, II, 1880-1898 (Calcutta, 1914), pp. 467-468, Address by the Vice-Chancellor, the Honourable Mr. H. J. Reynolds, on 10 March 1883. Satires on educated women are too numerous to list. Some indicative titles are Jogendracandra Basu, *Model bhaginī* (Calcutta, 1886); Durgadas De, *Miss Bino bibi bi e (onār in e kors)*

Opposition to tertiary education for women came not only from orthodox Hindus but from a faction within the Brahmo Samaj with a different educational philosophy. After 1878 the two groups were divided along fairly clear lines into the Sadharan Brahmo Samaj and the Nababidhan, the latter opposing advances made by the former. Objections were advanced on two grounds. One was the English-derived argument that higher education was unfeminine, and the other was the matter of loss of national identity. For instance, while accepting that Kadambini's success in the E.A. proved that the mental capacity of the sexes was the same, the opposition was "still firmly of the opinion that special teaching is necessary in the case of women for the education and refinement of that tender nature which God has given them for the purpose of softening and humanizing society."[130] They ridiculed the cause of higher education by pointing out the inappropriateness of the titles "Bachelor" and "Master" of Arts.[131] It was also pointed out that the British in India were in no hurry to send their own daughters to university, implying that the benefits were by no means generally acknowledged: "The fact is that the majority of the ruling race do strenuously object to subject their daughters to a conventional mode of examinations which neither fits them for worthy positions in life nor makes them better individuals in any sense of the expression."[132]

As a countermeasure, the Nababidhan group put up its own scheme for female education. The government grant had been withdrawn from the Native Ladies' Normal School, which after producing four teachers was no longer in a flourishing condition. After a temporary cessation of operation, it reopened in 1880 as the Metropolitan Female School, with thirty pupils.[133] This school languished,[134] but in the meantime the

---

(Barisal, 1898); Radhabinod Haldar, *Pāskarā māg* (Calcutta, 1888); Siddheswar Ray, *Boubābu* (Calcutta, 1889).

[130] *IMS*, 12 January 1879.

[131] *Liberal and New Dispensation*, 28 January 1883; 10 August 1884.

[132] *IMS*, 2 March 1879.

[133] *Ibid.*, 6 April 1879; Indian Reform Association Report 1879.

[134] *Ibid.*, 31 October 1880.

Committee of the Indian Reform Association came up with a replacement that would challenge the educational philosophy of the Bethune School. In 1882 it proposed a Native Ladies' Institution, "specially adapted to the requirements of the female mind and calculated to fit woman for her position in society." It declared that the awarding of degrees to women was "objectionable and unsexing." What was needed was a plan of education suited to the Hindu female character, a plan "at once natural and national."[135] The *Indian Christian Herald* proclaimed its approval of the new institution, as in its view "India wants her sons to be *sons* and her daughters to be *daughters* and *not* sons."[136] In fact, the curriculum differed little from that of the Bethune School. Juniors learned English (Toru Dutt's *Ancient Ballads and Legends of Hindustan*) and Bengali (*Sitār banabās*), arithmetic, science, drawing, ethics, domestic economy, and music. Seniors studied select passages from *Hamlet* and *The Merchant of Venice* and Addison for English, arithmetic, the history and geography of India, physical geography, Paley's *Natural Theology*, the laws of health, and the *Harmonium Sutras* parts one and two for music.[137] The Bible was also one of the English textbooks.[138] This specially formulated "feminine" curriculum was still too harsh to satisfy some critics. The *Liberty* of Lucknow complained that Addison was too antiquated and Paley too abstruse for women, and that such difficult texts ran counter to the Association's aim "not to turn our housewifes into pedantic blue-stockings and self-opinionated gentle *savants*."[139]

The popular Native Ladies' Institution and the failing Metropolitan Female School were amalgamated on 1 January 1883 as the Victoria College for Women.[140] Its managers declared proudly that "With a view to avoid masculine training and meet the special requirements and develop the softer suscep-

[135] *Liberal and New Dispensation*, 2 April 1882.
[136] *Ibid.*, 26 March 1882.
[137] *Ibid.*, 21 May 1882; 23 July 1882.
[138] *Ibid.*, 4 June 1882; 23 July 1882.
[139] *Ibid.*, 4 June 1882.
[140] *Ibid.*, 17 December 1882.

tibilities of the female mind, special subjects were included in the curriculum besides the ordinary course of studies, such as domestic economy, drawing, music, cookery, needlework, and laws of health." Weekly lectures were delivered at College Hall, in a popular and conversational style, which helped students in their home studies. In December 1882 thirty candidates presented themselves for examination, including three Christians, ten Hindus, and seventeen Brahmos. Most lived in Calcutta, but eight were from the *mofussil*. The bishop of Calcutta presided at the prize-giving, and gave his whole-hearted endorsement to this attempt to enable ladies to study at home amidst their domestic duties. In his address he said that "only one or two ladies might compete for University distinctions, but the great majority of women must always demand and ought to receive feminine training such as this institution imparted."[141]

Though more flexible in structure than the Bethune School, the Victoria College never had the same success. Despite protestations that it offered a truly national feminine education which was not against Hindu beliefs, it was firmly identified with Keshub Chunder Sen and the Nababidhan. Although it had accused the Bethune School of being westernized and un-Hindu, the Victoria College itself catered mainly to Brahmos, including the Anglicized families of some England-returned *bhadralok*. There was a European headmistress, Miss Pigot, and a boarding department was opened in 1883.[142] Girls were able to continue with higher studies to a certain extent. R. C. Dutt's daughters were educated to the standard of E.A. there.[143] The Victoria College managed to survive, but its fortunes fluctuated greatly over the next twenty years.[144]

[141] *Ibid.*, 1 April 1883.

[142] *New Dispensation*, 26 August 1883.

[143] Sushama Sen, *Memoirs of an Octogenarian* (Simla, 1971), p. 55.

[144] After Keshub's death it declined, but was revived by his daughter, the Maharani of Cuch Behar. *BP*, 4:2, 283 (August 1888). In *Mahilā*, 3, 10 (May 1898) there was an appeal to women for funds to maintain the school, and a call for volunteers for lecturing. The school probably closed between 1889 and 1895, and again between 1899 and 1901. Niranjan Niyogi, *Sādhan o sebā*, pp. 179-183. This volume also gives the subsequent early history of the

A noteworthy development in female education was the foundation of the Mahakali Pathsala in 1893. This school, established on orthodox Hindu principles by a female ascetic, Mataji Maharani Tapaswini, established a national form of education in a way the Brahmos never could. Upper-caste girls attended, in covered carriages, for a traditional education. The curriculum included Sanskrit, Bengali, arithmetic, and moral textbooks, but greater emphasis was placed on the learning of various *pūjā* rituals and the connected culinary skills. The best *pūjā* performer received a prize. The basic principles on which it was founded included the observance of *sāstric* injunctions in domestic life; the inculcation of *patibrata dharma* (devotion to one's husband) and the observance of the roles of a Hindu woman; the learning of literature and history from the *Kāvyas* and *Purānas*; and instruction in sewing, cookery, accounts, and the drawing of *ālpanā*. The school had its own textbooks. In its field it achieved a high standard. Girls who had reached the highest class were reading the *Rāghuvamsa* in Sanskrit. The school was supported solely by the Hindu community. Its patrons included wealthy native landowners such as the maharaja of Darbhanga[145] and the maharaja of Burdwan.[146] A further seal of approval, unusual in such an agressively Hindu context, was the official patronage of Lady Minto.[147] The school was also gladly accepted by its more progressive contemporaries.[148]

The Mahakali Pathsala had twenty-three branch schools in Bengal. The central school in Calcutta started with thirty pupils, and the number had increased to 450 by 1903, a higher enrolment figure than any other girls' school at the time.[149]

---

institution, as does the *Victoriā Institiusaner satabarsa smaranikā 1871-1971* (Calcutta, 1971).

[145] *BP*, 6:1, 387 (April 1897).

[146] *BP*, 8:1, 489 (May 1904). He gave 3,000 rupees to the building fund and promised a further donation of fifty rupees per month.

[147] *BP*, 8:2, 510-511 (February-March 1906).

[148] *BP*, 5:3, 362 (March 1895).

[149] M. G. Cowan, *The Education of the Women of India* (Edinburgh, 1912), pp. 112-115; Lotika Ghose, "Social and Educational Movements for and by Women," in *Bethune School*, pp. 145-146.

The nationalistic educational philosophy of the school was particularly acceptable in the period following the partition of Bengal in 1905.[150] The school's popularity was attributable to its compromise between education and orthodoxy, and its maintenance of continuity between home and school. The functioning of the school showed how Hindu orthodoxy and tradition had gradually been redefined to include female literacy, without occasioning any protest from the Hindu community. It is also interesting to note that despite the emphasis on education for a role in the home, many of the teaching functions of the home had been transferred to the school. The responsibility for teaching home duties was thus institutionalized, resulting to some extent in a change in the nature of domestic life. The success of the Mahakali Pathsala signified a general acceptance of the need for education for women.

There remain a few other trends to be noted. Coeducation was tried for the first time in 1897. Two *bhadramahilā* were admitted to the first year class at the prestigious Presidency College, but the experiment proved unpopular and was later discontinued.[151] Toward the end of the century a vogue for extreme westernization was current among parts of the *bhadralok* elite. Bethune School no longer seemed to provide the kind of training in accomplishments and languages needed by the future wives of high government officials. For a thoroughly English education, parents began to send their daughters to European schools like the Loreto House convent, which admitted a small quota of Indian girls. Loreto girls wore white

[150] Srinath Canda, *Brahmasamāje callis bathsar*, p. 320.
[151] Presidency College, *Centenary Volume 1955* (Calcutta, 1956), p. 19. See also the controversy this evoked in the press: *Bangabāsī*, 10 July 1897, *Hitaisi*, 13 July 1897, *Doinik-O-Samācār Candrikā*, 14 July 1897 in *RNNB* 17 July 1897; *Burdwan Sanjībanī*, 13 July 1897, *Pratikār*, 16 July 1897, *Saraswat Patra*, 17 July 1897 in *RNNB* 24 July 1897; *Sulābh Samācār*, 31 July 1897 in *RNNB* 7 August 1897; *Doinik-O-Samācār Candrikā*, 5 August 1897 in *RNNB* 14 August 1897; *Dacca Gazette*, 30 August 1897 in *RNNB* 30 August 1897. The two girls were Brahmos. The point was made repeatedly that coeducation was not accepted in either Britain or America, and so should not be imposed on Bengal. Two female students were also admitted to the B.A. class at Ravenshaw College, Cuttack, at this time. *Hitabādī*, 30 July 1897 in *RNNB* 7 August 1897.

frocks to school, were educated entirely in English, and learned French and music as accomplishments. The earliest pupils included the daughters of P. K. Sen (granddaughters of R. C. Dutt), Bihari Lal Gupta, and Sir Nilratan Sircar.[152] One early pupil recalled that her progressive Brahmo father, Dr. Prankrishna Acharya, had wanted her to attend a Bengali school, but her conservative mother favored Loreto House because she would learn more accomplishments there and thus make a better marriage. Her mother's hopes were justified. After matriculating from Loreto she married an England-returned I.C.S. officer.[153] Numbers at English schools were very small,[154] but indicate the kind of aspirations of the *bhadralok* elite.

The spread of female education generated discussion about the uses to which education should be put, and what the role of an educated woman should be. Authors began to quote Pope's dictum, "A little learning is a dangerous thing." Rajnarain Bose pronounced that it was better to remain in ignorance than to be "half-educated" and use that paltry knowledge to read obscene stories and plays.[155] The *Bāmābodhinī Patrikā* warned that

> to all those women in whose hearts there is no natural purity, who have no natural hatred of impure thoughts, in the making of whose hearts purity was not everlastingly united as an element, who are incapable of thinking independent thoughts—to all these pitiful women a little learning is totally disastrous—the cause of their downfall—and such examples are not rare.[156]

[152] Sushama Sen, *Memoirs*, p. 89. Also personal communication from Miss Bose, Calcutta, 10 March 1978. She was one of the third group of Bengali pupils at Loreto, around the turn of the century. Her parents sent her there to get the benefits of a western education.

[153] Interview with Usha Haldar, daughter of Dr. Prankrishna Acharya, Calcutta, 13 March 1978.

[154] There were twelve Bengali girls at Loreto House around 1910. Miss Bose has a photograph of this group—the girls in it included herself, her three cousins, the granddaughter of Sir Chandra Madhab Ghose, and the four daughters of Sir Nilratan Sircar.

[155] Rajnarain Bose, *Se kāl ār e kāl* (Calcutta, 1976), p. 60.

[156] "Nārīganer alpasiksā," Bāmāganer racanā, *BP*, 3:2, 242 (March 1885).

Increasingly parents considered a basic level of education to be essential for their daughters, so as to enable them to write letters, keep accounts, and read a few books. Marriage criteria had been substantially revised. The fact of literacy was no longer kept secret from the groom;[157] it became, instead, an important bargaining asset. As early as 1870 the deputy inspector of education in Dacca reported that the unmarried "in their selection of brides have come to consider beauty without education defective."[158] According to one women's journal, when people came to inspect a prospective bride one of the first questions was "can the girl read and write a bit?" The girl was usually able, with difficulty, "to write a half-page letter full of mistakes, and had learnt to turn over a few pages of *Durgesnandinī* or *Swarnalatā*, and thought of herself as having learnt a great deal, looking down on those who had not had the good fortune to learn all this as lesser creatures."[159]

The link between education and marriage raised a further issue connected with *alpa siksā* (little education). It was said that a woman with a little education would think of herself as an educated woman, and become unduly proud and arrogant.[160] A writer in the women's journal *Banga Mahilā* satirically ridiculed modern education, the aim of which was to enable girls to call themselves *siksitā*, or educated women. This title meant that they could do fancy work, recite a few prayers, and write poetry and prose for *Bāmābodhinī* or *Banga Mahilā*.[161] In many *bhadraparibār*, or good families, women wasted their time reading *Megnādbadh* or *Britrasanghār*, *Dvīpnirbān* or *Durgesnandinī*, but in very few households was there ever any educated discussion among women.[162] They were said to have no desire to read useful books such as

---

[157] W. Adam, *Reports*, first report (Rangpur, 1835), p. 110.
[158] Government of India, *Selections*, p. 387.
[159] *BP*, 6:1, 385 (February 1897).
[160] "Nārīganer alpasiksā," *BP*, 242.
[161] "Strīsiksā," *Banga Mahilā*, 1, 5 (September 1875).
[162] *BP*, 385.

biographies or books on child rearing, children's education, domestic medicine, or religion.[163]

Higher education for women prompted the question, "Will the woman, who has obtained the B.A. degree, cook or scour plates?"[164] It was feared that educated women would no longer be able to fulfil their natural role, which was still that of housewife, wife, and mother. Bengali society was in transition, and old and new elements had not yet blended. Female education became acceptable, but old functions still had to be carried out. Education was felt to train women in nonproductive activity rather than in needed skills, teaching them only to spend their leisure time reading novels. Writers chose to ignore the disapproval that had been expressed in the past at the degenerate, luxurious lives led by illiterate *zenana* women.[165] It was also commonly believed that education gave women aspirations to a western way of living and created dissatisfaction with their material conditions. The prevalent image of the Englishwoman was probably drawn from the stereotype of the *memsahib* in India, a purely social being who never did any housework. However, as a writer in the *Calcutta Review* remarked, such undesirable consequences were unlikely. Female education in England had only produced one of Miss Edgeworth, Caroline Fry, Hannah More, and Mrs. Somerville in many generations, therefore the creation of occasional *savants* was hardly a danger when weighed against the fact that there was nothing an educated lady could not do better than an uneducated one.[166] Others spent some effort finding examples of English women who were learned, pious, and also attentive to their household duties, such as Mary Lovell Ware[167] or Charlotte Brontë.[168] It was stated with approval that Mrs. Somerville was equally at home in calculating

---

[163] "Strī-siksār antarāy o taddūrīkaraner upāy," *Antahpur*, 7, 1 (May 1904).
[164] *Burdwan Sanjībanī*, 21 January 1890 in *RNNB* 1 February 1890.
[165] See Chapter One.
[166] "Native Female Education," *CR*, 25:49, p. 102.
[167] "Nārīcarit," *BP*, 5, 76 (December 1869).
[168] Mankumari Basu, "Nabyagrihinī," *BP*, 4:2, 287 (December 1888).

the aberrations of a comet and in mending her husband's stockings.[169] Whether such assurances did much to allay the fears of the *bhadralok* is unrecorded.

Writers, mainly male, idealized the "traditional" housewife, uneducated but skilled in her duties, contrasting her sharply with the stereotype of the new fun-loving, domestically incompetent educated woman. Champions of female education attempted to answer these charges. One writer argued that education made a woman better understand the dignity of housework, and appreciate the importance of her position as analogous to that of the ruler of a small kingdom.[170] A woman writer, the daughter of pandit Madan Mohan Tarkalankar, acknowledged the stereotype of the blue-stocking but attempted to discourage the phenomenon:

> Oh dear ones! If you have acquired real knowledge, then give no place in your heart to *mem-sahib* like behaviour. That is not becoming in a Bengali housewife. See how an educated woman can do housework thoughtfully and systematically in a way unknown to an ignorant, uneducated woman. And see how if God had not appointed us to this place in the home, how unhappy a place the world would be![171]

The debate over education raised the question of the "true" female role. Many of the arguments used were imported from Britain by different factions among the patrons of female education. For instance, the *Indian Mirror* discussed a "striking paper" on the future of English women by Mrs. A. Sutherland Orr, from the *Nineteenth Century* for June 1878. This lady advocated female education, but believed that the progress of female culture would prove detrimental to matrimony and lead eventually to the extinction of the species. The editor agreed with her, and condemned Calcutta University for sanc-

---

[169] "Native Female Education," *CR*, 25:49, p. 102.
[170] *BP*, 3:2, 239 (December 1884).
[171] Kundamala Debi, "Bidyā sikhile ki grihakarmma karite nāi?" Bāmā-ganer racanā, *BP*, 6, 86 (October 1870).

tioning a scheme of education that "tends to unsex women."[172] The *Brahmo Public Opinion* discussed the feminist Mrs. Fawcett's reply to Mrs. Orr in the August issue of *Nineteenth Century*. It came to the radical conclusion that "Let artificial restrictions be removed, let the same facilities for education be offered to women that are enjoyed by men and then natural forces will have fair play and women will find their fit career."[173] The *New Dispensation* maintained constant opposition to university education for women, predicting that lady B.A.s would be unable to find a place in society:

> What are we to do with them? Are they to cook, nurse, feed their children, attend to their husbands' wants, be good women in every respect? They might have done each and all of these things without becoming graduates. . . . Where then is the use of degrees for women, unless they be asked to unsex themselves and like men go to compete with them in all the active duties of life.[174]

The physical and moral evils much discussed by opponents of higher female education in England[175] were raised in the columns of the *New Dispensation*. One Dr. H. Hastings was quoted as saying "I venture to affirm, that it is physiologically impossible to have a learned girl and a healthy, robust mother, and strong children!"[176] This argument was not persuasive in Bengal, where the alternative of spending the whole of life in the *antahpur* was notoriously unhealthy, and one of the main reasons for advocating female education was that it would help produce strong children. The *Tattwabodhinī Patrikā* raised the familiar Comtean interpretation of women's "nature," governed by the heart rather than the intellect. The kind of education needed to attain a B.A. or M.A. was chiefly intel-

[172] *IMS*, 30 June 1878.
[173] *Brahmo Public Opinion*, 12 September 1878.
[174] *Liberal and New Dispensation*, 18 March 1883.
[175] See P. Atkinson, "Fitness, Feminism and Schooling," in S. Delamont and L. Duffin, *The Nineteenth Century Woman*; E. Davies, "The Influence of University Degrees on the Education of Women."
[176] *New Dispensation*, 29 July 1883.

lectual, not emotional, therefore considered unsuitable for women.[177]

Despite the strictures of disapproval from so many directions, most women appreciated the value of education without relinquishing their domestic role. Radharani Lahiri, trained as a teacher from the Native Ladies' Normal School, still wrote that "Helping others is a woman's ornament, and religion her life—taking these two sayings to heart a woman could be educated, and nothing other than good will result from it."[178] Women were grateful for efforts made to educate them, although many realized that in order to progress they would have to push themselves forward rather than rely on others.[179] The deep desire for education that was felt among women is illustrated in an incident related by one Nagendrabala Debi in the women's journal *Antahpur*:

> One day my son said to me, "Mother, please explain one of my lessons."
> What could I say, myself the very image of the goddess Saraswati!
> I said, "Memorize it, that will be sufficient."
> He said, "How can I learn if I don't understand?"
> I said, "Can't the private tutor explain it to you?"
> He did not answer. Then, having no other way out, I told him, "I don't know how to read."
> My son looked astonished for a moment, then said, "So you don't know anything."[180]

She prayed that all mothers educate their daughters to protect them from undergoing such humiliation.

Fortunately such incidents were becoming rare among the *bhadramahilā* by the turn of the century. By the 1880s many

---

[177] *Tattwabodhinī Patrikā*, 452 (Chaitra 1802 [1880]) in B. Ghose, *Sāmayikpatre*, part 2, p. 463.

[178] Kumari Lahiri, "Strīlokdiger abasya siksanīya ki?" *BP*, 142.

[179] Srimati Saratkumari, "Strīloker bidyā siksā," *Bāmāganer racanā*, *BP*, 11, 144 (August 1875).

[180] "Strīsiksā bisaye ardha siksitā hindu mahilādiger matāmat," *Antahpur*, 4, 4.

bhadramahilā were literate, especially in the cities. Census figures show a steady rise in the number and percentage of female literates for Calcutta over the period 1871-1901.[181] It is not possible, on the basis of these figures, to work out the level of education attained, or to ascertain the class or caste basis of educated females to see the proportion that were *bhadramahilā*. What stands out clearly is that there was a gradual extension of female education during the latter half of the nineteenth century. Although the total percentage of the female population receiving education was still extremely small,[182] and much less than the proportion of males, the achievements in the field of female education during the nineteenth century were phenomenal.

There had been a mere handful of literate women among the *bhadramahilā* early in the century, but by 1900 attending a public school had become an accepted part of a girl's life. The growth of female education was an institutional change with far-reaching implications for women's role, although the actual extent of disruption was much less than that envisaged and feared by many male critics. For women themselves, education was both a means of access to a far broader field of experience than had come within their reach before, and a stimulant and help in the performance of their domestic routine.

[181] Unfortunately the figures do not provide a good basis for exact comparisons. The number given as the total population fluctuates and the categories used in collecting statistics differ in each of the early censuses. However, the overall upward trend is clear. In 1876 there were 3,886 literate Hindu females in Calcutta; in 1881 there were 6,795 literate and learning, and in 1891 there were 10,162 in this category. In 1901 they formed 9.7 percent of the female population, compared with 3.36 percent in 1876. See *Censuses for Calcutta, Town and Suburbs*, 1872, 1876, 1881, 1891, 1901.

[182] By 1907 the number of women under instruction in Bengal had increased to 127,800, although this still only represented 3.1 percent of all girls of school age. The figure for 1907 is post-Partition, and does not therefore include numbers for East Bengal and Assam, as previous statistics did. H. Sharp, ed., *Progress*, p. 213.

ᢟ FOUR ᢞ

Changing Conjugal Relations

Whether educated or not, the first major event in the life cycle of a girl was marriage. During the latter half of the nineteenth century the nature of this institution began to change. A different style of marriage gradually developed, assimilating new qualities of romantic love and companionship. These changes were most significant at an individual, personal level. In the absence of other structural changes, the balance of power and authority in the "modern" conjugal relationship remained with the husband, as it had traditionally.

Traditional marriage relationships

The traditional Hindu ideal of marriage was expressed in the Hindu scriptures and in the epics and *purānas*. Sita, chaste and faithful heroine of the *Rāmāyana*, was the embodiment of the ideal wife. The *Laws of Manu* contain many well-known maxims on the role of the wife. Conjugal happiness was celebrated: "In that family, where the husband is pleased with his wife and the wife with her husband, happiness will be assuredly lasting."[1] But such happiness depended on the wife's acceptance of a position of subordination to her husband: "Though destitute of virtue, or seeking pleasure (elsewhere), or devoid of good qualities, (yet) a husband must be constantly worshipped as a god by a faithful wife."[2] Women were not considered twice-born. If married to a twice-born

[1] M. W. Pinkham, *Woman in the Sacred Scriptures of Hinduism* (New York, 1967), p. 72 (Manu 3.60).
[2] *Ibid.*, p. 76 (Manu 5.154).

man, a woman was to serve him and worship him as a divine being.[3]

Such prescriptions provided an overall framework of values for society, but social practice was more varied and complex. In traditional society, marriage was not viewed as a union between two compatible individuals, but as a social alliance between families. In Bengal, a bride became a part of her husband's family on marriage, and brought a substantial dowry with her. Marriages were arranged by the family elders with a view to maintaining or enhancing the power and prestige of the family. Negotiations were carried out by the *ghatakī*.[4] Marriage ceremonies were the occasion for lavish expenditure, because the magnificence of the affair was indicative of the status of the family.[5]

In the first half of the nineteenth century in Bengal, high-caste girls aged between eight and ten were married to men aged from fourteen to eighteen.[6] The young bride did not usually proceed to her husband's house immediately after the wedding ceremony. She stayed in her natal home for about a year before going to live with her new family.[7] The ceremony of consummation, or *garbhādhān*, took place at puberty when she was already a permanent resident in her husband's home. The belief that early marriage was directly related to early puberty was widely held and supported by the medical profession.[8]

[3] R. B. Inden, *Marriage and Rank in Bengali Culture* (Berkeley and Los Angeles, 1976), p. 31.

[4] See a discussion of *ghatakīs* in Chapter Two.

[5] S. C. Bose, *The Hindoos*, chapter five, has a very good detailed description of marriage ceremonies.

[6] I have not come across a single case of a woman married before 1860 who was married after the age of twelve.

[7] However, J. Kerr wrote in 1849 that in Bengal girls were married before the age of ten and immediately taken to reside permanently at their husbands' house. *Domestic Life*, pp. 202-205.

[8] In response to a questionnaire circulated by the Indian Reform Association in 1871, Dr. Mahendra Lal Sircar gave statistics he had collected on the age of menstruation in Calcutta. Out of 202 cases, 137 started menstruating between the ages of eleven and thirteen. (From the Annual Report of the Indian Reform Association 1870-71, included as Appendix II of P. K. Sen,

The impact of early marriage on the young bride is difficult to ascertain. There is no evidence on whether or not sexual intercourse was commonly a traumatic experience. Popular health manuals implied that it would not have been because Bengali girls grew up in an atmosphere so sensual that it precipitated early puberty. They were accustomed to hearing "obscene wedding stories" and salacious gossip.[9] According to one English observer, "From the time she can speak, a girl's mind is constantly directed to sex matters, and even deliberate stimulation of the organs is practised in many cases."[10]

Clearly traumatic was the young girl's sudden realization that she was about to leave the security of her natal home forever. She moved very rapidly from the relaxed atmosphere of her own home to the assumption of adult responsibilities among strangers. One old lady remembered vividly her terror on learning she was to be married:

> I was nine years old then. In the morning I used to carry the plates down to the *ghāt* to be washed. One day, as I was washing by the side of the *ghāt* two *bhadralok* carrying umbrellas and wearing sandals came by. They suddenly stopped in front of me. . . . They asked, "What is your name, mother, washing plates here all by yourself. What if you fell in?"
>
> I didn't know them, so I stammered fearfully, "I come every day to wash the plates. My name is Swarna. That is my house."
>
> "What is your father's name, mother?"
>
> I told them. One of them took two rupees from his pocket and put it in my hand saying, "Mother, I am going

---

Biography, II, 294-323.) This is not considered unduly early now, but the average age of first menstruation in Victorian England was around fifteen or sixteen. See P. Laslett, *The World We Have Lost* (London, 1965), pp. 89-90; and P. Branca, *Silent Sisterhood*, p. 139n.

[9] Bharatcandra Bandopadhyay, *Susrusā pranālī* (Calcutta, 1896), p. 147; and Kedarnath Sarkar, *Ritu-raksā* (Calcutta, 1891), p. 2.

[10] M. E. Staley, *Handbook for Wives and Mothers in India* (Calcutta, 1908), p. 67. I have found no other evidence of this practice.

to take you home with me, to be my daughter-in-law. Will you come?"

I was trembling with fear, and dropped the plates and ran home. As I was telling my mother what had happened the two *bhadralok* came in. . . . My father knew them . . . the marriage ceremony later took place. . . . After marriage washing plates, husking rice, nursing the cow, all had to be done. I was small, but I was not exempted from any work. I worked, but received no tenderness or affection.[11]

Not all young brides were treated so harshly, but the trauma of leaving home seems to have been a common element of their experience. Rassundari Debi was married at twelve. She enjoyed the wedding ceremonies, but when they were over she realized that she would have to leave home. At this point, she recollected,

I went and sat on my mother's knee and clung to her, saying "Mother, don't give me away."
Hearing this, and seeing my actions, everyone present began to cry. My mother took me on her knee and tried to console me by saying, "My Laksmi, you must understand, what is there to be afraid of, our god is there. Don't cry, after a few days I'll come and fetch you."
Even when she had calmed me down I was so scared that I was trembling, and I couldn't speak.[12]

Her mother-in-law turned out to be very kind, and tried to comfort her and welcome her to her new home. Nevertheless she spent her first few months there in misery. Girls were totally unprepared for the whole experience. At home mothers treated their daughters with indulgence, knowing the hardship of their inevitable fate, but did not attempt to prepare them by explaining beforehand what was to happen.

[11] Reminiscences of Santi Roy, recounting the experience of an old aunt of hers. The Bengali word *mā*, or mother, is used here as an affectionate term of address.
[12] Rassundari Debi, *Āmār jīban*, pp. 17-26.

The husband was not mentioned at all in either of the above accounts. In the mind of the new bride he was a much less significant figure than the mother-in-law. Custom did not foster any closeness between the newlywed couple. Husbands and wives were prohibited from meeting or talking to each other during the day. The only time they had together was a few hours at night, after the wife had finished the day's tasks and before she started on the next round at dawn. Under such conditions there was little opportunity for anything beyond a sexual relationship to develop. Proper wifely behavior had to be reverential. She had to cover her face if her husband came into her presence when others were there, and she was not supposed to speak to him in public.[13] She never referred to him by name, or familiarly, but by the honorific pronoun *uni*, "he."

The structure of the household was not conducive to the development of a close marital bond. The tie between mother and son was very strong in Bengali homes, and a son's first attachment was to his mother rather than to his wife.[14] A mother, dependent on her son for continuing support in her old age, saw the daughter-in-law as a future threat, and resented the presence of a rival for her son's care and affection. A wife who exerted too many claims on her husband was considered to be usurping the mother's position, upsetting the household equilibrium. As one writer put it,

It seems to the mother-in-law that since the coming of the new bride her son's behavior toward her is not as it was before. She thinks that this is *bou-mā*'s (daughter-

[13] The wife of Keshub Chunder Sen would never speak to him in public, her previous Hindu conditioning having been so strong. Jogamaya Goswami, even in the free atmosphere of the Bharat Ashram, was only seen speaking to her husband twice in four years.

[14] M. Roy, *Bengali Women*, pp. 101-103, gives an account of this relationship in contemporary Bengal, showing the persistence of some of the features described here. M. Wolf, "Chinese Women: Old Skills in a New Context," in M. Z. Rosaldo and L. Lamphere, eds., *Woman, Culture, and Society*, shows that the relationships within a typical Chinese family were very similar.

in-law's) teaching, because it is difficult for a mother to see her son in the wrong.

"Before this my son used to come to me and say, 'Mother, give me this, give me that.' Now he no longer does so."

Unnecessarily, these thoughts gather strength, and under the influence of a groundless belief she becomes dissatisfied with the young bride.[15]

The young wife's situation was strained. She had to cope with adult responsibilities while still having the interests of a child. Uprooted from her familiar environment, she was not easily able to find much companionship in her husband's home. She was often closer to her husband's younger brother, her *debar*, than she was to her husband, as this relationship was traditionally sanctioned.[16] Her status improved as she grew older. The brunt of adjustment and hard work was then moved onto the shoulders of successive new brides.

The husband had much more favorable conditions for adjusting to his new role. He remained in his own home after marriage, the object of the devoted attentions of mother and wife, adored by all.

The wife as helpmeet

To the British, the position of women in society was one of the yardsticks for measuring a nation's standing in the scale of civilization. Their view of the correct relationship between husband and wife was that in which the wife was the intelligent companion of her husband's daily life, giving him sympathy and encouragement, counsel and advice, solace and relaxation.[17] Many of the English-educated *bhadralok* were

[15] Srimati Satyabati Debi, "Ekāler sasurī bou," *BP*, 6:3, 407 (December 1898). See also "Bou-mā," *Antahpur*, 1, 7 (August 1898).

[16] The description of a woman's relationship with her *debar* in M. Roy, *Bengali Women*, pp. 106-109, is true of the earlier period as well.

[17] Sir J. B. Phear's opening address to the members of the Bengal Social Science Association, 1867, reprinted in B. Dutt Gupta, *Sociology in India*, Appendix V, p. 16.

attracted by this ideal, and their Anglicized education and colonial employment made it desirable to have a wife with some understanding of this new milieu. As a student of the Hindu College wrote in 1849 in a Bengali essay on the results of female education in India,

> as female education is not customary in this country, there is no happiness in Hindu families. Households break up, couples become estranged and quarrel, spoiling all happiness. Men follow one path, women another; men stop performing *pūjā* and paying reverence to gurus, but women do completely the opposite.[18]

Most *bhadralok* would have readily concurred with Archdeacon Baly when in an address to the Indian Reform Association he proclaimed that

> There can be no real happiness in the family, no real home life, no real companionship between two so unequally mated, the intellectual man and the unintellectual woman: the woman will be unable to share in the cultivated pursuits and enjoyments of the man, or intelligently to divide with him the serious cares and troubles of this life, and he will be compelled to seek outside his own home the true sympathy and companionship, which he ought to find, but misses within it.[19]

The element of English marriage that was most obviously missing, and the lack of which was most sorely felt, was that of companionship. Employment under British rule accentuated a sharp division between work and home, between business and pleasure or relaxation, a division less marked in Hindu society. The leisurely and cultured atmosphere of the Mughal administration was more harmonious than was the

[18] "Bhāratbarsīya strījātir bidyā siksār phal barnana kara" by Sitanath Ghose, reprinted in *GRPI from 1st May 1848 to 1st October 1849* (Calcutta, 1850), p. ccxxxviii.

[19] Archdeacon Baly, address to the Indian Reform Association, *IMS*, 20 April 1879.

separation of home and work in Victorian England, where the two were so distinct that it was necessary for the home to have a completely relaxed atmosphere to provide a counterbalance to the tensions associated with work.[20] Home had to be a haven from cares and worries, and the wife was there not only to minister to her husband's physical needs, but also to lend a sympathetic and understanding ear to his grievances. She was to enhance his leisure by joining him in it, constantly at his side. Bengali men generally spent their leisure time with other men, but English ideas stressed that qualities such as understanding and sympathy were particularly feminine. In a colonial situation, where the *bhadralok* were being subjected to constant humiliation in their working lives, there was an exceptionally strongly felt need for those qualities.[21] They required the type of wife who could provide sympathetic care and create the atmosphere of a peaceful haven in their own homes.

A Brahmo writer expressed the new need for companionship and its connection with British rule very succinctly:

Do what we may to resist the influence of Western civilisation, it is growing in upon us, and an educated Bengali, when he returns home, fagged and wearied by the day's over-work, wishes very much to be refreshed either with music, or with pleasant conversation on topics familiar to him, and feels very much disappointed when his hopes are frustrated. In several other matters, he very much feels the want of a help-mate.[22]

Especially in the first half of the century, and even later, the lives of the *bhadralok* presented a sharp contrast to this new ideal. Their own young wives still had the interests of children, and understood little of their husbands' world. Male response

[20] See L. Davidoff, *The Best Circles*, for a good discussion of this. See also E. Trudgill, *Madonnas and Magdalens*, chapter three, "Home Sweet Home."
[21] Innumerable accounts of humiliating incidents were reported in the vernacular press throughout the nineteenth century. See *RNNB passim.*
[22] "Female Education," *Brahmo Public Opinion*, 30 September 1880.

to this predicament was often frustration leading to complete withdrawal into ascetic religiosity and puritanism. The lot of their child wives was made even more miserable through their neglect. Durga Mohan Das, Khetra Mohan Dutt, Bijoy Krishna Goswami, and Keshub Chunder Sen all reacted in this manner.[23] Durga Mohan Das married Brahmamayi when he was nine and she was four. As he grew up he became disgusted with her, and used to treat her cruelly. It was only when he was studying at Presidency College in Calcutta, where he came into contact with Christianity, that he realized how much he had neglected his duties. From then on he made an effort to become closer to his wife.[24] Keshub Chunder Sen was married at eighteen to nine-year-old Jaganmohini. His total avoidance of her for the first four years of their marriage made her the object of ridicule. She was continually told by everyone that her husband did not love her. She could not stand the strain, and one day locked herself into a room and cried until forced out by one of the older ladies in the household.[25] At eighteen, Bijoy Krishna Goswami married Jogamaya, aged six. She used to try to interrupt his studies by putting her hands over his eyes, or covering the pages of the book he was reading, or, at night, by blowing out his lamp. Being a Brahmo, he attempted to instruct her on the Brahmo concept of a formless God. When he then asked her what she understood by it, she replied, "something round like a *sālgrām*."[26] He poured cold water over her in disgust.[27]

Victorian influence fostered the growth of puritanism among the *bhadralok*. The Brahmo Samaj epitomized this trend. It uncompromisingly condemned gambling, going to prostitutes, smoking, drinking, and the theater. Its members felt that if

---

[23] Amritalal Sengupta, *Jogamāyā Thākurānī* (Calcutta, 1916), p. 21; *Srī Khetramohan Datter jībanī* (Calcutta, 1919), pp. 7-8; Dwarkanath Ganguly, *Jībanālekhya*, and [Priyanath Mallik], *Brahma-nandinī Satī Jaganmohinī Debī* (Howrah, 1914).

[24] Dwarkanath Ganguly, *Jībanālekhya*, pp. 4-7.

[25] [Priyanath Mallik], *Brahma-nandinī*, pp. 35-36.

[26] A *sālgrām* is the black stone representing the god Visnu.

[27] Amritalal Sengupta, *Jogamāyā*, pp. 7, 19.

home and wife were made more agreeable they would form a counterattraction to such debauched habits. It would also mean less of a drain on family finances. An article on social reform in the *Bāmābodhinī Patrikā* edited by Brahmo Umesh Chunder Dutt said that

> the kind of pure enjoyment that is available to husband and wife in civilized countries is not present in our country. The husband does not receive enough from his wife to satisfy his expectations. Women are nearly all uneducated, and an educated person can never have a satisfying conversation with an uneducated person. Therefore the husband, having finished his official work, will go elsewhere for relaxation. For him the house is no longer a place of peace, but has become a place of discord.[28]

The Brahmo Samaj stressed the ideal of the happy family, a feature of English life that most impressed Keshub Chunder Sen on his visit there in 1870. In an address given on his return he said, "I do not think there is in any other part of the world such a thing as a sweet English home. Its sweetness, its purity must command our respect; the well-regulated English family deserves your imitation and study."[29] The ideal family portrayed in Brahmo literature was one in which children were brought up in morality and innocence, men and women could mix freely yet chastely, and the family as a whole would participate in joint activities like picnics and river excursions. In true English fashion, dogs were counted as family members, and given names like "Tiger."[30]

Mary Carpenter drew attention to the importance of the wife in any successful emulation of the English model. When she visited Sasipada Banerjea and his wife in Burranagore in 1866, she wrote that

[28] *BP*, 2:3, 198 (July 1881).

[29] Keshub Chunder Sen, "General Impressions of England and the English," October 1870. Reprinted in P. S. Basu, *Life and Works*, p. 270.

[30] Sibnath Sastri's novel *Nayantārā* exemplifies this. It was first published in 1899. In *Sibnāth racanāsangraha*, I (Calcutta, 1975).

for the first, and for the last time, during my whole visit, had I the happiness of being in a simple native dwelling, which had the domestic charms of an English home. The young wife came forward gracefully to welcome us to her pretty sitting-room, where well-chosen prints covered the otherwise bare walls, and a simple repast had been prepared for us. Her little boy, a fine child, was quite happy to see his father, and be noticed by him.[31]

Means of promoting family life were suggested. Home theatricals, apparently a common form of entertainment in middle-class English homes, were recommended as a harmless and pleasant means of enjoyment for ordinary Bengali families, and were promoted as a way of breaking down formal barriers between family members.[32] In practice they seem to have been taken up only by the wealthy.[33]

The task of creating the desired peaceful atmosphere in the home fell mainly on the wife. Women's magazines and household manuals instructed her on how to do so. One woman advised her readers,

> when your husband returns home from his official work or business, don't burden him with anything, but wholeheartedly try to drive away the cares of his labor. At that time no bitter or unloving words should be said, and he should not be pestered for better ornaments or good clothes. Speak sweetly to him. See, as God has placed the burden of caring for the wife on the shoulders of her husband, the Supreme Father has likewise given women the responsibility of driving away their husbands' cares.[34]

The necessary precondition for companionship between husband and wife was the possibility of shared interests: companionship supposed a field of common activity. Nayantara, heroine of the novel of the same name, was amazed at coming

[31] M. Carpenter, *Six Months*, p. 252.
[32] *BP*, 3:1, 220 (May 1883).
[33] *Ibid.* See also Sarala Debi, *Jībaner jharāpātā* (Calcutta, 1975).
[34] Umasundari Dasi, *Narīracit-kābya* (Calcutta, 1879), pp. 14-15.

across a passage in Kalidasa's *Rāghuvamsa* where a wife was hailed as a friend. She had thought that this was a new English idea, expressed in the English word "companionship," which she explained to her Sanskrit teacher as meaning "a woman who is a man's copartner in the household, in enjoyment, in happiness, in knowledge, in faith, in art and in literature."[35]

To attain this kind of mutuality, the existing gap between men's and women's interests had to be narrowed. In fact this meant further adjustment on the part of women. The primary means of bridging the gap was women's education. Later marriage, accepted to a much lesser extent, also helped to facilitate the process.

Beginning with Gyanendra Mohun Tagore in the 1840s, many *bhadralok* began to educate the wives they had married as child brides.[36] In joint families the lessons were necessarily haphazard because couples had no time for meeting during the day. Girish Chandra Sen could only teach his wife Brahmamayi after ten at night. In this manner he taught her to read parts I and II of *Barnaparicay*, the basic school reader.[37] Women themselves rapidly became enthusiastic about learning and would practice secretly in their spare time. Bala Shoondaree Tagore wanted to gain greater access to Christianity through a knowledge of English. She borrowed a spelling book from her husband's nephew, and used to ask him what he had learned each day. While pretending that it was only a matter of casual interest, she avidly tried to memorize every word.[38] Brahmamayi Sen used to read secretly in the kitchen in the one or two hours after the midday meal when everyone else had a rest.[39] One village girl used to go over the alphabet every evening by tracing the letters in the newly wetted cow-

---

[35] Sibnath Sastri, *Nayantārā*, p. 54.
[36] Bangkabihari Kar, *Bhakta Kālīnārāyan Gupter jīban-brittānta* (Calcutta, 1924), p. 4; Girish Chandra Sen, *Brahmamayī-carit*, pp. 4-6; Amritalal Sengupta, *Jogamāyā*; and Dwarkanath Ganguly, *Jībanālekhya*.
[37] Girish Chandra Sen, *Brahmamayī-carit*, pp. 4-5.
[38] E. Storrow, *The Eastern Lily Gathered*, p. 46.
[39] Girish Chandra Sen, *Brahmamayī-carit*, p. 6.

dung floor, rubbing it out quickly when she heard her mother-in-law approaching.[40]

Women educated in this manner did not usually achieve a standard of education even approaching that of their husbands. It took Bhramar, the child bride in Bankim Chandra Chatterjee's novel *Krishnakanta's Will*, three days to write a letter.[41] The level of education was not of great importance. Even a token education was an acknowledgment of the wife's participation in her husband's new life. With her husband as co-conspirator, the clandestine, exciting manner in which she was forced to obtain her knowledge encouraged a closer conjugal bond. Couples had a sense of shared adventure and rebellion.

In the 1850s and 1860s, and sometimes even after that, youths who became Brahmos were subjected to social ostracism, and had a special need for the support of their wives. Women had to know something of their husband's beliefs in order to make the choice between husband and family. Keshub Chunder Sen's wife Jaganmohini was forced to choose between her big house, friends, relatives, and possessions, and her husband. She chose him.[42] Harasundari Datta's husband Srinath married her when she was seven and he was fourteen. Four years later, when he was an initiated Brahmo studying in Calcutta, he arranged for her to escape from his village in Bikrampur to join him. He hired a boat to take her away in the middle of the night, but she refused to go. Over a year later he tried again, and this time was successful.[43] Again, the sense of shared daring and commitment was a strong reinforcement of the marital bond.

A less dramatic closeness in the new family patterns was encouraged by the British administrative practice of sending

[40] Interview with Roma Chatterjee, Calcutta, 6 October 1977. The woman mentioned was her great-aunt.

[41] Bankim Chandra Chatterjee, *Krishnakanta's Will*, translated by J. C. Ghosh (New York, 1962), p. 82. First published 1878.

[42] [Priyanath Mallik], *Brahma-nandini*, p. 43.

[43] Harasundari Datta, *Swargīya Srīnāth Datter jīban-kathā* (Calcutta, 1922), pp. 9-12.

government officials out to the *mofussil*, often to quite remote areas. To relieve their lonely existence, and as a belief in the importance of close marital bonds became more widespread, men began to take their wives and children with them, whereas traditionally the family would have stayed in the central joint family home in Calcutta or the ancestral village. Young husbands studying in Calcutta or *mofussil* towns sometimes brought their wives to join them there, too. Harasundari Datta was with her husband in the wilds of Assam, where he was managing tea estates, for seven years. After a spell in Calcutta they then went on to Mayurbhanj, Kanika, and Burdwan.[44] Satakari Haldar's wife Pramodini went with him to Chittagong, Kathi, Dinajpur, Banga, and Jessore. At many of these places they stayed for only a few months, because conditions were bad for Pramodini's health, but she insisted on accompanying him. They reveled in their freedom, running hand in hand into the waves at the beach near Kathura, or sitting under a tree looking at the beauty of the ocean, or walking together through the hills at Chittagong.[45]

Having a wife who could take part in public society was seen as a career asset for those who aspired to succeed under British rule.[46] The British often said that the reason they could not mix with Indians on equal terms was the seclusion of Indian women.[47] The more progressive members of the *bhadralok*, especially Brahmos, set out to remove this barrier. Englishmen were always very impressed by the presence of women at Brahmo gatherings, considering it a clear indication

[44] *Ibid., passim.*

[45] Satakari Haldar, *Pūrbba smriti* (Calcutta, 1898).

[46] From the nineteenth century onwards, in western middle-class society, many positions in a wide variety of professional fields were structured in the form of the "two-person career," where a wife has specific and important duties to perform in relation to her husband's work without being formally employed or remunerated. See Hanna Papanek, "Men, Women, and Work: Reflections on the Two-Person Career," in J. Huber, ed., *Changing Women in a Changing Society* (Chicago, 1973).

[47] See Sir J. B. Phear's speech on becoming president of the Bethune Society for 1866-1867 in *Proceedings*, p. lxxxvii.

of social progress. Saudamini Ray, wife of Brahmo Rakhal Chandra Ray, was present at a party her husband gave for English men and women he knew in Barisal in 1866. The district magistrate, Mr. Sutherland, was so impressed that he wrote to the lieutenant-governor, Sir Cecil Beadon, about it.[48] Brahmamayi Das was also invited to the meal, but felt she could not attend because she was unable to eat English food or speak English.[49] Saudamini Ray had been to Government House and had an English governess to tutor her.[50] Mary Carpenter organized the first mixed tea party in 1866, during her visit to Calcutta.[51] From then on there were occasional newspaper reports of functions of this kind. Women learned English partly for the purpose of being able to converse with English women and correspond with them, as well as for reading.[52]

Women increasingly took on the function of official hostess to actively aid and complement their husbands' careers. Jnanadanandini Debi, wife of the first Indian member of the Indian Civil Service, Satyendranath Tagore, was the first to take on such a role. Her husband, in his official capacity, sometimes had English civil servants or district officers to dinner, and "Mrs Tagore did the honours of the house with perfect propriety."[53]

It became part of a woman's role as wife not only to serve her husband, but to help his career as well. The *Bāmābodhinī Patrikā* published a series of articles entitled *Strī-saṅginī*, "wife-companion," on the lives of women who had substantially helped their husbands' careers by providing moral strength, sympathy, and cooperation, such as the wife of Sir Henry Lawrence. Another article mentioned that Garibaldi, Glad-

[48] Rakhal Chandra Ray, *Jīban bindu*, pp. 29-31.
[49] Dwarkanath Ganguly, *Jībanālekhya*, pp. 27-28.
[50] Rakhal Chandra Ray, *Jīban bindu*, pp. 100, 119.
[51] M. Carpenter, *Six Months*, pp. 183-184.
[52] *IMS*, 25 April 1875.
[53] M. Carpenter, *Six Months*, p. 70.

stone, and Napoleon, among others, had been encouraged by the pure love of their wives.[54] Protap Chunder Mozoomdar, a prominent Brahmo, said of his wife Saudamini,

> My wife has a wonderful power of work. If it had not been for her, I could not have got on at all, I am so absent-minded and impractical in the pursuits of life. Work which ought to have been mine in the administration and management of my affairs she has taken and fulfilled much better than I could have done.[55]

A Brahmo girl, with her advanced education and social accomplishments, became the perfect wife for a man with career aspirations in government service. The marriage of Bihari Lal Gupta, I.C.S., was obviously arranged on that assumption. Though said to be a man of no religious views, he was nominally a Hindu, but had no objection to marrying Saudamini Khastagir, daughter of Dr. Annada Charan Khastagir, once a prominent member of the "female emancipationist" wing of the Brahmo Samaj. Saudamini objected to the groom's religious position, but her father passed over her objections because all other aspects of the match were so suitable. She was reproved in an editorial of the *Bāmābodhinī Patrikā* for not having made better use of her emancipation by refusing.[56]

Marriage reform

One difference between traditional marriages in Bengal and English marriages was that in England the choice of partner was left up to the individuals concerned. A number of people in nineteenth-century Bengal began to voice objections to arranged marriages, where the partners had usually never seen

---

[54] "Bibāhita jīban," *BP*, 7:1, 433-434 (February-March 1901).

[55] P. C. Mozoomdar, *Heart Beats* (Indian ed., Calcutta, 1935). From the introduction by S. J. Barrows, 1894.

[56] "Socanīya ghatanār bibāha," *BP*, 8, 111 (November 1872).

one another before the marriage ceremony.[57] One writer for
the women's magazine *Banga Mahilā* lamented,

> When whatever qualities a person has or lacks, or how
> far their nature is similar to yours, are not known, there
> is no possibility of a full union in marriage. If, by the
> hand of fate, a well-suited couple are wed, there is a
> possibility of a close marital bond, not otherwise.[58]

Nagendrabala Mustaphi, a Hindu girl, wrote an essay in the
Bāmābodhinī Patrikā criticizing the way marriages were arranged with no thought for suitability or the future happiness
of the couple.[59] When it came time for Kumudini Ghose to
be married, her family worried about finding a groom for her
because she was less beautiful than her sisters. Insulted by
this, she contacted her brother, Brahmo Kunjalal Ghose, who
arranged with Dr. Nilratan Sircar to take her secretly away
to Calcutta to be educated.[60]

The question of arranged marriages raised a major point
of difference between Hindu and English ideals. The English
ideal of marriage was intertwined with notions of love and
romance. For Hindus, love and mutual attraction played no
part in marriage negotiations. Affection was a desirable part
of the ideal Hindu marriage, but it was assumed that this
would develop gradually through proximity. R. C. Dutt, in a
positivist defense of Hindu marriage in his novel *Sangsār*,
wrote that

> love springs in India after the marriage, when the young
> bride blooms into womanhood and becomes the mistress
> of the household, and when to all the devotion of a dutiful

[57] Mahesh Chundra Deb, "A Sketch of the Condition of Hindoo Women,"
read to the Society for the Awakening of General Knowledge in January
1839. Reprinted in G. Chattopadhyay, ed., *Awakening in Bengal*, pp. 98-
102.

[58] *Banga Mahilā*, 1, 12 (April 1876), 279.

[59] Nagendrabala Mustaphi, "Prayojanīya prārthanā," *BP*, 5:3, 357 (October 1894).

[60] Interview with Uma Ray, Calcutta, 29 November 1977. Kumudini was
her mother.

girl she adds the more tender and deeper love of a woman. The love so born lasts through life. The wife never forgets the duty she learnt in her tender years towards her lord, and the husband cherishes her who came to him as a girl, whose life he shaped to his until she bloomed, a loving woman, in his arms.[61]

The ideal of mutual growth in marriage was used as an argument to explain and defend the practice of child marriage, condemned by the British.[62] It was said that in a society where a woman had a definite role to fill in the household hierarchy, she had to be trained into that role when she was young and flexible, before she had developed independent ideas.

Although the British continued to harp on the barbarity of child marriage, among Hindus there was a marked resistance to raising the marriage age. In 1872 a Marriage Act was passed through Brahmo efforts, setting the minimum marriageable age for non-Hindus at fourteen for girls and eighteen for boys. The Hindu community was indifferent to this because it had no direct effect on them. Various measures were considered by the government to raise the marriageable age of Hindu girls. One indirect way suggested was that married students should be barred from government colleges. This was strongly objected to on the grounds of unwarranted interference with native custom.[63]

More direct measures were seen to be necessary, and were taken in the Age of Consent Bill of 1891. The agitation over this issue provides a case study of the way in which women in Bengal generally came to public prominence as symbolic objects rather than as a group speaking on their own behalf. The age of consent had been standardized at ten in 1860. That limitation provoked no objection, perhaps because by then the age of marriage had already begun to creep beyond ten.

[61] R. C. Dutt, *The Lake of Palms (Sangsār)*, p. 220.

[62] Leading Hindu *bhadralok* intellectuals, such as Bankim Chandra Chatterjee and Bhudeb Mukherjee, advocated this position. See *Sanjībanī*, 29 July 1893, and *Samāj-o-sāhitya*, 30 July 1893, in *RNNB* 5 August 1893.

[63] *Mursīdābād Patrikā*, *RNNB* 6 July 1878. The debate over the proposal continued for some time.

The 1890 bill proposed to raise the age of consent from ten to twelve. It was greeted by an enormous protest movement, with political significance beyond the immediate issue. The crucial objection to the age of twelve was that puberty nearly always occurred before then. Hindus were bound by scripture to have intercourse with their wives on their first menstruation, which constituted the ritual of *garbhādhān*. This was known as the "second marriage." Therefore, it was argued, the bill would be forcing millions of Hindus to sin.

In Bengal, the outcry and protest was carried on entirely by men. Women's point of view was not seriously taken into account at all. "A Woman" was the author of one pamphlet against the bill, but the political fervor permeating the tone of the arguments used suggests that it was probably by a man. The female persona was used for a conscious purpose: to convince the supporters of the bill that women themselves rejected it. The pamphlet took the form of a conversation between two women, Kamalkamini and Suresbhamini. At one point, Suresbhamini declared that

> we are women, and so we can well know, hear, and understand about woman's nature and wants. Girls who are hale and hearty ordinarily start menstruating at ten or eleven, and in this country most girls reach puberty at that age. There is no physical harm if a woman cohabits with her husband after menstruation. Rather, it is likely to be harmful if she does not do so. After beginning menstruation, if because her husband is abroad, or if for any other reason she is not fortunate enough to be able to cohabit with him, we can see that she becomes visibly worn-out and emaciated, and in feminine language we would say she had become "dāmāiyā." Not cohabiting with the husband at the appropriate time is among the causes of hysteria.[64]

[64] Meye kartrik likhit, *Āin! Āin!! Āin!!!* (Dacca, 1890), pp. 5-6. The word *dāmāiyā* is a female colloquialism that is now obsolete, meaning something like "as thin as a rope."

The writer went on to say that postponement of marriage until after menstruation would lead to unchastity, and furthermore, would cause great inconvenience to the husband. A wife who had not consummated the marriage after her first menstruation was in a state of ritual impurity which meant that she had no access to the kitchen and could not cook her husband's meals.

Although protest wisely centered on the exact age of puberty, in fact marriage ceremonies in Bengal were already anachronistic. The *garbhādhān* rite was often only a formality, intercourse having already taken place.[65] The custom of *phul sajyā* or wedding night, where the couple slept together in continence with female relatives standing guard outside, originated for the protection of the young bride. By the nineteenth century it had become merely an occasion of vicarious sexual release for the bride's female relatives, who spent the time singing obscene songs.[66]

The immediate cause of the raising of the marriage age issue at that time was the death of Phulmani, aged eleven, from being raped by her husband, Hari Charan Maiti. Much was made of the fact that Phulmani, like "crores of girls in this country," was accustomed to sexual intercourse, so it was said to be not that in itself which caused her death. Her misfortune was to have had a brutal ex-convict for a husband, but there was no need for the rest of society to be penalized because of his excesses.[67] Hindu writers extolled the Hindu marriage relationship and represented the bill as an attempt to introduce "unholiness" into this sacred bond by allowing

[65] T. Raychaudhuri noted that this was already so much earlier. *Bengal under Akbar and Jahangir*, p. 12.

[66] *Somprakās*, 30 November 1863 in *RNNB* 5 December 1863. A report in the *Burdwan Sanjībanī*, 27 January 1891, tacitly admitted that the *phul sajyā* was the night of first intercourse by saying that the bill would mean the abolition of the rite because of the risk of prosecution. *RNNB* 7 February 1891.

[67] *Sangbād Prabhākar*, 9 July 1890 in *RNNB* 12 July 1890, and *Dāccā Prakās*, 20 July 1890 in *RNNB* 26 July 1890. See *RNNB* June 1890-June 1891 for full coverage of the agitation.

the possibility of rape in marriage. It was pointed out that rape within marriage was not recognized under English law.[68] It was further argued that early intercourse could not be equated with rape because the distinctive features of rape "are not so much the physical pain caused to the woman, as the loss of her honour and chastity and the disgrace which is brought upon her husband and father," which were absent when it occurred within marriage.[69] The light dismissal of any physical injury and personal humiliation caused to the woman as insignificant showed the callously self-interested perspective of most Hindu husbands. Others demonstrated their deep-seated fear of losing control over women's sexuality by saying that a counter-agitation against late marriages was needed because a woman "feels the craving for sexual intercourse after her first menstruation, and if kept without marriage long after that, she is tempted to satisfy that craving by unlawful means."[70]

Protestors used nationalist and revivalist sentiment to mobilize public opinion against the bill, and in turn opposition to the bill became a symbol of nationalist resistance to government interference. A mass meeting was called on the Calcutta Maidan, and there were placards in the streets saying "Abolition of second marriage, Abolition of the Hindu religion, Protect us, Mother-Queen."[71] Despite the agitation, the bill was passed into law because the Legislative Council was almost entirely British in its composition. Census figures for 1891 and 1901 show a steady rise in the age of marriage. This trend reflects a gradual change in social custom, but may also have been helped by the passage of the bill.[72]

In this context, Brahmo marriage reforms were obviously not acceptable among the wider Hindu community, although

[68] *Dacca Gazette*, 29 January 1891 in *RNNB* 31 January 1891; *Doinik-O-Samācār Candrikā*, 10 February 1891 in *RNNB* 14 February 1891.

[69] *Sahacar*, 18 February 1891 in *RNNB* 28 February 1891.

[70] *Nabajug*, 2 October 1890 in *RNNB* 11 October 1890.

[71] *Sanjībanī*, 17 January 1891 in *RNNB* 24 January 1891.

[72] Figures for age and conjugal status given in the Bengal Censuses of 1891 and 1901 show this rise. The bill may have affected these statistics by causing people to disguise the real age of marriage for fear of prosecution.

they were in the vanguard of a slower general trend away from child marriage. Among Brahmos, especially after the 1872 Marriage Act, there was a marked rise in the marriage age. The community also evolved a flexible system of "facilitated" rather than arranged marriages. Some social mixing was permitted, especially at annual festivals. On these occasions young people came into contact with suitable members of the opposite sex. Arranged marriages still took place in the Brahmo community, but those responsible were concerned with individual compatibility and similarity of religious, moral, and even educational background. Lineage and wealth were no longer the determining factors in these marriages.

Nirmala Majumdar, whose parents were both Brahmo missionaries, met her future husband Nilratan Sircar at a Brahmo gathering. They were married when she was eighteen, in 1897.[73] Hemantakumari Chaudhuri, editor of women's journals, met her husband at the home of her guardian, Brahmo Sibnath Sastri. He was supposed to be meeting another prospective bride, but she was also present and he preferred her.[74] Krishna Kumar Mitra married Lilabati, fourth daughter of Rajnarain Bose, against her father's wishes, in 1881. Rajnarain was disturbed that the bridegroom intended the marriage to take place in the Sadharan Brahmo Samaj, not his own Adi Brahmo Samaj. He finally relented when, on asking the opinion of sixteen-year-old Lilabati, she expressed great eagerness for the marriage. He felt that she was of an age to make her own decision, and reluctantly gave his consent.[75] Sisir Kumari Bagchi, B.A., was married in 1898, at twenty, to a Brahmo geologist twenty years her senior. The marriage was arranged by her professor and family friend, Paresh Nath Sen. The high moral tone of a Brahmo marriage, and the new outlook it repre-

[73] Interview with Roma Chatterjee, Calcutta, 6 October 1977. The couple were her grandparents.

[74] Interview with Santa Deb, Calcutta, 18 March 1978. Hemantakumari was her mother.

[75] Krishna Kumar Mitra, *Ātmacarit*, p. 291; "Bibāha," *Tattwabodhinī Patrikā*, 457, Bhadra 1803 (1881), in B. Ghose, *Sāmayikpatre*, part 2, p. 601.

sented, are evident in the kind of gifts she received on the occasion. Among these were the Reverend F. W. Farrar's *Seekers after God*, from Professor Sen, and the poetical works of James Russell Lowell from another Brahmo friend.[76] Between 1872 and 1882, 149 Brahmo marriages were celebrated in accordance with the provisions of the 1872 Act.[77]

In many respects, a Brahmo marriage followed many of the conventions of a Hindu marriage. For instance, the bride's father paid all the marriage expenses as well as giving gifts to the groom. Some Brahmos felt that this ran counter to their notions of equality, and attempted to redress the balance. In the marriage of Candraprabha Biswas and Binaycandra Gupta in 1896, it was first decided that the bride and groom would each look after his or her own expenses. Later a more generous agreement was reached, that each would take care of the other's expenses. This was, however, an exceptional case.[78] At the marriage of Srinath Canda's widowed sister Sarada to Gopalcandra Ghose in 1873, he had Keshub Chunder Sen agree to change one part of the marriage ceremony. Rather than have the guardian "bestow" the bride in marriage, he used the words "charge over."[79]

One highly exceptional marriage was that of Sarala Ghosal, granddaughter of Debendranath Tagore. She had been brought up to be independent and to take part in the public male world of political affairs. She remained single until the age of thirty-three, when she accepted a marriage proposal to satisfy the wish of her dying mother, the writer Swarnakumari Debi, who wanted to see her properly settled. Her elder sister arranged a suitable marriage for her. The groom, Rambhuj Dutt

[76] Interview with Kalyan Dutt, Santiniketan, 16 November 1977. Sisir Kumari was his mother.

[77] A full listing of Brahmo marriages from 1861 to 1882, with the age, caste, and occupation of the parties as well as comments on any unusual features was given in the Register of Brahmo Marriages in the *Brahmo Year Book*, III, 1878; IV, 1879; V, 1881; VI, 1882.

[78] Srinath Canda, *Brahmasamāje callis bathsar*, pp. 294-296.

[79] *Ibid.*, pp. 93-94.

Chaudhuri, was a Punjabi nationalist lawyer belonging to the Arya Samaj. The marriage took place in 1905.[80]

Current satirical fiction depicted emancipated women as setting their own terms for their grooms. Miss Bino Bibi B.A., heroine of the play of that name, would not marry the groom arranged for her because he only had an E.A. (Entrance Arts) Pass, or university entrance. Her list of necessary qualities included being able to write plays like Shakespeare, novels like Scott, poetry like Byron, be a hero like Napoleon, rich like Rothschild, and a member of the Legislative Council and the Indian National Congress, among other things.[81]

Hindu newspapers predicted dire consequences for marriages in the English style, where courtship was all-important, which would lead to an overemphasis on external physical charms and qualities, and supposedly would be followed by aversion after marriage. The Hindu wife was said to begin with aversion from her dislike of going to her husband's home and end up loving him and creating a "happy home."[82] This ideal may have been realized earlier in the century, in the framework of a traditional social structure in which emotional satisfaction was not expected from a husband. However, the element of romance found in European marriages was emerging in the new Bengali literature of the later nineteenth century. It must have created expectations of love and romance in marriage even though the idea had not yet met with social approval. Literate women formed a large part of the readership of these romantic novels. A passage from Swarnakumari Debi's novel *Kāhāke*, translated into English as *An Unfinished Song*, aptly illustrates the new romanticism. The novel was set around 1882, and the heroine was nineteen years old and still unmarried. She boldly declared to the reader that

> this may be a source of surprise to one who understands this land of ours; but it is gradually changing, for are

[80] Sarala Debi, *Jībaner jharāpātā*, chapter 25, "Bibāha."
[81] Durgadas De, *Miss Bino Bibi B.A.*, p. 22.
[82] *Sahacar*, 13 January 1892 in *RNNB* 23 January 1892.

there not many maids unmarried in this advanced age who count as many years as I do? And if a surprise it be I have a still greater in store for my readers. I, a Hindu maiden, knew love before I entered wedlock. I loved a man without even expecting him to become my husband.[83]

Readers expecting scandal would have been disappointed. The man she loved was her doctor, and he eventually did become her husband because although unrecognized by her, he turned out also to be a childhood friend with whom her father had arranged her marriage.

Marriages like that of Sucaru Debi, third daughter of Keshub Chunder Sen, fulfilled this type of romantic expectation. In 1889, when she was fifteen, her marriage to the eighteen-year-old maharaja of Mayurbhanj was arranged. His relatives were opposed to the match. They sent him to England for seven years, and, on his return, had him married to a Hindu girl. Sucaru vowed never to marry anyone else. The story had a happy ending, however. The Hindu maharani died, releasing the maharaja to marry his true love, Sucaru, in 1905, when she was thirty.[84]

Cautionary notes were sounded even among the Brahmos. Protap Chunder Mozoomdar saw a problem in the independence and selectiveness of older girls, as these emphasized romantic ideas of love with the attendant distractions of "love letters, flirtations, rejections, and amorous fancies."[85] There was a fear that if late marriage was advocated on grounds of physical development, marriage would become entirely carnal.[86] In 1878 the *Indian Mirror* warned that "the time has really come to draw the line between reform and refined car-

[83] Swarnakumari [Ghosal] Debi, *An Unfinished Song* (London, 1913), p. 12. Translated from *Kāhāke* (Calcutta, 1898).

[84] Prabhat Basu, *Mahārānī Sucāru Debīr jīban-kāhinī* (Calcutta, 1962), pp. 67-80.

[85] "Mr P. C. Mozoomdar on Marriage Reform," *Liberal and New Dispensation*, 23 November 1884.

[86] *IMS*, 21 April 1878.

nality, and when moral and religious distinctions must be upheld as something different from social enjoyment."[87]

There were no grounds for such apprehension. Reformed marriages provided no public evidence of "carnality" or even sensuality. Traditional marriages were less puritanical in sexual matters, in fact. In a guide to letter writing for women, an example was given of a typical letter written by a semiliterate woman to her absent husband. Apart from being written in extremely flowery language and being full of spelling mistakes, a portion was excised and marked by asterisks indicating that it was considered too obscene to reprint.[88]

Despite the spiritual exaltation of the ideal Hindu wife, in practice she had greater knowledge and experience of sexuality than did most contemporary English women. Although puritanical Brahmos and Christians did exaggerate, much of the conversation of Hindu women seems to have revolved around sexual matters.[89] Sex was a major part of the traditional marriage relationship, whereas other qualities such as companionship and sympathy were only sought among members of the same sex.

The nineteenth century saw the creation of a new genre of modern medical textbooks and "scientific" marriage manuals, advising men on how to conduct their sex lives within marriage. Some information on sexual relationships can be gleaned from these.[90] Their exact readership is unclear. Women must have been part of it, because advice on general health and menstruation was sometimes addressed directly to them.

Marriage manuals declared that sex was not only a basic need, but also a source of great pleasure. They gave diverse advice on when to have and not to have intercourse. One

[87] *Ibid.*, 1 December 1878.
[88] Pyaridas Sarkar, *Strī siksā pratham kānta* (Calcutta, 1876), pp. 11-12.
[89] See Chapter One.
[90] Jogendranath Mukhopadhyay, *Jībanraksā* (Calcutta, 1887); Bharatcandra Bandopadhyay, *Susrusā pranālī*; Annada Charan Khastagir, *A Treatise on the Science and Practice of Midwifery with Diseases of Children and Women*, new ed. (Calcutta, 1878); Kedarnath Sarkar, *Ritu-raksā*; Surjanarayan Ghose, *Boijnānik dāmpatya-pranālī* . . . (Dacca, 1884).

manual proclaimed that it was "unscientific" for a man to have intercourse before the age of twenty-two, for the old to have intercourse with the young, to have intercourse purely for pleasure, or against either partner's will, among other things.[91] Another listed the wrong conditions for intercourse as being with a girl who has not yet menstruated, without a desire for children, against the woman's will, or during the first days of her period.[92] The menstrual taboo was found in all the manuals and textbooks, although the number of prohibited days varied. In all cases the woman's willingness was crucial in defining the most suitable time for intercourse. Simultaneous orgasm of husband and wife was described as the fullest form of sexual enjoyment.[93] If these manuals were taken as guidelines, the chances were that a woman would have had as much pleasure and fulfilment from intercourse as her husband.

Most women would have had experience of marital sex from puberty onwards, but some would have been denied this expression through *kulīn* marriage or early widowhood. Masturbation among Bengali women was acknowledged in medical textbooks. In "A Treatise on the Science and Practice of Midwifery with Diseases of Children and Women," a textbook written for the Bengali class at the medical school by Dr. Annada Charan Khastagir, it was noted that masturbation by young girls was a cause of hypertrophy of the clitoris. Apparently the practice was common in many schools, and was believed to be addictive and damaging to the brain. The Bengali practice of using an eggplant (*bārttāku*) for the purpose was said to be the cause of an infection called pelvic hesetolin [sic]. To stop masturbation, the remedy prescribed was a grain of opium and three grains of camphor made into a paste and taken three times daily, as well as the application of ice on the clitoris. The clitoris was medically recognized as the central organ of arousal. To increase desire, an electric

[91] Surjanarayan Ghose, *Boijnānik dāmpatya pranālī*, p. 38.
[92] Kedarnath Sarkar, *Ritu-rakṣā*, pp. 4-5.
[93] *Ibid.*, p. 10.

current through the clitoris was recommended, and to decrease it, the clitodorectomy operation; less drastically, a strong caustic lotion or ice could be placed on the clitoris.[94]

The preoccupation with sex in Bengali society created an aversion among some English educated youths. While many of their peers went openly to prostitutes, though warned against the dangers of venereal disease,[95] youths who joined the Brahmo Samaj were self-consciously puritanical and kept up a campaign against the vice-ridden lives of their Hindu contemporaries. Brahmos tended to go to extremes in their avoidance of sexuality. Keshub Chunder Sen had always stressed the spiritual nature of the bond between husband and wife,[96] and the emphasis gradually increased to the exclusion of all other facets of a relationship. Marriage was seen in negative terms, as an alternative to sin for those who could not "avoid uncleanness" and were "defiled with carnal thoughts." The most admirable people were those who took the vow of celibacy.[97] The concept was a curious mixture of Brahmo puritanism and Hindu asceticism.[98]

In practice not many Brahmos took up the challenge, but there is one particularly interesting and well-documented case of a couple who did. In 1882 Aghorekamini and Prakascandra Ray decided, after having had three sons and two daughters, not to have any more children because they distracted a woman from spiritual pursuits. They took a vow of chastity for six months. They had taken shorter vows in the past, but had never been able to extend them successfully. This vow was taken in trepidation, but they managed to keep it. At the end of it they decided to make it a lifelong commitment. It was a constant struggle for them, but seemed to deepen their love

[94] Annada Charan Khastagir, *A Treatise*, pp. 624-625.

[95] Jogendranath Mukhopadhyay, *Jībanraksā*, p. 30; Surjanarayan Ghose, *Boijnānik dāmpatya-pranālī*, p. 65.

[96] "Sukhī Paribār" (1874) in Keshub Chunder Sen, *Bidhān bhagnī sanggha*, new ed. (Calcutta, 1932).

[97] "New Social Code—Marriage," *New Dispensation*, 2 September 1881.

[98] The *Griha Sutra* recommended three or twelve nights of conscious abstinence every year for married couples; "Marriage," *IMS*, 7 July 1878.

for and understanding of each other. In 1891 they were formally united in *ātmīya bibāha* or "spiritual marriage." They
tested the limits of their physicality constantly. After some
years they decided to stop even embracing. Prakascandra wrote
in his diary that his ideal was the chaste kiss, devoid of all
sexual feeling. Aghorekamini's determination was the force
that kept them going. She had cried herself to sleep in the first
six months, but never told her husband about it.[99] Theirs was
a very happy marriage, in which they gave each other support
and sympathy in actively pursuing their individual goals. A
case of a Hindu couple who undertook a similar vow was less
successful. Motilal Roy was passionately attracted to his wife,
yet accused her of causing his spiritual ruin, and frequently
beat her in frustration at his own shortcomings. They took a
vow of celibacy in 1906, but he could never cope with his
conflicting impulses in a rational manner, and his wife suffered
for it.[100]

These cases were atypical. To gain insight into the new
quality of feeling in marriage one can turn to the letters exchanged between couples. Meant only for each other, they
indicate well the kind of affectionate closeness that could be
achieved in a marriage where women were given an image of
themselves as "help-mates."

Pramodini Haldar and her husband Satakari wrote daily
when apart, about simple matters like their own health and
that of the children, with injunctions to each other to look
after themselves. Contrary to traditional practice, she addressed him simply as "Dear Satakari," and signed herself
"Yours, Pramodini."[101] When he was in England, Srinath Datta
wrote to his child-wife Harasundari,

> Did I bring you from your home and parents to give you
> trouble? No! I brought you with great hopes of happiness.
> Now I see that instead of that I've given you endless

[99] Prakascandra Ray, *Aghor-prakās, passim.*
[100] Motilal Roy, *My Life's Partner* (Calcutta, 1945; Bengali original 1936).
[101] Satakari Haldar, *Pūrbba smriti*, pp. 33f.

misery, and thinking of this I feel distressed. But after some thought I gain consolation from knowing that you have greater mental strength than I. Isn't that so? Leaving your friends and relatives you willingly came with me and agreed to live among total strangers. Therefore I write to you so that by your love and self-restraint you can make my good sense prevail and keep me from temptation; then our relationship will be completely happy.[102]

The centrality of the marriage bond in their lives was expressed by the celebration of their wedding anniversary each year. They held a special service and feast to commemorate their silver wedding.[103] When Keshub Chunder Sen was in England, his correspondence showed that he was extremely anxious for letters from Jaganmohini. To his disappointment they were infrequent and often depressed in tone. After receiving one he wrote to her that

this time your letter was very good, and I was delighted to read it. What a strange union of hearts! You, there, saw me in your dreams and I, here, saw you in mine. You expressed a wish to see me during the *pūjā* time; I had also thought that I would travel from here before then. As I have written to you earlier, I will try to finish my work here as quickly as possible and return home. Don't be anxious about that.[104]

He always signed his letters to her "Yours everlastingly, Keshub." Aghorekamini Ray's love and determination are evident in her letters to Prakascandra. In one she described her romantic resolution of the domestic difficulties standing in the way of finding the time or implements to write a letter: "The straw of a broom was my pen, the juice of the seeds of the *pui sāk* creeper was my ink, the moon was my light."[105]

[102] Harasundari Datta, *Swargīya Srīnāth Datter*, pp. 1-2.
[103] *Ibid.*, p. 179.
[104] Letter from London dated 29 July 1870. In Manika Mahalanabis, ed., *Brahmānanda Srīkesabcandrer patrābalī* (Calcutta, 1941), p. 156.
[105] Prakascandra Ray, *Aghor-prakās*, p. 181.

Ananda Mohan Bose, one of the founders of the Indian Association, articulated the strength he derived from his wife in a letter written to her from Germany in 1891:

In my retrospect of the past, I have been thinking much of you too. I have thought of all the kindness and love and tenderness which I have received from you in these twenty-three years and more that we have been partners in life.

Accept again, my dear wife, all my gratitude for all your love and kindness. May the light of this love shine all the brighter in future! Help me in my struggle to be better, sustain my energies by sympathy and timely help, hold up my head when it droops, and under God be my strength in the straits of life. In woman's heart, when God shines on it, is a special lustre and comfort.[106]

The *bhadramahilā* had meaning for her husband's life beyond the domestic realm, even if she took no active part in it. She helped to give him the confidence necessary to sustain him in public life and in his dealings with the British. He genuinely valued her support, and depended on it. The exaggerated dependence of the kind expressed in the letter quoted above indicated the need for release and sympathy felt by the *bhadralok*. In an address to a newly married couple, the officiating Brahmo *ācārya* specified that the six most important characteristics of a marriage were the supportive qualities of mutual contentment, affection, trust, patience, self-sacrifice, and religious faith.[107]

The heightened importance of the marriage relationship, and the stress on mutuality, meant that the *bhadramahilā* also depended more on her husband. She no longer put such value on public signs of his approbation through gifts of clothes and ornaments, but gained sustenance from his presence and needed his companionship. Sarala Das, an Anglicized Brahmo

---

[106] H. C. Sarkar, *Ananda Mohan Bose* (Calcutta, 1929), p. 208.
[107] "Nabadampatir prati upades," *BP*, 8:1, 489 (May 1904).

girl who grew up in Burma, wrote in her diary that her love for her husband Satish was becoming obsessive: "Now I want Satish to think of me and love me and me alone and no one else. I sometimes feel afraid when I think that this morbid love I have for S will make me forget everything and everybody and God will be displeased and take him away from me."[108] The new relationship was not always perceived by women in such intense terms, however. Prabodhini Ghose, writing in the women's journal *Antahpur*, gave an enthusiastic account of the mental stimulation she received from her relationship with her husband:

> I have a few arguments with my husband. He can't get away with saying any old thing as though I were a fool. Certainly I argue with my husband, but our arguments are not proper quarrels. It is also a peculiar part of my nature that if I have an argument I feel very happy. If we have an argument at night, the next day will pass happily. We argue about our society. I do not always lose, but on numerous occasions I do. When he starts logic-chopping I can't stand up to his arguments. Anyway, I somehow intuitively think about society.[109]

Extramarital relationships

Scant evidence is available on unsuccessful marriages among the *bhadralok*. Even though Act III of 1872 had a provision for divorce, Sitanath Tattvabhushan wrote with pride in 1909 that it had never been used.[110] Nonetheless, separations did take place without legal sanction. Dayamayi Debi found her husband so rigidly conservative that it was the cause of many serious quarrels between them. When their children had grown up she left him and went back to her village. He came to take her back, but she was too proud and dignified to give in. She

[108] Amritalal Gupta, *Punyabatī nārī* (Giridi, 1923), p. 33.
[109] Prabodhini Ghose, "Bangamahilādiger arthakarī silpacarccā," *Antahpur*, 4, 1 (January 1901).
[110] S. Tattvabhushan, *The Philosophy of Brahmaism Expounded with Reference to Its History* (Madras, 1909), pp. 356-359.

lived separately from him for the rest of her life.[111] In 1874 the Brahmo correspondent of a vernacular newspaper dared to advocate separation for couples whose "tastes and feelings" no longer agreed. The editorial comment from the *Indian Mirror* was, "Those whom God has united let not such false logic put asunder."[112]

The first case of adultery among the "native gentlemen" to come before the court was the scandalous Bose versus Bose case of 1878. It provides some insight into an unsuccessful marriage.[113] Ksetramani Dasi was accused of adultery with her maternal uncle while her husband was away in the course of his duties as *munsiff*. She and her cousin Binodini, the go-between, gave evidence to the court from *pālkis*, or covered sedan chairs. Ksetramani pleaded not guilty, presenting herself as an innocent Hindu wife maligned by a jealous husband who would not let her communicate with any other males. Incriminating evidence was produced against her, and the jury passed a verdict of guilty. The uncle was sentenced to a year's imprisonment, and Ksetramani was returned to the mercy of her husband. Ksetramani was literate, letters being part of the evidence, and Binodini had done the rounds of all the best girls' schools in Calcutta, thereby discrediting the cause of female education by confirming its opponents' worst suspicions about its consequences. The editor of the *Somprakās* had not intended to "defile" the pages of his newspaper with the particulars of this "disgusting" case, he wrote, but did so because he felt that it exhibited a new feature in Hindu society. Parents and guardians had been led to permit lapses of this kind because of their mistaken notions concerning English education and freedom.[114] Free love became part of the stereotype of the emancipated woman.[115]

---

[111] Interview with Amita Sen, Calcutta, 25 November 1977. Dayamayi Debi was her grandmother. She commented that had it been today she would have gotten a divorce.

[112] *IMS*, 5 July 1874.

[113] *Indian Mirror* for July and August 1878.

[114] *Somprakās*, 12 August 1878 in *RNNB* 17 August 1878.

[115] Carucandra Acarya, *Sabhyatā-sangkat* (Calcutta, 1900). The heroine of

An article on the duties of a married couple in the *Bāmā-bodhinī Patrikā* began with a discussion of the evils of adultery. It admitted that, although theoretically equally bad for both men and women, in practice it was more damaging to a woman's reputation. To avoid the possibility, husband and wife should be solicitous of each other's happiness.[116] Men had a traditionally sanctioned escape from a wife whom they found unsatisfactory in any way. They were free to take a second wife, providing they could afford to maintain both.[117] The same freedom was never available to women. The new ideal of marriage was strictly monogamous. This led at times to a heavy and repressive puritanism. A new range of "suitable" literature was created, insipid and self-conscious, assiduously avoiding any erotic or sensual overtones. However, as traditional alternatives to monogamy had only served the interests of men, the puritanism that stressed a commitment to monogamy by both partners was of positive benefit for women at that time.

The institution of *kulīnism*, peculiar to Bengal, was frequently responsible for deviations from chastity among women. Marriage to a *kulīn* Brahmin by a non-*kulīn* girl brought honor and rank to her family; hence *kulīn* bridegrooms were in great demand. A *kulīn* Brahmin would marry between ten and fifty wives, visiting each only occasionally, if ever, after the marriage ceremony. Whatever their age, on his death the customary prohibition on widow remarriage sealed their future fate. The life of a widow was socially endorsed misery: the treatment of widows revealed the worst of society's attitudes to women. The Widow Remarriage Bill passed in 1856 carried little weight. It was not until the Brahmos took up

this farce, Kumudini, is called "the Wilberforce of women" by her lover. She tells her husband that her lover visits her for religious conversation—a jibe at Brahmos, who stressed the ultimate spiritual purpose of their social reforms. See also "Bangadesīya ramanīganer swādhīnatādān," *Somprakās*, 38, 22 Srāban 1279 (1872) in B. Ghose, *Sāmayikpatre*, part 4, pp. 263-265.

[116] "Gārhasthya darpan-dampatir kartabya," *BP*, 8, 111 (November 1872).

[117] See the short story "Kāsībāsinī" by Ambujasundari Dasgupta, *BP*, 8:2, 502-503 (June-July 1905). The heroine's husband dislikes her from the first because she is not beautiful. He takes another wife and sends her off to Gaya.

widow remarriage as part of their social reform platform that there was a large enough community to sustain and support couples who defied convention in this way. Vidyasagar's attempt to legislate against *kulīn* polygamy was unsuccessful, although the opposition in this case did not defend polygamy but argued that it was rapidly dying out of its own accord.[118]

Even if *kulīnism* were declining, there were still numerous widows in Bengal to whom the Brahmos could direct their efforts at social reform. A number of leading Brahmos married widows themselves.[119] The Brahmo Samaj, and to a lesser extent Christianity, held out hope for widows by waiving all the usual restrictions imposed upon them. On their own initiative, many widows escaped from their village homes to join a Brahmo community in one of the district towns or in Calcutta. Here they could experience greater independence, take a more active part in religious worship, and mix freely with others as an equal rather than a servant. There are records of a number of widows and *kulīn* brides who were attracted to the Brahmo Samaj.[120] Once they had joined, provisions were made for their education and vocational training, and sometimes also their remarriage.[121] Nabakanta Chatterjee arranged for the "deliverance" of fourteen widows between 1870 and 1873.[122] Sasipada Banerjea started a widows' home in Burranagore in 1887, where widows were educated and remarried.[123] Some cases were very dramatic, such as the renowned Bidhumukhi case. Bidhumukhi was a sixteen-year-old *kulīn*

[118] Bankim Chandra Chatterjee, "Bahubibāha" (1873), in *Bibidha Prabandha*, part 2, edited by Brajendranath Bandopadhyay, 3rd ed. (Calcutta, 1964 [1939]).

[119] Notable cases were Gurucharan Mahalanabis (*Ātmakathā* [Calcutta, 1974]); the second marriage of Sasipada Banerjea (A. Banerji, *An Indian Pathfinder*); and the first wife of Sitanath Tattvabhushan (*Autobiography*, [Calcutta, n.d.]).

[120] See, for instance, *Bāmā-carit* and *Swarger phul* (Calcutta, 1892), pp. 12-16. Islam may have had an attraction for widows similar to that of Brahmoism and Christianity, but I have no evidence of this.

[121] Of the 149 marriages recorded in the Brahmo marriage registers, 50 were with widows.

[122] Nalinikanta Cattopadhyay, *Nabakānta Cattopādhyāy, passim*.

[123] Kuladaprasad Mallik, *Brahmarsir jībane bhagabāner kripār jay* (Calcutta, 1918).

girl from a village in Dacca district. She did not want to marry the old *kulīn* with thirteen wives who had been selected for her, so she begged some Brahmo relatives to rescue her. They tried three times to arrange for her escape, and it was only on the third attempt, in September 1870, that one of the reformers was able to swim the river to give her a secret message telling her where to meet him. She was eventually rescued in a boat, and taken to Barisal, then Calcutta. A lawsuit was taken out against her rescuers on the false grounds that she was only thirteen. The case received wide publicity, and was eventually decided in her favor. At the age of twenty-one she married Brahmo Rajaninath Ray, M.A., according to Act III of 1872.[124]

Although some widows did manage to lead a bearable life, those who had no such means of escape were pushed to extremes. The social reform journal *Dāsī* gave a fictional but convincing story of a widow's life in the form of a series of letters between a widow and her sister. The widowed sister lived in despair because of the scorn, abuse, and mistrust heaped on her by her brother's wife, in whose house she lived. Yet she saw no real alternative:

> A widow should not be troubled by fasting, she should be able to sleep well with only the ground for a bed, a widow cannot be killed by abuse. If I am not able to bear these things nobly, then why should I keep living as a widow? The day when my aspirations turned to ashes at the Nimtollah *ghāt*, I could have quenched all my sufferings in the cold waters of the Ganges.[125]

A Hindu widow who committed suicide in 1875 wrote a note explaining that nothing was as miserable as the life of a widow. She planned her own death carefully, sending a boy out to buy one or two paise worth of opium each day until she had one rupee and five paise worth, which was enough to kill

[124] Accounts of her case were given in Nalinikanta Cattopadhyay, *Nabakānta Cattopādhyāy*, pp. 91-97, and *Brahmo Year Book*, III, 1878.

[125] *Dāsī*, 6, 1 (January 1897).

herself.[126] The fate of many other widows, following a lapse in chastity and subsequent social ostracism, was to end up as prostitutes. Brahmos also tried to rescue "respectable" widows from this fate, with varying degrees of success.[127]

The limits of change

As female education spread, the "traditional" ideal of womanhood underwent some modification. For instance, a manual on "The Instructive Lessons on the Career of Life of the Native Females" firmly laid down that a husband's first lesson to his wife must be to teach her the truest and fullest meaning of the word *swāmī*, or husband. In essence, it meant total obedience to his will. The same book also recommended a basic education, giving a woman at least enough literacy to read improving literature. The section on health care also took advantage of the latest ideas.[128] Kumudini Ray, an educated, articulate woman and a frequent contributor to the *Bāmābodhinī Patrikā*, still felt that it was part of a woman's duty to regard her husband as second only to God.[129] Another article in the same magazine maintained that the husband should make all decisions and the wife obey him, because he was the lord of the house and she was his subordinate.[130]

The fundamental similarity of the new ideology to what went before was apparent in High Court attorney Bhuban Mohan Das's address to his daughter Tarala on the occasion of her marriage in 1884. She was nearly sixteen. He reminded her that she was an educated woman, and therefore should have some understanding of the new duties that would fall on her. She should always see her husband as her most prized possession, "the lord of her heart." He would not acknowledge that she was a *sugrihinī*, or true housewife, unless she

[126] *Sulabh Samācār*, 3 Kartik 1282 (1875).
[127] Nalinikanta Cattopadhyay, *Nabakānta Cattopādhyāy*.
[128] Purnacandra Gupta, *Bāngālī bou* (Calcutta, 1885).
[129] "Hindu nārīr gārhasthya dharma," BP, 5:3, 359 (December 1894).
[130] "Gārhasthya darpan—patisebā," BP, 8, 110 (October 1872).

quenched her husband's thirst when he returned home tired and exhausted; unless she frugally saved from his earnings and unless she overcame her desire for superficial luxuries that would sink him into debt. He would be gratified when he heard that she did everything for her husband, and never did anything against his wishes.[131]

In fact a wife could exert pressure on her husband and influence his actions, but this was dependent on her strength of character, and was not encouraged by her role. For instance, Rakhal Chandra Ray, a Brahmo outcast from Hindu society, contemplated returning to it when subjected to emotional pressure from his family. His wife Saudamini reminded him that his duty to religion came before everything, so he withstood their entreaties.[132] Convention still required that wives defer to their husbands. The only socially approved way of exercising influence over a husband was by "redeeming" him. To do so was not only a woman's duty, but a challenge and an achievement. It had to be done with tact, and in a manner that would not offend him.[133]

Ultimately a husband had control over his wife's behavior, and defined the limits of her freedom. Banalata Debi's husband would not let her edit the women's journal *Antahpur* at first because he wanted her to help him with his own work.[134] In many ways, there was less scope for exercise of authority by the wife in a reformed Brahmo-type family than there was in a traditional Hindu household. A Brahmo husband spent more time in the home, and was involved in more joint decisions and activities with his wife than most typical Hindu husbands. Therefore a woman in that situation had less autonomy and independence than her traditional Hindu counterpart. A Hindu wife in a joint family suffered a great deal initially, but by

[131] "Subha bibāhopalakse kanyār prati upades," *BP*, 3:2, 237 (October 1884).

[132] Rakhal Chandra Ray, *Jīban bindu*, pp. 57-68.

[133] "Sahadharminī," *Antahpur*, 1, 6 (July 1898); Umasundari Dasi, *Nārīracit kābya*, p. 14; Purnacandra Gupta, *Bāngālī bou*, pp. 55-57; Tarakanath Biswas, *Bangīya-mahilā* (Calcutta, 1886), pp. 38-40.

[134] Kuladaprasad Mallik, *Brahmarsir jīban*, p. 33.

middle age was generally in a commanding position of authority over the household. That kind of authority never came to a woman in the reformed family, as her husband shared her power in the domestic sphere. She did not gain equivalent access to his public sphere of influence in exchange.

In practice, as well as in theory, a mature educated woman often showed the same revence for her husband that she would have done had she been born decades earlier. An educated man was still capable of accepting such devotion from his wife. Prabhabati Debi, an educated woman, ceased to perform the Savitri Puja because gradually the image of the goddess was replaced in her mind by that of her husband. She no longer felt the need to worship any other god than him.[135] Dayamayi Sen, an accomplished Hindu *bhadramahilā* with some education, used to drink her husband's *caranāmrita*, the water in which his feet had been washed, daily. He left her with a supply of it in a metal pot whenever he went away. Many people told her that this was unrefined and superstitious, but she replied that to regard one's husband as one's all was inherent in the thinking of a faithful Hindu wife.[136] Such extremes were regarded as anomalous among the *bhadramahilā*, but they were not much more than the physical expression of a spirit of submission still prevailing in marriages. It was presumably quite acceptable for Sarala Das to write in her diary in 1898 that

> I want my husband to be my conscience and guide in everything. All great thoughts should progress from him. In this is man's natural glory. . . . Seeing or hearing my husband do anything which I do not think is good hurts me very much. Because I want to believe that my husband is better than me in everything. Truly, he *is* better than me in everything.[137]

[135] Prabhabati Debi, *Amal-prasūn* (Jessore, 1900).
[136] Saraccandra Datta, *Dayāmayī Sener sangksipta jīban carit* (Sylhet, 1890), pp. 25-26.
[137] Amritalal Gupta, *Punyabatī nārī*, p. 18.

After the death of their husbands, some Brahmo women lived in the style of a Hindu widow. There would, however, have been a fundamental difference in their self-esteem arising from the attitude of members of their own community toward them.[138] They were advised to take the good qualities of a Hindu widow—her devotion and self-sacrifice—without accepting her degradation.[139]

The British model that provided some of the inspiration for the change in marriage customs was not one that itself encouraged a great deal of female independence. The nineteenth-century English woman may have seemed advanced to the Bengali *bhadralok*, but she too played a primarily domestic and supportive role in the family. The sense of constriction inherent in a Victorian marriage was expressed with sensitivity by English Unitarian Elizabeth Sharpe, in a letter to her friend Rajnarain Bose:

> I am going to be married. This will change my life completely from what I thought it might have been. I shall never come to India now, which I thought I might possibly have been able to do, indeed I shall be able to do very little for your country, though I shall always care very much for her welfare, for I shall be so much occupied in my own home, and shall feel it my first duty, to spend all my best energies there. An English lady at the head of a household, has seldom much time or thought for objects beyond her home. I have hitherto had an unusual amount of leisure-time, living in a quiet home, well-ordered by my good mother, and sharing with my sisters the small domestic duties. In my new home I shall be more than usually occupied. Mr Henry Cobb, to whom I am now to be married in a few weeks, is a London lawyer. He has been married before, and has four little

---

[138] See, for instance, the lives of Saratkumari Deb (*Āmar sangsār*, Calcutta, 1942, Introduction) and Bamasundari Debi (*Bāmā-carit*).

[139] Muralidhar Bandopadhyay, *Srīmatī Saraswatī Sener sangksipta jībanī*, pp. 76-78.

children, to whom I am to supply the place of the mother they have lost so early. I am very happy in the thought of my new and life-long duties. It is, of course, impossible to leave any old course of life and enter a new one without some regrets, but I believe I am doing what is right, and as God would have me do.[140]

Tennyson's "The Princess" gave poetic expression to an idea that was very popular with the Victorians, that of equality in separate spheres.[141] This idea was eagerly taken up by the Bengali *bhadralok*, who were satisfied with the belief that women should be equal with but complementary to their husbands, rather than competing with them in similar roles on equal terms. Srinath Datta, an "England-returned," was only in favor of female education if it did not create unrest in the family by the wife's refusal to be subordinate to her husband.[142] Men were not advocating an equality that would upset their own domination. They had made efforts to "elevate" their wives not only from altruistic motives but because having such a wife was beneficial to them. Michael Madhusudan Dutt eulogized the prospect in an essay written in 1841: "The happiness of a man who has an enlightened partner is quite complete. The very idea of so sweet a possession awakens even in the most prosaic bosoms feelings truly poetical."[143]

[140] Letter from London, dated 18 July 1872. From Rajnarain Bose, *Ātmacarit*, 4th ed. (Calcutta, 1961 [1909]), p. 130.

[141] Tennyson's poem includes such thoughts as:

> For woman is not undevelopt man,
> But diverse: could we make her as the man
> Sweet love were slain: his dearest bond is this.
> Not like to like, but like in difference . . .
> . . . "Dear, but let us type them now
> In our own lives, and this proud watchword rest
> Of equal; seeing either sex alone
> Is half itself, and in true marriage lies
> Nor equal, nor unequal." (1847)

Alfred, Lord Tennyson, *Tennyson: Poems and Plays* (London, 1973), p. 199.

[142] Harasundari Datta, *Swargīya Srīnāth Datter*, p. 175.

[143] Michael Madhusudan Dutt, "An Essay on the Importance of Educating Hindu Females, with Reference to the Improvement Which It May Be Ex-

By the end of the century the "enlightened partner" was a *fait accompli*, but the notion of "possession" still remained.

Often traditional features persisted in new contexts, and underwent a fundamental change in meaning. In similar fashion, although situations sometimes appeared to be totally different because of the trappings of a new context, the underlying traditional concept frequently remained almost intact. As these processes were happening simultaneously, it is futile to attempt to find clearly demarcated areas of "change" and "tradition," although it is still possible to indicate broad trends and isolate completely new features.

Attitudes had not remained static. During this period a new mutuality had emerged in the way couples perceived their marriages. Marriage had become a conscious partnership. The feeling of companionship this gave rise to led to an impression of equality in marriage. Examples have already been given which show that the equality was largely illusory. However, the illusion was convincing because of the contrast between the position of the new *bhadramahilā* and that of more traditional women in the surrounding society. Education, and for some a later age of marriage, set the *bhadramahilā* apart. Gains that may now seem limited were seen by them as liberating. Women accepted the dominant ideology that gave them a "separate but equal" role. They believed in the importance of their function as wives and mothers. Their closer relationship with their husbands was a pleasant feature of their married lives. If there was discontent, it was not articulated. All anger and dissatisfaction at the treatment of women was directed at traditional Bengali society rather than at the reformed sector. Looking back at the past, and at the traditional society around them, they felt that they had made considerable advances.

---

pected to Produce on the Education of Children, in Their Early Years, and the Happiness It Would Generally Confer on Domestic Life," in Brajendranath Bandopadhyay, ed., *Madhusudan racanābalī* (Calcutta, 1965), p. 519.

FIVE

Motherhood and Child Rearing

As the churning of the ocean gives forth nectar,
so the churning of the ocean of language produces
the sound "*mā.*" The imagination of a poet holds
no sweeter image than this.[1]

Motherhood was the most important function in the life of a Hindu woman. The birth of children sanctified the marriage bond. Although daughters were not highly valued, the birth of a son was of pivotal importance to the family. Temporally, he was the provider and inheritor of property; spiritually, he was the only one who could perform the ritual offering of oblations to ancestors. The son was the perpetuator of the family lineage. Barrenness in a woman, or her failure to bear a son, were grounds for a husband to abandon her and take another wife.[2]

Hindu thought personified and exalted the idea of woman as mother in the image of the Mother Goddess, recognizing her importance as the progenitrix of sons and her association with fertility and creation. Brahmos emphasized the fatherhood of God in the manner of Christianity, but the pervasiveness of the Mother Goddess cult in Bengal prevented them from relinquishing the Hindu concept of God as Mother. The idea of divine maternity was integrated with the Brahmo view of women in the following manner:

[1] "Mā," *BP*, 3:3, 265 (February 1887).
[2] See S. C. Bose, *The Hindoos*, chapter two, "The Birth of a Hindoo," on the difference in birth rituals for sons and daughters. The birth of a daughter was greeted with sorrow, but that of a son was heralded with the conch and presentation of gifts to relatives.

When he the Mother of all mothers becomes our supreme Mother, all women partake of that divine motherhood, and man looks upon woman as gifted with a deeper and tenderer divinity than what he himself possesses. These various considerations force upon us the necessity and the advantage of the distinctive recognition of God in the capacity of our blessed Mother. This relation, therefore, is at present most popular and most constantly impressed upon the Brahmo Samaj.[3]

For Bengali men, who enjoyed a particularly close relationship with their mothers, motherhood evoked a fund of nostalgic memories and emotional outpourings that was readily transferred to devotion to the deity taking the form of Mother.

Childbirth: traditional practices and suggested reforms

To benefit from this reverence for maternity, it was necessary for a woman to begin having children shortly after marriage. Often she would start bearing children not long after reaching puberty. Despite the discomforts, pregnancy may have been welcomed by a young bride, as it was a time when she was treated with greater care and affection than usual. Sometimes for the period of her confinement a woman would return to her natal home, where she could relax fully. In the fifth, seventh, and ninth months of pregnancy she underwent certain rites, all of which allowed an indulgent gratification of her appetite for special foods or sweetmeats.[4] The purpose of such indulgence was not simply the anticipation of the joy and status to be had from her possible production of a son; it was also spurred by the realization, based on experience, that the woman might not survive the throes of childbirth.[5]

[3] "Divine Maternity," *Theistic Quarterly Review*, 5 (May 1880).
[4] S. C. Bose, *The Hindoos*, Appendix A, "Observances and Rites during Pregnancy," pp. 293-300.
[5] *Ibid.*, pp. 293-294.

In all parts of the world in the nineteenth century, child-bearing was hazardous and painful.[6] Babies were generally delivered at home, by midwives without scientific knowledge. Very little was known about prenatal or postnatal care.[7] In Bengal, there were traditional rituals to ensure a safe delivery, but prenatal customs such as not wearing clothes over which birds had flown, spitting on the breast once a day before washing, and wearing a reed in the hair to stave off evil spirits could not have been of any practical benefit.[8] Traditional medical treatments, based on herbal compounds, may have been more efficacious. These included the taking of a few grains of asafoetida with water to prevent miscarriage, and tying a string of the *lajjābatī* creeper around the waist to ensure an easy birth.[9]

Birth took place in the *sutikāgriha*, or *āturghar*. This was always the smallest, darkest room in the house, a physical embodiment of the impurity associated with childbirth. Following the delivery the midwife placed the mother on a strict diet, excluding cold water or cooling drinks even in the hottest months. *Jhāl*, a compound of drugs, was prescribed as an antidote against cold, puerperal fever, and other diseases.[10] A fire was lit in the *sutikāgriha* immediately after birth. The lack of air would have offset the supposed beneficial effects of the heat treatment, by creating smelly, suffocating conditions not conducive to the good health of either mother or child. Upper-caste women were required to spend one month in the *sutikā-griha* because of fear of contamination from their ritual im-

[6] In England in 1868, 26 percent of children still died before the age of five. P. H. Chavasse, *Counsel to a Mother* (London, 1869), p. 3. See also J. H. Miller, " 'Temple and Sewer': Childbirth, Prudery, and Victoria Regina," in A. S. Wohl, ed., *The Victorian Family, Structure and Stresses* (London, 1978), and P. Branca, *Women in Europe since 1750* (London, 1978), pp. 76-81.

[7] B. Ehrenreich and D. English, *Complaints and Disorders: The Sexual Politics of Sickness* (London, 1976; New York, 1973), p. 23.

[8] S. C. Bose, *The Hindoos*, p. 293.

[9] See *BP*, 6:2, 388 (May 1897), for a number of traditional remedies connected with pregnancy.

[10] S. C. Bose, *The Hindoos*, pp. 22-23. He said that *jhāl* was often effective.

purity.[11] A woman's period of confinement in the *sutikāgriha* could only have been made bearable by the thought of the future rewards of motherhood. A professor of the Calcutta Medical College in 1847 expressed horror at the "filthy, smoky, and crowded hovels, to the straw of which the unfortunate Bengallee females are condemned by native usage in the hour of suffering."[12] The health officer for Calcutta in 1876 gave a more detailed but equally disturbing account of traditional practices:

> A chamber, a few feet square, so situated that at the best of times its atmosphere must be close, has every aperture carefully shut. It is crowded with relatives and attendants, so that there is often barely room to sit, and a fire of wood embers, or even charcoal, is burning in an open vessel. The atmosphere is principally smoke, which is increased by herbs scattered on the fire for the purpose. The woman is lying, generally on the ground, in the midst of this. The feeling on entering the room is that of impending suffocation.[13]

Custom forbade the use of a bed, mattress, or additional garments. Conditions were observed regardless of the weather, and dry cowdung or wood fires were kept going day and night. It was also prohibited for the child to wear any sewn covering during this month. Although generally a woman remained sheltered,[14] immediately after birth she was supposed to take a cold bath in the tank or *ghāt*. At times the effect of this, in her weak state, sent her into a raving delirium, in which case an *ojhā*, or exorcist, was brought in to exorcise the spirit possessing her by beating her with a torn slipper.[15]

The mother was attended during and after birth by a mid-

[11] "Dhātrī bidyā," *BP*, 3, 52 (December 1867).
[12] Dr. Stewart, Report on the Statistical History of the Female Hospital, *GRPI for 1846-47*, Appendix E No. 10, p. clxxv.
[13] Bengal Census 1881, part II, p. 120.
[14] S. C. Bose, *The Hindoos*, pp. 23-24.
[15] Nanibala Dasi, "Sutikāgāre prasūtir susrusā," *Antahpur*, 7, 1 (May 1904).

wife, usually a woman of the Dom or Bagdi caste.[16] During delivery, midwives sometimes interfered with natural labor in a way that could jeopardize the health of both mother and child. Cases were reported of midwives who began pulling the infant's head as soon as it appeared,[17] and of others who removed the placenta by hand as soon as the infant had fully emerged.[18]

Giving birth under such unfavorable conditions meant that a woman was extremely susceptible to subsequent infections, even if the birth itself was uncomplicated, and death in childbirth was common among all classes.[19] Cases of *sutikā-rog*, or puerperal fever, were frequent, and were the most common cause of death in childbirth all over the world.[20] The rate of infant mortality was also extremely high.[21]

Men were not allowed into the *sutikāgriha* during the thirty-day period of ritual impurity. Husbands therefore had no contact with their wives during this time, or even children with their mothers. This rigidity may have placed some emo-

[16] S. C. Bose, *The Hindoos*, p. 23; "Sutikā-griha," *Antahpur*, 5, 7 (November 1902).

[17] "Dhātrī bidyā," *BP*, 4, 57 (May 1868).

[18] Annada Charan Khastagir, *A Treatise*, p. 167.

[19] A number of biographies of the *bhadramahilā* record deaths in childbirth: S. Sen, *Memoirs*, p. 28; Satakari Haldar, *Pūrbba smriti*, pp. 19-30; Rakhal Chandra Ray, *Jīban bindu*, pp. 123-129; Dwarkanath Ganguly, *Jībanālekhya*, p. 78. The latter biography describes the death in childbirth of Brahmamayi, wife of Durga Mohan Das. An official announcement, moving in its brevity, appeared in the newly instituted Birth and Death columns of the Sunday edition of the *Indian Mirror*:

November 12, 1876. Domestic. Birth. Wife of D. M. Das. Still-born daughter, premature. Night of 3 November.

Death. Morning 6 November, at residence 1 Lower Circular Road. Brahmamoyi Das, beloved wife of D. M. Das, deeply mourned by husband, children and friends.

[20] See Rakhal Chandra Ray, *Jīban bindu*, p. 42, and "Swargatā Kusumkumārī," *Mahilā*, 3, 1 (August 1897). P. Branca, *Silent Sisterhood*, pp. 86-89, records that this was the case in England, even though some Bengalis thought that European women had overcome most of the difficulties of childbirth by observing the rules of health. See Mohendracandra Gupta, *Strībodh*, p. 59.

[21] Gopal Chunder Dutt, *Sulochona or the Examplary Wife (A Story of Bengal Domestic Life)* (Calcutta, 1882), pp. 186-190, is a vivid fictional account of a mother's grief over the birth of a stillborn child.

tional strain on a woman, as she had no control over her situation. Sitanath Tattvabhushan recollected that his mother died in 1860 at the age of 25, shortly after giving birth to her fourth child, which also died. Realizing that she was dying, she called repeatedly for young Sitanath to come to her, but his father forbade him because of the fear of her impurity: he was suffering from fever at the time and would not have been able to undergo the ritual purificatory bath. Consequently his mother died in a state of mental anxiety as well as physical pain.[22]

In the earlier part of the nineteenth century, women in England were still attended by midwives, but at the same time the medical profession was developing and elevating midwifery into a medical science. Obstetrics and gynecology became legitimate areas of specialization for doctors. Books of advice to women on how to handle confinement and pregnancy were published from 1833. As far as women were concerned, the most important medical advance was the discovery of chloroform in 1847, which considerably reduced the pain of delivery.[23]

Doctors studying in the Calcutta Medical College took midwifery as part of their training. The Midwifery Hospital of the Medical College introduced the use of ether and chloroform in delivery, but it is not known whether it was used in home births as well. Only the poorest low-caste women entered hospitals for childbirth, and even then many were only sent there by midwives after complications had developed. The *bhadramahilā* gave birth in the *sutikāgriha* in her own home.

The *bhadralok* showed an eagerness to use new medical knowledge, although it was only accessible to the few who could afford the high cost. In 1848, the report of the Midwifery Hospital announced with pride that all of their six or more college graduates now settled and practicing in Calcutta were "habitually called to take charge of the women of the

[22] Sitanath Tattvabhushan, *Autobiography*, p. 18.
[23] See P. Branca, *Silent Sisterhood*, chapter five, "The Dynamics of Victorian Motherhood" and J. H. Miller, " 'Temple and Sewer.' "

families they attend during their confinements, and that though not required to render manual assistance, except in cases of difficulty, they are always requested to undertake the medical management of every case, both during and after delivery."[24] The report also said that the practice of confining women to "some filthy outhouse, enveloped in the fumes of charcoal, and drenched with heating tisannes" had been "entirely abandoned by all the respectable Natives in Calcutta." That was far too sweeping an expression of optimism, but it does show that some of the *bhadralok* were anxious to try to relieve the sufferings of women in childbirth by employing doctors, and that women acquiesced. From this report it seems that, at least around the middle of the century, doctors and midwives shared their skills; the doctor supervised while the midwife came into closer contact with the patient.

Recent studies of the medical profession in nineteenth-century England and America have criticized it for defining women's health in terms of their satisfactory fulfilment of the accepted stereotype of feminine weakness. The care of the midwife is thought to have been more in harmony with a woman's needs.[25] There is some validity in this, as midwives would have been more experienced than doctors, and as women who had had children themselves they may have had more empathy with their patients. Many Bengali women were skeptical about the capacities of a doctor: "What do doctors know? Ask a woman who's had many children what to do and she'll give you the right answer."[26] However, midwives did not spare the young mother's feelings, either, and comparing her labor with their own, they would often scold her sharply for the slightest deviation from their advice. Experience was their sole guide, and they firmly resisted innovation.

In an attempt to solve the problem of the very high infant

[24] *GRPI for 1847-48*, Appendix E No. VII, p. cl.

[25] B. Ehrenreich, *Complaints and Disorders*; L. Duffin, "The Conspicuous Consumptive: Woman as an Invalid" in S. Delamont and L. Duffin, eds., *The Nineteenth Century Woman*; J. S. and R. M. Haller, *Physician and Sexuality in Victorian America* (Urbana, Illinois, 1974).

[26] Nanibala Dasi, *Antahpur*, 7, 1.

and maternal mortality rate, women began to turn to doctors for solutions. Dr. Jadunath Mukherji, author of *Dhātri siksā*, the best seller on midwifery first published in 1867,[27] advertised his skills as accoucheur, physician, and surgeon. He saw lady patients at his house in Bowbazar Street between 2 and 4 p.m. daily.[28] There is no evidence that during this period doctors achieved any substantial lowering of the mortality rate among *bhadramahilā*, but the increasingly frequent use of their services showed a desire to alleviate the suffering of childbirth by taking advantage of new medical techniques. A textbook for medical college students first published in 1868 showed the uses of surgery in obstetrics, including detailed diagrams explaining how to carry out a forceps birth or a caesarian using surgical instruments.[29]

Despite their medical knowledge, doctors called in to manage cases in *bhadralok* families were often unable to diagnose or treat complications in pregnancy. In 1874 Saudamini Ray was treated by doctors for chest and back pains, but they could not find the cause of her illness. They were unable to tell that she was about to give birth to twins. After the birth, the placenta did not follow as it should have, and Saudamini was in such agony that she begged her husband not to prolong her life by any further treatment. The placenta was eventually expelled, but Saudamini did not survive. A European doctor was called in to attend her, but could do nothing.[30] In 1896, Pramodini Haldar had heart failure as she was about to give birth. A European doctor and a midwife were both called in, and helped deliver her of a son, but she died.[31]

The latter case showed the continued dependence on the

---

[27] It was in its third edition by 1875. *Bengal Library Catalogue of Books—Quarterly Appendix to the Calcutta Gazette*, 1875, I. He also wrote *Sisu sarīr pālan*, on child rearing, in 1874.

[28] *IMS*, 30 March 1879.

[29] Annada Charan Khastagir, *A Treatise*.

[30] Rakhal Chandra Ray, *Jīban bindu*, pp. 123-129. Kailaskamini, wife of Umesh Chunder Dutt, died of anaemia in 1898 because she was pregnant with twins. Rajanikanta De, *Caritamādhurī (Chayjan brāhmikā sādhbīr jībanābhās)* (Calcutta, 1919), p. 21.

[31] Satakari Haldar, *Pūrbba smriti*, pp. 20-30.

midwife while the modern knowledge of the doctor was also used. There was still great demand for the services of a midwife because her fee was much lower than that of a doctor. A midwife also had the advantage of being able to have close physical contact with women. An article on midwifery in the *Bāmābodhinī Patrikā* in 1868 raised the question of whether the midwife should stay with the patient after having ascertained readiness for delivery by a digital examination of the cervix. The answer was no if the midwife was a man (male-midwife presumably meaning a doctor), but yes if it was a woman, because the patient would not be ashamed to perform any bodily functions in front of her.[32] In fact, this answer demonstrated that the permissible contact between a woman and a male doctor was considerable, if this was the only point at which he was excluded.

The introduction of retraining programs for midwives was an attempt to combine practical experience and scientific knowledge. Despite her experience, a midwife was often ignorant of basic sanitary principles. The Calcutta Medical College Hospital and the Mitford Hospital in Dacca first opened courses for midwives in 1870.[33] A European midwife attended the delivery of R. C. Dutt's third daughter in 1873—an instance of compromise between a traditional midwife and a doctor, as well as a status symbol.[34]

One way of improving health conditions was for mothers themselves to know something of the new medical principles. In 1857, the first of a continuing stream of mother and child care manuals, based generally on English prototypes, appeared under the title of *Sisu pālan*, subtitled *Infant Treatment*. The author, Shib Chunder Deb, claimed that the "ignorance on the part of Hindoo females of the Proper management of infants, and the great mortality which arises from this cause" compelled him to write the book.[35] His own

---

[32] "Dhātrī bidyā," *BP*, 3, 55 (March 1868). See also J. H. Miller, " 'Temple and Sewer,' " pp. 29, 34, on "man-midwifery" in England.
[33] "Dhātrī bidyālayer bibaran," *BP*, 6, 89 (January 1871).
[34] S. Sen, *Memoirs*, p. 54.
[35] Shib Chunder Deb, *Sisu pālan*, I (Serampore, 1857), iii. The preface was

4. Saratkumari Deb (1862-1941),
daughter-in-law of Brahmo reformer
Shib Chunder Deb.

experience of having lost two sons because of the ignorance
of midwives, inadequate conditions for birth, and the lack of
after-care was a contributing motive.[36] He was not a doctor,
but had adapted Andrew Combe's *Treatise on the Physiological and Moral Management of Infancy* to the circumstances
of Hindu society in an "easy and familiar style."[37]

This work, and those that followed it, recommended re-

written in English, possibly to draw British attention to Bengali efforts at
self-improvement.

[36] Saratkumari Deb, *Āmār sangsār* (Calcutta, 1942), p. 2. Saratkumari was
Shib Chunder Deb's daughter-in-law.

[37] Shib Chunder Deb, *Sisu pālan*, p. iii.

forms and made knowledge of the need and means for improvement known to the *bhadramahilā*. A manual of general instruction for women, published in 1862, stressed the importance of prenatal care.[38] Shib Chunder Deb recommended extensive changes in arrangements for the *sutikāgriha*. He said that it should be removed to a higher floor, where there was some movement of clean air to ventilate it, and where conditions could be dry and sunny. Later manuals echoed him in this matter. The first of a series of articles on midwifery in the *Bāmābodhinī Patrikā* was on the *sutikāgriha*, advising that it should be situated on the second story of the house in a place that was neither too dark nor too windy. The room should have windows that allowed the passage of fresh air from north to south, should get plenty of sun, and be removed from any smelly, unsanitary places.[39] Care was to be taken in opening and shutting doors to prevent sudden draughts.[40] A fire should be kept going in cold weather, but it should be a wood or coal fire rather than cowdung. It was to be lit outside the room so as to control the amount of smoke.

Before literacy among the *bhadramahilā* had become widespread, however, initiative for improvement of conditions came from men, who had some knowledge of alternative possibilities. Durga Mohan Das had read many books on childbirth. When his wife gave birth to their first child in 1861 he decided that he could not subject her to the rigors of the *sutikāgriha*. Instead, he let her lie on his own bed, on a mattress, to the consternation of his family.[41] In 1872 the Tagore family's *sutikāgriha* was a sunny room on the third floor of their Jorasanko house.[42]

The new medical wisdom laid down that a mother should not remain in the *sutikāgriha* for longer than one week, but it is not known how many families would have dared to defy

[38] Mohendracandra Gupta, *Strībodh*, pp. 60-65.
[39] "Dhātrī bidyā," *BP*, 3, 52 (December 1867), and Mohendracandra Gupta, *Strībodh*, p. 63.
[40] *Soi* (Calcutta, 1890), p. 142, section on "Gārhasthya bidyā," hint 49.
[41] Sarala Ray Centenary Committee, *Sarala Ray*, p. 85.
[42] Sarala Debi, *Jībaner jharāpātā*, p. 1.

traditional taboos on this matter. Injunctions such as the following would have been easier to observe: a woman was to
be allowed to wear warm clothes, and was to take care with
her diet; traditionally approved foods such as pepper, lime,
hot ghee, fish, meat, *roti, luchi,* and *parotā* were considered
harmful; a medically recommended diet included milk, arrowroot, barley, sago, boiled rice, and *mug dāl* broth. In extreme cases, brandy could be taken for relieving pain.[43] By
the turn of the century, although women's health during childbirth had not yet markedly improved, there was some recognition of the importance of postnatal care.

Progressive *bhadralok* husbands took a close interest in the
health of their wives, and ignored the period of ritual impurity
after birth. Rakhal Chandra Ray was by the side of his wife
Saudamini when she died in childbirth. Pramodini Haldar's
husband was with her for a tender farewell when she died
after giving birth to a son.[44]

The *bhadramahilā* were encouraged to take up midwifery
themselves. There was no dearth of literature to instruct them.
Had they absorbed all that was available, they would have
been extremely well qualified. Bengali women were less ham-
pered by false notions of delicacy than their English contemporaries, and therefore had access to fuller information. In
England in 1854 the publication of *Female Physiology* by Dr.
Sturt elicited the following comment from a reviewer in the
leading medical journal, *The Lancet*:

> What? Is it to be tolerated that a medical practitioner, a
> man above all others who should be imbued with true
> modesty . . . shall unblushingly give to the ladies of Eng-
> land drawings of the vagina, uterus, spermatozoa, various
> stages of labour etc. . . . I was nauseated by the task of
> perusing this offensive volume.[45]

[43] "Dhātrī bidyā," *BP*, 4, 59 (October 1868); Nanibala Dasi, *Antahpur*,
7, 1; "Sutikā-griha," *Antahpur*, 5, 7.
[44] Rakhal Chandra Ray, *Jīban bindu*, and Satakari Haldar, *Pūrbba smriti*.
[45] L. Duffin, "The Conspicuous Consumptive," p. 46.

This kind of prudery could have been detrimental to women's health. Fortunately, Bengalis were not plagued by an inability to reconcile the anatomical facts of pregnancy with the pure state of motherhood.[46] In 1867 the *Bāmābodhinī Patrikā* published a series of detailed and informative articles on midwifery, covering pregnancy, its symptoms and treatment, and delivery.[47] An article in the same journal in 1872 published essential information for a pregnant woman on the growth and development of the fetus. Illustrations in black, white, and red showed the fetus from the time of conception through each month of pregnancy.[48] Manuals on household hints, and collections of essays for the purpose of female education, generally contained sections on midwifery.[49] Doctors wrote more detailed books of advice for expectant mothers.[50]

Mothers took notice of the new information insofar as they could. The first practical test of the efficacy of the new theories was the birth of the son of Shib Chunder Deb, author of *Sisu pālan*. He was born prematurely, when his mother had only completed the seventh month of pregnancy. At that unexpected time all the other women in the family were away on a pilgrimage. The child was delivered "scientifically," and reared according to the rules laid down in his father's book. This shocked the women of the neighborhood, skeptical of a man's claim to expertise in these matters, but Shib Chunder's wife followed her husband's advice with good results, and proved their scorn to be groundless.[51] Kumudini Sinha tried to rear her children by following the rules of health laid down in Dr. Annada Charan Khastagir's manual for women. She even committed some sections of the book to memory.[52] A *bhadramahilā* helping with a delivery early this century fol-

[46] For an interesting discussion of this dichotomous view of women in Victorian England see J. H. Miller, " 'Temple and Sewer.' "
[47] *BP*, 3, 4 (1867-1868).
[48] "Mātrigarbha o garbhasisu," *BP*, 8, 109 (September 1872).
[49] *Soi*; Pyaridas Sarkar, *Strī siksā.*
[50] Pulin Sanyal, *Saral sisu pālan* (Calcutta, 1885).
[51] Saratkumari Deb, *Āmār sangsār*, pp. 1-3.
[52] *Kumudinī-caritra*, pp. 28-29.

lowed the "modern" practices of bandaging the mother's stomach soon after birth, disinfecting the vaginal area with antiseptic lotion, and bathing the newborn infant with soap immediately after the birth.[53]

Unfortunately, there is no direct evidence that would prove conclusively that the kind of knowledge demonstrated by women in these instances filtered down to the majority of the *bhadramahilā*.[54] However, there is enough inferential evidence to believe that this was the case. *Bāmābodhinī Patrikā*, which often carried articles on midwifery and child rearing, had a circulation of over 1,000 by the mid-1880s. The actual readership would have been much greater than the number of subscribers alone would indicate. Books on medical care, hygiene, and simple midwifery, written especially for women, were printed in runs ranging from 500 to 2,000 copies, and often went into many editions.[55] Available knowledge was certainly widely disseminated, although practice may have been slow to change in accordance with new theoretical principles. For the most part, recommendations were of the kind that could be adopted without too great a break with tradition. These reforms were essentially improvements of a utilitarian nature that did not conflict with women's traditional role, although they may have helped alleviate her suffering. The changes reflect a desire on the part of educated Bengalis to benefit from modern scientific knowledge, and a growing humanitarian concern for the welfare of mother and child.

[53] Renuka Ghose, *Sarojinī-carit* (Calcutta, 1936), pp. 71-72. However, in 1914 Sudha Mazumdar found when giving birth that most of the "traditional" practices referred to earlier were still carried out. S. Mazumdar, *A Pattern of Life*, p. 130.

[54] Jay A. Mechling, in "Advice to Historians on Advice to Mothers," *Journal of Social History*, 9, 1 (Fall 1975), cautions against using childcare manuals as either reflecting or causing child-rearing patterns. In his view, manuals reflect the values of the writers, and can only be used to generalize about social beliefs. This would certainly largely be true of nineteenth-century Bengal. However, biographical evidence shows that some women did try to follow the advice given in manuals.

[55] *Bengal Library Catalogue*, from 1867 onward.

Contraception and family size

Childbirth was such a risky venture throughout the nineteenth century, and so detrimental to the health of the mother, that it is not surprising that many women preferred to have longer intervals between pregnancies. Direct information on their methods of avoiding child-bearing is scarce, but can be pieced together from diverse sources.

Research has shown that both the rising economic and social aspirations of the middle class, and "domestic feminism," or the desire of women to control their own fertility, were factors in the adoption of contraception to limit family size in nineteenth-century England.[56] The *bhadralok* also aspired to a middle-class style of life, characterized by expenditure on long-term benefits with little immediate return. The education of sons to a tertiary level, and the education of daughters were considerable expenses. The pain and misery of childbirth would have made the *bhadramahilā* reluctant to repeat the experience very frequently. At the same time, other factors worked against these reasons for limiting family size. The high rate of infant and child mortality tragically diminished the number of children in a family. For instance, the wife of Brahmo Kalinarayan Gupta bore sixteen children, of whom six died in infancy and early childhood.[57] Annapurna Cattopadhyay had ten children, but two were stillborn and one died after a few weeks.[58] The traditional association of status with the ability to display wealth made a large family a symbol of prosperity. The *bhadralok* may have been caught between the urge to display status by having a large family and the desire to give each member maximum opportunities by limiting family size.

Universal medical ignorance over the process of conception made effective contraception impossible in the nineteenth century. There was total confusion regarding the "safe period."

[56] See J. A. and O. Banks, *Feminism and Family Planning in Victorian England* (Liverpool, 1964), and A. McLaren, *Birth Control in Nineteenth-Century England* (London, 1978).
[57] Bangkabihari Kar, *Bhakta Kalinārāyan Gupter*, p. 19.
[58] Srimanta Cattopadhyay, *Annapūrnācarit* (Calcutta, 1893), *passim*.

What was then designated as such has since been proved to be the time most likely to result in conception. Nineteenth-century doctors calculated that conception took place shortly after menstruation.[59] Bengali marriage manuals all gave the same misleading information on the connection between menstruation and pregnancy. One method of ascertaining pregnancy attributed to "European scholars" was that a woman must have had intercourse during her menstrual period.[60] An article on menstruation in the *Bāmābodhinī Patrikā* warned women not to sleep with their husbands during menstruation or for three or four days before or after, because of the likelihood of pregnancy.[61] Scientific prohibitions were reinforced by the *Laws of Manu*, which prohibited intercourse during the first four days of menstruation because of ritual impurity.[62] A manual written as late as 1908 fixed the "sterile week" at precisely the most fertile period—from 14 days after one menstrual period to five days before the next.[63]

Nonmedical methods such as condoms, pessaries, and douches were more effective, but may not have been readily accessible to the *bhadramahilā*. They could also cause various infections.[64] It is likely that there were traditional methods of birth control that would have been widely known. The 1901 Bengal census commented on the falling birth rate, and speculated that one reason for this was the "deliberate avoidance" of child-bearing.[65] Prolonged nursing, known to be connected

[59] J. S. and R. M. Haller, *The Physician*; A. McLaren, *Birth Control*.

[60] Jogendranath Mukhopadhyay, *Jībanraksā*, p. 38.

[61] "Ritur abastāy ki ki niyom pālan kariya calā ucith," *BP*, 2:1, 180 (January 1880); Surjanarayan Ghose, *Boijñānik dāmpatya-pranālī*, p. 35; Jogendranath Mukhopadhyay, *Jībanraksā*, p. 20.

[62] Kedarnath Sarkar, *Ritu-raksā*, p. 3.

[63] M. E. Staley, *Handbook*, p. 94.

[64] *Ibid.*, pp. 93-94 mentioned the harm caused by greasy, germy pessaries, injections of cold unsterilized water with solutions of strong drugs, or mechanical devices impossible to sterilize. She recommended a douche of warm sterilized water with a solution of boracic acid, Lysol, or Creolin.

[65] Bengal Census, 1901, part II, pp. 215-221. It was said that the family of the landless laborer could only be smaller than that of the cultivator because of preventive methods. Among cultivators, family size varied with the size of the holding. This also illustrated the fact that in traditional society, a large family was a sign of prosperity.

with the delayed resumption of the menstrual cycle after birth, was very common in Bengal. Postpartum abstinence also helped to space births.[66] Abortion was also used as a means of birth control. A letter in the *Statesman* in 1878 from a "medical man" referred to the prevalence of abortion and infanticide in Bengal, in cases where pregnancy was the result of an illicit liaison.[67] In 1901, the *Dāccā Prakās* reported a case of a fifteen- or sixteen-year-old girl who had been made "enceinte" [sic] by a wealthy man. He procured an abortion for her "by the application of some drug," but she died three days later.[68] Other evidence shows that methods of abortion were known and practiced. Books on abortion were available.[69]

Despite the use of contraception by various sections of the population, birth control was never a public issue in nineteenth-century Bengal. The Malthusian debate going on in England was known to some of the *bhadralok*, and had come into brief prominence in 1883, after Moncure Conway visited India. He had recommended the adoption of Malthusian population control, which he defined as the exercise, by a couple, of "common sense, prudence, and self-restraint, while studying carefully the physiological and moral laws of their own constitution"—presumably meaning abstinence and the so-called "safe period."[70] Apart from this the issue was ignored.

Motherhood redefined

Even if contraceptive methods were used to space births, the major part of a woman's life was still taken up with childbirth and child rearing. Her chief role and occupation had always

---

[66] Jogendranath Mukhopadhyay, *Jībanraksā*, p. 38; Surjanarayan Ghose, *Boijnānik dāmpatya pranālī*, pp. 65-66.

[67] "100 Years Ago," *Statesman*, 13 September 1978. The correspondent referred to Dr. Norman Chevers' *Medical Jurisprudence* for evidence.

[68] *Dāccā Prakās*, 25 August 1901 in *RNNB* 31 August 1901.

[69] See *Bengal Library Catalogue*, 1875, II—*Garbhinī bāndhab* and 1885, III—*Nārī jīban*.

[70] The debate went on in the *Liberal and New Dispensation*, 13 April 1884, attacking Conway. He replied in the issue for 8 June 1884. See also a letter from A. D. Tyssen, London: "A Pilgrimage to Malthus," in *IMS*, 19 December 1880.

been to bear and rear a family. In the west, the nineteenth century saw the culmination of a redefinition of both motherhood and childhood. As middle-class women had no productive function in the economic system, motherhood was elevated into a full-time occupation. Increasingly it was stressed as the noblest function of woman, not to be approached casually but with semi-religious awe.[71] The child was a miracle of creation, care of whom required "more gentle handling, and thought, and knowledge, than that of keeping in repair a beautiful chronometer,"[72] a precious gift entrusted to the mother by God. In a time of rapid social change, the role of mother was sacralized and made into an emblem of the security of the family in the face of external upheaval. Both child and mother were symbols of unblemished innocence, in contrast with the impurity of the world at large.

The traditional Hindu reverence for the concept of mother made the *bhadralok* particularly receptive to the Victorian elevation of motherhood. The role of the mother was pivotal in leading the way from "superstition" to "enlightenment" in a situation in which modernization and the advance of "civilization" were seen as future goals. Motherhood as a woman's duty was not a new idea, but the way that duty was defined differed. Duty was to go beyond simple loving care and guidance by chastisement. Child rearing, with the production of an enlightened citizen as its aim, was a solemn burden. The fulfilment of this aim necessitated the absorption of new theories of child care, adapted mainly from Victorian models and modified by the vastly differing traditional family system upon which they were imposed. The traditional mothering role seemed inappropriate to a society in which children were to be educated by English methods, and was thus redefined to suit the new circumstances. The elevation of motherhood in this way gave the *bhadramahilā* an enhanced sense of purpose and boosted their self-esteem. Moreover, it was a means of bring-

---

[71] P. Branca, *Silent Sisterhood*, chapter five.
[72] P. H. Chavasse, *Counsel to a Mother*, p. 3.

ing them into the same mental world as the *bhadralok*, and a recognition that they shared the responsibility of shaping the future under colonial rule.

A writer in the *Bāmābodhinī Patrikā* blamed the structure of the joint family for Bengali failings of cowardice, dependence, laziness, and apathy. The need for change within the family was pointed out:

> In these times, if a new family and social organization are not laid on the foundations of a pure ethical system, then the old stability of Hinduism will not be seen again. The need for family order is even greater than the need for social order, because the foundation of the lives of men and women are laid in the family, and those patterns continue throughout their lives.[73]

The influence of mothers upon the great men of history was a popular theme in didactic literature in nineteenth-century Bengal.[74] The idea of filial duty, already strong in the Hindu family, was matched by a newer idea of parental duty. Traditionally, parental duty was implicit, expressed in the socialization of the child through domestic duties and religious rituals. Different expectations of the goals of life required a conscious adoption of new methods of socialization. A paper on "The Educated Natives of Bengal; their position and responsibility," read to the Bethune Society in 1869 by Gopal Chandra Dutt, criticized the traditional father in terms that could also be applied to the mother: "It is not given to him to think of the responsibilities which devolve upon a parent of qualifying his children for the duties of life. . . . He calculates only upon the objections of filial duty. It never occurs

---

[73] "Sāmājik ebang paribārik sāsan," *BP*, 8, 108 (August 1872).
[74] Nagendrabala [Saraswati] Mustaphi, Cuttack, "Samājonnatite nārī-jāti," *BP*, 8:1, 498 (February 1905); "Strījātir bises kārjya," *BP*, 4, 59 (July 1868); Sukatara Datta, "Madālasā bā ādarsa jananī," *Antahpur*, 2, 14 (February 1899). This was also a popular theme in England. See C. A. Halsted, *The Obligations of Literature to the Mothers of England* (London, 1840).

to him that the duty is mutual. It is enough that he has given birth [sic] to children."[75]

Bengali mothers needed to be schooled to a realization of their new responsibility and importance. An English female well-wisher who had established a correspondence with some Brahmo women wrote in one letter: "You said that you are unable to accomplish any good work, but here in England when a woman marries and becomes a mother the training of a child to be tender, obedient, loving and full of zeal for learning is considered more important than anything else."[76] By the end of the century, the *bhadramahilā* had fully internalized the "grave responsibility" of motherhood.[77] It was endowed with importance on a national scale. The significance of motherhood had expanded beyond being merely a home function to being a public duty:

> Even though we are women and we are weak, when God has given us such great responsibility he will also give us the necessary strength. For better or for worse, the future of society and of the nation rests on these children of ours. If they are properly educated then the nation will follow the path of progress. . . . Therefore, sisters, come let us join together and give of our strength to fulfil this great vocation, and though we are weak, let mutual co-operation give us collective strength.[78]

New methods of childcare

Childcare manuals and numerous articles in periodicals, especially women's journals, conveyed the specific means of building a healthy and enlightened generation. In 1885 a monthly journal devoted to infant management and the treatment of disease by European and native methods began pub-

[75] Bethune Society, *Proceedings*, p. 192.
[76] "Bilāter patra," *BP*, 6, 86 (October 1870).
[77] "Jananī," *Antahpur*, 1, 3 (April 1898).
[78] Saralabala Debi, "Santān-siksā," *Antahpur*, 4, 9 (October 1901).

lication.[79] The literature covered all aspects of child rearing from infancy to around five years of age. The proliferation of advice would indicate that women were in need of guidance in an area that had never previously been perceived as problematic. For many women, especially those who had separated from the larger joint family to accompany their husbands, there was a real need for very basic guidance on childcare. For others to whom the advice of generations of older women was available, the manuals performed a "modernizing" function, often explicitly condemning traditional practices and urging the adoption of new methods.

Breast feeding may be singled out as an issue symptomatic of the conflict between old and new advice. The advantages of modern ideas on the duration and regulation of breast feeding, and the disadvantages of traditional ones, were widely discussed. Both traditional wisdom and modern advice shared the view that all mothers should breast feed. New writers advised women to systematize breast feeding in a quasi-scientific manner, but warned them against giving it up altogether.

The employment of a wet nurse for feeding infants had been routine practice in Europe until the late eighteenth century.[80] Although in some countries it continued until much later, it was dying out among middle-class women in England by the mid-nineteenth century.[81] Despite this, the Bengali stereotype of Englishwomen typified them as regarding breast feeding as degrading. The *bhadramahilā* was warned against falling under English influence in this matter.[82] The stereotype may have been based on the persistence of wet-nursing among the ar-

---

[79] *Bengal Library Catalogue*, 1885, II—*Prasūtisiksā nātak*, edited by Pramatha Nath Das. The summary of contents noted that it seemed especially designed for Bengali ladies, and was written in the form of a dramatic dialogue.

[80] L. DeMause, "The Evolution of Childhood," in L. DeMause, ed., *The History of Childhood* (New York, 1974), pp. 34-35.

[81] *Ibid.*, p. 35; P. Branca, *Silent Sisterhood*, pp. 100-101. Branca points out, however, that there is no clear statistical evidence on this.

[82] *Bhāratī*, February 1878; "Sisupālikā," *Gārhasthya*, 11 (1886).

istocracy, and also by the public exposure of the practice of "baby farming" in England in the early 1870s.[83] It may also have been common for English women in India to employ wet-nurses.

In Bengal wet-nursing was not simply a caricatured form of Anglicization, but was an established practice among the wealthy.[84] However, in the nineteenth century general opinion was solidly in favor of breast feeding by the mother alone. Women were only to resort to a wet-nurse if they were too ill to feed the child themselves.[85] Even then, bottle feeding, in special bottles obtainable from "any good dispensary," was regarded as a preferable alternative.[86] There is scant evidence on how women themselves felt about breast feeding. It was said that when a European doctor forbade the wife of Brahmo district official Ananda Mohan Barddhan to breast feed because she was pregnant with her next child, she was extremely upset.[87]

In practice, resorting to wet-nurses was not common among the *bhadramahilā* and was therefore not a matter worthy of the attention it received in England. According to doctors, Bengali mothers were guilty not of neglecting the feeding of the child, but of breast feeding it too frequently and weaning it too late. In the west, nursing beyond two years had always been exceptional.[88] By the nineteenth century, an authority such as Mrs. Beeton's *Book of Household Management* recommended nine to fifteen months of nursing.[89] In Bengal, children were commonly breast-fed for three, four, or even

[83] See a discussion of "baby farming" as a consequence of women entering the work force in "Strīganer sāmājik sambandha o adhikār," *BP*, 8, 112 (December 1872).

[84] Sarala Debi, *Jībaner jharāpātā*, p. 1.

[85] *BP*, 8, 108 (August 1872).

[86] *Bhāratī*, March 1878.

[87] Kusummala Datta, *Swargīya Ānandamohan Barddhan Mahāsayer jībaner katipoi smriti* (Tippera, 1927), p. 27.

[88] L. DeMause, "The Evolution," p. 35.

[89] P. Robertson, "Home as a Nest: Middle Class Childhood in Nineteenth Century Europe," in L. DeMause, ed., *The History of Childhood*, p. 410.

five years.[90] Medical opinion declared that prolonged breast feeding was responsible for deteriorating health in mothers and children, and tried to encourage a lower weaning age. Preferably this was to be around one year, or a few months later if the infant were weak, but not beyond the age of two.[91] One European woman doctor in India, attempting to explain prolonged nursing habits, observed that the conditions of life of Indian women made them better able to breast feed than European women. Whereas an Englishwoman was unable to nurse her child for more than nine months because of the mental and physical strain it imposed on her, the sedentary and secluded life of an Indian woman was such that she could safely continue to nurse for up to twelve or fourteen months.[92] Another European doctor disagreed, stating that *antahpur* women were less likely to be able to breast feed than women who did outside work.[93] In his autobiography, Sibnath Sastri recounted how tensions within the joint family caused his mother's supply of milk to dry up, with the result that he became seriously ill.[94] The strains of breast feeding were not readily acknowledged, although there were numerous side effects that could cause considerable discomfort.[95]

As noted earlier, the practice of prolonged nursing was used by Bengali women as a means of spacing births. They may not have welcomed the injunction to wean the child at nine months, since it opened up the prospect of more frequent pregnancies. Even in England doctors used the contraceptive

[90] P. Chapman, *Hindoo Female Education*, p. 13; Shib Chunder Deb, *Sisu pālan*, 1, 91; Hemangini Kulahbi, "Aniyamit stanya dān," *Antahpur*, 8, 1 (May 1905).

[91] *BP*, 8, 108 (August 1872); Surjanarayan Ghose, *Boijnānik dāmpatya pranālī*, p. 113; Dr. Cleghorn of Lucknow, "Bhāratbarse sisupālan," *Mahilā Bāndhab*, 2, 14 (July 1887).

[92] M. E. Staley, *Handbook*, p. 225.

[93] Dr. Cleghorn, *Mahilā Bāndhab*, 2, 14.

[94] Sibnath Sastri, *Ātmacarit*, pp. 8-9.

[95] P. Branca, *Silent Sisterhood*, pp. 103-104, mentioned that Mrs. Beeton recognized that "lactation is always an exhausting process," and cited the problems of milk fever, engorged breasts, cracked nipples, and general fatigue.

aspect of breast feeding as an incentive for adopting it.[96] Faith in nursing as a form of birth control would help to explain the unusually long nursing period among Bengali women. Therefore it was either shortsighted or naive of medical advisors, who were predominantly male, to condemn the practice without suggesting any alternative forms of contraception. Unfortunately there is no biographical evidence on the age of weaning to establish whether the *bhadramahilā* followed this advice, which was, in respect to fertility control, working against their own interests.

Other medical advice was more readily acceptable. Women had often delayed initial feeding because the first milk was said to be harmful,[97] but in fact doctors said it served a useful function, cleansing the infant's bowels of accumulated waste. Traditionally feeding was delayed until the mother's milk started to appear, but doctors pointed out that if the child was put to the breast within six to twelve hours after birth, the milk would begin to flow freely.[98] Medical advice of this nature would have made breast feeding easier for the mother and bypassed the need for a wet-nurse or other temporary feeding measures.

A value that permeated and dominated the whole child-rearing process in the nineteenth century was the importance of a regular routine. This notion was applied to breast feeding, in an attempt to supplant the established practice of feeding the infant on demand. An article by one Hemangini Kulabhi on "irregular breast feeding" was published in *Antahpur* in 1905, warning women of the terrible consequences that could result if they were not fully mindful of their responsibility to feed according to a schedule. She claimed that infants had been known to die because they were given too much milk at their first feed, or if fed at night when the mother herself was still half-asleep. Even educated women were castigated for believing that the more milk an infant was given the better

[96] *Ibid.*, pp. 100-101.
[97] Dr. Cleghorn, *Mahilā Bāndhab*, 2, 14; *Bhāratī*, November 1877.
[98] Dr. Cleghorn, *Mahilā Bāndhab*, 2, 14.

its health would be. They were also found guilty of too readily interpreting the infant's cries as hunger pains, rather than as the result of other common causes of discomfort such as stomach aches. The writer's chief concern was to show that irregular feeding was harmful to the health of both mother and child. She recommended feeding every two hours for a newborn infant, lengthening the time between feeds as it grew older.[99] Another writer advised feeding every four hours, starting from 5 a.m. and going through to 10 p.m. If the infant cried at night it was not to be fed, but to have its diaper changed, be turned over, or be given a drop of water.[100] After weaning, a child could begin a diet of nourishing foods, eating four or five times a day but not at night. The "correct" diet excluded anything oily or unripe, and sweetmeats.[101]

A childcare manual directed mainly at English mothers in India emphasized that the absolute regularity and punctuality of a fixed routine were essential to the child's progress.[102] It is doubtful whether the clockwork functioning of an English nursery could ever have been applied in a Bengali family, where the fixed routine of daily activities was not rigidly measured by the clock. It would have been very difficult for a woman to institute a routine of childcare if it did not fit in with the routine observed by the rest of the family. It was only possible in a situation where the senior members of the family saw some value in the establishment of a routine. Shib Chunder Deb, anxious to carry out the precepts he had laid down to guide others, made sure that his son was fed at regular intervals, literally timed by the clock.[103] By the end of the century many ordinary Hindu *bhadramahila* were following similar routines.[104]

---

[99] Hemangini Kulabhi, *Antahpur*, 8, 1; *BP*, 8, 108 (August 1872). See also Nandakrisna Basu, *Bāmābodh* (Calcutta, 1879), "Sisur sarīr pālan," pp. 55-61.

[100] *Bhāratī*, February 1878. Much of this advice is still current.

[101] "Sisuder āhār," *BP*, 2:2, 33 (May 1866).

[102] M. E. Staley, *Handbook*, p. 282.

[103] Saratkumari Deb, *Āmār sangsār*, p. 2.

[104] Renuka Ghose, *Sarojinī-carit*, p. 25.

Apparently Victorian reticence prevented much discussion of toilet training in England, but an article in the *Bāmābodhinī Patrikā* in 1872 was explicit in recommending that toilet training start from the age of three or four months. At this age the infant was to be taken out of bed for the purpose eight or ten times a night.[105] Following the routine suggested would have been a great strain on the mother, and it was unlikely that she would have responded favorably to this part of the new system of childcare. In any case, the joint family situation still common to most *bhadramahilā* meant that responsibility for child rearing did not fall on the mother alone. Therefore unless all family members were equally committed to the importance of a fixed routine, the system would have broken down when the child was out of the mother's direct care.

Another drawback of the new methods was that they were an added cost to the family, both directly and indirectly. Infancy, which had not previously involved any expenditure at all, now required the buying of diapers and feeding bottles, as well as the payment of doctor's fees. An article in *Bhāratī* stated plainly that the family which observed new methods of childcare would have to be prepared to spend money. A mother needed at least two dozen cotton and one dozen flannel sheets, among other things.[106] Indirectly, the fixed routine placed so many new demands on a woman's time that she would no longer have had as much time to do her normal household duties. The resolution of this would probably have meant that she coped with an extra burden rather than spending any money on hiring servants to take over her work. In a large family it may have been possible for her normal household duties to be done by other family members, but this was unlikely. She was expected to carry out her normal domestic duties with the child either within reach or being cared for by others. The child would have fitted in with the routine observed by adults in the household, rather than the reverse.

The new definition of motherhood gave the mother full

---

[105] P. Robertson, "Home as a Nest," p. 419; *BP*, 8, 108 (August 1872).
[106] *Bhāratī*, November 1877.

responsibility for the moral as well as physical management of her children. Their strengths and weaknesses were all attributed to her. Many English women felt this to be a burden,[107] but for the *bhadramahilā* the wider distribution of responsibility within the joint family would have lessened the pressure on her alone. The new responsibility was more likely to have been a source of strength, since a mother's status was enhanced by the attention paid to her role.

Praise for a mother's capabilities was less forthcoming than advice and criticism. Articles told her that not only was she to blame if her child did not turn into a reliable citizen,[108] but she was also guilty if it fell ill because she had carelessly allowed it to eat what it liked or had neglected to dress it properly.[109] From the time of pregnancy and nursing, a mother's state of mental as well as physical health was said to influence the child.[110] The *Indian Mirror* quoted with approval the words of an English mother, "I'm a missionary in my nursery; there six pairs of little eyes are watching me, and six little hearts are acquiring ideas of truth from my works as well as words," following them with the pious injunction, "It would be a happy day if an Indian mother could say as much."[111]

Shib Chunder Deb was again a pioneer in the field of literature on the moral training of children. In 1862, he added to his volume on the physical aspects of infant treatment with a second part on the moral management of infancy. His sources included selections from *Letters on Early Education* by Pestalozzi, the Swiss pioneer of new child rearing methods.[112] It was followed by a stream of books such as *Mātrisiksā* in 1871, and *Saral sisu pālan* in 1885.[113] Even a "Mohammedan work" on the duty of parents to children was translated into Ben-

---

[107] P. Branca, *Silent Sisterhood*, chapter six, "A New Model of Child Care."

[108] "Sisubinayan," *BP*, 2:1, 183 (April 1880); "Pitā mātār dāyitwa," *BP*, 2:2, 191 (December 1880). The latter held the father responsible as well.

[109] "Kusumhār," *Mahilā*, 3, 8 (April 1898).

[110] Pulin Sanyal, *Saral sisu pālan*, "Prasūtir prati upades."

[111] *IMS*, 1 June 1879.

[112] Shib Chunder Deb, *Sisu pālan*, II (Calcutta, 1862).

[113] See review of *Mātrisiksā* by Gangaprasad Mukhopadhyay in *BP*, 7, 93 (May 1871), and Pulin Sanyal, *Saral sisu pālan*.

gali.[114] The writings of Herbert Spencer and Samuel Smiles were referred to for additional authority on the importance of instilling moral principles from early childhood.[115]

Childhood as an age of innocence

In the west, the nineteenth century saw the culmination of a new idea of childhood that had its origins in the fifteenth century.[116] The child was seen as an innocent being, to be protected against the corruption and moral laxity of the world by strict discipline and careful moral instruction. The Victorian writer of a manual of *Counsel to a Mother* described childhood thus: "the happiest time of life [is childhood,] before sin has blotted and smutched a child's pure and innocent mind, and before care has wrinkled and ploughed up his fair brow, and when all is blooming, bright, and beautiful."[117] In Bengali society, children were coddled and indulged for the first few years of life, but then assumed adult responsibilities in relation to the succeeding infant. They were disciplined by physical punishment rather than by moral admonition. They were not presumed to be pure, nor were they separated and excluded conceptually from the world of adults. Childhood was for them a brief but enjoyable phase of life, from which they gradually assumed responsibilities of their own in the family hierarchy. The division between child and adult was even less marked for girls than for boys. Whereas a boy would go to school for many years before taking up an occupation, a girl was trained from an early age in the domestic duties she would be expected to fulfil throughout her life. For her the transition in status was marked by marriage and taking up residence in her husband's home.

The new idea of childhood was taken up by the Bengali

---

[114] See review of *Sisusantānganer siksā bisaye pitā mātār kartabya*, translated by Girish Chandra Sen, *BP*, 12, 153 (May 1876).

[115] Candicaran Bandopadhyay, *Mā o chele* (Calcutta, 1887).

[116] P. Ariès, *Centuries of Childhood*, English tr. (London, 1962).

[117] P. H. Chavasse, *Counsel to a Mother*, p. 66.

5. Amala (1891-   ?) and Santipriya (1885-1933),
children of Saratkumari Deb.
They had a "progressive" upbringing as part of
a Brahmo family. Note their Anglicized
clothes, including boots and stockings.

bhadralok, especially the Brahmos. They were attracted by
the emphasis on morality in the education of the child. As
education for both sexes became more widespread, and extended for a longer duration, the idea of the child as a separate
entity was reinforced. Journals especially for children were

started. Keshub Chunder Sen edited the children's magazine *Bālak Bandhu* from 1878. *Sakhā*, a monthly for children, was started by a young Brahmo in 1882.[118] Jnanadanandini Debi edited *Bālak*, an illustrated monthly for children, from April 1885. A year later it was incorporated into the adult journal *Bhāratī*.[119] Ladies of the Sadharan Brahmo Samaj edited *Mukul* for children from 1895,[120] and an illustrated monthly magazine for girls, *Sakhī*, was started in 1900.[121] Punyalata Cakrabarti, daughter of the well-known author of children's books Sukumar Ray, remembered how she used to enjoy reading *Mukul*. It was attractively printed, and full of stories and poems, simple explanations of scientific findings, travel tales, biographies, and jokes.[122] The women's journal *Antahpur* tried to have a regular children's page, with illustrated nursery rhymes and stories.[123] A new genre of children's literature was created. Stories familiar through the oral tradition were published in abridged versions made "suitable" for children. The *Choto Rāmāyan* and *Choto Mahābhārat* were very popular among children of the *bhadralok* first learning to read.[124]

Brahmos had separate organizations for children, which combined entertainment with a strong dose of moral guidance. Both the Band of Hope and the Sunday School Movement

[118] Sibnath Sastri, *History of the Brahmo Samaj*, 2nd ed. (Calcutta, 1974), pp. 302-303. From 1885 it was edited by Sastri himself, then from 1887-1893 by Annada Charan Sen.

[119] She had hoped that the children of the Tagore family would run it entirely with their contributions, but as that was not enough, she made it up with her own compositions and those of Rabindranath. Brajendranath Bandopadhyay, *Sāmayikpatra-sampādane banganārī* (Calcutta, 1950), p. 8; Rabindranath Tagore, *Reminiscences* (Madras, 1971), pp. 242-243.

[120] Sibnath Sastri, *History of the Brahmo Samaj*, p. 334.

[121] National Library, Calcutta, *Catalogue of Bengali Books*.

[122] Punyalata Cakrabarti, *Chele belār din guli*, 2nd ed. (Calcutta, 1975), pp. 33-34.

[123] For instance "Gowālā bou" in *Antahpur*, 4, 4 (May 1901). A footnote explained that *Antahpur* aimed to provide for the entertainment and instruction of children, as well. That had been done in its first year, but had not been kept up in the second and third years, and was therefore starting again.

[124] Punyalata Cakrabarti, *Chele belār din guli*, p. 35. Her father wrote and illustrated these books.

were started in Calcutta for Brahmo children. The Sunday School children had their own miniature hymn book of selected Brahmo songs.[125] Many Brahmos were impressed by the kindergarten movement in Europe. When Sibnath Sastri visited England he bought all the literature he could find on the subject, including a biography of Froebel, founder of the movement.[126]

Writers became eloquent in echoing Victorian sentiments on the pristine state of childhood innocence: "When a child drops from heaven like a pure blossom it is untouched by the corrupt winds of the world. Then both its body and mind are as malleable as clay and can be shaped with ease."[127] To maintain this original state of grace, special care had to be taken to instil moral principles from an early age.[128] The child was to be treated as a rational being, but one with a simplified understanding. Reasons for beliefs and morality had to be explained to it, but in uncomplicated terms. Hindu parents may not have felt the same need to instil religious beliefs in their children that Brahmos did, being able to rely on their absorbing them through established rituals pervasive in daily life. However, for the stabilization of a new creed such as Brahmoism, the specific inculcation of the principles it represented was necessary. In Brahmo households, children said daily prayers for their own betterment. Bibhubala, daughter of Umesh Chunder Dutt, said the following prayer every morning: "Oh God, I thank you for keeping me safely throughout the night, and I pray that today you will keep me well and make me a good girl."[129] Lilabati Mitra taught her

---

[125] [Sadharan Brahmo Samaj], *Sangīt-mukul*, 2nd ed. (Calcutta, 1886).

[126] Sibnath Sastri, *Ātmacarit*, p. 175; *IMS*, 27 April 1879; 18 May 1879. By 1904, the kindergarten system had been introduced in Bengal, and *Bangīya kindergarten* was an approved vernacular textbook. See *Hitabādī*, 9 September 1904 in *RNNB* 17 September 1904; *Hitabādī*, 4 December 1904 in *RNNB* 10 December 1904.

[127] Saralyamayi Dasi, "Sisusanggathan," *Antahpur*, 1, 2 (January 1898).

[128] "Gārhasthya bisaye naranārīr kartabya," *BP*, 6:3, 401 (June 1898); "Mātār prati kayekti upades," *BP*, 11, 150-151 (March-April 1876); "Bālak dharmmārthīdiger prati," *BP*, 8:2, 502-503 (June-July 1905).

[129] "Sukanyā Bibhubālā," *BP*, 7:2, 441-442 (October-November 1901).

children to say prayers of thanksgiving and safekeeping on waking in the morning, before meals, and before bed at night. When they reached the age of six or seven they were sent to Sunday school.[130]

Numerous articles stressed that the mother should make a concerted effort to take the responsibility for child rearing into her own hands. Writers disapproved of the care of children by servants, which was common practice in wealthier households,[131] both because it was regarded as a dereliction of duty and because servants were thought to perpetuate the old system of child rearing based on threats and superstition.[132] Supposedly less scrupulous than mothers, servants were known to use opium to stop a child's cries and put it to sleep.[133] Servants, and "old-fashioned" mothers, were accused of using fear as a disciplinary force, a practice frowned upon in the later nineteenth century as scarring the child's future perception of life.[134] The bogey of ghosts or spirits was commonly used as a threat to ensure good behavior.[135] The harm this did to children was said to be the cause of characteristic Bengali timidity.[136] New disciplinary methods stressed honesty and openness, which were seen as the triumph of reason over superstition.

The central position accorded to the child in the new idea of the family affected the conduct of the parents. They had to regulate their behavior to make sure that they never set a bad example to the child. Moralists instructed parents not to quarrel in front of their children, to show their anger openly, or to scold their children in front of strangers.[137] Children

---

[130] *Līlābatī Mitra* (Calcutta, 1924), pp. 15-18.

[131] Rabindranath Tagore, *Reminiscences*, chapter four, "Servocracy."

[132] "Pitā mātār dāyitwa," *BP*, 191.

[133] Sibnath Sastri, *Grihadharma*, p. 57.

[134] See L. DeMause, "The Evolution," pp. 11-17. The practice of frightening children with ghosts was common from ancient times, but was coming into question by the eighteenth century.

[135] *BP*, 5:3, 352 (May 1894); Candicaran Bandopadhyay, *Mā o chele*, pp. 32-33.

[136] Saralyamayi Dasi, *Antahpur*, 1, 2.

[137] Candicaran Bandopadhyay, *Mā o chele*, p. 36; *Paricārikā*, 1, 6 (16

were to be controlled not through anger but through reason. Punishment was supposed to be more effective when it was mental rather than physical, and the removal of special pleasures or privileges as a disciplinary measure was recommended.[138] Parents who deceived children by promising them false rewards would instil deceitful habits in the children.

In certain areas, honesty was replaced by falsehood, supposedly for the child's own good. A childcare manual by an English woman doctor disapproved of the way in which children in an Indian household were permitted to see and hear everything their elders did or said, shortening their period of "real childhood" in which such matters as sex, money, sickness, and suffering did not intrude.[139] Modern parents were not to mention "obscene conjugal matters"—in effect anything connected with sex—in the child's hearing.[140] At times these instructions seemed contradictory, as a mother was also expected to answer all a child's questions fully and truthfully so that it did not learn habits of deceit and mistrust.[141] The confusion remained unresolved. It resulted from an uncertainty as to the real place of the child in the family. While Sibnath Sastri encouraged parents to be friends with their children, in order to gain their full confidence, he also warned against including children in adult discussions or social gath-

---

October 1878); Renuka Ghose, Sarojinī-carit, p. 65; "Mātār prati kayekti upades," BP, 11, 150-151.

[138] "Sisu binayan—sisudiger abādhyatādi," BP, 3:2, 242 (February 1885); Sibnath Sastri, Grihadharma, p. 59; Nandakrisna Basu, Bāmābodh; "Sisu-binayan," pp. 93-99; P. C. Mozoomdar, Strīcaritra, 3rd ed. (Calcutta, 1936), pp. 23-24.

[139] M. E. Staley, Handbook, pp. 300-301.

[140] Saralyamayi Dasi, Antahpur, 1, 2.

[141] "Sisu santāner prati mātār kartabya," BP, 5:1, 334 (November 1892). This is not to say that honesty was only an attribute of "modern" mothers. The mother of Sir Gooroodass Banerjee was said to be ignorant of all new childcare theories, but nevertheless always reproved her daughters-in-law for disciplining their children with threats of dire punishments that could not be carried out, on the grounds that it would lead them into habits of falsehood. Candicaran Bandopadhyay, "Jananī Sonāmani Debī" (1913), in U. C. Banerjee, comp., Reminiscences, Speeches and Writings of Sir Gooroo Dass Banerjee Kt (Calcutta, 1927), p. 15.

erings of adults where they could be corrupted.[142] Protap Chunder Mozoomdar took Victorian puritanism to extreme lengths when he advised Indian mothers to make sure that their children always wore clothes.[143]

The father had a share in parental control in the new family model. He was not expected to involve himself in specific details of childcare, but to assume an overall responsibility, especially in matters of moral guidance.[144] Prankrishna Acharya, a Brahmo doctor, was typical of the new kind of father. He personally went over his children's studies with them every day, letting them ask him as many questions as they wished.[145] His son regarded him as his closest friend.[146]

By the turn of the century, motherhood had been invested with new meaning for the *bhadramahilā*. It had been raised from a natural function to an exalted duty. Motherhood had attained the status of an occupation, a vocation so complex that only a well-educated woman could manage it. This had also happened in England. In Bengal, reformers propagated the new duties and methods of motherhood with enthusiasm, because they believed the educated mother to be a crucial link in the process of modernization. The new career expectations of the sons and daughters of the *bhadralok* could only be met with the help and cooperation of mothers in creating a suitably "modern" home environment.

The spread of female education also created higher aspirations in women that had to be fulfilled. Women needed to feel that the knowledge they had acquired was not simply ornamental, but fitted them for taking on the role of the enlightened woman. The proliferation of advice to women on

[142] Sibnath Sastri, *Grihadharma*, p. 59.

[143] P. C. Mozoomdar, *Strīcaritra*, p. 24, no. 7.

[144] "Gārhasthya bisaye naranārīr kartabya," *BP*, 401.

[145] See the reminiscences of his daughter, Usha Haldar, in *Dāktār Prānkrisna Ācārja-jībanprasanga o upadesābalī*, 2nd ed. (Calcutta, 1973 [1936]), p. 21.

[146] See the reminiscences of Bijaykrisna Acarja, *ibid.*, pp. 24, 26. The idea of parent-child friendship is also lauded in Nandakrisna Basu, *Bāmābodh*, p. 95.

their role as mother suggested that the way they would traditionally have handled this role was inadequate, and needed to be transformed. The educated woman was eager to respond to a recognition of her qualifications. Although the mother had always been a central figure in Hindu society, the *bhadralok* initiated a redefinition of her traditional role. New ideas of motherhood placed a greater burden on the *bhadramahilā*, but compensated for it by acknowledging her importance for the progress of "civilization" in Bengal.

৩৫ SIX ৩৫

Domestic Life: The Role of the *Bhadramahilā* as Housewife

Men recall pictures of homely households in earlier times, and imagine that such things are, or might be, going on still. They forget the prosaic fact, that the continually increasing use of all sorts of machinery for the supply of household wants has completely altered the aspect of our domestic interiors. The rounded life of our grandmothers, full of interest and variety and usefulness, is a thing of the past. Some of us may look back upon it with regret, but it can never be recalled. How can women, living in towns where they can buy almost every article in domestic use cheaper than they could make it, unless they reckon their time and eyesight as worth nothing at all, work with spirit at tasks which are obviously futile? It is not in human nature. It is not in *women's* nature even, mysteriously inconsequent as that nature is believed to be.[1]

The frustration underlying the words of English feminist Emily Davies, speaking for women of the English middle class, could also have applied to a growing number of women in Bengal by the late nineteenth century, when the stereotype of a "new woman" who was disdainful of domestic skills and inept at housework was current. This was usually contrasted with an

[1] "On Secondary Instruction as Relating to Girls," read at the Annual Meeting of the National Association for the Promotion of Social Sciences, 1864; in E. Davies, *Thoughts*, p. 69.

186

idealized portrait of the woman of the past, the perfect housewife. In all those areas of the housewife's role which came under criticism, namely, the employment of servants, the arrangement of the house and domestic hygiene, cooking, household medicine, and the management of finance, extremely complex changes were taking place, a result of the transformation of the world of the *bhadralok* rather than of any faults of character in the "new woman."

Financial responsibility

In 1891-1892, the minimum taxable income was 500 rupees per annum, and one in every thirty-one people in Calcutta was paying income tax. A majority of the urban *bhadralok*, professionals and salaried government employees, would have fallen into this taxpaying category.[2] Although they must be considered affluent when compared with the 97 percent of the population whose incomes were below the taxable level, in fact they were often struggling to make ends meet. In traditional society, conspicuous consumption in the form of occasional lavish expenditure on feasts and festivals was an accepted indication of social status. In the latter half of the nineteenth century, the urban *grihastha bhadralok* were adopting a lifestyle that placed less value on grand displays of wealth. Instead of spending money in sporadic outbursts, they had to maintain a constant level of expenditure on newly perceived areas of importance such as education and health.

On account of the scarcity of available figures, and the wide variations in wages over the course of a career, it is difficult to determine an average wage for the urban *bhadralok*. A salary of 150 rupees a month seems to have been considered reasonably comfortable. The fluctuations in salary and in employment experienced by many *bhadralok* are illustrated in the career of Srinath Datta. When he returned from studying

[2] B. B. Misra, *The Indian Middle Classes. Their Growth in Modern Times* (Delhi, 1978 [1961]), pp. 243-244, 363-367. These groups were only brought under the operation of the Income Tax Act from 1886.

agricultural science in England, he could only get part-time employment as professor of mathematics at Albert College, earning 100 rupees per month. Then he was appointed manager of a tea estate in Assam at 150 rupees per month, which increased to 300 rupees after some years. During this time he paid off the debts he had incurred in England, but found it a struggle to maintain his growing family. Returning to Calcutta, where the rent on their house was 80 rupees a month, he had to supplement his meager teaching income by selling the milk of the family's cow, and by pawning all of his wife Harasundari's gold ornaments. His next position was as settlement officer in Mayurbhanj, on 200 rupees per month. After five years there, with eight children, they were in debt again. He took up a position as settlement officer for the Raja of Kanika for 150 rupees, and in 1891 was made assistant manager of the Burdwan estate on a salary going from an initial 300 rupees a month to 500. He held this position for eleven years. Afterwards he again held short-term posts in various places.[3] Srinath Datta was not a very successful member of the *bhadralok*, but his earnings were probably typical of most. His case also represents the particular difficulties that would have been encountered by a reforming or Brahmo family with a distinctively "progressive" lifestyle. Their expectations and aspirations were always higher than their means.

In Bengal, a lifestyle in accordance with progressive attitudes was only possible for the wealthier *bhadralok*. The material prosperity that made possible the changing mode of life of the English middle class was only found among the *bhadralok* elite. An article in *Abalābāndhab* drew attention to the rising cost of living in a *bhadralok* family.[4] Not only was there the expense of education for boys—ranging from an average of 100 rupees a year, to 1,000 rupees for education in England—but also the even higher cost of female education. Food had become more elaborate, and the reformed woman's dress,

[3] Harasundari Datta, *Swargīya Srīnāth Datter*, passim.

[4] "Abasthānusāritā," *Abalābāndhab*, 1, 5 (March 1879). See also "Eto rog o akāl mrityur kāran ki?" *BP*, 3:2, 250 (November 1885).

including petticoat, chemise, and often shoes, was far more costly than a simple sari. Houses had more furniture—pictures, basins, couch, piano, sofa, easy chairs, and reading lamps. Servants were employed, and the cost of doctors and medical treatment was high. There were also obligatory subscriptions to progressive causes, and to newspapers and journals. Apart from this there were other expenses such as rent, for those who had left the family home, and the obligation to send money back to the family if one was a breadwinner.[5]

Newspaper advertisements help to give an idea of the cost of purchasing some fashionable and prestigious items. Advertisements in the *Indian Mirror* in the 1870s show that "harmoniflutes" were priced from 40 to 55 rupees, while harmoniums were 80 rupees each. Bronze kerosine table lamps cost from 48 to 70 rupees, cut-glass models went from 85 to 130 rupees, and reading lamps from 27 to 86. Clocks ranged from 40 to 100 rupees, and watches varied from 35 for a "railway guard" keyless watch to 200 for one in a gold case. Solid gold watch chains could be bought for 50 to 250 rupees. A magic lantern cost 85 rupees, and the slides that went with it were 1 to 5 rupees each—alternatively, a "show" could be hired for 6 rupees for two hours. In 1878, a subscription to the *Indian Mirror* itself was 24 rupees annually for town-dwellers, and 32 for *mofussil* subscribers, with an extra charge for the Sunday edition.[6]

In a review of *Surucīr kutīr* by Dwarkanath Ganguly, an archetypal middle-class moralistic novel on the virtue of thrift, a Brahmo writer summarized the problem thus:

> Western civilisation has created many domestic wants; we now aspire to a mode of living which is more costly than the one we were used to. The mind of our young men and women have been filled with western ideas about clothing and living which are leading us fast into extrav-

---

[5] Prakascandra Ray sent 30 of the 80 rupees per month that he earned in 1875 back to his mother. Prakascandra Ray, *Aghor-prakās*, p. 33.

[6] See the advertisement section of the *Indian Mirror* in the 1870s.

agance. Our young women have learnt to wear costly dresses before learning the science of domestic economy. Our desire to live in good, comfortable and well-ventilated houses leads us to cast our eyes on some of the big houses in, what are called English quarters, the rents of which are exceedingly high, but we do not care to learn the art of making a house, wheresoever located, comfortable, neat, clean and well ventilated. We always set before our eyes the residence of a well to do European without caring for our means, and we would often times go to spend every pice that we earn to live according to our ideal. But an Englishman would never exceed his means, but would try to save something out of his earnings and yet live better—have better and more substantial food. The secret of all this is the English wife. She is well versed in domestic economy. Thrift is a part of the education of an English wife. She knows how to make her husband and her children comfortable and yet to save something.[7]

On such a small margin, a woman's role as consumer and as financial manager was crucial.

In most households, the husband gave his wife a portion of his earnings to manage according to her own judgment of priorities. The ability to keep accounts was a quality sought after in the new housewife. In the past, women may have had some control over household finances, but the ability to keep accounts and manage money in a rational fashion was seen as a benefit of female education.[8] Women had to learn the need for a rising middle class to maintain its position through thrift, in contrast with the traditional way of establishing sta-

---

[7] " 'Surucheer Kuteer' or Thrift in Indian Homes," *Brahmo Public Opinion*, 19 February 1880. *Surucīr kutīr* was first published in 1878, and went into a second edition of 1,000 copies by 1881. *Bengal Library Catalogue*, 1881, I.

[8] "Gārhasthya darpan," *BP*, 8, 104 (April 1872); "Gārhasthya darpan," *BP*, 11, 145 (September 1875). Swarnamayi Gupta, *Ūsā-cintā* (Calcutta, 1888), p. 73.

tus by lavish expenditure on festivals and ceremonial occasions. They were frequently lectured to on the need for thrift, economy, and living within their means.[9] This capacity would have been essential for the management of finances in lower-income *bhadralok* families. An article in the *Bāmābodhinī Patrikā* in 1876 gave instructions on the correct method of keeping precise accounts. It drew up a sample balance sheet, with categories of food, clothing, education, wages, customs (festivals), charity, and medicine on the expenditure side. These categories were then subdivided. For instance, education included the cost of fees, books, paper, and so on. Under income, the suggested categories were savings, rent, interest, salary, and commercial profit.[10] The whole process was one of rationalization of expenditure for long-term gain.

Articles advised readers of various ways of saving money. It was supposed to be cheaper to hire a gardener to grow vegetables for four rupees a month than to buy them in the market, and to be more economical to buy paddy and husk one's own rice.[11] Women were warned against extravagant purchases. If a man gave his wife twenty rupees a month for household expenses and she only spent sixteen rupees, she was to save the rest instead of spending it on a "wool box."[12]

Although she had no earnings, a woman's role in the household economy was a contributing factor to a family's wealth. Unaccounted for even now, there was the "hidden" value of her housework. The gold jewelry she brought with her on marriage was regarded as an investment. In addition, women were often able to save money of their own through careful management of the household allowance. They were advised to invest this in gold ornaments, company shares, money-lending, or business capital. It was stressed that apart from

[9] Ramtanu Gupta, *Strī-sikṣā*, p. 16; "Abasthā o sangsār," *BP*, 3:3, 261 (October 1886).

[10] "Gārhasthya darpan," *BP*, 12, 154 (June 1876).

[11] "Ādarsa hindu paribār," *BP*, 400.

[12] Jogendranarayan Ray, *Banga-mahilā* (Chinsurah, 1881), p. 64: "Banga mahilār sangsār jātray sahāyta."

this self-advancement, a portion should be spent on charity.[13] Women were able to carve out some independent means through this form of saving.

Biographical evidence confirms that women played a very important role in family finances. By "judicious economy," Shib Chunder Deb's wife made a small fortune out of the household allowance her husband gave her. She used the money for charitable works—a bathing *ghāt* with covered landing place in memory of her father, and a charitable homeopathic dispensary.[14] Her savings gave her an opportunity to establish and promote her own area of interest. Kailaskamini Dutt saved some money and pawned some of her gold ornaments—a woman's main source of capital—to buy land and build a house.[15] She was a clever business woman, managing the finances of the *Bāmābodhinī Patrikā* and paying her husband his salary as editor. When they went into debt to buy a printing press, she pawned more of her ornaments to keep the journal afloat.[16] Harasundari Datta was also a better financial manager than her husband Srinath. She saved from the monthly housekeeping allowance without letting him know. He used to spend his own portion and then ask her for money, but fear of going into debt made her tell the lie that she had none. Eventually her determination was rewarded, and they were able to buy some land in Calcutta from her savings.[17] Similarly, Kumudini Sinha sold her ornaments and costly clothes to help her husband raise the sum of more than 800 rupees needed to build a house on land in the Brahmo Mangalpara that he had purchased for 600 rupees.[18] When her husband's family became insolvent, Brahmo Atarmani Debi sold her ornaments to help pay the debt. In 1903 she decided to economize by moving the whole family to Giridi, a hill station

---

[13] "Byay," *BP*, 5, 79 (March 1870).
[14] M. N. Ghosh, ed., *The Life of Grish Chunder Ghose*, p. 62.
[15] Her brother shared in the purchase. *BP*, 6:3, 401 (June 1898).
[16] *BP*, 6:3, 402 (July 1898).
[17] Harasundari Datta, *Swargīya Srīnath Datter*, pp. 103-104.
[18] *Kumudinī-caritra*, pp. 24-25.

much favored by Brahmos, where the cost of living was lower than that in Calcutta.[19]

Women were gratified by the responsibility of keeping accounts and the chance for financial independence it provided. It was also a recognition of their capabilities, and constituted a position of trust. Prakascandra Ray used to do the monthly estimates himself, until Aghorekamini asked him why he could not trust her with this task. He replied that he had not done so because he thought it would be too complicated for her. She took up the challenge and handled the accounts very competently from then on.[20]

Women's position as financial managers meant that they were able to make decisions on the adoption of various new methods of performing old tasks in the household. Their main purchasing power was in basic items like food, but they would also have had a part in buying household furnishings. Labor-saving devices, which were already beginning to change the nature of housework in England in the nineteenth century, were barely evident in India. The main item under this category was the sewing machine. It was a product of the new technology, used increasingly by housewives in Victorian England.[21] For the Bengali housewife, it represented a potential money-saving rather than labor-saving item. Ordinarily she would have had her children's and husband's clothes sewn by a tailor, at some cost, but now she was urged to sew them herself to economize.[22] The idealized heroine of *Surucīr kutīr* bought a sewing machine and started a tailoring company. The *pārā* women who worked with her were supposed to be able to earn 5 or 6 rupees per month, which she invested for them with a return of 100 rupees per annum.[23] Sewing ma-

[19] Amritalal Gupta, *Punyabatī nārī*, pp. 60-61.

[20] Prakascandra Ray, *Aghor-prakās*, p. 65.

[21] P. Branca, *Silent Sisterhood*, chapter three, "The Modern Homemaker."

[22] Kumudini Ray, "Hindu nārīr gārhasthya dharmma," *BP*, 5:3, 359 (December 1894).

[23] See the plot summary given in " 'Surucheer Kuteer' or Thrift in Indian Homes," *Brahmo Public Opinion*, 19 February 1880.

chines first appeared in Calcutta in 1853.[24] An advertisement for Singer sewing machines in 1878 offered an instruction booklet with every machine purchased, and, for "lady purchasers residing in Calcutta," free personal instruction was given as an added incentive.[25] Harasundari Datta was given a sewing machine, costing 84 rupees, by the wife of an English estate manager in Mayurbhanj. She sewed all of the family's clothes on it, from the children's cotton wrappers to her husband's overcoat.[26] The high initial cost of purchasing a machine would have prevented many *bhadramahilā* from benefiting from the long-term economy. As consumers, women wanted to partake of the novel goods and services available in Calcutta and urban centers, yet their financial control over a limited income and the continual injunctions to thrift would have held them back from spending on items other than minimal necessities.

The ideal of the *sugrihinī*

The *sugrihinī*, or good housewife, was presented as an ideal in all literature directed toward women. She was one who toiled ceaselessly from morning till night, delighting in such labor.[27] Mindful of others' comfort and not preoccupied with her own, she was hospitable and generous without being extravagant, skilled in the culinary and medicinal arts and able to control a large household. Banalata Debi, daughter of Sasipada Banerjea, was described as an *ādarsa grihinī*, or ideal housewife. It was said that she supervised the most minute details of the household even while seriously ill. She kept an eye on the accounts and the kitchen, and saw to it that her husband and young son were properly looked after and that

---

[24] Six machines were imported from America by the wealthy Rajendra Datta in 1853. Their speed and efficiency was marveled over in an article "Selāiyer kal," in *Sangbād Prabhākar*, 18 June 1853, in B. Ghose, *Sāmayikpatre*, part i, p. 91.

[25] Advertisement section, *IMS*, 1 December 1878.

[26] Harasundari Datta, *Swargīya Srīnāth Datter*, pp. 39-40.

[27] "Subhabibāhopalakse kanyār prati upades," *BP*, 3:2, 237 (October 1884).

6. Banalata Debi (1879-1900), an "ideal housewife" or *ādarsa grihinī*. The daughter of Brahmo reformer Sasipada Banerjea, Banalata edited the women's journal *Antahpur* from its inception in 1898 until her death in 1900.

order was maintained. A week before her death, even though she was very weak, she was not satisfied unless she made out the marketing list and supervised the cooking herself.[28]

The topic set by Sasipada Banerjea for a prize essay in 1881 was "*Ādarsa grihinī*." The winning entry, by Parbati Basu, described her as one who woke early and cooked the morning meal. In the "free" time she had before beginning to cook the evening meal, the *ādarsa grihinī* would not be idle: "Any shirt without a button, any torn clothing, can be worn again for some time if mended; any pillow without a cover, any dirty sheet, any things that haven't been moved and need dusting—she attends to all these things with care."[29]

Yet, in the eyes of numerous social commentators, the *nabīnā*, or new woman, of the later nineteenth century was not living up to the rigorous standards set by the *prācīnā*, or woman of old. It was repeated endlessly and became a matter of conventional wisdom that the new woman disdained housework.[30] Bankim Chandra Chatterjee wrote an article comparing the two types. In contrast with the hardworking *prācīnā*, he satirized the *nabīnā* as utterly lazy, floating on the surface of the water like a lotus, admiring her own reflection. He expressed concern that her attitude would have disastrous results, such as the deterioration of women's health, because housework was a form of exercise; a decline in the health of children, because they were born and reared by weak mothers; and a loss of skills needed for housework. To him, "the woman who, coming into the world, spends her time rolling out of bed, arranging her hair in front of the mirror, doing carpet work, reading *Sītar banabās*, and having children, contributing to no one's happiness but her own, may be a little better

[28] *Antahpur*, 3, 12 (December 1900). Supplement on the death of editor Banalata Debi.
[29] Parbati Basu, "Ādarsa grihinī," Bāmāracanā, *BP*, 2:2, 194 (March 1881).
[30] "Nārīcarit," *BP*, 5, 76 (December 1869); *BP*, 10, 129 (May 1874); "Grihinīganer grihakārjya karā cāi," Jogendranarayan Ray, *Banga-mahilā*; Tarakanath Biswas, *Bangīya-mahilā*, p. 18; "Grihakarmma karibār kathā," Candranath Basu, *Gārhasthyapāth*, 2nd ed. (Calcutta, 1887).

than an animal, but her birth as a woman is in vain."[31] Rajna-rain Bose echoed him, claiming that women of "those days" were far more hardworking than the housewives of "these days," who were educated and looked down on physical effort.[32] Swarnamayi Gupta, a critical and analytical female writer, agreed that women were no longer as competent in domestic skills, but questioned whether it was not the method of education, rather than education itself, that was to blame.[33]

The past time referred to was not clearly located, but by inference it was a time before women had any interests outside the house. The "new woman" not only had the audacity to dislike hard work, but she preferred to read novels or do woolwork. In effect, the perfect past time was before the spread of female literacy. The criticisms by earlier writers of the laziness of women of former times and the futile manner in which they spent their leisure time had been forgotten.[34]

The positing of a "golden age" when women were better than in the contemporary age was not a phenomenon peculiar to Bengal. An English woman wrote in 1883 that "things are getting worse not better, and our young women are less useful than their mothers, while these last do not as a rule, come near the housekeeping ladies of older times, who knew every secret of domestic economy."[35] The generality of this kind of outcry indicates that the anxiety was not necessarily caused by particular changes in women's attitudes to housework, but by a nebulous panic at the rapidity of social change, and an uncertainty as to how to adapt to it. Women became symbols of stability, tradition, and continuity, and therefore any change in their role or mode of living was interpreted as a threat to the social order.

[31] Bankim Chandra Chatterjee, "Prācīnā ebang nabīnā," *Bibidha praban-dha* (Calcutta, 1964), p. 156. First published in *Banga Darsan* in 1874.
[32] Rajnarain Bose, *Se kāl ār e kāl*, p. 86.
[33] Swarnamayi Gupta, *Ūsā-cintā*, pp. 67-69.
[34] For some of these criticisms see Chapter One.
[35] E. Lynn Linton, *The Girl of the Period and Other Social Essays* (London, 1883), quoted in P. Branca, *Silent Sisterhood*, p. 23.

The employment of servants

One important element of social change, not caused by women but affecting them closely, was the increased employment of servants. Traditionally, only *zamindari* families or large urban households employed a retinue of servants. In most cases these were not internal household servants, but external servants expected to do menial work or help with *zamindari* affairs. The *ginnī* directed the women of the household in the domestic chores, which included cooking enough food to feed the servants as well as the family. Rassundari Debi described this kind of arrangement from her experience.[36] Servants were considered to be part of the extended family, and enjoyed with its members a relationship of mutual obligations of service in exchange for patronage and maintenance. Apart from this, particular caste and occupational groups performed certain essential services—for instance, sweepers removed refuse and *dhobās* washed clothes. In rural areas, the *jajmani* relationship was operative, and artisan castes were bound by ritual ties to give their services.

Unfortunately, there is little information on the subject of servants, wages, and incomes in Bengal. Available evidence indicates that there was an increase in employment of servants among the *bhadralok*. In England, the middle class had the material wealth enabling them to afford to employ servants, although frequently aspirations to higher status were ahead of the financial capacity to hire domestic help.[37] In theory, the employment of servants left the mistress of the house unoccupied. Women were severely castigated for the purely imaginary vice of laziness:

A young girl complains now-a-days that she has nothing to do? Nothing to do! ... Why, if a girl will do it, she has plenty to do! Not if she will leave all to servants—not if she be afraid to soil her fingers—not if she think

[36] Rassundari Debi, *Āmār jīban*, pp. 27-29.
[37] P. Branca, *Silent Sisterhood*, pp. 53-57.

it vulgar to attend to household duties—not if she deem
it derogatory either to make a pudding or to nurse a sick
person—not if she consider a young lady ought to be a
drone in this busy hive of England.[38]

In practice, even if she could afford to employ enough servants
to do all the work, in order to direct them the mistress of the
house needed to know as much about domestic skills as would
have been necessary if she had to perform their duties herself.[39]

In Bengal, the *nabīnā* was accused of being a drain on family
finances because she had withdrawn her labor and forced the
family to hire servants in her stead. In 1892, a writer in *Banganibāsī* claimed that missionary teaching had encouraged girls
to spend all their time in reading, writing, and needlework,
and that therefore the cost of living had increased because
servants had to be engaged. This increase in cost was said to
threaten the viability of the joint family unit, which had relied
on the contribution to household work by the women of the
family.[40]

The increase in employment of servants by the *bhadralok*
was partly due to a concern with establishing social status.
This was indicated by a writer in 1887, who criticized both
men and women for laziness and for abrogating their household responsibilities:

Now many of both men and women amongst us, inclining
to refinement and affectation, are employing servants to
do the housework. Now many women think it degrading
to wash plates, sweep, or cook. And many men think it
is an insult to have to do the marketing or pour a glass
of water from the water-pot themselves.[41]

[38] P. H. Chavasse, *Counsel to a Mother*, pp. 161-162.
[39] T. McBride, *The Domestic Revolution. The Modernisation of Household
Service in England and France 1820-1920* (New York, 1976), p. 28;
P. Branca, *Silent Sisterhood*, chapter two.
[40] *Banganibāsī*, 19 August 1892, in *RNNB* 27 August 1892.
[41] Candranath Basu, *Gārhasthyapāth*, "Grihakarma karibār kathā," pp.
63-64.

A woman writer in 1898 severely criticized other women for living above their means in order to enhance their status by hiring servants and giving up housework. She said that in some families, the wife hired a servant or a cook as soon as her husband earned twenty-five to thirty rupees a month. She cited the case of a Brahmo family with six or seven children where the husband, earning only eighteen rupees a month, still insisted on hiring a servant for six to seven rupees of his salary. Disapprovingly, she commented that the housewife was perfectly healthy, and could have saved family finances by doing everything herself.[42] Jnanadanandini Debi recollected that in the 1860s the wages of a maidservant were around two rupees a month, and those of a manservant around two and a half rupees, but that the cost of employing servants gradually rose above this.[43]

In nineteenth-century England, there was a proliferation of manuals on how to deal with servants because of the novelty of the employer role for middle-class women.[44] In Bengal there were also numerous articles in magazines and manuals on dealing with servants. It seems unlikely that the role of mistress and employer was entirely unfamiliar to the *bhadramahilā*, who occupied a superior position in the caste hierarchy and therefore were used to dealing with subordinate service castes. Advice may have been needed, however, because of the changing nature of the relationship between mistress and servant. Change was taking place in the composition of the servant population, as well as in the status of their employers. Formerly servants had been "old retainers," an integral part of

[42] *Mahilā*, 3, 6 (January 1898).

[43] Reminiscences of Jnanadanandini Debi in Indira Debi Caudhurani, *Purātanī*, p. 27.

[44] See T. McBride, *The Domestic Revolution*, chapter one; P. Branca, *Silent Sisterhood*, chapters two, three. E. Ellis, *The Wives of England, Their Relative Duties, Domestic Influence, and Social Obligations* (London, 1843), chapter two, "Treatment of Servants and Dependants," gives an idea of the way in which obligations and rights were formalized. F. P. Cobbe, *The Duties of Women*, 2nd ed. (London, 1882), pp. 149-151, discussed the change from patriarchy to contract in the master-servant relationship.

the larger family structure. In the nineteenth century, both the increased pressure on land and expectations of employment in urban areas brought an assortment of people into the towns and cities of Bengal. They were hired as servants on a contractual basis, and nothing was known about their background. Housewives were warned to be very careful when hiring servants. In order to find out more about the prospective servant's character, it was desirable to have a reference from their previous employer about their abilities and their reasons for leaving the job.[45] Protap Chunder Mozoomdar advised prospective employers that to get a good servant they would have to be prepared to pay competitive wages. If they did, the servant would work harder and be more likely to stay on. He cautioned against employing "all those people from Monghyr and Gaya, decrepit gluttons from the trail of the tea estates, or expelled from the jute factories, who have come seeking jobs in Calcutta: they are utterly stupid workers, who devour like Yama and sleep like Kumbhakarna. Keeping that kind of person on would be like trying to teach a camel to read the *smritisāstra*."[46]

The manuals instructed housewives to treat servants with affection, and to speak nicely to them. They should give their servants an exact idea of their duties and how to perform them correctly, and should reward them when they had worked well.[47] Banalata Debi, the *ādarsa grihinī* mentioned earlier, never addressed even young servants by the familiar pronoun *tui*. Tears came to her eyes if anyone spoke harshly to the cook.[48] Subodhbala Debi never raised her voice to give orders to servants, yet managed to retain a firm authority.[49] Other women were less exemplary, and their behavior perhaps re-

---

[45] "Gārhasthya darpan," *BP*, 8, 115 (March 1873).

[46] Yama is the god of death. Kumbhakarna is the second brother of Ravana in the *Rāmāyana*, who kept awake for one day after sleeping six months. P. C. Mozoomdar, *Strīcaritra*, p. 102, "Dāsdāsī."

[47] Sibnath Sastri, *Grihadharma*, pp. 64-66, "Prabhu-bhrityer sambandha"; "Gārhasthya darpan," *BP*, 115.

[48] *Antahpur*, 3, 12, special supplement.

[49] Subodhbala Debi, *Nīrab sādhanā* (Calcutta, 1913), p. 6.

flected the mistress-servant relationship more realistically. An article in *Paricārikā* complained that although it was considered *abhadra*, or unladylike, to fight with the maidservant, it was hard to avoid it when she stole one paise in every three. In jest, a *Cākarāni Hitakārinī Sabhā*, or benevolent association for maidservants, along the lines of the Brahmo Samaj or the Indian Reform Association, was suggested as a solution to the problem. The writer declared that, without some improvement in the situation, it would be impossible for the *bhadramahilā* to remain *bhadra*.[50]

In a paternalistic fashion, writers stressed that servants were also human and needed sympathy and love, and that in many respects they were like children, who needed moral instruction. The English practice of including servants in regular family worship was commended.[51]

Despite the outcry over women's laziness, the great majority of the *bhadramahilā* continued to be closely involved in the work of the household. Koilasbasini Debi wrote in 1863 that among the *madhyabitta griha*, or middle-class households, the wife did the work of cook, maidservant, and midwife.[52] In 1873, a correspondent of the *Indian Mirror* who was proposing a change in the timetable at the Bharat Ashram Ladies' School gave further credence to this. He said that the times were inconvenient for "every middle class female" who was not a boarder there. Whereas in the Bharat Ashram housework was done systematically and with the aid of "menials," "in families of insufficient income no such aid can be obtained and the poor ladies having performed all the works themselves find very little time at their command to devote to the acquisition of knowledge."[53]

Biographical evidence suggests that in many *bhadralok* families the housewife had to do all the work herself because they

[50] "Āmāder jhī," *Paricārikā*, 16 July 1878.
[51] Sibnath Sastri, *Grihadharma*; "Gārhasthya darpan," *BP*, 115.
[52] Koilasbasini Debi, *Hindumahilāganer hīnābasthā* (Calcutta, 1863), pp. 54-55.
[53] *Indian Mirror*, 16 October 1873. Letter from P.K.R. Chowdry, Calcutta.

could not afford to employ a servant. A paid servant was not taken for granted, but was a sign of well-being. For example, when Sasipada Banerjea lost his job in the post office, he had to dismiss their servant, and his wife Girijakumari had to take over all the housework.[54] Similarly, when Srinath Datta returned from England in 1876 he could only get part-time employment, earning 100 rupees a month. His wife Harasundari did all the cooking, and a friend who shared their rented house did the marketing. They could employ only an occasional maidservant and a *darwan*. However, when he got a position as settlement officer for the maharaja of Mayurbhanj in 1884, on 200 rupees per month, the family went to live there and employed a maidservant. Harasundari continued to do the cooking and sewed all the clothes for their large family.[55] Families would often start out unable to employ servants, but would gradually become employers once their position and income improved.

The first generations of Brahmo women went without servants for some time for social as well as financial reasons. Traditional servant castes would no longer serve them because they had been ostracized by the Hindu community. In most cases the ostracism eventually broke down,[56] as it would have been difficult to maintain such sanctions in urban areas with a mobile servant population. Keshub Chunder Sen's wife Jaganmohini did most of the housework and cooking throughout her life because of continued difficulty in getting servants. This was especially so when they lived in the joint family house, where the servants showed the same contempt toward them as the rest of the household.[57]

Even with servants, the housewife often continued to do much of the work herself. Despite the popular image of the

[54] Rajanikanta De, *Caritamādhurī*, p. 15.

[55] Harasundari Datta, *Swargīya Srīnāth Datter*, pp. 17, 37-39.

[56] Rakhal Chandra Ray, *Jīban bindu*, pp. 69-71; Dwarkanath Ganguly, *Jībanālekhya*, pp. 22-24; Prakascandra Ray, *Aghor-prakās*, p. 25; Sibnath Sastri, *Ātmacarit*, pp. 58-59.

[57] [Priyanath Mallik], *Brahma-nandinī*, pp. 91-99, 117.

nabīnā, good housekeeping remained a mark of virtue, and the good housewife was extolled as an ideal woman.[58] Most *bhadramahilā* still aspired to the ideal of the *sugrihinī*. When Umesh Chunder Dutt was principal of City College, his wife Kailaskamini still did all the housework. They did not employ a maidservant or a cook.[59]

There are many explanations for the trend toward increased employment of internal household servants by the *bhadralok* in nineteenth-century Bengal. One is that traditional patron-client relationships could only function in a small-scale rural setting, and servants had to be employed on a contractual basis for the same services to be performed in cities and towns. The spread of female education left women with less time to devote to household work. More importantly, the capacity to employ servants was an indication of social status. The rapid pace of urbanization and change created a confusion of mind that linked the high cost of living, including the added cost of servants' wages, with the supposed idleness of the educated female.

Domestic order

In fact, the educated *bhadramahilā* was being schooled in a different range of domestic duties, and had to bear the burden of responsibility for the smooth functioning of the household even if there were servants. In the traditional family structure, the *ginnī* was responsible for household organization. It was not to her, however, but to younger women who may have been setting up their own homes, or marking out their own domain in a larger household, that the household manuals and magazine articles on domestic organization were addressed. Subjects discussed ranged from the location of the house to the layout of rooms within it and the arrangement

---

[58] Nalinikanta Cattopadhyay, *Nabakānta Cattopādhyāy*, p. 20; *BP*, 6:3, 402 (July 1898).
[59] Rajanikanta De, *Caritamādhurī*, p. 18.

of furniture in each room. The theme underlying all instructions was the importance of order, routine, and cleanliness.

The proper use of time, central to the Victorian work ethic, exercised an influence in Bengal through colonial administrative practice and Brahmo puritanism. In some "progressive" households, each day was rigidly divided into separate activities by a timetable. The schedule prescribed for inhabitants of the Bharat Ashram typified this concern for precise allocation of time.[60] The list of activities in an average day in the life of Aghorekamini Ray showed a similar concern with marking out boundaries for each activity. Her routine was set out thus:

1) Supervise the children's meal. 2) Study. 3) Worship. 4) Look after the sick. 5) Go to school. 6) Give clothes to the washerman. 7) Supervision. 8) Make a quilt. 9) Visit a new friend. 10) Arrange for shoes. 11) Make estimates and give out wages.[61]

Hygiene was also a governing principle. In this respect, Bengal did not lag far behind Britain, where the discovery of germ theory was still recent and not widely known among the general populace. Most accounts of the typical traditional house commented on the disregard for hygiene and cleanliness it exhibited. Although the outer apartments were usually reasonably commodious and airy, the *antahpur* was dingy, and

cooking-rooms without proper chimneys, and smoky outlets generally, form part of these dwelling apartments; in addition to which source of mischief is the *aus takoor* [sic], or place for throwing the refuse of the cooking-house. It may be easy to imagine the noxious quality imparted to the atmosphere by stagnant water and decaying vegetables and animal matter. It is now generally acknowledged, that this noxious quality is in reality a subtle poison, which acts on the human system through

[60] See Chapter Two for an account of this schedule.
[61] Prakascandra Ray, *Aghor-prakās*, p. 172.

the medium of the lungs, producing fevers and other ep-
idemics. . . . There are also the odious privy-houses, one
sufficing for a whole family. They are seldom or never
cleared, and are a perennial source of disease and un-
healthiness. . . . It is now also generally known, that tanks,
and collections of water of every kind, are dangerous
beneath or near a house, because, unless their contents
be constantly in a state of change, which is rarely the
case, their tendency is to send up exhalations of a noxious
kind. But to a native house, contiguous to the female
apartments, is generally attached a tank, in which the
women perform their ablutions, wash their cooking utensils, and the water of which they use for culinary and
domestic purposes. It is, however, nothing better than a
kind of millpond, into which every kind of refuse is
thrown.[62]

The correct locality for a house was a place where there had
never been a tank; a clean cowshed beside the house should
have a sloping cement floor.[63] In the cities it was also necessary
to have, at some distance from the house, or at least away
from the kitchen and dining areas, a toilet that should be
cleaned daily with water and disinfected with lime.[64] The bed-
rooms needed to be airy, and the kitchen was to be at a
distance from the living rooms, with a storeroom beside it.[65]

The interiors of Bengali houses were contrasted unfavorably
with English houses, where cleanliness was almost an obses-
sion.[66] Although Bengali women swept their houses twice a
day, they were accused of neglecting the overall cleanliness,

[62] Kanny Loll Dey, sub-assistant surgeon, in an address to the Bengal Branch
of the British Medical Association in March 1866, quoted in M. Carpenter,
Six Months, I, 62-63. See also the opening paragraphs of Peary Chand Mitra's
novel *Bāmātosinī* (1881) in Asitkumar Bandopadhyay, ed., *Pyāricād racanābalī*, p. 559, and P. Chapman, *Hindoo Female Education*, pp. 2-3.

[63] "Grihasthālīr kathā," *Antahpur*, 5, 5-6 (September-October 1902).

[64] In villages a hole in the ground, with dry earth to be put on after each
use, was considered sufficient. "Nārīr kartabya," *BP*, 4:1, 268 (May 1887).

[65] "Gārhasthya darpan," *BP*, 10, 133 (September 1874).

[66] *BP*, 2:2, 195 (April 1881); Pyaridas Sarkar, *Strīsiksā*, p. 29.

and of contributing to unsanitariness by wiping their fingers on the walls, floors, or pillows after preparing betel, or by spitting on the wall or floor.[67] In the interests of better health, women were advised to wash and air all bed linen, and to clean and dust twice daily, even under the bed.[68] Drinking water was to be purified, either by collecting rain water, boiling well water, or putting it through a filter.[69]

The new sense of order showed a preoccupation with the adage "a place for everything and everything in its place." One writer on "Women's Duties" complained of the inconvenience of never being able to find things in the disorder prevailing in a Bengali household. A towel might be placed over the water-pot in the morning, hung on the door at midday, left in the kitchen in the afternoon and then placed on the bed at night, leaving a dirty and wet mark. Things would be much better if the housewife told everyone to put objects back where they found them, so that they would always remain in the same place.[70] All items in the storeroom were to be listed and labeled for increased efficiency.[71]

Order and hygiene were not the only considerations. The *bhadralok* displayed a new kind of taste and aesthetic style. In general, Bengali homes were simply and sparsely furnished, the only decoration being the traditional *ālpanā* designs on the floor or walls. An article written in 1892 noted that the traditional house plan was changing, especially in the towns. The most fashionable type of house had drawing rooms in the inner and outer apartments; dining rooms were coming into vogue, and separate "suites of apartments" were provided for each married couple in a large household. The women's drawing rooms would include such items as a piano or har-

[67] Candranath Basu, *Gārhastyapāth*, pp. 1-5, "Griha pariskār rākhibār kathā."

[68] "Nārīr kartabya," *BP*, 2:3, 196 (May 1881).

[69] Kumudini Ray, "Hindu nārīr gārhasthya dharmma," *BP*, 5:3, 359 (December 1894); "Swāsthya raksā," *BP*, 2:2, 188 (September 1880).

[70] "Nārīr kartabya—bās bhaban," *BP*, 3:3, 265 (February 1881).

[71] "Nārīr kartabya," *BP*, 196.

monium.[72] Wealthy *bhadralok* imbibed the Victorian predilection for heavy furniture. One writer commented on the tendency for "Anglicized baboos" to go to excess, cramming their houses full of chairs, tables, and sofas, covering the walls with wall-shades and mirrors, and hanging chandeliers from the ceiling.[73] The apparent lack of organization in a Bengali house disturbed British visitors, who had their own fixed Victorian ideas of taste. Annette Akroyd felt "heartache" at the sight of the discomfort and untidiness of Dr. Annada Charan Khastagir's house. The "complete absence of order" baffled her. When she visited Brahmamayi, wife of Durga Mohan Das, she noted that her house was just being furnished in the English fashion. Her verdict was that W. C. Bonerjea, Monomohan Ghose, Dr. Goodeve Chuckerbutty, Dr. Ghose, and Dr. Russic Lal Dutt, among non-Brahmos, and Dr. G. C. Roy and Durga Mohan Das among Brahmos, were the only Bengalis living in an "enlightened" way, which she defined confidently as the preference for comfort, convenience, and individual liberty over the "disgusts" of a genuine Bengali family home.[74]

It is not surprising that Bengali housewives lacked the skills needed for coping with the new *bhadralok* house. They were not used to so much furniture or to the accumulation of household ornaments, and therefore they did not realize the need for dusting them, either.[75] Traditional household skills were of little use when dealing with the new paraphernalia. The

[72] Guru Proshad Sen, "The Hindu Family," *CR*, 95, 190 (October 1892), 307-308.

[73] J. Kerr, *The Domestic Life*, p. 166.

[74] Annette Akroyd, *Diary and Notebook in India 1872-1878*. Entries for 28 December 1872 and 16 March 1873. Letter to Fanny Mowatt, her sister, 9 May 1873, in Akroyd-Beveridge Papers.

[75] "Gārhasthya darpan," *BP*, 11, 141 (May 1875) complained that Bengali housewives did not dust regularly, as Englishwomen did. M. Urquhart, *Women of Bengal*, noted that westernization meant houses were encumbered with heavy furniture and carpets that rotted and became dusty because women were not trained to cope with them. "Emancipated" women, she said, had more modern houses and a better idea of how to keep them in order (pp. 20-21).

articles in manuals and journals therefore fulfilled the important function of teaching women how to manage their changed environment. For instance, oil paintings were a novel decorative item in wealthier households, and required special care and handling. One household magazine, *Gārhasthya*, gave instructions on how to clean oil paintings.[76] Women also had to be educated in the new aesthetic. To this end, they were lectured on such topics as "The Arrangement of Household Furniture."[77] Household manuals recommended that the home should be decorated with flowers, in garlands or in vases, and with pictures and paintings on the walls.

Despite Miss Akroyd's condemnation of his own home, Dr. Annada Charan Khastagir gave some lectures on health and hygiene to the Native Ladies' Institution. Kailaskamini Dutt attended these, and was so impressed that she made an effort to observe the rules of health in her own home, in such matters as ensuring that the water was pure and clean.[78] The modern *ādarsa grihinī* was to be imbued with both a notion of hygiene and a decorative sense. A biographer of Girijakumari Banerjea praised her for being a skilled housewife, arranging the house so that it looked beautiful as well as clean.[79]

Sarojini Ghose, a Hindu *bhadramahilā*, was a perfect example of the modern *ādarsa grihinī*. When she moved into a new house with her husband and children in 1896, she put a table, chairs, and pictures in the drawing room and a clothes-horse in the bedroom. The bed was brought out, placed in the sun, and cleaned with hot water to get rid of bugs, before being put back in its place. Necessary articles were placed on a table beside the bed. The *almirah*, clothes trunk, mirror, and comb were all put in suitable places. All provisions in the

[76] *Gārhasthya*, 1, 7 (1884). In some cases the instructions would have been passed on to servants. The *Indian Mirror* in 1880 commented disapprovingly on the lascivious pictures of women in the drawing rooms of houses of educated natives. *IMS*, 23 May 1880.

[77] Lecture to the Sunday School for Girls in Bhagulpore, *Liberal and New Dispensation*, 7 September 1884.

[78] *BP*, 6:3, 401 (June 1898).

[79] Rajanikanta De, *Caritamādhurī*, p. 14.

storeroom were labeled and arranged. The kitchen was spotlessly clean. The toilet had clean water, and a lump of clay for handwashing, as well as soap; the bathroom had a bucket, basin, wooden stool, soap, and oil. The kitchen had its own separate bucket and basin, which were not to be mixed up with those used in the bathroom.[80]

Culinary skills

Cooking was another area in which the capacities of the "modern" woman came under attack from the 1870s onward. It was said that the *nabīnā* was no longer able to cook, and relied on the skills of professional cooks to perform a function she would formerly have handled herself.[81] A chorus of voices proclaimed that the *bhadramahilā* would not cook because she regarded it as beneath her dignity, and had to hire a cook. In 1876, one writer remembered wistfully that in his childhood all *bhadramahilā* could cook, but claimed that this was no longer the case. Now women hired cooks, no matter how low their husbands' incomes.[82] Rajnarain Bose agreed, commenting caustically that things would only change in the wake of changes in England, as Bengalis always followed the English. He thought it fortunate, therefore, that in England cooking was being actively promoted by lectures, societies, and royal patronage.[83]

Traditionally, girls learned how to cook from their mothers or from other older women. Early in the nineteenth century, Rassundari Debi learned from an old woman living nearby,

[80] Renuka Ghose, *Sarojinī carit*, pp. 22-23.

[81] D. N. Pal, *The Hindu Wife*, 2nd ed. (Calcutta, 1911), p. 45: "It is a modern innovation that cooks are retained in some Hindu households." A woman writing in 1878 said that in the past, in both rich families and those not rich, the women of the family did the cooking but that now in all educated families there was a cook. *Abalābāndhab*, 1, 9 (July 1879).

[82] "Strīsikṣā," *Tattwabodhinī Patrikā*, 394 (June 1876) in B. Ghose, *Sāmayikpatre*, part 2, p. 441.

[83] Rajnarain Bose, *Se kāl*, pp. 86-87. See also "Supakka grihinī," *Paricārikā*, 1, 8 (January 1879). The writer remarked that even the Queen of England taught her daughters how to cook.

by helping her with preparations and watching her cook until she picked up the skills herself.[84] Sudaksina Sen learned to cook when she was seven or eight, in order to cook for her grandfather when he visited places as a Brahmin priest.[85] Bamasundari Debi learned cooking as a game, by playing with toy utensils in imitation of her mother, until she was old enough to be entrusted with real ones.[86] Punyalata Cakrabarti, at the turn of the century, learned to cook by making miniature copies of the dishes her mother prepared.[87]

The increasing prevalence of formal schooling for girls of *bhadralok* families undoubtedly disrupted the organization of traditional learning. Recognizing this, an article written in 1887 suggested to mothers that they teach their daughters to cook during the school holidays.[88] The normal routine of school between 9 a.m. and 3.30 p.m., followed by a period of rest and then further study, did not leave any time for learning domestic skills.[89] It seems unlikely, however, that most mothers would not still have found some time to transmit cooking skills to their daughters. Whatever the reality, it is significant that a decline in cooking ability was perceived, and seen as a result of "modernization" and women's education.

However, the laments about the incompetence of modern women were supplemented by some attempts to deal with the problem. There were calls for cooking to become part of the school curriculum for girls, thus institutionalizing the transmission of a traditional domestic ability.[90] Schools in Bengal were urged to follow the precedent of some schools in England, where cooking had already been added to the curriculum.[91] The Utterparah Hitakari Sabha included cooking in its

[84] Rassundari Debi, *Āmār jīban*, pp. 15-16.
[85] Sudaksina Sen, *Jīban smriti*, pp. 39-40.
[86] Candrakanta Sen, *Bāmāsundarī*, p. 13.
[87] Punyalata Cakrabarti, *Chele belar din guli*, pp. 101-102.
[88] "Nārīr kartabya," *BP*, 4:1, 270 (July 1887).
[89] Priyambada Debi, "Strī-siksā," *Antahpur*, 4, 5 (May 1901).
[90] *Somprakās*, 25 July 1887 in *RNNB* 30 July 1887.
[91] *Bhāratbāsī*, 23 July 1887 in *RNNB* 6 August 1887; "Randhan kārjya," *Abalābāndhab*, 1, 8 (June 1879).

list of subjects for study, and a cooking prize was awarded by the Madhya Bangla Sammilani in 1889.[92]

What made these lessons necessary was as much a change in taste and food habits as a loss of competence. As the *bhadralok* became less insular, through moving to different parts of India and through contact with non-Bengalis and Europeans, greater experimentation in cuisine became the rule. The modern *sugrihinī* was one who was skilled in the new ways of cooking as well as the old.[93] Girish Chunder Ghose noted of Bengali women in 1868 that

> in the art of cooking they are remarkably advancing. It is no longer a simple soup or a dish of porridge which establishes the fame of a Hindu woman as a cook; she must master the mysteries of pillaos and know exactly the true colour of a kabab in order to pass for learned in the art; some even aspire to the glory of preparing fowl curry and cutlets in exact imitation of the Great Eastern Hotel.[94]

Formerly these exotic foods would have been prepared by specialist cooks, or brought in from outside. Different kinds of food were an added expense, so housewives could economize by learning to prepare these delicacies themselves. A writer in the *Bāmābodhinī Patrikā* in 1874 enumerated the types of cooking a *bhadramahilā* should learn:

> native Brahmin dishes of rice and curry; meat in the Moghul style; sweetmeats made from *chānā*, coconut, semolina, lentils, pumpkin, and thickened milk; western-style pickles and jams, cakes, biscuits, puddings, and bread; and Indian *roti, luchi,* and *puri*.[95]

[92] *IMS,* 7 July 1878; *BP,* 4:3, 296 (September 1889).

[93] It was said in praise of Girijakumari Banerjea that she was a skilled housewife who knew how to cook both old and new ways. Rajanikanta De, *Caritamādhurī,* p. 14.

[94] G. C. Ghose, "Female Occupations," in B. Dutt Gupta, *Sociology in India,* pp. 58-59.

[95] "Gārhasthya darpan," *BP,* 10, 130 (June 1874); "Grihasthālīr kathā," *Antahpur,* 5, 5-6.

They also needed to know how to prepare special diets for children, nursing mothers, and invalids—the latter included broths of sago, arrowroot, barley, or Benger's Food.[96] There were no established channels for transmitting foreign recipes. Articles urging the need to cook bemoaned the lack of cookbooks to instruct women.[97] The first Bengali cookbook, *Pākrajeswar*, appeared in 1874. It was brought out by the raja of Burdwan, and was therefore not suitable for use in ordinary *bhadralok* homes.[98] The gap was soon filled. *Pākprabandha*, a Bengali book of "well-tried recipes for the preparation of rare and delicate Mahomedan, Hindu, and other dishes," by "a Bengali Lady" was advertised at a price of five annas in 1879.[99] In 1889, Bipradas Mukhopadhyay brought out *Soukhīn-khādya-pāk*, part one, which included instructions on the cooking of *khecāranna* (rice, lentils, spices, and fat), pullao, rich curry, korma, shish kebab, kofta, cutlets, and chops. The author's stated purpose was to revive the lost art of cooking. Part two included English food.[100] It became standard practice for books on general household topics to include recipes for special cooking.[101]

From 1883, Bipradas Mukhopadhyay also edited *Pāk-Pranālī*, a monthly magazine devoted entirely to cooking. Its aim was not only to teach women the culinary skills they were said to have lost through education and refinement, but also to help them to keep up with changing tastes in food, to teach

---

[96] "Gārhasthya darpan," *BP*, 130; "Gārhasthya darpan," *BP*, 10, 131 (July 1874); Manorama Das, *Antahpur*, 5, 8-9 (December-January 1902-1903); Swarnamayi Gupta, *Usā-cintā*, p. 97.

[97] "Gārhasthya darpan," *BP*, 130; "Randhan-kriyā," *Abalābāndhab*, 1, 8 (June 1879).

[98] *Bengal Library Catalogue*, 1874, II. It was in its third edition by 1881. "Randhan-kriyā," *Abalābāndhab*, 1, 8. There were some cookbooks in English, one of which—*Dainty Dishes for Indian Tables*—was even translated into Urdu for the use of servants. These were of no use to the *bhadramahilā*. See, for example, the advertisements in the *Indian Mirror*, 31 July 1879.

[99] *Indian Mirror*, 21 March 1879.

[100] Bipradas Mukhopadhyay, *Soukhīn-khādya-pāk*, part one (Calcutta, 1889). He also wrote many other cookbooks.

[101] See for instance *Soi*. It had recipes for sweets, fifty vegetarian, and fifty non-vegetarian dishes, pulaos, and puddings.

them new cooking methods, and to enable them to save money by preparing food at home themselves.[102] The journal was illustrated, and recipes were clearly set out, with a list of ingredients followed by the method, and often gave a brief history of the dish, as well. A very wide range of recipes was covered, from local dishes using the banana flower, to duck egg moglai kofta, Jewish pulao, Portuguese sweets, Swiss cake, German coconut pudding, and Italian meatballs. Inevitably there was a large proportion of English recipes, including fried fish with white sauce, mutton chops, custard, omelette, bread, and, ironically, the recipe for Arnott's curry powder, to make "English curry."[103]

Women's journals took up the duty of teaching women different ways of cooking. *Bāmābodhinī Patrikā* had an occasional recipe column from 1884, and *Mahilā* had one from 1895. *Punya*, which was not specifically for women, carried recipes by the editor, Prajnasundari Debi, from its inception in 1897. She had achieved such mastery over the new cooking that she invented her own variations, naming them after eminent men. Her inventions included the "Rammohun pulao" and the "Vidyasagar barfi."[104] Her recipes always listed the price of the ingredients. For instance, "Lady Canning" sweets could be made at home for about three rupees, and a Bombay curry for one rupee.[105] *Antahpur* also had a regular cookery column from 1900, written by women contributors.[106]

Women felt strongly about the cooking columns in these journals. They became the subject of a minor controversy when the editor of *Punya* criticized a recipe for guava jelly published in *Antahpur*. She said that readers would be better off buying it for eight to ten annas in the market than following

---

[102] *Pāk-Pranālī*, 1, 1 (Calcutta 1883).

[103] *Pāk-Pranālī*, 1-6 (1883-1903).

[104] *Punya*, 1, 2 (November 1897); 2, 1-2 (October-November 1898).

[105] *Punya*, 1, 4-5 (January-February 1897); 1, 12 (September 1898).

[106] See, for instance, Saralabala Sarkar, "Randhan—kumud phuler byānjan"; Sarayubala Ghose, "Ilis māch porā," *Antahpur*, 3, 4 (April 1900), and Kamalekamini Gupta, "Randhan—chicken pulao and Irish stew," *Antahpur*, 7, 7 (November 1904).

the recipe in *Antahpur*. Her criticism of the recipe was that it had said that the guava seeds should be thrown out, when they could have been saved to make "guava cheese," an expensive item in the marketplace. "A reader of *Antahpur*" replied spiritedly that there was no need to give the recipe for cheese in a recipe for jelly. She also said that because all the contributors to *Antahpur* were women, all their recipes had been tested, whereas although the editor of *Punya* was a woman, the fact that it was mainly written by men explained the ignorance it displayed in domestic matters.[107]

A woman writing in *Abalābāndhab* in 1878 about women's surrender of cooking to professional cooks did not see it as a difficult problem to solve. In her view, elementary cooking skills sufficient to make a few kinds of *tarkārī* could be picked up within a few days, and subsequently improved upon. She did not think a cookbook would be of any use.[108] Her observation, coupled with the fact that all the recipes published in books and articles were for exotic dishes, indicate that the literature was used for widening the repertoire of women's cooking rather than for teaching them basic proficiency. Biographical evidence supports this. Sarojini Ghose learned how to cook some English dishes from the Madrasi cook of the English headmaster of Kanchantola school. She was very glad when *Pāk-Pranālī* and other cookbooks appeared. She invited some English ladies, the wives of local district officials, to try her attempts at English cooking, for which they praised her highly. In exchange for learning how to cook English dishes, she showed them how to cook Bengali ones.[109] Dayamayi Sen used to send her own recipes to *Pāk-Pranālī*. In return for her interest, the editor gave her a complimentary subscription to the journal.[110]

[107] The disputed recipe was given in "Randhan," *Antahpur*, 4, 1 (January 1901), and the response to criticism of it came from "Janouk Antahpur pāthikā," "Samālocanā khāti noi," *Antahpur*, 4, 3 (March 1901).
[108] "Randhan kārjya," *Abalābāndhab*, 1, 8.
[109] Renuka Ghose, *Sarojinī-carit*, pp. 52-60.
[110] Saracchandra Datta, *Dayāmayī Sener*, p. 9.

It had always been the mark of a *sugrihinī* to be able to cook well, and to cater for large numbers and diverse occasions. Although standards were said to be dropping as the nineteenth century progressed, the evidence suggests the contrary. In fact, the culinary skills expected were becoming more exacting to suit different social requirements.

Medical expertise

Medicines and medical treatment were other areas in which modern women were said to have lost the skills and knowledge of their predecessors. In the past, women had been conversant with local herbal remedies for common ailments, and were able to treat themselves and their families. It was claimed that by the later nineteenth century women no longer knew these remedies, and called the doctor for even the simplest complaints.[111] Remoteness from the family home and the increasing amount of time spent on education played a part in creating this disjunction, but it was only partially connected with the changes in women's situation. A bewildering array of methods of treatment was available—not only folk medicine, but also the Hindu *kabirāji* system, the Islamic *hākimi*, and the recent discoveries of homeopathy and allopathy. In addition, the growth of the modern medical profession in the nineteenth century, and the resultant professionalization of medical knowledge, helped to encourage a dependence on doctors and eroded the self-reliance that had characterized past generations of Bengali women.

It was often said, both by Indians and by Englishmen, that Indian women would not agree to be treated by male doctors. The accuracy of this assertion for Bengal is doubtful, as there are records of numerous cases in which doctors were called in to treat women. A writer in the *Doinik-O-Samācār Candrikā* in 1892 declared that

[111] "Strīsiksā," *Tattwabodhinī Patrikā*, 394; Lilabati Mitra, "Grihaswāsthye ramanīr dristi," *Antahpur*, 7, 9 (January 1905); *Paricārikā*, 1 (16 September 1878); Rajnarain Bose, *Se kāl*, p. 87.

there is no respectable Hindu family which will deny an elderly *vaidya* admission into its zanana [sic]. At no time were such *vaidyas* denied such admission. . . . As a general rule physicians are men who can be safely trusted. But it may be objected that this is true of villages only. . . . As regards towns, too, we can say that our maternal grandfather, who was a very famous *kaviraj* of his time, had access to the zanana of many high families in Calcutta.[112]

Although women consulted doctors frequently, the degree of actual contact between the doctor and a female patient was often limited. Apparently it was not uncommon for a male doctor to have no contact with his female patient, but to use an intermediary such as a male relative or maidservant to enquire after symptoms, and to prescribe drugs on the basis of that information.[113]

The cost of medical treatment was high, and evidently some men had to be persuaded that proper medical treatment for their womenfolk was a necessary expense.[114] In 1878, the normal fee was from three rupees to as much as ten rupees a visit for a native doctor, and sixteen for a European doctor.[115] Lady doctors charged ten rupees a visit.[116] Within the Brahmo community there were a number of prominent doctors who often treated their coreligionists for a reduced fee.[117]

[112] *Doinik-O-Samācār Candrikā,* 19 May 1896 in *RNNB* 23 May 1896. Unfortunately, the author's bias was evident. His eagerness to show that women accepted male doctors stemmed from his horror at the prospect of female doctors. This attitude was shared by many. See also *Nababibhākar Sādhāranī,* 30 May 1887 in *RNNB* 4 June 1887.

[113] *Indian Mirror,* 13 August 1878. This came up in the 1878 Bose versus Bose adultery case, in the evidence given by an assistant surgeon who had been asked to treat Ksetramani Dasi for leukorrhea. She denied having it.

[114] Swarnamayi Gupta, *Usā-cintā,* pp. 73-75.

[115] "Abasthānusāritā," *Abalābāndhab,* 1, 5. The well-known Dr. Jadunath Mukherji advertised that he charged four rupees a visit. It is not clear whether this meant a home call or a consultation at his surgery. *Indian Mirror,* 2 February 1878.

[116] *Sanjībanī,* 22 February 1890 in *RNNB* 1 March 1890. This referred to lady doctors of the Lady Dufferin Fund, but may not have been the general rate.

[117] Dr. Annada Charan Khastagir treated the wife of Brahmo missionary

Despite this, biographies indicate that in cases of serious illness of any member of the family, male or female, doctors were called in.[118] Even the high cost of European doctors did not deter people from making use of their services in serious cases. They seem to have been considered more proficient and better qualified than Bengali doctors. Saratkumari Deb wrote in a biographical account of her family that she and her husband Satyapriya were treated by an English surgeon, at considerable cost, for postpartum illness and piles, respectively.[119] When Kailaskamini Dutt dislocated her thigh while living in the Bharat Ashram she was not treated by the regular Brahmo doctor but by a European doctor.[120] The *bhadramahilā* did not use hospitals, but were treated at home.[121]

A striking feature of the period was the variety of medical treatment people availed themselves of. When Dayamayi Sen, a Hindu *bhadramahilā*, fell ill, she was treated first by a doctor, then by *kabirājes*, as well.[122] After Saudamini Ray was treated by doctors without success, the village *ojhā* was called in. On a later occasion she was attended by a European doctor.[123] On one occasion Aghorekamini Ray became seriously ill. The doctors who examined her diagnosed a disease of the womb, but could do nothing for her. *Kabirājes* were then called in, who said that she had an incurable abdominal tumor. Her husband was advised to bear the further expense of consulting a European doctor, and summoned the well-known surgeon Dr. Charles. He correctly diagnosed that she was six months pregnant and had no other ailments.[124] Both Kumudini Sinha

---

Kedarnath De (Swarnalata Debi, *Mātri-tarpan*, p. 7), and many others. Dr. Dukuri Ghose was the doctor attached to the Bharat Ashram. Sudaksina Sen, *Jīban smriti*, p. 93.

[118] Prabhabati Debi, *Amal-prasūn*; Amritalal Gupta, *Punyabatī nārī*, p. 41; Harasundari Datta, *Swargīya Srīnāth Datter*; Gurucharan Mahalanabis, *Atmakathā*.

[119] Saratkumari Deb, *Āmār sangsār*, p. 29.

[120] *BP*, 6:3, 401 (June 1898).

[121] *Sanjībanī*, 22 February 1890 in *RNNB* 1 March 1890.

[122] Saracchandra Datta, *Dayāmayī Sener*, p. 18.

[123] Rakhal Chandra Ray, *Jīban bindu*, pp. 42-43, 123-129.

[124] Prakascandra Ray, *Aghor-prakās*, pp. 39-41.

and Srinath Canda's nephew were treated by the famous homeopathic doctor D. N. Ray after they felt that allopathic treatment had been unsuccessful.[125] Surgery was only used occasionally, and with varying results. Girijakumari Banerjea had
a kidney stone surgically removed. The operation brought
temporary relief, but she did not survive.[126]

Writers accused women of having lost the expertise in native
folk medicine held by women of previous generations. The
problem was not as simple as they made it appear. Loss of
skill in native medicine had not been succeeded by a void. The
nineteenth-century *sugrihinī* had a far wider choice of types
of medicine and treatment than was available to her predecessors. Apart from folk medicine, women were expected to
know a little about each of the four forms of treatment current
in the later nineteenth century: allopathy, homeopathy, *kabirāji*, and *hākimi*.[127] In 1871 there were still relatively few
books putting this knowledge into simple Bengali for the purposes of a housewife, so *Bāmābodhinī Patrikā* undertook to
include a regular feature on elementary medical remedies.[128]
Household manuals and other women's magazines often included a section on native medical remedies,[129] which were
widely promoted as the cheapest form of treatment available.
Women who had mastered basic native medicines could save
the family a lot of money in doctors' fees and expensive prescriptions. Remedies given included the use of the leaves of
the *bisatārak*, or a paste of *hābalamālī*, for clearing sinuses.
The leaves of the *tulsī* plant, or basil, relieved symptoms of
malaria. The juice of the leaves mixed with honey and fed to
a child every morning would cure a cough. If a child fell over
and hurt itself, the leaves of the *gādā phul*, or marigold, ap-

---

[125] *Kumudinī-caritra*, pp. 37-43; Srinath Canda, *Brāhmasamāje callis bath-sar*, pp. 259-261.
[126] Rajanikanta De, *Caritamādhurī*, p. 13.
[127] Bharatcandra Bandopadhyay, *Susrusā pranālī*, p. 27.
[128] "Gārhasthya cikitsā pranālī," *BP*, 8, 100 (December 1871).
[129] *Soi; Gārhasthya*, 1, 2, 1884. *Antahpur* had an occasional medical column.

plied to the injured part would stop the bleeding.[130] Native
medicine had itself absorbed modern principles. A health manual by a *kabirāj* stressed the need to restrict the number of
people allowed in the sickroom, to allow air and light into it,
and to change clothes daily and bedding regularly.[131]

Homeopathic medicines were popular, and were recommended as being much cheaper than allopathic medicines. In
the smallpox outbreak of 1895, the homeopathic medicines
Vaccineus and Lactose Tinctura were recommended, along
with vaccination and the eating of a paste of *kantakarī* root
mixed with black pepper.[132] A treatise on menstruation also
gave information on how to prepare and dilute homeopathic
medicines for any menstrual complications.[133]

Although allopathic medicine was also very widely used,
there was some criticism and suspicion of its effects. One
writer claimed that women had greater longevity than men
because they took fewer western medicines. He said that quinine affected the bones.[134] Rajnarain Bose said that recent
generations of children were weaker than in the past because
their mothers treated them with western rather than native
medicines.[135]

Despite these dissenting voices, most women had learned
the rudiments of treating common ailments with western medicine. The well-equipped house of 1885 was supposed to have
measuring glasses, scales and weights (for measuring grains
of medicine), a wooden syringe, and a thermometer, as well
as a long list of basic drugs including quinine, bromide of
potash, diluted sulphuric acid, diluted nitric acid, soda, mus-
tard, castor oil, magnesia carbonate, and carbonate of am-
monia.[136] Women had to learn to dispense new drugs using

---

[130] "Grihacikitsā," *BP*, 5, 77 (January 1870); 'Sahaj musti jog," *Antahpur*,
3, 4 (April 1900).
[131] Kabiraj Candrakisor Sen, Ayurvedic Vidyalay and Osodhalay, *Rogi-
carjyā* (Calcutta, 1895), pp. 37-38.
[132] *BP*, 5:3, 363 (April 1895).
[133] Kedarnath Sarkar, *Ritu-raksā*, pp. 12-13.
[134] "Grihacikitsā," *BP*, 77.
[135] Rajnarain Bose, *Se kāl*, p. 87.
[136] Pulin Sanyal, *Saral sisu pālan*, p. 120.

a different system of measurement. Many of the remedies given in journals and manuals assumed a familiarity with western medicines. For instance, to treat convulsions in a child, a woman was first to administer castor oil, then put cold water on its face and sit it in a tub of warm water. If this was not effective, then she was to rub chloroform liniment on its back and spine. If the condition lingered, a dose of bromide of potassium was recommended.[137] Girish Chunder Ghose graphically portrayed the kind of confusion women must have felt in coming to grips with the new form of medicine: "When English medicine is had recourse to, with its perplexing programme of mixtures and pills and embrocations alternating in constant whirls by the hour, the mother is generally the sole dispenser of doses, for the father is absent·on his outdoor work."[138]

Lilabati Mitra was an example of someone at the end of the nineteenth century who had acquired confident mastery over all types of medicine. She advocated the "common-sense" observance of certain rules of hygiene, with the use of cheap native medicines where possible, as well as the use of western drugs. Her suggestions for prevention of malaria included sleeping under a mosquito net, drinking boiled water, and taking regular doses of quinine. Once malaria was contracted, eau-de-cologne or cold water on the forehead could be used to allay the fever. The area surrounding the house should be free from jungle, and pits and pools had to be covered to prevent them from becoming breeding grounds for mosquitoes. She recommended regular exercise, because she had heard of a *saheb* who had cured himself of malarial attacks by going horseback riding wearing a flannel coat to make him sweat; after coming home and resting in a closed room for an hour, he was cured.[139]

Occasionally women were confident enough to bypass all systems and follow their own judgment. One woman wrote

[137] "Grihacikitsā," *BP*, 8, 106 (June 1872).
[138] G. C. Ghose, "Female Occupations," in B. Dutt Gupta, *Sociology in India*, p. 58.
[139] Lilabati Mitra, "Grihaswāsthye ramanīr dristi," *Antahpur*, 7, 9.

to the *Bāmābodhinī Patrikā* saying that for eczema, allopathic and homeopathic medicines had proved useless. Her son had had it for two years, and doctors had been unable to help him, but she had eventually found her own cures. These were either to bathe the child with soap, then dry it and cover its body with arrowroot, in which case the rash would disappear in seven or eight days; or to bathe the child in a salt lake or river, and rub it with coconut oil one or two hours later, which would clear the rash in two weeks.[140]

From the 1870s the book market was inundated with books on all types of medicine, many written specifically for women. Dr. Khastagir wrote a health primer in 1882, based on lectures he had delivered to the Native Ladies' Institution. Their efficacy was proved by "the fact that many of the fair hearers of the author have completely changed their modes of household management after hearing them."[141]

Women were also bombarded with advertisements for medicines and patent remedies of all kinds. An average monthly number of *Bāmābodhinī Patrikā* contained a high proportion of medical advertisements, such as Binod Batika for malaria and fevers connected with the spleen; Sarbbamangala Ghrita for ringworm and skin diseases; cough mixture for curing asthma; Gajasinghe for all fevers; Dr. Sitalacandra Pal's Santan Raksak oil for preventing miscarriages, ensuring safe births and healthy children; and Kabiraj Nagendranath Sen Gupta's oils for epilepsy, earache and skin disease. Mahalanabis and Company, druggists of Cornwallis Street, advertised that besides their patent remedy for rheumatism, "all allopathic medicines, spectacles and surgical instruments" were available. Mitra and Company was a homeopathic library and dispensary in College Street advertising a cheap range of medicines. Lahiri and Company, a big homeopathic firm with six branches other than the central one in College Street, advertised among its wares a small "box" for the treatment of cholera, which

[140] "Griha cikitsā—ekjimā nāmak carmmarog o tāhār cikitsā," *BP*, 6:2, 393 (October 1897).
[141] "Notices of Books," *Liberal and New Dispensation*, 3 December 1882.

was made up of twelve phials of medicine, a book, and a phial of special medicine, all for five rupees. A larger version of this box, with twenty-four phials, a book on home medicine, camphor, and a dropper, cost eight rupees. Some advertisements were accompanied by testimonials from eminent people, guaranteeing the genuineness of the various healing properties.[142]

Advertisements for doctors and medicines also appeared in English and Bengali dailies. A typical issue of *Brahmo Public Opinion* had advertisements for Dr. M. M. Bose, M.D., L.R.C.P., whose consulting hours were between 7 a.m. and 8 a.m. daily; for Hari Charan Roy Kobiraj's dispensary with genuine native medicines and drugs, and for Mahalanabis and Company, established in 1862, with its "far-famed patent remedies" such as "Dr. Rubini's Spirit of Camphor," a specific for cholera, selling at twelve annas for a one-ounce phial, or one rupee six annas for *mofussil* orders.[143] The *Indian Mirror* advertised Dr. B. M. Sircar's Arroma Augustum, for curing dysmenorrhea and bringing on conception, for three rupees eight annas.[144] Doctors advertised their own patent remedies. Dr. Annada Charan Khastagir listed his qualifications—prompt cures of recent and acute fevers, holder of Lord Northbrook's first prize on Burdwan Epidemic Fever and its treatment, and successful operations on "thousands of urinary stones, tumours of testicles" with "charge for treatment suited to circumstances"—in order to launch the following patent medicines:

> for acute fevers, first medication eight annas, second and third medications one rupee each; for malarious fevers with spleen or liver, one rupee each for first or second medication; one rupee each for medicine for coughs, looseness of bowels, dysentery; and eight annas each for

[142] Advertisements in *BP*, 6:4, 417 (October 1899). The sampling is a good indication of the kind of advertisements printed in most journals.
[143] *Brahmo Public Opinion*, 7 August 1879. Mahalanabis and Company was run by Gurucharan Mahalanabis, a prominent Brahmo. Dr. M. M. Bose was the brother of Ananda Mohan Bose.
[144] *IMS*, 17 October 1880.

sweet and tasteless medicine for children for fevers, coughs,
looseness of bowels and dysentery.[145]

Not all patent medicines were from so reputable a source.
Many were sheer quack remedies, sometimes dangerous, prepared by shrewd but unscrupulous racketeers. There was no
legislation governing the sale or advertising of patent medicines.[146]

The widespread use of patent remedies and doctors' services
by the later nineteenth century indicates that the medical and
pharmaceutical professions had secured a place in the consumption patterns of the average *bhadralok* household. Much
of the advertising of these goods and services was directed to
women, in recognition of their importance as consumers. In
such circumstances, women may easily have been pressured
into losing confidence in their own medical skills. In addition,
in an urban setting patent medicines would have been more
readily available than the ingredients for folk medicines, and
therefore were more convenient for the housewife. The prevalence of manuals of instruction in folk medicine showed that
the conditions for this kind of expertise to be handed down
no longer existed for many *bhadramahilā*, who had to resort
to self-education from books. To accuse the nineteenth-century *sugrihinī* of ignorance of folk medicine was to ignore the
familiarity with modern medical knowledge that she had acquired.

The educated woman of the second half of the nineteenth
century had been accused of having lost touch with house-
wifely skills. The assertion contains an element of truth, yet
overlooks the complexity of her situation. With much of her
youth spent in formal education, then marriage, which was

[145] *IMS*, 28 November 1880.

[146] The *Samay*, 25 August 1893, called for legislation to restrict the sale
of patent medicines, and to check the practice of fraudulent doctors and
kabirājes numerous in the *moffusil*. *RNNB* 2 September 1893. The *Nabajug*,
19 September 1903, gave names of a number of people who had been selling
patent medicines in Calcutta under assumed English names. *RNNB* 26 September 1903.

often followed by a break not only with her own family but also with that of her in-laws, a woman would have had little opportunity to pick up domestic skills. Dayamayi Sen lamented that she had lost touch with some traditional skills when she had to set up a separate household with her husband, on his official duties.[147] Annette Akroyd commented that the "advanced" wives of England-returned husbands, separated from their families, had no means of learning household skills.[148] A Hindu woman educated at Loreto House at the turn of the century, Miss J. Bose, admitted that she was not trained to do anything domestic. Neither she nor her mother could cook ordinary food.[149] Educated women also developed interests other than housework. It was said disapprovingly that one such educated *bhadramahilā* used to tie her child to the veranda post with a string while she read a book.[150]

Despite the fact that opportunities for training were less, the expectation that the *bhadramahilā* would perform the traditional domestic role remained. As the *bhadralok* developed a distinctive lifestyle, a woman's duties became more complex. It was no wonder that she showed some confusion. By the later nineteenth century, the idea that the home was a woman's "kingdom" was a cherished belief.[151] Traditionally the home had always been her sphere, but education created rising expectations that had to be fulfilled, without going to the extent of providing alternative roles. In response to this, household servants were employed increasingly to elevate the function of housewife to a managerial plane. The transmission of skills was institutionalized in "modern" forms to suit changed circumstances—through lectures, books, journals, and school curricula instead of through imitation of existing models in the home. Another reason for institutionalization was that

[147] Saracchandra Datta, *Dayamayī Sener*, p. 9.
[148] Annette Akroyd, *Diary*, 5 May 1873.
[149] However, her mother could cook sweets and other special dishes. Interview with Miss J. Bose, Calcutta, 10 March 1978.
[150] Gurucharan Mahalanabis, *Ātmakathā*, p. 74.
[151] "Ramanīr kārjyaksetra," *BP*, 7:1, 424 (May 1900).

women had not simply lost certain skills, but were required to master a whole new set of household abilities that were part of maintaining the *bhadralok* image.

In nineteenth-century England, the concern for order in the house was connected with the beginnings of industrialization. The consequent rationalization of housework, attempting to increase its efficiency, followed the industrial work pattern.[152] In Bengal, the order that was part of the English middle-class lifestyle may have been reflected in the functioning of the British administration, and therefore had some influence in moderating the lives of those who worked under its discipline. Apart from that, however, society continued to operate in a traditional way, unmarked by the middle-class concerns of thrift, order, efficiency, and absolute cleanliness. The *bhadra-mahilā* was supposed to perform the difficult task of "modernizing" a sphere that was more integrated with a traditional society that functioned in a collective, cooperative manner than with a mechanized industrial society. Even in Europe, the abundant supply of servants for the middle classes limited the necessity for rationalizing housework. In Bengal, this was even more the case, indicating that the advice on modern housewifery was not given only because of the pressure of economic necessity, but because of the need to elevate and professionalize the role of housewife.

The professionalization of housework in the nineteenth century through institutional channels was directed both toward satisfying the expectations and making use of the talents of literate and educated women, as well as toward the creation of a new lifestyle. To make female education worthwhile, and its benefits apparent, the educated woman had to keep house differently from her forbears. Much more was expected of her than of her illiterate predecessors. In view of the responsibilities and new choices faced by women, the attempts to contrast the incompetence of modern women with the ideal women of a past golden age seem unfair and fatuous.

[152] See T. McBride, *The Domestic Revolution*, chapter one.

Women mounted a staunch defense of their position in response to the barrage of attacks. After Bankim Chandra Chatterjee's article "Prācīnā ebang nabīnā" appeared in *Banga Darsan* in 1874, three replies from women were printed. The first, from Candikasundari Debi, turned the argument back onto men, comparing them unfavorably with men of old. Laksmimani Debi, the second respondent, accepted the criticisms but argued that men's egotism had forced women to adopt these "faults." The third writer, Rasamayi Dasi, scathingly challenged men to reverse roles:

> If we die, you can perform *ekādasī*, eat vegetarian food, and wear coarse white cloth; if you die we'll have a "second family"—you can give birth to children, and supervise the kitchen—if there is a marriage in the house you can cover your moustache with your sari, carry the ritual articles on a tray on your head, perform women's rites, and keep the bride awake with ribald jokes in front of the bride-chamber. Your happiness will know no bounds. As youths, we'll go off to college, books in hand—as we grow older, we'll wear our hair in a Firingi bun, topped by a turban at a jaunty angle, and go to the office—make speeches in the Town Hall with our nose rings dancing— arouse the audience with charming yet penetrating looks from behind our spectacles. . . . Come to the *antahpur*— we'll go to the office. It is these men, who have been oppressed by conquerors for seven hundred years. Doesn't this shame you?[153]

[153] Letter from Rasamayi Dasi, in Bankim Chandra Chatterjee, *Bibidha prabandha*, p. 162.

᳥᳥ SEVEN ᳥᳥

The Erosion of Purdah

The institution of purdah, described earlier, exercised fundamental control over the social behavior of the *bhadramahilā* in the nineteenth century. It was commonly believed during the nineteenth century that it had been introduced as a protective measure during the Muslim invasion.[1] Later it came to be an indication of status in imitation of the custom of the ruling Muslim power. Upper-caste Hindu women observed purdah, whereas most lower-caste women did not. Observance of purdah seems to have been a feature of upward mobility.

Purdah was a form of social control by men over women's behavior which implied a view of women as simultaneously sexually vulnerable and in need of protection, and sexually aggressive and in need of control. Contact through the colonial system with the social patterns prevailing in the west led the *bhadralok* to question the justification for controlling women by segregation and seclusion. Ideological systems controlling women's behavior were possibly equally powerful in the west, but they functioned in a more subtle form. Women were not physically confined, and sexual control was exerted as much through the mechanism of individually internalized "guilt" as through that of "shame" dependent on "sanctions imposed

[1] Tarakanath Biswas, *Bangīya-mahilā*, p. 51; Mohesh Chundra Deb, "A Sketch of the Condition of the Hindoo Women," read to the Society for the Acquisition of General Knowledge, January 1839, in G. Chattopadhyay, ed., *Awakening in Bengal*, pp. 94-95; Satyendranath Tagore, "Āmār bālyakathā," in Indira Debi Caudhurani, ed., *Purātanī*, p. 191. See also the essays in the sections "The Analysis of Purdah and Sex Segregation" and "The Social Structure of Purdah Institutions" in H. Papanek and G. Minault, eds., *Separate Worlds*.

228

by members of a group with whom there is frequent interaction," which operated in traditional Hindu society.[2]

The symbolic importance of purdah, and its actual integra-
tion with the rest of society through links with marriage arrangements, property ownership, and inheritance, made it an
institution that could not be violated without major upheaval.
Even marginal alterations to strict purdah touched off rever-
berations of panic throughout Hindu society. Those who supported and defended it envisaged total anarchy as a result of
any lessening of its restrictions. The breakdown of purdah
was implicitly seen as an unleashing of the pent-up sexuality
of men and women by jettisoning all social controls and notions of correct morality. Explicitly, it was feared that women
would be subject to humiliation and degradation from "uncivilized" men because society was not yet ready to cope with
this kind of freedom.

By the end of the nineteenth century there had been some
modifications in the purdah system, however. In general, these
were part of the process of "westernization" associated with
rising status under British rule. Lower-caste women, who were
less able to afford it, still adopted purdah as part of the process
of "sanskritization."[3] Among the *bhadramahilā*, the few who
went furthest in the direction of discarding purdah altogether
were those for whom such a move was a determinant of their
distinctive group identity, such as Christian and Brahmo women.
The paradoxical nature of emergence from purdah is well
illustrated by these groups. Although noticeably socially freer
than orthodox Hindus, they were also more puritanical.

A combination of external pressures and responses from
within Bengali society brought about changes in purdah. The
arrangements of the colonial administration and the provision

---

[2] H. Papanek, "Purdah," p. 316, characterizes "impulse control" in these
ways.

[3] The term "sanskritization" illustrates the process, but is not entirely apt
because the original institution of purdah is most closely associated with
"islamicization," part of a Hindu strategy of maintaining status under Islamic
rule.

of a transport network for travel were outside forces that eventually helped to bring about modifications in the purdah system. Dress reform and emergence into public society were consciously adopted by the progressive section of the *bhadralok* and gradually taken up by a wider group. These changes had a dramatic impact in the context of the segregated society of nineteenth-century Bengal.

Administrative discouragement of purdah

The British government was generally unsympathetic to purdah and to the extra burden of separate arrangements that it entailed. Administrative measures sometimes meant that strict purdah had to be modified. The vernacular press often protested against the government's lack of sensitivity to Indian social customs, typified by its subjection of the *bhadramahilā* to due processes of law with no special concessions to purdah. When, in 1884, a "lady of a respectable family" was imprisoned for an offense relating to her estate, the press reacted strongly against the decision, claiming that for a purdah woman such a sentence was equivalent to capital punishment.[4] The courts also required that *pardānasīn* (ladies observing purdah) be present, not only as plaintiffs or in voluntary attendances, but also as witnesses. The suggestion from the press that provision be made for *bhadramahilā* to be represented by their legal counsel empowered to make statements on their behalf was not adopted.[5] In 1901 the plaintiff in a rape case begged to have her case heard in chambers, but her request was refused. This elicited the comment from the editor of *Sanjībanī*

---

[4] *Bangabāsī,* 1 August 1884, *Surabhī,* 4 August 1884 in *RNNB* 8 August 1884.

[5] *Doinik-O-Samācār Candrikā,* 26 March 1893 in *RNNB* 1 April 1893. However, in some areas, purdah in the courts may have been the rule. In 1905, the *Sandhyā* warned the *bhadralok* that sending women to Lady Fraser's purdah party would set a precedent for law courts to ask women to give evidence publicly. *Sandhyā,* 2 December 1905, 5 December 1905 in *RNNB* 9 December 1905. Precedents were probably scarce because "respectable" women would not have had much business with the courts. Female *zamindars* would have had transactions handled by their agents.

that in future "no respectable ladies will be willing to seek the protection of law against their oppressors."[6] In 1905 the Bank of Bengal also declined to make special concessions to purdah, by stipulating that two persons known to the bank had to witness the signature of a *pardānasīn* who wished to receive interest on government promissory notes.[7]

Official indifference to the observance of purdah in administrative transactions forced women to abandon it in certain circumstances. Although this may not have changed the purdah system with regard to informal, unofficial life, it created an awareness that women had to discard purdah when dealing with impersonal institutions. Purdah was best suited to controlling women within the home. Major adaptations were required to maintain purdah arrangements on an official, public scale. When the ruling power did not believe in the ideological premises of purdah, it was not prepared to go to the lengths required to maintain it.

Modification of purdah through travel

Emergence from purdah was hastened by the geographical mobility of the *bhadralok* under British rule. *Bhadralok* professionals pursued career opportunities all over India, often taking their wives and families with them. Brahmo missionaries, on tour or in residence, also took their families traveling. Even if these domestic arrangements were not permanent, their womenfolk would often join them for short visits. The growth of the railways facilitated exchanges of this kind, and helped maintain close links between the "expatriate" *bhadralok* and his family and region. Bholanauth Chunder's comment on Bengali men in 1860 could equally be applied to women:

the long vista, that is opening from one end of the empire to the other, will, in a few years, tempt him out-of-doors to move in a more extended orbit, to enlarge the circle

[6] *Sanjībanī*, 27 June 1901 in *RNNB* 6 July 1901.
[7] *Bengalee*, 17 December 1905 in *RNNB* 23 December 1905.

of his terrene acquaintance, to see variety in human nature, and to divert his attention from the species Calcutta-wallah to the genus man. The fact has become patent, that which was achieved in months and days is now accomplished in hours and minutes, and celerity is as much the order of the day as security and saving.[8]

Rail travel for women was fraught with greater trouble than it was for men. The collective anxiety over railway travel by women as expressed in the press indicates the kind of fears and practical problems encountered in the transition from a strict purdah society to one that allowed greater physical mobility. While broadening their horizons through travel, women were also exposed to hitherto unknown dangers. They were brought into direct contact with the larger, impersonal society beyond the normal narrow scope of the *antahpur* and its immediate locality.

The difficulties of rail travel for women were a frequently recurring subject in all newspapers throughout the later nineteenth century. Before 1870 there do not appear to have been any special arrangements for female rail passengers, which made it very difficult for women to travel by rail and yet remain socially acceptable. In 1869, the *Dāccā Prakās* suggested "private carriages for native females," with female guards. The vulnerability of women passengers was emphasized by the concern that strict measures be taken to ensure that no "men in female garb" gained admittance. Carriages were also to be provided for a woman's close relatives, and for women who wished to travel in the company of their relatives but not of other men.[9] By the end of that year, separate carriages had been provided for the *bhadramahilā*. It was also possible to arrange for observance of purdah when boarding and alighting from the train. The arrangements were still incomplete: there were no purdah rest rooms, and the *bhadramahilā*

[8] Bholanauth Chunder, *The Travels of a Hindoo to Various Parts of Bengal and Upper India* (London, 1869), I, 140.

[9] *Dāccā Prakās*, 23 May 1869 in *RNNB* 29 May 1869.

who could not afford to travel intermediate class was not catered for.[10]

The press reported frequent cases of sexual assaults on women, often by Eurasian railway guards. Opinion was divided as to how the situation should be remedied. The debate was fueled by racial feeling against Eurasians. As a group, Eurasians were not only perceived as an obstacle to the professional advancement of Bengalis, but now also as a threat to their personal control over their womenfolk. Some papers used the issue of assaults on women travelers to call for the dismissal of Eurasians from the position of railway guards on moral grounds. Others used it to direct venom against "enlightened Babus who feel no hesitation in allowing the female members of their houses to travel by rail without a male companion," and "those shameless native women who venture out of their homes without a proper companion."[11] It was suggested that female ticket collectors be appointed, and that severer penalties be imposed on offenders.[12] Only a small proportion of the total number of cases was reported. Given the tendency to blame women for exposing themselves to danger by breaking purdah through rail travel, few women would have dared besmirch their reputation by reporting assaults, especially if they consisted of insults and provocation rather than rape. A report in *Hitabādī* in 1896 confirmed this, commenting that "ticket examiners have touched the breast,

[10] The female carriages specifically excluded low-class women (*itar strīlok*); *Dāccā Prakās*, cited in *BP*, 5, 76 (December 1869). The exclusiveness of the *bhadramahilā* was manifested again later, with complaints that because there was only one intermediate ladies' compartment, some women with intermediate tickets had to travel with third-class women. *Mihir-O-Sudhākar*, 16 May 1896 in *RNNB* 23 May 1896; *Samay*, 6 November 1903 in *RNNB* 14 November 1903; *Banga Mahilā*, 13 April 1870 in *RNNB* 15 April 1870.

[11] *Sanjībanī*, 26 September 1891, *Bangabāsī*, 26 September 1891 in *RNNB* 3 October 1891; *Somprakās*, 25 November 1895 in *RNNB* 7 December 1895.

[12] *Bikrampur*, 7 May 1896 in *RNNB* 16 May 1896; *Hitabādī*, 12 November 1895 in *RNNB* 23 November 1895; *Bankurā Darpan*, 16 December 1895, *Sulabh Doinik*, 23 December 1895 in *RNNB* 28 December 1895; *Hitabādī*, 31 January 1896 in *RNNB* 8 February 1896; *Bengalee*, 8 June 1901 in *RNNB* 15 June 1901.

pinched the cheek or kissed the faces of many young women, who have slunk away more dead than alive, weeping tears of shame and anger, not venturing to tell anybody of their disgrace."[13]

In the novel *Nayantārā*, Sibnath Sastri graphically exposed the kind of discomfort frequently encountered by female rail passengers. The heroine Nayantara was to travel from Chinsurah to Hughly with her brother, but he missed the train. Alone in a second-class compartment, she was subjected to rudeness and insults from two "*bābus*" in the same carriage. On arrival at the station, their predatory intentions became clear, and she was saved only by the arrival of a relative.[14] The rise of militant nationalism, which advocated the growth of self-defense among Bengali men, encouraged increasing physical militancy for women as well. An article in the Brahmo paper *Sanjībanī* in 1905 entitled "Mother, who holds the scimitar and the skull in her hands, it is for thee to heal the wound of insults" gave this advice:

> Travelling on railways cannot be avoided. But it is difficult to count up the cases of outrage on females which occur every year. Except the use of the sword, we do not see any means of preserving our women-kind from such intolerable insults.
>
> We therefore request our women-kind to take to the use of arms. Let each female, when intending to travel by rail, conceal a long knife inside her clothes before she leaves home. Whenever she sees anybody preparing to make any attempt on her virtue, let her save herself by thrusting the knife with force into the breast of that man. There is no other way except this of preserving the honour of women on railways and steamers.[15]

Despite its many hazards, travel was advocated as a way of broadening the mind beyond a narrow provincial outlook.

[13] *Hitabādī*, 31 July 1896 in *RNNB* 8 August 1896; *Sanjībanī*, 15 August 1896 in *RNNB* 22 August 1896.

[14] Sibnath Sastri, *Nayantārā*, pp. 60-61.

[15] *Sanjībanī*, 27 July 1905 in *RNNB* 5 August 1905.

It was regarded as an educational experience providing a means of learning about other regions and customs.[16] Travel gave women a much wider sphere of interest, as well as an opportunity to observe the living conditions of women in other regions and to compare them with their own.

Brahmo women were among the first to realize the educational benefits of travel. In 1871, Saudamini Mozoomdar and Mahamaya Basu visited northwest and western India and recorded their impressions for the *Bāmābodhinī Patrikā*. They met Panjabi women in the Panjab, and noted the dress habits of Gujerati and Parsi women in Bombay. The relative social freedom of Bombay women, who walked about in public and attended mixed meeting places, impressed them, and they speculated on how long it would be before Bengali men would be civil enough to react to this with the indifference of the men of western India.[17] Their Brahmo puritanism was disturbed by the women of the Panjab, who were known to bathe naked in the lake and to sing obscene songs publicly at certain festivals.[18] In 1905, a description of a trip to Bombay was printed as a series of letters. By this time, Bengali lady travelers were more active. They visited public places of interests such as the Tata Palace and the art school, and commented on subjects that ranged from the social advancement of the Parsi to the difficulties of life for the Bengali middle classes in Bombay.[19]

The means of travel—by rail or by steamer—exposed women

[16] P. C. Mozoomdar, *Strīcaritra*, pp. 119-122, "Desbhraman."

[17] Anandibai Joshee, who gained fame as the first Indian woman to study for a medical degree in the United States, was unpleasantly struck by the incivility of Bengali men when she came to Calcutta from western India in 1881. When she walked in Calcutta with her husband, unveiled, as she was accustomed to doing in Bombay, she was rudely stared at and even insulted. See Mrs. E. F. Chapman, *Sketches of Some Distinguished Indian Women* (London and Calcutta, 1891), pp. 58-59.

[18] *BP*, 8, 100 (December 1871); *BP*, 8, 109 (September 1872); *BP*, 8, 115 (March 1873). Krishna Kumar Mitra was also taken aback to see Panjabi women bathing naked in full public view. *Ātmacarit*, p. 104.

[19] Sri Ni . . . , "Patra," *BP*, 8:1, 493-494 (September-October 1904); "Patra," *BP*, 8:1, 495 (November 1904); "Bombāi bhraman," *BP*, 8:1, 498 (February 1905).

to a range of people outside their own small circle of kin. When traveling in a ladies' compartment, they had the novel feeling of taking responsibility for themselves. Aghorekamini Ray was very scared the first time she traveled by rail, in the ladies' carriage. Her husband, seated in the adjoining carriage, got out and reassured her at every stop, and gradually her fears evaporated. She eventually became so intrepid that she traveled by rail to Lahore alone with her two daughters.[20] Women were often placed in difficult situations, in which they proved very capable of responding to the challenge. Kamalekamini Gupta wrote in *Antahpur* in 1902 of a rail journey she had made five years previously, on which half the carriages had been disconnected along the way, separating her from her male companion. She was left to fend for herself, with the additional responsibility of looking after a young girl and her baby, the other occupants of the ladies' carriage. Taking charge of the situation, she demanded to see the stationmaster, sent off a telegram arranging to rejoin her companion at Asansol, and made sure that they caught the next through train.[21] The episode must have given her confidence in her ability to look after herself. Travel continually placed people in new situations. Lilabati Mitra described a trip to Waltair, south India, which had given her firsthand experience of the arrogance of the British in India. A British traveler in her compartment had beaten up a native stationmaster for not providing ice to go with his lemonade and soda.[22]

Travel made Bengali women conscious of nationalism, in that it made them realize that their own region was but a small part of a much larger entity. Subodh Kumari Majumdar's experience was typical of many. She wrote of her frustration at not being able to communicate with Sindhis in the Panjab,

[20] Prakascandra Ray, *Aghor-prakās*, pp. 46-47.

[21] "Relebipad—(satya ghatanā)," *Antahpur*, 5, 4 (August 1902).

[22] Lilabati Mitra, "Oalteyār," *Antahpur*, 7, 6 (October 1904). This story may have been fictional, but the vivid description suggests that it was based on experience.

or to follow the Brahmo service in Sindhi that she attended.[23] Exposure to the people and customs of other parts of India often forced women to revise their preconceptions and stereotypes. One woman recalled how she had been told from childhood that people from Orissa were savages. In Calcutta she had only seen them as *pālki* bearers, servants, or gardeners. It was not until she visited Orissa that she found that they had their own culture, with its own pandits and *bhadralok*.[24]

This type of nationalism increased women's awareness of the resources available in different parts of India. In 1878, a twenty-one-year-old Maratha woman, Ramabai, created a sensation in Calcutta by debating in Sanskrit with learned pandits. A welcome meeting was held at the house of Ananda Mohan Bose and was attended by about twenty *bhadramahilā*. Radharani Lahiri read a Bengali address, stressing that Ramabai provided them all with a model of national womanhood:

> Not we alone, but the whole of the inhabitants of India ought to be proud of you. You are an example of in what an elegant garb higher education can dress the heart of a woman. Formerly the name of foreign ladies of learning had to be cited as examples, now seeing you, we shall not have to search for illustrious examples in a foreign country. . . .
>
> No public meeting has ever been convened for doing honor to a lady of this country. Your propitious advent to this part of the country has laid the foundation for such meetings.[25]

During her stay in Calcutta, Ramabai also delivered a lecture in Hindi on the subject of "education and travel" at the Barabazar Literary Club.[26]

[23] Subodh Kumari Majumdar, "Kārācir patra," *BP*, 8:1, 490 (June 1904).
[24] "Urisyā bhraman," *Antahpur*, 5, 2-3 (June-July 1902).
[25] "Report of a Meeting Held at the House of Baboo Anund Mohan Bose for the Reception of Roma Bai," *Brahmo Public Opinion*, 19 September 1878.
[26] *Ibid.*, 23 January 1879.

In subsequent years Bengali women proceeded to take advantage of opportunities in other regions that were unavailable in Bengal. Abala Das went to Madras to study medicine in 1882 because Calcutta Medical College had not yet opened its doors to female students.[27] In 1891, Aghorekamini Ray attended the Isabella Thoburn College in Lucknow for nine months of a teacher training course, before starting her own girls' school in the district of Bankipur, Bihar.[28]

The idea of travel as enjoyable in its own right, and of visiting another place for a holiday rather than for business, gained currency toward the end of the nineteenth century. The *bhadralok* gradually adopted the British way of seeing holidays as a time for rest and recreation in a different environment. The *pūjā* vacation was no longer only used as an opportunity to visit the ancestral village, but as the time to go away for a holiday. Sarasibala Ray described her excitement at the prospect of a trip to Murshidabad in the *pūjā* holidays of 1900, which she looked forward to as an escape from the normal conventions of the *antahpur*. The novelty of the experience led her to delight in the smallest details, and her account of the journey itself formed a substantial part of an article she wrote about it in *Antahpur*.[29]

The British idea of a holiday was linked to a belief in the beneficial effects of a change of air. In his autobiography, Surendranath Banerjea noted that admiration for the English practice of spending summer holidays at the seaside or on the Continent had led to the development of similar health and holiday resorts among the Bengalis. The annual British exodus to the hills was also a powerful impetus to the adoption of the practice by the *bhadralok*. Surendranath built a holiday house at Simultolla in 1898. Other Bengali hill stations were

[27] Sarala Debi, *Jibaner jharāpātā*, p. 216.
[28] P. C. Mozoomdar, *Strīcaritra*, "Sādhbī Aghorkāminī," pp. 164-171; Prakascandra Ray, *Aghor-prakās*, pp. 109-111; "Swargīya Aghorkāminī," *BP*, 6:1, 378 (July 1896).
[29] Sarasibala Ray, Chinsurah, "Mursidābād bhraman," *Antahpur*, 3, 9 (September 1900).

Madhupur, Deoghar, Baidyanath, and Darjeeling.[30] Giridi became very popular as a resort among the Brahmo community. There was a Brahmo Samaj there, and also in Darjeeling.[31]

Only a very few *bhadramahilā* were able to travel beyond India's borders, but this minority had a significance beyond its numbers. They performed the function of intermediaries, as informants for English women wanting to know more about the women of India, and for Indian women curious about the lives of women abroad. The first Bengali women to go to England and Europe were Christians from Anglicized families. For instance, Toru and Aru Dutt were taken to England and France by their parents as young girls.[32]

Women in England who took up the "cause" of Indian women were eager to see their Indian sisters. When Mary Carpenter came to Bengal in 1866, she visited Sasipada Banerjea and his wife in Burranagore. She invited them both to pay her a return visit in England, in order to raise interest there in the cause of female education in India. Sasipada's wife Rajkumari accompanied him to England in 1871. The social disapproval she incurred by going must have been very difficult to bear. They were stoned by caste Hindus when they paid a farewell visit to his ancestral home before departure. She spoke no English, and the fact that her visit was used by both her husband and Miss Carpenter to prove a theoretical point cannot have made her stay very enjoyable. Sasipada wrote to Miss Carpenter initially that "I accept your kind invitation to take her with me, not that she will be able to do

[30] Surendranath Banerjea, *A Nation in Making* (Madras, 1925), pp. 159-160; P. C. Ray, *Life and Experiences of a Bengali Chemist*, p. 86.

[31] Atarmani Debi and her family went to Giridi regularly from 1892. Amritalal Gupta, *Punyabatī nārī*, p. 47. Kalyan Dutt's parents were Brahmos. As a geologist, his father spent six months each year in the jungle, during which time his mother and the children remained in Calcutta or Giridi. Interview, Santiniketan, 16 November 1977.

[32] H. Das, *Life and Letters of Toru Dutt* (Oxford, 1921). Other Bengali Christian families who spent some time in England were those of Dr. Goodeve Chuckerbutty and Gyanendra Mohun Tagore (in his second marriage). See Jnanadanandini Debi, "Smritikathā" in Indira Debi Caudhurani, *Purātanī*, pp. 34-35, 38-39, 42.

anything to satisfy your friends, but only to show to my country women that they could have their due position in Society," and Miss Carpenter wrote of Rajkumari's visit in similar terms: "If she learned nothing here, the simple fact of her braving all difficulties and persecutions courageously to devote herself with her husband to take the first great step for the emancipation of her sisters is most important, and has a significance which can hardly be exaggerated."[33]

While he was still a student in London in 1863, Satyendranath Tagore had hoped that his wife Jnanadanandini would be the one to take that "first great step." His attitude, however, showed greater sensitivity to Jnanadanandini's feelings than Sasipada appeared to show for his wife. Satyendranath clearly missed his young bride very much and longed to see her, as well as wanting to show her the sights of England. For her own good, he wished to take her away from what he saw as the stifling atmosphere of the *zenana* and to introduce her to the freedom of English social life. His solicitude for her reaction and his excited plans for her stay in England were expressed in his letters to her. After he had written asking his father's permission to let her go to England, he wrote to her asking

> Jnanada, will you be unhappy at what I've written to father about you? I am not motivated by selfish desires, but am only thinking of your good. Doesn't it seem to you that our women are married too young, at an age where they don't know what marriage is, and they are not able to make an independent decision. . . . Won't we be happy when we enter into marriage with a new and free love? I have only said to father that I want to bring you to England for your education. . . . As much as you will progress yourself, your countrywomen will also benefit from your example.[34]

[33] Albion Banerji, *An Indian Pathfinder*, pp. 16-19.
[34] Letter from Satyendranath Tagore to his wife from London, 11 January 1864: "Strīr prati patra" in Indira Debi Caudhurani, *Purātanī*, pp. 48-50. See also the letters dated 18 January 1864, 18 February 1864, 26 February 1864, 8 March 1864, and 2 July 1864.

Debendranath refused permission on that occasion, but Satyendranath eventually succeeded in taking her out of the *antahpur* and away with him when he returned to India as an I.C.S. officer. He also fulfilled his dream of sending her to England. She went in 1877, with her three children. He was unable to accompany her, but joined her during her two-and-a-half year stay. Although one of her children died there, she appeared to have enjoyed her English sojourn. She was able to increase her proficiency in English, and even learned a little French. Her memories, recorded sixty years after the event, describe people and places in straightforward terms, with little impressionistic comment.[35] Her stay in England seems to have been of less benefit to her countrywomen than Satyendranath had hoped earlier. After her return, her main innovation was to introduce the celebration of "birthday parties" in the Tagore family and other Brahmo homes.[36]

Jnanadanandini's visit was not as controversial as that of Rajkumari Banerjea in 1871. The ground had already been broken, so orthodox indignation over the issue may have been dissipated. The Tagore family held such a commanding position in society that any breach of convention by one of its members was perhaps less subject to social disapproval or ostracism. However, her freedom to go to England showed that within the Tagore family the strict purdah enforced by Debendranath in the early 1860s had been substantially modified.

A small but growing number of Bengali women continued to visit England, for studies as well as for social purposes. The expense of such a journey restricted it to the wealthy *bhadralok* elite. Sunity Debi first visited England with her husband the maharaja of Cuch Behar on the occasion of Queen Victoria's Diamond Jubilee in 1897, and made a number of subsequent visits.[37] In 1886, Romesh Chunder Dutt's wife and four youngest children accompanied him to England. She ex-

---

[35] Jnanadanandini Debi, "Smritikathā," in Indira Debi Caudhurani, *Purātanī*, pp. 38-42: "Bilāter kathā."

[36] Sarala Debi, *Jībaner jharāpātā*, pp. 49-53.

[37] Sunity Devee, *The Autobiography of an Indian Princess* (London, 1921).

perienced at firsthand the difficulties of engaging servants there. Her husband hired a "lady's companion" for her to help her become accustomed to English life.[38] Kadambini Ganguly went to Edinburgh for further studies in medicine in 1893.[39] As early as 1884, three years after her graduation, six scholarships for Indian students to study in England had been announced. The *Bāmābodhinī Patrikā* had expressed the hope that they would be open to women because there were some suitably qualified Bengali ladies.[40]

The identity of the first Bengali woman to publish her impressions of England was hidden. Her book, *Inglande Banga Mahilā*, was published anonymously in 1885. Her account was interesting because she was a sharp and critical observer. She expressed her admiration for family relationships in England, from the freedom of choice in marriage partners to the relations between parents and children, and brothers and sisters, all of which she saw as characterized by equality and mutual respect. On the other hand, she criticized the English for their worship of self-interest and money. She noticed the class distinctions in English society and the contempt that forced the poor to act like "uncivilized beasts." Her balanced, objective account led at least one reviewer to claim that it was the best book of its kind in the Bengali language.[41]

The communications network built up by the British in India in the nineteenth century made travel more convenient for all. Among the *bhadralok*, the attraction of Calcutta as a cosmopolitan urban center, as well as the need to pursue employment opportunities in other parts of India, meant that

[38] R. C. Dutt, *Three Years in Europe 1868 to 1871 with an Account of Subsequent Visits to Europe in 1886 and 1893*, 4th ed. (Calcutta, 1896), pp. 107-112.

[39] *BP*, 5:1, 339 (April 1893).

[40] *BP*, 3:2, 236 (September 1884).

[41] "Critical Notices, Vernacular Literature. Inglande Banga Mahila, By a Bengali Lady. Calcutta 1885," in *CR*, 82, 164 (1886). The author was also praised in the *Report on Publications Issued and Registered in the Several Provinces of British India during the year 1885*, as penetrating "deeper into English life than the majority of Bengali writers of this class" (p. 35).

travel was an essential part of their lifestyle. As the ideal of the *bhadramahilā* as helpmeet became widespread, women also had to traverse these distances to be with their husbands. Extensive rail travel by women had become necessary for maintaining family contacts. Through travel, they gained a broader experience of life and an enhanced confidence in their ability to deal with the world outside the *antahpur*. Practical conditions of travel inevitably led to some modifications of purdah. On the level of ideas, travel to other regions and to other countries gave the *bhadramahilā* a wider perspective on their own lives by fostering a consciousness of nationhood and exposing them to alternative ways of life in which purdah was less central.

Dress reform and ideas of modesty

The purdah system of the early nineteenth century allowed some freedoms that seem to have been essential outlets in an otherwise rigid system. Ironically, it was these areas of freedom that proved most shocking to opponents of purdah. Most *bhadramahilā* were able to appear at public places such as religious shrines or bathing *ghāts* without self-consciousness. Although most of the bathing *ghāts* in Calcutta were designated for one sex or the other, some were mixed.[42] Kasi Mitra's *ghāt* was one such place, where modest Hindu women who would insist on covering their faces in the presence of men "shamelessly" bathed in public.[43] In the *mofussil* all women bathed at mixed *ghāts*.[44] The Dacca magistrate issued an order forbidding anyone to bathe in certain *ghāts* at certain hours, because of the "shameless way which some women used to go through the process."[45] What was interpreted by nine-

[42] Radharaman Mitra, "Gangār ghāt," *Oitihāsik*, 4 (January 1977), 50.

[43] Ambujasundari Dasi [Dasgupta], "Kalikātār Gangāsnān," *BP*, 8:1, 495 (November 1904). See also "Abagunthan," *BP*, 2:2, 42 (February 1867).

[44] "Strīlokdiger snān pranālī," *BP*, 5, 72 (August 1869). See Chapter One for discussion of the greater freedom of women in the *mofussil*.

[45] *Dāccā Darpan*, 27 April 1864 in *RNNB* 4 May 1864; *Dāccā Prakās*, 28 April 1864 in *RNNB* 11 May 1864 indignantly called for a repeal of the

teenth-century puritans as lasciviousness is more likely to have betokened a straightforward lack of inhibition about normal bodily functions. An article on mixed bathing in the *Bāmā-bodhinī Patrikā* revealed the author's own obsessions in describing how "obscenely" women rubbed their bodies and washed the saris they were wearing. It noted that these women would not dare go into mixed society when their clothes were dry, but would unabashedly expose themselves to the public gaze when they were wet and practically naked.[46] In a composition on "Modesty" in the *Bāmābodhinī Patrikā*, a young Brahmo girl was very censorious of the "immodesty" of women who wore thin saris, even in front of the servants, and who bathed, publicly. She recommended that servants should not be allowed to enter the house without permission and that baths should be taken secretly.[47]

Another aspect of purdah that presented itself as an affront to those outside the system was women's clothing. An upper-caste woman would habitually wear a sari of fine transparent muslin.[48] It was a single piece of cloth, draped around the body. No undergarments were worn.[49] The only other component of a woman's dress was her ornaments.[50] This clothing seemed well suited to the hot climate of Bengal, yet the wearing of such a revealing form of dress, even if only in front of male relatives, appears incongruous in a strict purdah system. However, it may have served to reinforce purdah by exposing female sexuality and then demarcating sharply the boundaries within which it could be expressed. Women themselves probably preferred their traditional dress for reasons of comfort,

---

order, which was only for the benefit of English ladies whose modesty was shocked at seeing nude bodies of natives in the water.

[46] "Strīlokdiger snān pranālī," *BP*, 72.

[47] Kumari Saudamini, "Lajjā," Bamabodhini Sabha, *Bāmāracanābalī. Prathom bhāg* (Calcutta, 1872), pp. 22-24.

[48] P. Chapman, *Hindoo Female Education*, p. 18.

[49] In the seventeenth century women wore a *kanchali* or bodice under the sari. Rich women also wore *ijar* as underwear. T. Raychaudhuri, *Bengal under Akbar and Jahangir*, p. 221. The women standing on the verandas of the *antahpur* in Plate 3 were wearing the "traditional" sari.

[50] S. C. Bose, *The Hindoos*, pp. 298-299.

but Bengali men were also reputed to have a "jealous repugnance" to "any alteration in female attire."[51] Once women came to symbolize tradition and continuity, any changes in their condition were forcefully resisted by men. As "reforms" in female dress would have enabled a lessening of purdah restrictions, the retention of traditional dress may have served to buttress the existing system.

The preoccupation with women's dress in the nineteenth century was a result of taking a fresh look at traditional clothing through the puritanical perspective of Calvinist Christianity and Victorian England. Compared with the thick gowns worn by English women, the type of sari worn by Bengali women appeared to leave them practically unclad. The Reverend Krishna Mohan Banerjea declared in 1841 that to wear such a garment in public would be a breach of decency.[52] Shib Chunder Bose expressed the view that "it would be a very desirable improvement in the way of decency to introduce among the Hindoo females of Bengal a stouter fabric for their garment in place of the present thin, flimsy, loose *sari*, without any other covering over it."[53] Another writer ventured to suggest that women could at least wear silk saris when they appeared in public. They were as beautiful as muslin, yet less transparent and more modest.[54]

A puritanical concern for decency was frequently expressed by the British in Bengal. In 1850 J.E.D. Bethune wrote to Lord Dalhousie that he made "occasional presents of dresses, when any of the little girls appeared in rather too primitive a state to correspond with my notions of decency."[55] To Annette Akroyd, even when women were well covered, "the very bundling of themselves up in swathes of muslin suggest immodesty."[56]

---

[51] K. M. Banerjea, *Native Female Education*, p. 80.
[52] *Ibid.*
[53] S. C. Bose, *The Hindoos*, p. 194.
[54] Jogendranarayan Ray, *Banga-mahilā*, p. 35.
[55] He was referring to pupils at the Bethune School. Letter of 29 March 1850, in J. A. Richey, ed., *Selections*, part II, p. 53.
[56] Akroyd-Beveridge Papers, *Diary and Notebook*, 26 December 1872.

7. Nirmala (1878- ?), eldest daughter of
Saratkumari Deb. Her blouse, chain, and locket
were typical of the style favored by educated
Bengali women.

Traditional dress was seen by the *bhadralok* as a stumbling
block in the way of reforming the condition of women. They
wished to promote female education and female participation
in public social events. Traditional dress had evolved within
a purdah society and was unsuitable for appearing in front
of men outside the intimate family circle. Women would need
to feel their dress provided protective covering if purdah were
to be discarded. Koilasbasini Debi, one of the first Hindu

246

female authors, thought it necessary for women to dress differently if they wanted to benefit fully from public education.[57]

The progressive *bhadralok*, especially the Brahmos, actively sought a solution to the problem. In 1865 the Brahmo young men's group, the Sangat Sabha, met to discuss a suitable form of dress for modern women. The problem was of immediate importance to them because they wanted to bring their wives into public society, but at that stage they were not able to form any definite conclusions.[58] In 1871, the Brahmo women's auxiliary group the Bama Hitaisini Sabha discussed the same topic. Some of the views presented by members were published in the *Bāmābodhinī Patrikā*.[59] One member, Saudamini Khastagir, said of traditional dress that

> if the kind of thin clothing customary here at present is worn the whole body can be seen clearly. This kind of shameless dress cannot be worn in polite society. If a person was preaching or lecturing in a place, it would be possible that if we wore this dress there we would not hear any of the fine talk. Considering this, the extent to which progressives object to this dress will be understood.

She considered the adoption of English dress, but dismissed the idea as too costly and impractical. Saudamini favored the costumes of Bombay and northwest India, but felt that direct adoption of their dress would confuse regional identity. Rajlaksmi Sen, another member of the Bama Hitaisini Sabha, expressed similar views. She noted that women dressing in the reformed style had to avoid not only "denationalization," but also the danger of being mistaken for prostitutes, some of whom wore chemises, jackets, and shoes with their saris. Her idea was for a *bhadramahilā* to be distinguished from them by wearing an additional *cādar*, or wrap, covering her from

[57] Koilasbasini Debi, *Hindu mahilāganer hīnābasthā*, p. 66.

[58] *BP*, 1:2, 17 (January 1865).

[59] Letters from Saudamini Khastagir and Rajlaksmi Sen, and editorial comment, in "Bangānganāganer paricchad," *BP*, 8, 97 (September 1871).

head to foot. The editor made the final recommendation for the reformed dress:

> At home: *ijār* (short trousers) *pirān* (blouse) and sari; or long *pirān* and sari
>
> Outside: *ijār*, *pirān* and sari, *cādar*, *pyjāmā* and shoes (optional)

Two months later, a woman from Bombay wrote to the editor of the *Bāmābodhinī Patrikā* giving her views on dress reform. The anonymous correspondent was clearly identifiable as Jnanadanandini Debi, one of the first Bengali women to act as official hostess at public functions hosted by her husband. The dress question was therefore of direct practical relevance for her. Her suggestion was to improvise a new form of dress that drew inspiration from diverse groups, including the English, Muslims, and Bengalis, which would take on a distinct Bengali identity if all Bengali women started wearing it. She said that many Calcutta women, when visiting each other, had already adopted a dress very similar to that suggested in the *Bāmābodhinī Patrikā*. For herself, she wore shoes, stockings, bodice (*āngiyā kācali*), blouse (*jāmā*) and a short skirt (*ghāgharā*) or *ijār* with a sari over the top at home, and a *cādar* covering her head in addition when she went out. As women may have had difficulty envisaging all the garments she described and may have felt uncertain as to how to wear them, she offered to make a set for anyone who was interested, or to send them a picture of how the clothes should be worn.[60] The style she invented became known as the "Brahmika sari."[61]

Increasingly women adapted their clothing along the lines suggested, although the quest for a definitive style continued throughout the century. An advertisement in the *New Dispensation* in 1881 under the heading "Woman's Dress" asked readers, "Have you any idea as to what the reformed Hindu

---

[60] "Bangānganāganer paricchad," Bāmāracanā, *BP*, 8, 99 (November 1871).
[61] Sarala Debi, *Jībaner jharāpātā*, pp. 53-54. Plates 6, 8 and 9 all show women wearing the "Brahmika sari."

woman's dress ought to be? Put it upon paper; if possible, draw and paint the design and let us see it. Decent not costly."[62]

The direct adoption of European dress, favored by some, was seen to have numerous drawbacks. It was too costly, as well as being too bulky for the average Bengali home.[63] Some men objected to it on the grounds of immodesty, with reference to the amount of bare flesh exposed by a low-cut evening gown.[64] Others noted its unhealthy aspect, including the fact that tight lacing was coming under attack from doctors in England.[65] Bengali Christian women were the only group who wholeheartedly adopted English dress.[66] Even Annette Akroyd, a staunch opponent of the traditional sari, said that she had no temptation to put her girls into English dress because it made them look "irretrievably common."[67]

The model for a reformed dress was derived from other parts of India rather than from England, and was a result of the wide exposure to other Indian regional cultures gained through travel. As early as 1865, it was noted in a news item in the *Bāmābodhinī Patrikā* that women in western India were able to move around with greater freedom because they had suitable clothes.[68] A lady writing from Bombay in 1904 described in detail the different modes of dress she saw there. Women draped their saris differently, and wore a jacket called a *celi* underneath. They wore brighter colors than Bengalis, and rich women always wore silk saris. Parsi women wore

---

[62] *New Dispensation*, 31 March 1881.

[63] "Bangānganāganer paricchad," *BP*, 97.

[64] See *Sanjībanī*, 20 January 1894 in *RNNB* 27 January 1894; and P. C. Mozoomdar, "The Emancipation of Women in Bengal," *CR*, 118, 236 (April 1904).

[65] "Mahilār paricchad," *Antahpur*, 4, 6 (July 1901). See also P. H. Chavasse, *Counsel to a Mother*, p. 135, on the ill effects of tight lacing. He said that it caused diseases of the lungs, fainting, indigestion, offensive breath, purple complexion, red noses, impurities of the blood, and constipation.

[66] A few Anglicized Hindu and Brahmo *bhadramahilā* also wore gowns. Monomohan Ghose's wife was one of these. Sarala Debi, *Jībaner jharāpātā*, p. 53.

[67] Akroyd-Beveridge Papers: letter to Fanny Mowatt, 10 February 1874.

[68] *BP*, 1:2, 17 (January 1865).

trousers and a long shirt underneath, with a silk sari and jacket on top, and shoes. On their heads they wore a white cloth or handkerchief.[69] The Parsi woman's dress inspired Jnanadanandini's "Brahmika sari."[70] Her design and its popularity transcended regional boundaries. It could even be said to have fostered a sense of national awareness by creating a fashion for Bengal that drew its inspiration from western India, and that eventually came into vogue all over the country.[71]

As the first group to take up the reformed dress, Brahmo women would initially have been clearly distinguishable from the Hindu *bhadramahilā* by their clothing. In his autobiography, Brahmo Gurucharan Mahalanabis recalled his quest for a reformed mode of dress for his wife. As it used to cost him two rupees or so to send her to weekly meetings of the Brahmika Samaj, even though it was within walking distance of their home, it struck him as unfair that his wife was not free to walk there. After discussing the matter with a group of friends, he concluded that the chief obstacle to her mobility was her dress. He decided to get her to wear a chemise, jacket, and full-length *cādar* over her sari, as well as shoes. Wearing "pantaloons" himself, he then walked with her to the Brahmika Samaj, where they were greeted with surprise by all the women present. Still uncertain, he later got her to wear gown, boots, and veil in the manner of a Bengali Christian friend. This caught on among other Brahmos, and Bijoy Krishna Goswami made his wife follow suit. He sold a gold amulet of hers to buy her a gown, which she wore back to her home in Santipur. Being only eleven or twelve years old at the time, she was too young to be embarrassed by the stir she caused among her relatives, who mistook her for a *memsaheb*. Even Keshub Chunder Sen's mother was surprised by this kind of Anglicized garb, and once asked Gurucharan's wife if that was the dress of her region in East Bengal.[72]

[69] "Patra," *BP*, 8:1, 495 (November 1904).
[70] "Mahilār paricchad," *Antahpur*, 4, 6; Gurucharan Mahalanabis, *Ātmakathā*, pp. 101-102.
[71] Sarala Debi noted this. *Jībaner jharāpātā*, p. 54.
[72] Gurucharan Mahalanabis, *Ātmakathā*, pp. 100-104.

After a visit to Bombay, Keshub Chunder Sen introduced a new form of dress to the Bharat Ashram. He proposed that women wear sari, chemise, and jacket at home, with the addition of a petticoat and piece of net over the hair for going out. Harasundari Datta, who was living in the Bharat Ashram at the time, felt that petticoats were an inessential extra expense for middle-class families.[73] Many women must have shared her objection to the additional cost of the new items of clothing, which would have made a considerable difference to the family budget.

Annette Akroyd objected to the reformed mode of dress because she sensed that women's normal aesthetic judgments foundered when dealing with an unfamiliar form, and her puritanism remained unsatisfied with the level of decency attained. She remarked that "the prevalent fashion among those who are emancipated at all, of placing a wreath of flowers over the veil, looks very tawdry and is most unbecoming. There must be a decided change too in at any rate the lower garments."[74] She, too, urged the adoption of petticoats, and tried to devise a new kind of undergarment that would be "from the shoulders, all in one piece." She also cut squares of Brussels net for girls to cover their heads with when going out, and made them wear boots. Despite her awareness of the dangers of "denationalization," her reforms were not generally well received because they were too Anglicized. Her concept of modesty was an alien imposition for many women. For instance, a new pupil at the Banga Mahila Bidyalaya was depressed by the thought that emancipation seemed to consist in always wearing a petticoat. The girls' resistance to her reforms, and the realization that her own views on the subject were not shared by many, shook Miss Akroyd's customary confidence and complacency. In 1873 she visited the wife of Ananda Mohan Bose, who was sick at home. She found her dressed in muslin "swathing" with no shoes or stockings, her hair down, and surrounded by young men. Afterwards she

[73] Harasundari Datta, *Swargīya Srīnāth Datter*, pp. 158-160.

[74] Akroyd-Beveridge papers, *Diary and Notebook*, entries for 26 December, 27 December, 28 December 1872.

wrote to her sister with genuine puzzlement that "I am thrown back on radical questions of modesty and delicacy often, and have to ask myself why are such sights so shocking to me?" However, she felt that she had made some progress. She had become "so accustomed to dhutie that when properly worn I do not notice it."[75]

Non-Brahmo women did not begin to change their dress habits on a large scale until the end of the century. The chemise was worn mainly by city women, and by a few in the *mofussil*, but was not regarded as essential.[76] Older women, especially, resisted the imposition of a less comfortable form of dress. Enthusiasm among promoters of dress reform sometimes reached absurd proportions. At one stage progressive young men were said to have taken bodices and chemises home to their old mothers and grandmothers in the villages to wear while doing their daily round of domestic duties.[77]

There was some discussion on the wearing of jewelry as a part of dress reform. Apparently rich ladies would sometimes wear six or seven pounds of gold ornaments as an indication of their wealth and status. Shib Chunder Bose noted, however, that by 1881 the spread of English education had "improved" their taste, creating a preference for elegance over weight.[78] Newspapers were filled with advertisements for the new type of jewelry. Hamilton's, the most famous jewelers in Calcutta, had illustrated advertisements of the latest fashions, including dangling gold earrings from 20 to 40 rupees, broad gold band bracelets from 120 to 200, and engraved gold lockets from 16 to 50 rupees.[79]

[75] *Ibid.*, letters to Fanny Mowatt: 20 March 1873, 20 October 1873, 10 February 1874.

[76] S. C. Bose, *The Hindoos*, p. 194; Jogendranarayan Ray, *Banga-mahilā*, p. 37; *Paricārikā*, 1, 7 (December 1878).

[77] *Sandhyā*, 9 May 1905 in *RNNB* 13 May 1905.

[78] The new taste showed a preference for ornaments of "delicate diamond cut workmanship" set with pearls and precious stones rather than for old-fashioned solid gold ornaments. S. C. Bose, *The Hindoos*, pp. 298-299.

[79] Advertisements in *Liberal and New Dispensation*, 1882-1884. See the chain and locket worn by Nirmala Deb in Plate 7. For the rich, there were far more expensive items. Sarala Debi was given a diamond and ruby necklace

8. Saudamin Mozoomdar (1843-1931), wife of Brahmo
missionary Protap Chunder Mozoomdar, wearing the "reformed
dress" of the *bhadramahilā*. Note the Brahmo style of
draping the sari; the long-sleeved, high-necked blouse;
the headcloth, and the shoes.

Brahmos, with their puritanical and thrifty habits, disapproved of the traditional practice of investing in ornaments and ostentatiously wearing them as a visible proof of wealth.[80] An article in the *Bāmābodhinī Patrikā* in 1865 suggested alternative forms of investment—in shares, banknotes, railway holdings, or land. It added that the wearing of so many ornaments was not only unsafe but also unhealthy, because it stopped the blood circulation.[81] The editor of *Somprakās* concurred with this disapproval, and called on managers of girls' schools to desist from giving jewelry to school girls as prizes.[82] It was said that women preferred the "immodesty" of traditional dress because of a desire to display their ornaments, and they were reminded that with English dress they still had their necks, ears, feet, and even possibly parts of their arms exposed as areas for display.[83] Swarnamayi Gupta attempted a much deeper analysis of the reasons behind women's partiality for ornaments. She contended that in the present state of society husbands soon lost interest in their less educated wives, and women felt that they could only retain their husbands' affections by enhancing their own physical attractions with the help of ornaments. In addition, she pointed out that ornaments were often a woman's sole source of support after the death of her husband, and therefore meant far more to her than a mere item of adornment.[84]

Another debated aspect of dress reform was the wearing of shoes. Orthodox women never wore shoes. Apart from the practical consideration that in a hot climate wearing shoes and stockings inside the house was unnecessary, shoes were

---

with a matching pair of bracelets worth 1,000 rupees, from the shop next door to Hamilton's. Sarala Debi, *Jībaner jharāpātā*, p. 80.

[80] P. C. Mozoomdar, *Strīcaritra*, p. 87.

[81] "Alangkār paridhān," *BP*, 2:1, 23 (July 1865).

[82] *Somprakās*, 25 March 1867 in *RNNB* 30 March 1867.

[83] Jogendranarayan Ray, *Banga-mahilā*, p. 37; the editor of *Somprakās, ibid.*, said that the wish to exhibit their jewels led women to wear such flimsy clothes.

[84] Swarnamayi Gupta, *Ūsā-cintā*, pp. 86-88.

associated with immoral women.[85] Shoes would also have been a further costly addition to the family budget. In 1881, ladies' plain elastic-sided boots were advertised for four to six rupees, and kid leather or glove-kid boots sold for ten to fifteen rupees.[86]

However, most dress reformers, with their Anglicized perspective, insisted that women be taught to wear shoes and stockings. To middle-class Victorians such as Annette Akroyd, bare feet were a sign of barbarism. The first time she saw Jaganmohini Sen, dressed in the style of a well-to-do Hindu *bhadramahilā*, she remarked that she was "dressed like a poor wife of some uncultivated Hindoo—in red silk wrapper, no shoes and stockings, and a barbaric display of jewels, necklaces, chains, great earrings etc."[87]

Jnanadanandini Debi wrote in the *Bāmābodhinī Patrikā* that from the point of hygiene shoes might be necessary, but not stockings. The editor added that the wearing of shoes was optional. He said that if women did not have to do much walking outside, then stockings covered with a strong "preserver" would be sufficient to keep the feet clean.[88] Another writer noted that Hindu ladies outside Bengal had adopted the practice of evening walks, for which shoes and stockings were essential for beauty and comfort.[89] Others were of the opinion that shoes and stockings were unnecessary.[90] It was said in praise of Sarojini Ghose that she had never worn shoes in her life, a proof of her simplicity and orthodoxy.[91]

During the nineteenth century, wearing shoes was a dis-

---

[85] The distinction was made in ancient literature and sculpture, where shoes were interpreted as a sign that women did not keep to the home. See M. M. Urquhart, *Women of Bengal*, pp. 96-99.

[86] *Indian Mirror*, 18 August 1881.

[87] Akroyd-Beveridge Papers, *Diary and Notebook*, 27 December 1872. At a later date her reaction was more mellow. Keshub Chunder Sen and his wife dined with her on 6 March 1873, and she commented that Jaganmohini "looked very pretty in her saree, but not wearing shoes or stockings."

[88] "Bangānganāganer paricchad," *BP*, 99.

[89] "Bangīya Hindumahilār paricchad," *BP*, 7:2, 443 (December 1901).

[90] Jogendranarayan Ray, *Banga-mahilā*, p. 38.

[91] Renuka Ghose, *Sarojinī-carit*, p. 34.

tinctive trait of the Brahmo *bhadramahilā*. Punyalata Cakrabarti recounted that when her mother, a Brahmo, went to her in-laws' house as a young bride, they expected her to wear shoes. They told her she was free to follow her own customs, but she eventually convinced them that she was used to going barefoot and happy to do so.[92] Nalinibala Chaudhuri, a Brahmo living in Assam at the turn of the century, was criticized for being a *memsaheb* because she wore shoes. She must have been an imposing sight—she had to wear men's boots because ladies' shoes were only available in Calcutta.[93]

Dress reform was initiated by Bengali men, under the influence of alien concepts of modesty, but was soon taken up by women themselves as they perceived that it was a necessary prelude to greater freedom from the restrictions of purdah. Although initially limited to a small group, the new form of dress was gradually adopted by all middle-class women.

Participation in public society

One of the most heated controversies concerning the *bhadramahilā* in the nineteenth century was over their role in public society. Opponents of the breaking of purdah argued that Bengali society—Bengali men—were unable to cope with the social freedom of women. Debate over the issue showed a confusion of thought. The repression of sexuality inherent in the institution of purdah fostered a belief in the dangerous effects of uncontrolled female sexuality. It was feared that women's entry into male society would unleash pent-up sexual frustrations: the threatening specter of the powerful sexual temptress. On the other hand, the modest purdah woman was seen as needing protection from male lust. There was a general apprehension that since Hindu males were unaccustomed to female society, they had no experience of resisting temptation, and would respond to the social presence of women with

[92] Punyalata Cakrabarti, *Chele belār din guli*, p. 123.
[93] Interview with her daughter, Manika Ray, Calcutta, 14 February 1978.

obscenity.[94] One writer believed that the English language did not have the vocabulary of obscenity available to Hindus, and that hence English women did not face the same obstacles in entering society. The same writer also argued, more credibly, that the European concept of chivalry and the corresponding attitude of respectful deference to women in acknowledgment of their weakness was unknown in India.[95]

Resistance to any change in strict purdah was not only a reflection of male jealousy and possessiveness, but showed a fear of widespread social disruption. The immediate introduction of women into traditionally male social groups was feared because there were no guidelines for social behavior in such situations. New skills were required to mix socially with women. In traditional Bengali society the *bhadralok* only had contact with women as relatives or prostitutes. Mixed society put men and women in an unprecedented relationship to each other, as friends and acquaintances rather than kin, and required new attitudes and behavioral adjustments.

A growing number of *bhadralok* were eager to see the establishment of freer social mixing between the sexes, but views differed as to how this should be achieved. A sketch on "Quarrelsome Reformers" in 1881 caricatured the differences. One speaker in the *āddā* of young *bhadralok* made a spirited speech calling for women to be brought into the streets, the squares, railway stations, zoological gardens, and the Agricultural Exhibition. They were also to ride horses and bicycles, skate, dance, jump, and practice gymnastics. The next speaker rejected these proposals, but wanted women to have public and political lives—"to write, memorialize, and obtain their rights." The author's sympathies lay with the final speaker:

> Those who by violence want to force out the Hindu woman into public life offend against that very law of liberty which they plead for in their reforms. She does *not* want

[94] "Naranārī," *BP*, 8, 115 (March 1873).
[95] "Edeśīya bāmāganer bahirbhraman": letter from Janakinath Sarkar, *BP*, 8, 98 (October 1871).

to mix with men promiscuously. She is naturally bashful and retiring. Admitting for argument's sake she does want to mix as freely with men, and in public life, as is the custom in other parts of the world, may I ask what protection there is for her from those insults which are sure to be heaped upon her by unprincipled men? Allow me to ask you how many of our countrymen know due respect for the other sex; how many of them can look or think chastely about them? ... I would rather mistake on the side of conservatism, than on the side of radicalism where the question of woman's moral safety is concerned. I would not trust every big official into my household, I would not trust every reformer into the presence of my wife and sister. But I would introduce good men like Christian Missionaries, and others like them, whether Hindu or European, most gladly to see the ladies of my house.[96]

Progressive *bhadralok* were in broad agreement about the low state of segregated male society, but looked to the moral influence of women to bring about a change in it. They believed that women's presence was uplifting and ennobling, and hoped that the presence of women at social occasions would help to "eradicate those vices which a partial adoption of European ideas has introduced," such as intemperance.[97]

The volume of discussion tended to outstrip the number of occasions on which women did appear in mixed society. In 1864, a gentleman discussing Girish Chunder Ghose's lecture to the Bethune Society on "The Bengali at Home" confidently said that no "respectable native" had yet ventured to bring his female relatives into male society or to any public places of amusement. In countering this claim, the Unitarian Reverend C.H.A. Dall could only state that Vidyasagar had taken

[96] "Quarrelsome Reformers. A Social Sketch," *Theistic Quarterly Review*, 6-7 (January 1881), 27-34.
[97] Monomohan Ghose, "The Effects of English Education upon Bengali Society," Lecture to the Bethune Society 29 April 1869, in *Proceedings*, p. 271.

his mother to Mr. Hudson's studio to have her portrait painted.[98] In fact, there had been at least one instance prior to this, with major ramifications. To mark his appointment as *ācārya* in the Brahmo Samaj in 1862, Keshub Chunder Sen had taken his young wife to a function at the home of Debendranath Tagore. They were ostracized from the family home for this offense, and had to take refuge in the Tagore household for some time.[99]

The first noteworthy social occasion on a larger scale was the tea party given by Mary Carpenter on her first visit to Calcutta in 1866. Keshub Chunder Sen organized the event, but his preoccupation with the broader social significance of the party led him to overlook some minor details. He had ordered a carriage to pick up all the invited guests, but forgot to send it for his own wife, who was left alone and in tears. The situation was saved when someone found her, and arranged transport. About sixteen Brahmikas and their husbands were present. Ladies were served tea and coffee, and entertained by Miss Carpenter. Although two English ladies had been invited as interpreters, there was some difficulty in communication. Miss Carpenter wrote that

I had relied on various albums and scrap-books which I had brought with me, but when I observed a lady look at one upside down, without any possibility on my part to make her understand its meaning, a different mode of proceeding was evidently necessary. I therefore explained a portfolio of prints and drawings to a circle of gentlemen, and then requested them to do the same to the ladies. This was accomplished satisfactorily. Then the England-returned daughter of their host, Bengali Christian Dr. Goodeve Chuckerbutty, played the piano and sang for the guests, after which they dispersed.[100]

[98] Meeting of the Bethune Society, 14 January 1864, *ibid.*, p. lviii.

[99] [Priyanath Mallik], *Brahma-nandinī*, pp. 42-48. They had also broken caste by dining with the Tagores, who were Pirali Brahmins.

[100] Accounts of the event were given in Mary Carpenter, *Six Months*, pp. 183-184, entry for 26 November 1866; [Priyanath Mallik], *Brahma-nandinī*, pp. 105-107; "Miss Mary Carpenter," *BP*, 2:2, 41 (January 1867).

Miss Carpenter also witnessed Jnanadanandini Debi's presentation to Lady Lawrence at a drawing-room reception at
Government House. Jnanadanandini showed exceptional
courage in attending the function alone, as her husband was
ill. The Tagore family was opposed to her going. Even Mary
Carpenter recognized that the occasion would have been a
"trying ordeal" for her, although she showed "great self-pos-
session" throughout. It may have been some consolation to
her to know that "her demeanour and appearance were the
objects of much admiration, and the event was considered an
important one in social progress."[101]

Even among the Brahmos there were differences of opinion
as to the degree of social freedom to be permitted. During the
1860s women held their own prayer meetings, separate from
those of men.[102] By the 1870s, men and women in the Bharat
Ashram mixed freely, establishing the atmosphere of a large
family wherein such closeness was acceptable. However in a
public, formal event such as the weekly service, women still
sat behind a curtain, maintaining purdah. This seemed anomalous to one sector within the Brahmo Samaj, often referred
to as the "female emancipationists." Taking the principle of
religious equality literally, Annada Charan Khastagir and Durga
Mohan Das dared to sit with the women of their families in
the general body of the congregation. Conservatives reacted
strongly, and accused the ladies involved of acting out of a
"love of ostentation." The inability of others to see that their
action stemmed from a "genuine result of the most natural
impulse and the most valued privilege of the human mind—
love of personal liberty," forced them to secede and establish
a rival congregation.[103] Keshub Chunder Sen kept out of the
debate by maintaining that he did not want to offend the

[101] M. Carpenter, *Six Months*, p. 220; Jnanadanandini Debi, "Smritikathā"
in Indira Debi Caudhurani, *Purātanī*, p. 33.
[102] M. Carpenter, *Six Months*, p. 179. She described a women's prayer
meeting that she attended in Calcutta on 24 November 1866.
[103] See Ananda Mohan Bose's comments on the situation, which took place
while he was studying in England, in a letter to S. D. Collet cited in H. C.
Sarkar, *Ananda Mohan Bose*, pp. 31-32.

sensibilities of any part of the congregation. He eventually intervened in order to restore harmony, and conceded to the demands of the "female emancipationists" by reserving seats for women within the main body of the *mandir*. He told his followers that he believed in the equality of men and women, and that as mixed worship had been proven possible in the west there was no reason why it should not be acceptable in India.[104]

Initially, women's emergence into society was characterized by sporadic attendance at quasi-official public functions. Through this, the elite of the *bhadramahilā* became familiar with the etiquette of English society, although it remained alien to them. Whereas social etiquette was used by English women as a way of preserving class distinctions and asserting status in a rapidly changing society, in Bengal Anglicized social graces were a veneer, and were not part of the structure of social relationships. Despite the fact that the adoption of English manners, especially among the lower-income *bhadralok*, was considered by conservative Hindus to be an affectation and was a subject of ridicule, the "veneer" was a significant social phenomenon. It represented the aspirations of a sizable sector of the *bhadralok* and differentiated them from the surrounding society. Variations in practice thus did not matter, as they did in England, because the assumption of Anglicized habits in itself symbolized social position. In that way it functioned as a new and visible sign of social classification, grafted on to the symbols and indicators of hierarchical rank that were an inherent and universally understood part of traditional social organization.

Attempts were made to familiarize women with English etiquette in order to train them for the role of official hostess and helpmeet. Part of Annette Akroyd's socialization of the girls in her boarding school was to teach them those skills

---

[104] P. C. Mozoomdar had questioned whether the purity of religious worship could be maintained if women were present. Gurucharan Mahalanabis, *Ātmakathā*, pp. 85-87. All histories of the Brahmo Samaj give an account of the "Mandir seating controversy."

which she considered necessary for entry into society, such as eating at table with knives and forks. She invited English women to dine with the girls, and took them to public social functions. In July 1874 she took them to dine with Mrs. Hobhouse, and in January 1875 to an entertainment arranged by her.[105] In February 1876 about a dozen Brahmikas attended another of Mrs. Hobhouse's entertainments, where there was music and a magic lantern show.[106] Miss Akroyd also introduced her girls to the English institution of paying "calls"— the social ritual of visiting people as a planned event in a semiformal manner.

This kind of social interaction was confined to a small group, most of whom were Brahmos. Orthodox society remained disapproving, and attendance at such gatherings was regarded unfavorably. In the Bose versus Bose adultery case of 1878, Binodini, one of the accused, vowed at the trial that she had always been a *pardānasīn*. Although she was an ex-pupil of Miss Akroyd's school, she made a point of swearing that she had never heard of Lady [sic] Hobhouse or been to her garden party. She was queried closely on this—"Be careful, did you not go with Miss Akroyd to Lady Hobhouse"—but still denied it.[107] It was significant that her alleged attendance at public social functions was used as evidence against her, and that she claimed to be a *pardānasīn* in order to establish her good character.

Mixed social events continued, and even increased, despite public disapproval. The Anglicized nature of these occasions persisted, however, as the purpose of discarding purdah was often to facilitate dealings with English colleagues and superiors. The *bhadralok* realized the advantage of having wives who were a social asset. To the British, the presence of women at social functions was such an indicator of "civilization" that mixed gatherings were seen as a means of bridging the cultural

[105] Akroyd-Beveridge Papers, *Pocket Diaries* 1873, 1874, 1875; letter to Fanny Mowatt 20 March 1873.
[106] *IMS*, 13 February 1876.
[107] *Indian Mirror*, 13 August 1878.

gap between English and Bengalis, and of reducing racial tension. The *Brahmo Public Opinion* in December 1879 reported a "small but select social gathering" of native ladies and gentlemen, some girls from Bethune School, and some Europeans at the house of Sir Richard Garth, the chief justice. All sat at the supper table with no distinction of race or color—"The closer, warmer and freer such intercourse becomes, the better for the mutual understanding of the two races."[108]

The rise of nationalism temporarily arrested this kind of social interaction between the two races, and gave new impetus to the defenders of purdah. The wife of the lieutenant-governor of Bengal, Lady Fraser, had planned a purdah party at Belvedere to mark the visit of the prince and princess of Wales at the end of 1905. The press made a concerted effort to isolate and ostracize anyone who agreed to send their womenfolk to the function. Objections were varied. It was said that ladies would lose their modesty and be shamed by such "reckless exposure"; that they would be embarrassed at their awkwardness in the midst of European ladies; that their presence would go against long-established social usage, and, finally, that in the political context of the recent partition of Bengal, their attendance would be an act of disloyalty. The men and women involved on this occasion were not the usual targets of public ridicule, the Brahmo "emancipationists," but were scions of established Hindu families. Twenty-five women did attend, including members of the families of Kumar Girindra Narain Deb, grandson of Raja Radakhanta Deb; and of Raja Binay Krishna of the Sovabazar Raj, and the wife of Pandit Haraprasad Sastri.[109] However, the correspondence between the lieutenant-governor, Sir Andrew Fraser, and Sir Gooroodass Banerjee on the subject of the purdah party provides an interesting reminder that in some circles any innovation was still firmly resisted. The lieutenant-governor wrote to Sir Gooroodass on 9 September 1905, with details of the

[108] *Brahmo Public Opinion*, 25 December 1879.
[109] See *RNNB* for November and December 1905, and January 1906.

purdah arrangements that had been made. Sir Gooroodass's reply made it clear that no matter how strictly it was to be observed, it was not possible for a *zenana* Hindu lady to attend a public party of this nature. She was only able to visit places of pilgrimage or houses of near relatives and intimate neighbors.[110]

By the end of the century, the *bhadralok* elite had created a social circle of their own, in which women were free from many of the conventional restrictions on their behavior. For instance, Sarala Ray, wife of Professor P. K. Ray and daughter of "female emancipationist" Durga Mohan Das used to hold a kind of "salon" at her home, which was a meeting place for prominent social and political figures from all over India. She was also one of the first women to smoke publicly.[111] Freedom was also greater in proportion to the distance from one's immediate social context. When Romesh Chunder Dutt's daughters visited him in Baroda in 1905, he entertained them with tennis and badminton parties, concerts, songs, and picnics.[112] Among the elite, social interaction took a very westernized form, in imitation of the British in India. The maharani of Cuch Behar, daughter of Keshub Chunder Sen, was regarded by the British as a "popular and successful hostess," but Hindus disliked her adoption of the public, Anglicized role of official hostess. Although she had not grown up in purdah, after marriage the maharaja would not allow her to meet any Indian men whose own wives were still *pardānasīn*. Her guests were therefore mainly English people and some Brahmos.[113]

The new career requirements of the *bhadralok* working for the British meant that different models of social behavior were increasingly adopted, even at lower levels. Greater social mix-

[110] Bhola Chatterji, *Sir Gooroodass Banerjee and His Times*, unpublished monograph, Indian Statistical Institute (Calcutta, 1976), pp. 317-320.

[111] Sarala Ray Centenary Committee, *Sarala Ray*, p. 106.

[112] J. N. Gupta, *Life and Work of Romesh Chunder Dutt* (London, 1911), p. 418.

[113] Sunity Devee, *Autobiography*, p. 80; Mrs. E. F. Chapman, *Sketches*, pp. 88-89.

ing was also taking place on a wider scale in nonofficial circles. Hospitality had always been part of a Hindu woman's duties. The Brahmos and progressive *bhadralok* transformed this obligation. A modern woman not only cooked for her husband's guests, but entertained them with her conversation, as well. She would also receive hospitality by attending functions at the homes of his friends and colleagues. In 1866, Saudamini Ray's attendance at a party given to repay the hospitality of European officials by her husband, *zamindar* Rakhal Chandra Ray, created a scandal even among the Brahmos.[114] Her presence was so exceptional that it was brought to the attention of the lieutenant-governor, Sir Cecil Beadon, who expressed his admiration. By the turn of the century, Sarojini Ghose, wife of a jute merchant in East Bengal, willingly gave hospitality to Muslim and European colleagues of her husband in her own home.[115] Annapurna Debi, wife of Dr. Srimanta Cattopadhyay of Bogura, participated fully in her husband's social circle. She was an intelligent woman, with an inquiring mind, who took advantage of her husband's social position to broaden her horizons. When well-known writers came to Bogura she invited them to her house and discussed literature with them. She knew all the educated men in the town, from the deputy magistrate to the schoolteachers, and used to talk with them about literary, religious, and social topics. She had interesting discussions with such eminent visitors as Surendranath Banerjea and Dwarkanath Ganguly.[116]

Emergence from purdah was a corollary of female education. Women who attended schools were inevitably unable to maintain strict purdah. In addition, it was proposed that women should be taken on organized excursions to public places in order to extend their general knowledge. Keshub Chunder Sen was one of the first to advocate this kind of education, con-

[114] Rakhal Chandra Ray, *Jīban bindu*, pp. 79-83. Apparently Keshub Chunder Sen disapproved. See Sibnath Sastri, *History of the Brahmo Samaj*, p. 130.

[115] Renuka Ghose, *Sarojinī-carit*, pp. 97-98.

[116] Amritalal Gupta, *Punyabatī nārī*, pp. 82-83.

sciously modeling his program on the activities of working men's institutes in England. He proposed that

> Competent and experienced English ladies may occasionally invite together five and twenty native ladies and proceed with them to such places as the Asiatic Museum and Botanical Gardens, and explain to them the varied and interesting objects that are to be found there, for the benefit of their minds and hearts, with illustrations. Such practical lessons will do them immense good, which no mere amount of book knowledge will ever be able to achieve.[117]

Keshub put his plans into action, and made a special appointment for pupils of the Native Ladies' Normal School and other *bhadramahilā* to visit the Asiatic Museum.[118] Ordinarily women were admitted to the museum, but *bhadramahilā* did not go.[119] In 1876 more than a dozen Brahmo women were taken to the Art Gallery, at a time when it was closed to the rest of the public.[120] Keshub's pioneering efforts were followed by other organizers of cultural events and institutions. A fine art exhibition in 1879 advertised that Friday was reserved as viewing time for *zenanas*, at a cost of four annas per person. Mrs. Monomohini Wheeler, inspectress of schools, was to be present to explain the subjects of the pictures "to those whom the English catalogue may not enlighten."[121] The appearance of women at public events without incident increased confidence that modifications in purdah could be incorporated into the changing social structure without ill effects. At the First International Exhibition in Calcutta in 1884, purdah arrange-

[117] Keshub Chunder Sen, "The Improvement of Indian Women," delivered to the Bengal Social Science Association, 24 February 1871, in B. Dutt Gupta, *Sociology in India*, Appendix V, p. 216.

[118] *BP*, 6, 92 (April 1871).

[119] A report in *BP*, 7, 95 (July 1871) mentioned that a large number of visitors to the picture gallery of the Asiatic Museum were women, but not *bhadramahilā*.

[120] *IMS*, 7 May 1876.

[121] *Ibid.*, 2 February 1879.

ments were made, but when women found that they could enter among general visitors without being molested or annoyed, they freely did so. Fifty thousand native ladies visited the exhibition.[122]

While social arrangements were gradually changing in this manner, groups that set out with the specific purpose of challenging traditional social mores were subjected to public ridicule. In 1892, a group of 125 Brahmo men, with 30 women and 25 children, went to the Botanical Gardens "for purposes of prayer." A few of the men were assaulted by some drunken *darwans*, who used obscene language within hearing of the party. The English officer in charge of the gardens took no notice of the Brahmo complaint. Public sympathy for the Brahmos was not forthcoming, either. The *Bangabāsī* declared that "the Brahmos have suffered disgrace for taking their women with them to the Botanical Gardens." Following the incident, a writer in the *Doinik-O-Samācār Candrikā* addressed "a few words of advice" to Brahmo women:

> The Brahmos ought not to go anywhere and everywhere to hold religious service. They have their Samaj building and their houses and they can hold their religious service there. Moreover, it is improper to go anywhere and everywhere accompanied by ladies. And if the Brahmos have not understood this still, they will never understand it. European ways will never suit this country. To travel publicly with women, under the idea of giving them the same rights as are enjoyed by men, will always lead to trouble in this country.[123]

[122] Presumably not all of them were *bhadramahilā*. Convocation address by H. J. Reynolds, 15 March 1884, University of Calcutta, *Convocation Addresses*, II, 1880-1898, pp. 486-487.

[123] For a report of the original incident, see *Sanjībanī*, 2 April 1892 in *RNNB* 9 April 1892. For comment see *Bangabāsī*, 9 April 1892, and *Doinik-O-Samācār Candrikā*, 14 April 1892 in *RNNB* 16 April 1892. The writer went on to say, "Were not the Brahmos insulted in the same way as on the present occasion on the Calcutta International Exhibition grounds, and that simply because they had ladies with them?"

Hindu women emerged from purdah in a less noticeable manner than the Brahmos. By 1886, a Hindu writer defined freedom for a woman in terms of being able to go out with her husband and talk to his friends. He acknowledged that a certain level of freedom had already been accomplished: women now talked to their husbands in the presence of others, traveled in open carriages, and attended the theater and the circus.[124] *Zenana* women were said to sustain the existence of the Calcutta theater. If men were to stop their wives from going, many theaters would have had to close down. Many *bhadramahilā* also attended *jātrā* performances. These women must have been Hindus rather than Brahmos, who strongly disapproved of the theater. The plays staged were often ribald satires or romantic epics considered unsuitable for women. The fact that most actresses were prostitutes or courtesans also offended the puritanical Brahmo sensitivities.[125]

In part, these changes were the result of a consciousness among the progressive *bhadralok* that purdah was a form of oppression of women. Reformers had managed to introduce change into their own circles without the ensuing social anarchy that had been predicted, by replacing purdah restrictions with new puritanical norms: collective "shame" mechanisms were reinforced by a sense of individual morality and personal "guilt." The positive and enthusiastic way in which women took advantage of social freedom while remaining within the acceptably passive image of womanhood considerably facilitated the process of gradual erosion of strict purdah.

Women's own preferences played an important part in determining the ways in which purdah would be modified. The public social role modeled on that of the Victorian wife may not have appeared congenial to them, yet they were clearly interested in doing and seeing more than the limits of purdah permitted. They followed their own interests with determination. Therefore, although few women were willing to attend

---

[124] Tarakanath Biswas, *Bangīya-mahilā*, pp. 51-52.
[125] "Thiyetār o banganārī," *Antahpur*, 7, 2 (June 1904); *Candrikā*, 5 April 1866 in *RNNB* 11 April 1866.

a formal public social gathering, they would attend the theater in large numbers. The theater was particularly attractive as an escape world where their fantasies could be played out. It did not involve the strain of personal participation in a public social role for which most *bhadramahilā* were inadequately prepared.

Many women in England were dissatisfied with the kind of social role that was put forward as a model for the *bhadramahilā*. In the tract "Cassandra," Florence Nightingale recorded a frustration with it that many others would have echoed:

> The ideal life is passed in noble schemes of good consecutively followed up, of devotion to a great object, of sympathy given and received for high ideas and generous feelings. The actual life is passed in sympathy given and received for a dinner, a party, a piece of furniture, a house built or a garden laid out well, in devotion to your guests— (a too real devotion for it implies that of all your time)— in schemes of schooling for the poor, which you follow up perhaps in an odd quarter of an hour, between luncheon and driving out in the carriage—broth and dripping are included in the plan—and the rest of your time goes in ordering the dinner, hunting for a governess for your children, and sending pheasants and apples to your poorer relations.[126]

Some Bengali *bhadramahilā* also realized that public appearance did not in itself signify emancipation. An article in the *Bāmābodhinī Patrikā* in 1886 commented that "many well-meaning gentlemen are saying that women should be given freedom, but they do not entrust women with the power to make decisions on heavy responsibilities in their own lives."[127]

Although external changes such as the growth of the school

---

[126] Florence Nightingale, "Cassandra" (1859), in R. Strachey, *The Cause. A Short History of the Women's Movement in Great Britain* (London, 1928), Appendix I, p. 415.

[127] "Strī swādhīnatā," *BP*, 3:3, 261 (October 1886).

system and the increase in rail travel contributed to the process of erosion of purdah, the impact of this process was lessened by the continued emphasis on the idea of the "separate world." By the end of the nineteenth century the purdah system had been considerably modified. The modern *bhadramahilā* had a redefined role in the household and in society, and was no longer rigidly confined to a separate space, but she was not challenging hitherto male spheres, and therefore the balance of social control remained substantially unaltered.

EIGHT

Between Domesticity and Public Life: Voluntary Associations and Philanthropic Activity

Skills, knowledge, and awareness of social concerns that had been developed through education and exposure to a wider public life needed an arena of operation. Neither the *bhadralok* nor Hindu society was ready to grant women the same freedoms as men, but the energies that had been generated by social change could not be ignored. The *bhadramahilā* began to imitate the *bhadralok* in setting up organizations among themselves for social and philanthropic purposes. The trend was encouraged by male reformers, who endorsed the values of spending time usefully and helping to uplift the less fortunate. The women's organizations of nineteenth-century Bengal managed to break new ground in their structure and interests, without challenging the parameters of acceptable female concerns. The growth of women's organizations, their changing nature, and their often divergent aims and methods, were closely integrated with social developments in the world of the *bhadralok*.

Women's voluntary associations

For the first few decades of the existence of women's organizations, only Brahmo women were involved. As members of a new "sect," Brahmos had cut themselves off from participation in the household and communal rituals of Hinduism. Instead of these, they celebrated their group consciousness through the ritual of congregational worship, and affirmed

271

their commonly held principles in formal discussion groups or voluntary associations. Brahmo women would have experienced some of the same problems of alienation from the Hindu community as their menfolk, especially in the 1860s and 1870s. However, their customary mode of establishing social contact was through informal channels, and therefore the initiative for the establishment of formal women's organizations came from men. Women may have welcomed the opportunity to consolidate their recently acquired identity as Brahmos that was thus presented, but this was not the primary aim of the men who established voluntary associations for women. They envisaged the broader social purpose of raising women above the state of oppression in which they were said to exist in Hindu society. Women's voluntary associations were discussion groups creating a sense of common purpose among the participants, as well as forums for molding the consciousness of the "new woman" and indicating directions for change in her position.

Formal meeting procedures followed those of men's organizations, and thus furnished women with skills that were to be of use in breaking into previously male domains such as politics and public administration.[1] Brahmo women soon became familiar with such formal procedures, thus moving into an ideal position for participation in public affairs at a later date. In addition, women's organizations, by their very existence, emphasized women's distinctness and separateness, and introduced serious consideration of issues concerning the role and status of women. In some respects this was merely a continuation of the "separate world" of the purdah system, but by the end of the nineteenth century, women's successful mastery over the form of the voluntary association had created among them confidence in their ability to understand and

[1] Brian Harrison makes a similar point about the value of skills learned by women in conservative philanthropic organizations such as the Girls' Friendly Society; "For Church, Queen and Family: the Girls' Friendly Society 1874-1920," *Past and Present*, 61 (November 1973).

function within the public institutional framework of colonial India.

The first Bengali women's organization was the Brahmika Samaj, founded on 15 July 1865.[2] It was primarily religious, consisting of a weekly women's service followed by a discussion of spiritual matters. Keshub Chunder Sen preached sermons on moral and spiritual questions, which were generally attended by fifteen or sixteen women.[3] Secular activities were added soon after its inception: Bibi Miss Pikari taught women sewing for two to three hours every Saturday, the day of the women's service.[4] Miss Pigot, a missionary of the Church of Scotland, attended regularly in order to get to know Bengali women. She also invited them to her home.[5] One participant, Srimati Swarnalata, was concerned by the fact that many women were unable to attend the services. For their benefit, she jotted Keshub's sermons down from memory when she got home, and sent them to the *Bāmābodhinī Patrikā* for publication.[6] There is no coherent record of the continued existence of the group, but it seems to have kept going sporadically.[7] In 1866 a Brahmika Samaj was started in Bhagalpur, through the efforts of Dr. Krishna Dhan Ghose. It was less exclusively religious than its mentor, and aimed at social reform and educating its members to mix socially and to acquire "habits of freedom."[8] Other Brahmika Samajes were created in the wake of Brahmo Samajes in the *mofussil*.

The Bamabodhini Sabha was founded in 1863 by male reformers concerned with the condition of women. Its most important function was the publication of the women's jour-

[2] Sibnath Sastri, *History of the Brahmo Samaj*, p. 105; BP, 2:1, 24 (August 1865).

[3] *BP*, 2:1, 25 (September 1865).

[4] *BP*, 2:1, 26 (October 1865).

[5] *BP*, 2:1, 28 (December 1865).

[6] *BP*, 2:1, 30 (February), 31 (March), 33 (May), 34 (June), 35 (July 1866).

[7] The *IMS* announced the revival of the Brahmika Samaj and its weekly service on 22 March 1874.

[8] S. D. Collet, *Brahmo Year Book*, 1882, cited in Prabhatcandra Gangopadhyay, *Bānglār nārī-jāgaran*, pp. 44-45.

nal *Bāmābodhinī Patrikā*. In 1870 the Sabha held a meeting
at which Protap Chunder Mozoomdar suggested the establishment of a ladies' society, run by women, for the discussion
of religious and social questions. It was thought that about
twenty-five Brahmo women would attend meetings. The Sabha
would provide funds for transport. Sasipada Banerjea was put
in charge of the plan, and Protap Chunder was delegated to
enlist the assistance of Miss Pigot.[9] The scheme was not realized at the time, however, and there was no further mention
of a specific women's group connected with the Bamabodhini
Sabha. By the 1880s some women were actively involved in
the general affairs of the sabha, but it was still an overwhelm-
ingly male organization.[10]

The suggestion of a separate women's society was taken up
in 1871 under the auspices of the Indian Reform Association.
With the assistance of Keshub Chunder Sen and Miss Pigot,
the Bama Hitaisini Sabha was formed. It aimed at improving
the general welfare of women, although men were included
as members. Fortnightly meetings consisted of lectures, discussions, and readings of works considered suitable for women.
At its second meeting, English benefactors Mrs. Phear and
Miss Pigot were present, along with thirty Bengali women. In
keeping with his position in other organizations to which he
belonged, Keshub Chunder Sen took on the role of president.
Bijoy Krishna Goswami delivered a lecture on the spiritual
progress of women, and four students of the Native Ladies'
Normal School read their own compositions to the assembled
gathering.[11]

At the first anniversary of the Bama Hitaisini Sabha, Keshub
Chunder Sen addressed the group, setting the parameters for
the kind of activity he expected of it. He said that men were
strong and bold, women affectionate and merciful. In ac-

[9] "Bāmābodhinīr bises adhibesan," *BP*, 6, 87 (November 1870).

[10] For instance, Kamini Sen, B.A., was one of those present to discuss plans
for the twenty-fifth anniversary issue of the *Bāmābodhinī Patrikā*; *BP*, 4:1,
268 (May 1887).

[11] "Bāmā hitoisinī sabhā," *BP*, 7, 93 (May 1871).

cordance with these biologically determined differences, women should not aim at competing with men by being great scholars, but should concentrate on being good wives, mothers, daughters, and sisters.[12] At meetings of the sabha, however, its sixteen or so members were expected to express their own opinions and to ask questions,[13] though presumably the questioning was only possible within the limits permitted by Keshub, whose objective seems to have been one of indoctrination rather than exploration.

The progress of the sabha was intermittent. In June 1873 the *Bāmābodhinī Patrikā* was already speculating on whether it still existed.[14] The following month the second anniversary report of the sabha was published. The anniversary proceeded in a familiar fashion, with lectures from men, and readings by female members of their own essays on "the pleasures and advantages of studying science" and "the duties of educated women." The annual report noted that during the year there had been discussions on the following topics: the ideal qualities of women in ancient India and contemporary civilized England, child rearing, mercy, ideal women, the present condition of Bengali women and the duties of English women toward them, the appropriateness of secular education for women, the system of education best suited to furthering the progress of women, and the aims of a woman's life.[15] The sabha seems to have continued sporadically until 1878. In April of that year the *Indian Mirror* mentioned a meeting of the sabha at which Father Lafont lectured about the telephone,[16] and *Paricārikā* published a letter of thanks sent to Father Lafont on behalf of the sabha in December.[17]

Some time prior to 1878—the exact date is uncertain—there was an ideological split in the Bama Hitaisini Sabha.

[12] "Bāmā hitoisinī sabhā sāngbathsarik uthsab," *BP*, 8, 105 (May 1872).
[13] "Bhārat āsram," *BP*, 8, 107 (July 1872).
[14] English supplement, *BP*, 9, 118 (June 1873).
[15] "Bāmā hitoisinī sabhā," *BP*, 9, 119 (July 1873).
[16] *IMS*, 28 April 1878.
[17] Letter in English dated 26 December 1878, printed in *Paricārikā*, 1, 8 (January 1879).

The controversy was well-hidden, and reference was only made to it in an article in *Abalābāndhab*, organ of the "female emancipationist" group in the Brahmo Samaj.[18] The article discussed the split in detail and severely criticized the Bama Hitaisini Sabha for being male-dominated. The anonymous author of the article said that what women wrote or discussed followed the directives of men, and that women barely dared to express themselves at meetings where males were present and vocal. To show their dissatisfaction, some women decided to break away and (still with the help of male relatives) founded a new group called the Nari Hitasadhini Sabha, run entirely by women. Its female president had to send out notices, write reports, and read reports at meetings. Women discussed topics freely, and although men were present, they could only intervene to question decisions they strongly disagreed with. Women then argued the point, and made the final decision. This description of the Nari Hitasadhini Sabha gives an insight into the robust spirit of some Brahmo women, as well as into the heavily male-dominated nature of women's organizations prior to this. No records exist to show whether matters discussed by the Nari Hitasadhini Sabha differed substantially from those discussed by the Bama Hitaisini Sabha. The emphasis on independence and "constitutional" procedure indicates a connection with the 1878 split in the Brahmo Samaj as a whole. The Nari Hitasadhini Sabha would have been the female counterpart of the Sadharan Brahmo Samaj. Even in the more conservative atmosphere of the Bama Hitaisini Sabha, many women would have gained some familiarity with organizational procedures; Radharani Lahiri, secretary of the Bama Hitaisini Sabha, certainly did. The shift in the balance of power in favor of control by women was, however, a welcome initiative attributable to the Nari Hitasadhini Sabha.

A group of women, probably associated with the progressive faction, met at the home of Ananda Mohan Bose in 1877 to honor the late Mary Carpenter. A newspaper report com-

---

[18] "Nārī samāj o bratabidhi," *Abalābāndhab*, 1, 8 (June 1879).

mented that it was "remarkable" that the whole business of the meeting was conducted by educated native ladies.[19] A society for the "improvement of Brahmica ladies" was announced in 1879. It may have been the same group as the Nari Hitasadhini Sabha, but seems to have been less innovative. This society was presided over by a man, albeit the "venerable" Ramtanu Lahiri. Weekly meetings were divided as follows: the first and third weeks were to be devoted to "prayer and religious and moral instruction of the ladies," the second was to be a discussion group for women only, and the fourth was to be a social gathering including men, with lectures, scientific experiments, readings, music, and "other useful entertainments."[20] At the first women-only meeting, two ladies read papers on how women could make best use of their time in the present state of society. One outcome of the meeting was the appointment of a "ladies' working committee" to visit different Brahmo families at least twice a month, to attend and nurse the sick, to carry out home teaching, and to contribute to charity. Members were to do needlework, which would be sold for charity.[21] Thirty ladies joined as members. The following meeting was a mixed social gathering, at which thirty-five women and twelve men were present. Some of the men addressed the group on topics of current interest

such as the Zulu war and the death of Prince Imperial with an account of South Africa, anniversary of the National Orphan Home in London, tour of Roma Bai in Assam and her lectures on female improvement, the distress in East Bengal, the threatened inundation in Orissa, the recent meeting on Mass education, and the London meeting on India presided over by Mr. Bright &c.

[19] *Bhārat Sangskārak*, 16 July 1877 in *RNNB* 28 July 1877.
[20] *Brahmo Public Opinion*, 7 August 1879.
[21] This was modeled on the philanthropic activities of English women in India, who held "fancy fairs" to raise money for charity. See reports in *BP*, 1:2, 18 (February 1865); 2:1, 30 (February 1866).

The proceedings continued with

> a short lecture on Blood. After this the views of various places in Europe and America, Illustrated Papers, Photographs of natural objects, Microscopic views &c., were shown, and refreshments were handed round. Then came a series of most interesting electrical experiments and the exhibition of some scientific apparatus. Conversation and music concluded the proceedings.

The final editorial comment shows the rather anxiously paternalistic view men had of the organization—"We cannot but think that meetings such as these will produce a beneficial educational influence on the minds of our ladies."[22] The tone of the society stressed "improvement" rather than "emancipation." At subsequent meetings it was proposed and carried that the Ladies' Association should publish biographies of good women and selections from sacred writings.[23] The first book chosen for publication was *Prabandha-latikā*, a collection of moral essays by Radharani Lahiri.[24]

The above organization was the precursor of the better-known Banga Mahila Samaj, founded on 1 August 1879.[25] Its format was the same as that of its unnamed predecessor. On the occasions when women ran their own meeting sessions, they showed their grasp of organizational procedures: they chaired meetings, prepared reports, and made resolutions. The group's constitution was drawn up in April 1880, covering points such as the committee's right to decide on whether members needed to be Brahmos, loss of membership for members who had fallen four months behind in their payment of dues, and the election of office-bearers. There were to be a president and two secretaries, one of whom would be the treasurer, elected at six-monthly intervals. To an extent the

[22] *Brahmo Public Opinion*, 28 August 1879.
[23] *Brahmo Public Opinion*, 18 September 1879.
[24] Calcutta, 1880. Five hundred copies were printed in the first edition.
[25] See Prabhatcandra Gangopadhyay, *Bānglār nārī-jāgaran*, pp. 82-83; Lotika Ghose, "Social and Educational Movements," in *Bethune School*, p. 143.

power structure reflected that of the Sadharan Brahmo Samaj: Swarnaprabha Bose, wife of Ananda Mohan Bose, was first secretary and then president of the Banga Mahila Samaj for many years. The Banga Mahila Samaj also provided some scope for activity to single women and widows. Saraswati Sen, a widow who had been initiated into Brahmoism by Keshub Chunder Sen in 1875, presided over some of the meetings.[26] She took a personal pride in the samaj as a sign of women's achievement: "It must be said that it is our great good fortune to have an organization. Like our learned menfolk, we have the right to express our opinions and work for society. Whenever I think about this I am overjoyed." Radharani Lahiri, another of Keshub's protégées, was also active in the Banga Mahila Samaj.[27]

The activities of the association were less impressive than the aims outlined in the program. Miss Collet commented in 1880 that the work done by ladies had not been what was expected, although some members had done their duty and "occasionally rendered help to their poorer sisters." Christian ladies had joined the samaj to cooperate in social and philanthropic work.[28] This contact may have directed the organization toward a fuller consciousness of the scope for women's activity in the realm of social work, a field that had been taken up by women in England. In general the samaj stressed women's domestic civilizing mission. At one of the meetings, Bijoy Krishna Goswami addressed the group on the need to establish a "domestic altar" at which the whole family could worship together and create an "abode of peace and happiness."[29]

The first annual report in 1881 indicates that the activities of the samaj centered on issues of moral reform and improvement rather than on social work in the sense of helping others outside the immediate sphere or class to which members be-

---

[26] Muralidhar Bandopadhyay, *Srimatī Saraswatī Sener*, pp. 56-62; *Brahmo Public Opinion*, 13 November 1879.

[27] *Brahmo Public Opinion*, 25 December 1879.

[28] *Brahmo Year Book*, 1880.

[29] *Brahmo Public Opinion*, 25 December 1879.

longed. In the preceding year, the Banga Mahila Samaj had published its second book, *Saral nīti pāth*, a collection of moral teachings for children. Sasipada Banerjea donated twenty rupees as a prize for the best essay on "Ādarsa grihinī," in memory of his late wife.[30] Durga Mohan Das gave ten rupees for a scholarship for needy widows as a memorial to his wife. He also gave the same sum to the National Indian Association to further its efforts for the education of Bengali women. Many of the Sadharan Brahmo Samaj men who were involved in the Banga Mahila Samaj also belonged to the Bengal branch of the National Indian Association. The British parent branch had been founded in 1871 by Mary Carpenter, to promote social progress in India and to encourage harmonious relations between the two nations. The central organizers of the association were English women. Although no Bengali women were active in the National Indian Association, its close connection with the Banga Mahila Samaj, and its function of printing suitable books for Bengali women, probably made it an influential prototype organization.[31]

The dominant function of the Banga Mahila Samaj was social. Apparently "elderly" ladies enjoyed the meetings.[32] It was claimed by sympathetic men that "such social and intellectual gatherings cannot but impart a salutary influence upon the members, who long after these meetings with eagerness."[33]

By 1881, the list of the samaj's activities was not much more extensive. The committee of eight still included three men, although they did not hold office. Radharani Lahiri had started a children's group, but it had run down because of her ill health. A library had been established, with English books contributed by Miss Manning on behalf of the National

[30] The sole entrant, Parbati Basu, won the prize. *Brahmo Year Book*, 1881. An extract from her essay is given in Chapter Six.

[31] *BP*, 2:2, 193 (February 1881); *Brahmo Public Opinion*, 2 September 1880. The latter report also mentioned that Sasipada contributed a silver medal to be awarded annually for the encouragement of female education in Bengal.

[32] *Brahmo Public Opinion*, 8 July 1880; 2 September 1880.

[33] *Ibid.*, 2 September 1880.

Indian Association. Bengali books were also purchased, because most women were not conversant with English. During the year women had delivered lectures on a standard series of topics—social harmony, the progress of nature, the proper use of time, beauty, work and talk, and perseverance.[34]

Despite the commonplace and superficial titles, the texts of some women's speeches show an acute awareness of the complexities and subtleties of the issues under discussion. Radharani Lahiri, in an address given on the fifth anniversary of the Banga Mahila Samaj, showed her concern with establishing the real purpose of "emancipation" for women:

> Learned sisters! You may find it natural to dress like an elder *bou* in locally made bell-shaped earrings, bracelets, ornaments, and a Dacca sari—or you may wear "earrings," brooches and bracelets from Hamilton's, costly ribbons from Moore Company, and a gauze sari. It is doubtful whether there is any substantial difference between these. The uneducated *bou* travels in a closed carriage, and I, an educated woman, in an open carriage. Is this the ultimate product of civilization, is it by this that the country's well-being will be demonstrated? If that were so, then who would suffer? Today Bengali women would be counted as products of progressive civilization, but sisters! don't be offended if I say that thinking about our society pains me.[35]

Her speech indicated a genuine disenchantment with the superficial westernizing trend of reforms, without arguing for a reversion to the ideal of submissive Hindu womanhood. Her final call was for a mixing of the spirit of Sita and Savitri with the western woman's interest in charitable activities and helping others. Throughout its existence, the Banga Mahila Samaj remained an association for instruction rather than for action, holding meetings with lectures by eminent guests such as Father

[34] *BP*, 2:3, 205 (February 1882).
[35] "Bangīyamahilā samājer sāngbathsarik uthsab," *BP*, 3:1, 224 (September 1883).

Lafont and Sir Jagadis Chandra Bose.[36] By 1905 the samaj was defunct, having been superseded by other more active bodies.

The Arya Nari Samaj was founded by Keshub Chunder Sen in May 1879 as a "Ladies' Union" based upon "national principles."[37] Its object was to carry out reform "in accordance with the pure manners and customs of Aryan Hindu women of ancient times." It was against imitation of "foreign manners," but was willing to "accept liberally whatever is beneficial in foreign countries." Yet as was so often the case, nationalism for women was presented not as an affirmative state of self-reliance, but as one of intensified "femininity": "the main object of all endeavours of female improvement is to develop the female nature according to the laws of nature." Other objects were the study of health and hygiene, science (to reveal the "wisdom and mercy of God"), and biographies of good women, as well as engagement in congregational worship and daily prayer. Under the heading "social and domestic duties," the first mentioned was that "to serve the husband is the highest virtue of woman in this world." Women were also expected to eschew extravagance and be domestically proficient. The editor of the *Indian Mirror* commented that none of the rules violated "any of the progressive tendencies of the age." Tennyson's "The Princess" was invoked to emphasize the soundness of the point.[38]

The Arya Nari Samaj was designed to fit women for the position they would fill in society as good mothers, wives, and sisters, steering a middle course between the "outlandish habits and airs of *memlog*" and the "superstitious old village grandmother." At one of the early meetings it was resolved to form a small circulating library for women, and to contribute to charity by donating money, old clothes, and furniture to the secretaries for distribution to the poor. A distinctive feature of the Arya Nari Samaj was the adaptation of

[36] *BP*, 3:3, 260 (September 1886).
[37] *IMS*, 11 May 1879.
[38] "The Ladies' Union," *IMS*, 18 May 1879.

Hindu *bratas* to new objectives. There were the Maitreyi *brata* for those who wanted to cultivate religious fellowship with their husbands; the Savitri *brata* for self-sacrificing devotion to the husband; the Draupadi *brata* for household duties, and the Lilavati *brata* for those seeking knowledge. The Victoria *brata* was to teach women how to love and help servants, and the Nightingale *brata* was for offering relief to suffering humanity.[39] It is difficult to take these *bratas* seriously when their content is more closely examined. The "knowledge" acquired by those taking the Lilavati *brata* consisted of the following:

> Seven striking phenomena in nature illustrative of God's wisdom and love; seven important facts in history; seven wonders in the world; seven Sanskrit texts enjoining the duties of women.[40]

However, the samaj did engage in some outside work. The Metropolitan Female School was revived in 1880, and put under the charge of the Arya Nari Samaj. By November four Brahmo ladies had volunteered their services as teachers in the school.[41]

There is no extant list of office-bearers to show who really ran the samaj. In the initial stages, at least, it was controlled firmly by the president, Keshub Chunder Sen. The account of the samaj given by one of Keshub's biographers consisted entirely of selections from the sermons and addresses Keshub gave to the group.[42] By April 1880 the Arya Nari Samaj had twenty-two members. Fortnightly meetings were held at the home of the president. Although its professed aims were different, the meetings of the Arya Nari Samaj bore a marked resemblance to those of the Banga Mahila Samaj. Father Lafont lectured to both samajes on the uses of electricity. The

[39] *IMS*, 8 June 1879.
[40] *Ibid.*, 6 July 1879.
[41] *Ibid.*, 14 November 1880.
[42] Gour Gobinda Roy, *Ācārjya Kesabcandra*, middle, part 6 (Calcutta, 1897), pp. 1,140-1,148; end, part 2 (Calcutta, 1901), pp. 163-184.

committee of the Arya Nari Samaj agreed on a variety of social resolutions, such as that girls should not marry against their will although their guardians would guide their choice; that only properly dressed ladies could go into society; that "no fallen woman be allowed to marry, unless she has been thoroughly reclaimed under proper care and discipline, and kept in trial for a sufficiently long period." Most resolutions were replete with moralistic Brahmo-Victorian puritanism, explicitly stated in the final point that "frivolity and levity shall not be tolerated, and preference shall always be shown to the regulated freedom and becoming modesty which European society enjoins upon the wives and daughters of the clergy."[43]

Predictably, the Arya Nari Samaj and the Banga Mahila Samaj saw each other as rivals and opponents. While the Arya Nari Samaj declared itself against westernized emancipation, an implicit criticism of women in the Sadharan Brahmo Samaj, the *Brahmo Public Opinion* expressed equally strong objections to the Arya Nari Samaj. It accused Keshub of imposing on women directions that they did not themselves want, and maintained that the public activities of its members disproved the assertion that women chose to restrain their own liberty.[44] Although in substance the criticisms were justified, each side tended to caricature the position of the other. Keshub had never stood in the way of a certain degree of public involvement on the part of women in the women's associations set up by him. He did not object to their becoming teachers, or preachers in the Brahmo Samaj. His wife Jaganmohini preached to the Arya Nari Samaj each Sunday, and kept the group going after Keshub's death.[45] His daughter Manika Mahalanabis kept the organization going into the twentieth century. It was still in existence in 1904, when Sushama Sen was joint secretary.[46]

The Banga Mahila Samaj and the Arya Nari Samaj were

[43] *IMS*, 11 April 1880.
[44] *Brahmo Public Opinion*, 28 September 1880.
[45] [Priyanath Mallik], *Brahma-nandini*, pp. 174-229.
[46] Sushama Sen, *Memoirs*, p. 318.

the two most significant women's organizations of the later nineteenth century. Their membership was small, but they represented prototypes for other associations. Other interest groups formed their own women's organizations. The Bangiya Khristiya Mahila Samaj was founded by Bengali Christian women in 1880. It published its own journal, *Khristīya Mahilā*.[47] There were thirty-five members by 1881, and three hundred women were present at the annual meeting in 1882. The society was run by women.[48] Swarnakumari Debi, daughter of Debendranath Tagore, founded the Mahiladiger Tattwajnan Sabha as a women's branch of the Theosophical Society in 1882. The society attracted no public attention, and may not have progressed much beyond publishing a booklet setting out its rules and objectives.[49]

Swarnakumari Debi also started the Sakhi Samiti in 1886. It was the first organization run by women to have a clear commitment to social welfare. Its object was to take in destitute widows and unmarried girls and give them vocational training.[50] Its initial aim, reported in the *Bāmābodhinī Patrikā*, was to send out suitable teachers to Hindu *zenanas*.[51] Women's inexperience in running such projects probably contributed to the eventual failure of the scheme. Girls taken on had to sign a contract promising to teach for the same number of years as they were trained, or to pay back the cost of their tuition. However, all the girls merely took advantage of the education they had received to make a good marriage, and neglected to fulfil their part of the bargain. The samiti could have taken legal action, but decided instead to discontinue the scheme. The only person who did teach under the auspices of the samiti was Sarala Ray, the well-educated daughter of Durga Mohan Das. After her marriage she taught for the samiti in

[47] *BP*, 2:2, 191 (December 1880).

[48] *BP*, 2:3, 204 (January 1882).

[49] Mahiladiger Tattwajnan Sabha, *Uddesya o niyamābalī* (Calcutta, 1882); Sarala Debi, *Jībaner jharāpātā*, p. 221.

[50] *Bhāratī O Bālak*, cited in Sarala Debi, *Jībaner jharāpātā*, p. 221.

[51] *BP*, 3:2, 261 (October 1886).

her spare time, giving it her earnings.[52] As the samiti was run entirely by Swarnakumari Debi and some of her relatives and close friends, its influence was limited. Swarnakumari's daughter Hiranmayi had lost a number of her own children and personally took in many of the samiti's homeless girls and raised them as her own.[53] Under her impetus, the defunct society was revived in 1906 as the Bidhaba Silpasram.

In 1890 the samiti organized a charity bazaar, which was opened by its patron Lady Lansdowne.[54] This function, modeled on those held by philanthropic English ladies in India, was an important feature of later women's associations. Such bazaars were organized by women, staffed by women, and sold handicrafts made by women, such as *kāthā* work, embroidery, sweetmeats, and *ālpanā* designs.[55]

In 1892 Krishna Bhabini Dasi, who had lived in England with her husband for some years, broached a plan to set up a society for relieving the distress of "poor native women." Whether she was able to do so or not is unknown, as there is no further mention of her work.[56]

All the women's organizations mentioned so far were situated in north Calcutta. A need was felt for a similar group in south Calcutta, where many of the *bhadralok* householders were living by the end of the nineteenth century. In 1903, Sarala Ray and Kamala Bose started a Mahila Samiti in Ballygunge.[57] This seems to have been a discussion group rather than a charitable organization.[58] Some educated women yearned for greater mental stimulation than most women's groups provided. For instance Sarala Debi, B.A., daughter of barrister

[52] Sarala Debi, *Jībaner jharāpātā*, pp. 84-85.

[53] *Ibid.*, p. 60.

[54] *BP*, 4:3, 302 (March 1890).

[55] Lotika Ghose, "Social and Educational Movements" in *Bethune School*, p. 148. Ladies of the New Dispensation held their "Ananda Bazaar" along these lines. [Priyanath Mallik], *Brahma-nandinī*, p. 153.

[56] *Sanjībanī*, 2 January 1892 in *RNNB* 9 January 1892.

[57] Sushama Sen, *Memoirs*, p. 318.

[58] *Punya*, 5 (October-November 1905) published a paper on women's duty and the progress of *swadeshi* that had been read to the Mahila Samiti by Manisa Debi.

Purna Candra Sen of Rangoon, wanted to attend Sibnath Sastri's Monday discussion group, but did not wish to be the only woman present. She was going to ask Sibnath to run a similar group for women, but marriage interrupted her plans.[59] Men's groups were probably conducted at a higher intellectual level than those of women because they were not restricted by a preoccupation with "suitable" topics.

Within the Brahmo Samaj, there were women's auxiliary groups. In 1884 Brahmo women started a Sunday School for Brahmo children. The "lady workers" set the textbooks, conducted examinations, gave conduct prizes and handed out "conduct books" to be filled in weekly by the child's parents to ensure supervision of moral conduct at home.[60] As time went on, their range of activities expanded to include excursions and entertainments. A library was formed, with contributions from Unitarian ladies of the Sunday School Union in England.[61] They started the children's journal *Mukul* in 1896.

The Bharat Mahila Samiti was established in 1895 by Kadambini Lahiri, a Brahmo widow, and by 1904 it had ninety-five members. The high moral tone exhorted women to maintain "purity of feeling" within the home and family, and to read the newspapers, and seek new forms of knowledge. Their social duties were recognized in a token fashion. Members who were overburdened with their own home duties were requested to spend at least one hour each month doing useful work for another family.[62] The organization also supported a widow's home, which became a part of the Tagore family's Mahila Silpa Samiti in 1906, after the Bharat Mahila Samiti had become a discussion group to replace the defunct Banga Mahila Samaj.[63]

[59] Amritalal Gupta, *Punyabatī nārī*, p. 25.
[60] Sibnath Sastri, *History of the Brahmo Samaj*, p. 307.
[61] *Ibid.*, p. 329. The ladies were those pillars of the National Indian Association, Mrs. J. B. Knight and Miss Manning (p. 344).
[62] Amritalal Gupta, "Mahilādiger sabhā samiti," *BP*, 8:1, 496-497 (December 1904-January 1905).
[63] The Banga Mahila Samaj was declared defunct in the 1901 Sadharan Brahmo Samaj annual report. S. Sastri, *History of the Brahmo Samaj*, p. 347.

The Bharat Mahila Samiti was briefly mentioned in Sibnath Sastri's definitive *History of the Brahmo Samaj*. Despite the stress on equality in the Sadharan Brahmo Samaj, women's activities seem to have been of a subsidiary nature. They were not influential in the running of the samaj as a whole, in matters such as the distribution of funds or the making of policy decisions. Although Sibnath wrote that "women enjoy seats in the Executive Committee," there is no record of any women holding office during the period to 1905. The limited idea of equality envisaged by even the progressive Brahmos was aptly expressed by Sibnath:

> And let it be solemnly averred here, that during the pretty long course of their experience they [men in the Sadharan Brahmo Samaj] have had no cause for regret for having allowed their women the amount of social liberty they enjoy. It has elevated the relationship between the sexes, and has infused new life in the minds of their women, many of whom have come forward to be the sharers of their labour. Nay, the conviction is daily strengthening in them that women are the proper guardians of peace and purity in human society, and that the freer they are, the better is that duty performed.[64]

Although initially most voluntary associations were limited to Brahmo women, they sometimes organized functions in which educated Hindu women also participated. For instance, when Vidyasagar died they organized a meeting that was attended by three hundred women. Meeting procedures were strictly adhered to: resolutions were made and seconded, then debated. Swarnamayi De proposed that funds be collected for a memorial to Vidyasagar in Bethune College. Saraswati Sen seconded the proposal, and a committee was appointed to carry this out. Dr. Kadambini Ganguly thought that Bethune College was the most appropriate place for his memorial. Jnanadanandini Debi proposed that a refuge for homeless

[64] *Ibid.*, p. 364.

women be founded in his name, but some Hindu women disagreed. It was clearly a matter of pride to women that they could run their own meetings with male efficiency and precision.[65]

There were numerous small women's groups in the *mofussil*.[66] Susila Debi, daughter of Annapurna Cattopadhyay of Bogura, came to Mymensingh when her husband was posted there as a teacher. Among other activities she founded a Bhagini Samaj.[67] Banalata Debi, daughter of Sasipada Banerjea, founded the Sumati Samiti in 1892, when she was only thirteen, as a women's welfare organization.[68] It raised subscriptions to care for a few homeless girls, and tried to forge links with Hindu women in *zenanas* by initiating a correspondence with individual women. Banalata Debi herself received piles of letters from these women, and replied personally to each one. Her elder sister Sukatara took over as secretary after her death in 1900. Hemantakumari Chaudhuri started a women's group in Shillong, with a library of Bengali books, which was kept going even after she left. About fifty people came to each discussion meeting. She started a similar association when she moved to Sylhet.[69]

In 1901 *Antahpur* requested women's organizations to send in descriptions of their activities, in order to carry out a survey of the field, but no response was published.[70] In 1905 the *Bāmābodhinī Patrikā* called on Sarala Debi, of the Tagore family, to provide educated women with a new nondenominational organization with branches in the *mofussil*.[71] There was a growing need among educated women for a forum

---

[65] *BP*, 4:5, 320 (September 1891).
[66] "Mahilā samiti," *Antahpur*, 4, 12 (December 1901).
[67] Srinath Canda, *Brāhmasamāje callis bathsar*, p. 257.
[68] Special supplement, *Antahpur*, 3, 13 (December 1900).
[69] "Mahilā samiti," *Antahpur*, 4, 12.
[70] *Ibid.*
[71] Amritalal Gupta, "Mahilādiger sabhā samiti," *BP*, 496-497. She eventually did form such an organization, the Bharat Stri Mahamandal, in 1910. See Lotika Ghose, "Social and Educational Movements" in *Bethune School*, p. 150.

where they could meet each other for discussion and engage in some form of useful philanthropic work, and through which they could maintain contact with the outside world.

There was a marked shift in the nature of women's organizations over time. By the 1890s, all societies were run by women rather than men. Women had gained enough confidence, and experience in procedural technique, to take over. Apart from women's initiative, the growing lack of interest on the part of men hastened the transition. As men were increasingly drawn into nationalist political associations and activities, their interest in social reform and the "condition of women" issue waned. The ideological force of the Hindu revival tended to deemphasize the advancement of women, identifying it with westernization. No male organizations were still concerned with this issue by the end of the century.

Although most social reform institutions, such as schools, welfare homes, and charity organizations were still run by men, the burden of responsibility for social work was passed increasingly to the growing number of educated *bhadramahilā*. They had the advantage of being in a position to deal directly with women, but in many other ways were handicapped by the limitations on their own female role. Their lack of contact with the outside world meant that their activities had to be confined to a very narrow sphere, and as a result, women's philanthropic efforts during the period up to 1905 were piecemeal and amateur. The main purpose of most women's associations was to act as a support group for the benefit of educated women. At the same time, their consciousness of a new concept of social duty for the educated woman was growing, fostered by the responsibility gained from being in control of their own organizations. Whereas in earlier women's groups the *bhadramahilā* had been passive recipients of instruction, by 1905 they were actively involved in making their own decisions about what their social function should be.

There was no dearth of models for this type of active involvement, in other parts of India as well as in the west. The activities of Ramabai and Mrs. Ranade in Bombay were well publicized. Women's journals often carried reports of the work of British women reformers such as Harriet Martineau, Josephine Butler, Miss Manning, and Mrs. Fawcett. Mary Carpenter, one of the pioneers of social work in Britain, visited Bengal three times. However, it is interesting to note that she regarded the *bhadralok*, rather than the *bhadramahilā*, as her colleagues and equals.[72]

The development of women's organizations in Bengal followed its own momentum, and was only marginally affected by the kinds of activities middle-class women in England were undertaking. British associations provided an overall framework to operate in, but the activities of women within Bengali associations were different. In later nineteenth-century Britain, a large number of middle-class women were engaged in voluntary philanthropic activity. Sometimes their efforts were entirely individual, but often they carried out their work under the auspices of a larger charitable organization, most frequently connected with a religious body. The larger organization was usually dominated and run by men, but most of the routine work was done by women.[73]

In the predominantly segregated society of nineteenth-century Bengal, women were unable to participate in large male-run organizations, but they did not compensate for this by extending the scope of their own associations to take in wider social concerns. Many possible explanations can be offered for this. The *bhadramahilā* were still less at ease than the *bhadralok* at functioning in a regulated organizational framework. They had not been fired by the social conscience and attendant philanthropic spirit expounded by evangelical missionaries and Unitarian reformers to the same extent as their

---

[72] See her address to the Bethune Society on "The Reformatory School System, and Its Influence on Female Criminals," 11 December 1866, in Bethune Society, *Proceedings*, pp. lxxxix-xcvii. Her contact with Bengali women, on the other hand, was purely social. See her *Six Months, passim.*

[73] See R. G. Walton, *Women in Social Work* (London, 1975); K. Heasman, *Evangelicals in Action* (London, 1962).

menfolk, and were more influenced by a traditional idea of social responsibility that consisted in direct gestures of munificence to the poor without the mediation of an impersonal charitable institution.

Despite their limitations, nineteenth-century women's associations did foster a sense of group identity. The lead given by Brahmo women was taken up by Hindu women in the twentieth century. In later organizations the social purpose was much more clearly formulated than it had previously been. The growing involvement of men in the political arena created a vacuum that educated women were able to fill, especially as their access to other areas of public work was limited. After 1905, women's social welfare organizations mushroomed.[74]

It was only by this stage that women's associations had developed an autonomy independent of men. It could no longer be said, as it had been in 1880, that

> as yet, our women have no independent existence. Their opinions, views and sentiments are moulded, shaped and governed by those who lord over them. If their husbands, brothers and friends are Hindus, they are Hindus also. If those relations happen to be conservatives, they are conservatives also. If those relations are liberals or radicals, they are also liberal and radical in their opinion. We dare say the Arya Nari Samaj will only reflect the opinion of the ascetic Brahmos on this question, just in the same way as the Banga Nari Samaj or the Ladies' Association will, if consulted, reflect the opinion of the "extreme radical" section of the Brahmo community in this matter.[75]

[74] The most notable of these were the Hiranmayi Bidhaba Asram, 1906; the Bharat Stri Mahamandal, 1910; Saroj Nalini Mahila Samitis from 1913 on; the Nari Siksa Samiti, 1919; and the Bengal Women's Educational League, 1927. The culmination of all these efforts was the foundation of the All-India Women's Conference in 1929. See Lotika Ghose, "Social and Educational Movements" in *Bethune School*, pp. 148-165.

[75] *Brahmo Public Opinion*, 16 September 1880.

Philanthropy

Philanthropy, in the form of assistance to the poor and needy, had always been a traditional obligation of those in the upper echelons of Hindu society. Important family occasions or religious festivities were marked not only by celebrations and feasts, but also by a ritualized feeding of the poor. This was a religious and social obligation rather than the result of personal generosity or a charitable impulse to improve the lot of others. During the nineteenth century, however, charitable activity was partially transformed along western institutional lines.[76] Women would have found it difficult to participate in this new system, which was alien to their customary mode of operating. For the most part, they continued to participate in charity in the traditional manner, distributing clothes, grain, money, or medicine directly to the poor.[77] Women who did have large sums of money at their disposal, usually widowed owners of *zamindari* estates, were better able to fit in with new patterns of charitable activity, although some of their decisions were actually made by their male agents. One of the best-known and generous benefactors in the nineteenth century was Maharani Swarnamayi of Cossimbazaar.[78] Her donations amounted to *lakhs* of rupees. On a more moderate middle-class scale, Sarojini Ghose would feed between 100 and 125 beggars every Sunday. She would also distribute clothes to those who needed them, and feed the sick with sago, barley, and boiled rice.[79]

Women's activities did not remain static simply because they operated outside an institutional framework. In the later nineteenth century women used their newly gained education

[76] R. Sanyal, "Indian Participation in Organized Charity in Early Calcutta, 1816-66; A Response to the Poverty Question" in *Bengal Past and Present*, 96, part II, 183 (July-December 1977).

[77] See, for instance, the life of Kailaskamini Debi, wife of Umesh Chunder Dutt, in *BP*, 6:3, 402 (July 1898).

[78] For a brief biographical sketch and an outline of some of her charitable activities, see U. Chakraborty, *Condition of Bengali Women*, pp. 113-116.

[79] Renuka Ghose, *Sarojinī-carit*, p. 111.

and scientific knowledge to enhance their individual efforts to serve others. Many *bhadramahilā* mastered midwifery and modern medical treatment, which they put to use not only among friends and relatives but also among their subordinates. Sarojini Ghose and Annapurna Cattopadhyay both learned medicine from husbands who were trained as doctors. Doctors treating patients whom Annapurna was nursing would discuss the most suitable form of treatment with her.[80] Sailabala Sen learned midwifery from a doctor, and used her skills to serve the poor as well as her own family and neighbors.[81] Her mother also was a skilled midwife. Although she had mastered the subject through books, she was renowned for being able to manage even difficult deliveries.[82] Nalinibala Chaudhuri learned midwifery from her doctor husband, and eventually set up a center for training midwives in Sylhet.[83] An anecdote from the life of Aghorekamini Ray illustrates the way in which the *bhadramahilā* could, in an individual capacity, be socially useful and responsible for changes in living conditions. It is said that once Aghorekamini was told that a low-caste woman had fallen very ill after a difficult birth:

> She quickly went there and saw that the woman was the wife of a coal-seller, living in a dirty little hovel, half of which was filled with heaps of ashes. It was terribly smelly, without a bed, clothes, medicine, or invalid food. As soon as she arrived she sent someone for a doctor known to her, and for a bed and clothes from her own home, then she swept the floor clean herself. When the poor householder tried to restrain her, she said "What are these two hands for?" The woman was quickly nursed back to health, and looked after properly till she had regained her strength.[84]

[80] *Ibid.*, p. 93; Amritalal Gupta, *Punyabatī nārī*, pp. 81-82.
[81] Amita Sen, interview, Calcutta, November 1977.
[82] Hemlata Gupta, interview, Santiniketan, 15 November 1977.
[83] Manika Ray, interview, Calcutta, 14 February 1978.
[84] "Sādhbī Aghorkāminī," P. C. Mozoomdar, *Strīcaritra*, p. 166.

Many Brahmo women provided a backbone of support for the social reform activities of their menfolk. In the early 1870s, when concern with social reform was at its height, a number of Brahmos were engaged in performing dramatic rescue operations to save unhappy widows from a life of misery, or to retrieve *kulīn* girls from disastrous marriages. These girls were taken away from their villages and brought to Calcutta or other *mofussil* towns to live. The wives of their deliverers provided the actual hospitality and daily care for these girls, and often a close and filial relationship developed between them.[85] Girijakumari Banerjea was her husband Sasipada's partner in the running of the Burranagore Hindu Widows' Home and Female Boarding School.[86] During the outbreak of plague in Calcutta in 1898, some Brahmo women stayed behind and tended the sick alongside their husbands.[87] Ramananda Chatterjee and his wife returned to Calcutta from Allahabad, leaving their children behind, to help in the plague camps.[88]

Through their participation in women's organizations the *bhadramahilā* became attuned to channeling their charitable activities through the new institutional structure. Rather than donating what funds they had to traditional religious bodies or directly to the poor, increasingly they directed their donations through institutions. In 1884, two ladies of the New Dispensation sent forty seers of ice, fifty watermelons, and other items to patients in the Calcutta Medical Hospital. Another lady sent fifty fans she had embroidered herself to be distributed among the patients.[89] Sarala Das of Rangoon gave away most of the money she had won from scholarships to the poor through the Brahmo Samaj. When she received 100

[85] See, for instance, the part played by Rukmini Debi, wife of Gurucharan Mahalanabis, in his *Ātmakathā*, pp. 136-137; or by Brahmamayi Das, in Dwarkanath Ganguly, *Jībanālekhya*, pp. 51-71.

[86] Albion Banerji, *An Indian Pathfinder*, p. 59.

[87] An article in *Sanjībanī*, 21 May 1898 exhorted more people to do so. *RNNB* 28 May 1898.

[88] Roma Chatterjee, interview, Calcutta, 6 October 1977.

[89] *Liberal and New Dispensation*, 6 April 1884.

rupees for the Keshub Chunder Sen prize in the Entrance Arts examination to spend on books, she donated half of it toward a home for the poor. After her marriage, her independent income dried up, and she persuaded her mother to continue the donations for her.[90]

The Dasasram, a home for the destitute in Calcutta, published monthly reports in its journal *Dāsī* listing donations. Many of the donors were women, who contributed small amounts according to their means.[91] After reading a report in *Antahpur* on Brahmo relief efforts in the famine in Ajmer in 1900, Subala Acharya, wife of a Brahmo doctor, pledged 100 rupees per month toward this relief work. She calculated that since 10 rupees would keep a middle-class family from starvation, 100 rupees should keep eight to ten families. Following her example, Srimati Hemnalini and Srimati Hemangini, the wives of two *zamindars* of Tangail district in East Bengal, donated 500 rupees each for famine relief work, and the wife of a Calcutta *zamindar* presented another 20 rupees.[92]

In general, female charity was of necessity less public and ostentatious than that of men. Women had to save what money they could, usually from the family budget, and often made their donations anonymously. Atarmani Debi, a Brahmo housewife, always saved from household expenses. When she heard of famine or distress anywhere, she would secretly send a donation from this store.[93] In 1905, the honorary secretary of the Rajkumari Kusthasram in Baidyanath, Deoghar, a female leper hospital, wrote thanking women donors to hospital funds. The range of gifts varied enormously, from sixty-one rupees given by the poet Mankumari Basu to a regular contribution of four annas per month from 1903 on given by Srimati Kuntimani Debi of Gobindapur, Manbhum. Harasundari Debi of 203 Cornwallis Street gave five rupees a month from January 1904; the wife of the deputy magistrate of Ku-

[90] Amritalal Gupta, *Punyabatī nārī*, pp. 30, 39.
[91] *Dāsī*, 6, 1-9 (January-September 1897).
[92] "Bhīsan durbhik," *Antahpur*, 3, 8 (September 1900).
[93] Amritalal Gupta, *Punyabatī nārī*, p. 67.

rigram, Rangpur, gave two rupees per month from January 1902, and Hemantakumari Chaudhuri, editor of *Antahpur* living in Assam, gave eight annas per month from 1902.[94]

In Bengal, as well as in the west, philanthropy was considered particularly well suited to the feminine role.[95] Although it has been shown that women were involved in philanthropy on an individual basis within traditional society, male reformers were continually looking for ways to draw women into greater involvement in organized charitable activities. One major obstacle was the absence of a sizable group of unmarried women, the group most closely involved with philanthropic activity in England. Even an activist like Frances Power Cobbe, herself unmarried, felt that motherhood had to be a full-time occupation for married women:

> So *immense* are the claims on a mother, physical claims on her bodily and brain vigor, and moral claims on her heart and thoughts, that she cannot, I believe, meet them all, and find any large margin beyond for other cares and work. She serves the community in the very best and highest way it is possible to do, by giving birth to healthy children, whose physical strength has not been defrauded, and to whose moral and mental nurture she can give the whole of her thoughts. This is her *function*, public and private at once,—the *profession* which she has adopted ... it is a misfortune to all concerned, when a woman, under such circumstances, is either driven by poverty or lured by any generous ambition to add to that great "Profession of a Matron" any other systematic work, either as bread-winner to the family or as a philanthropist or politician.[96]

Among the *bhadramahilā* there were very few women who never married, although toward the end of the century the

[94] "Baidyanāth kusthāsram," *BP*, 8:1, 489 (May 1904).
[95] Protap Chunder Mozoomdar wrote that "of all the good qualities for which woman's nature is esteemed in the world, the service of the others is the greatest." *Strīcaritra*, p. 160, "Parasebā."
[96] Frances Power Cobbe, *The Duties of Woman*, p. 190.

rising age of marriage meant that women could devote a few more years to extensive philanthropic activity before marriage and motherhood intervened. Bengali widows did form a group that was in some ways comparable to that of unmarried women in England. It was a large group, and although many were also mothers, some were widowed at an early age and were condemned to a life of self-denial with little outlet for constructive activity. In 1860, Bishop Cotton gave an address to the Bethune Society on "The Employment of Women in Religious and Charitable Works" in which he suggested that widows in Bengal should take on the function of ministering to the sick and bereaved in society, as unmarried women did in England.[97] Bengali women admired the philanthropic work of women in the Salvation Army and the Little Sisters of the Poor, and lamented the lack of similar groups within their own society.[98]

Despite the social values that elevated motherhood into a full-time occupation, there was a consciousness among the educated *bhadramahilā* that they should put their education to some use in a sphere beyond the home. The limited leisure time available, however, and their restricted mobility, meant that most schemes suggested were rather impromptu and disjointed. For instance, in 1884 an Englishwoman wrote "A Hint to Ladies of Leisure" in the *Brahmo Public Opinion*, suggesting that educated women hold classes at their homes for at least two hours each week, to teach other women about the rules of health, infant management, geography, and sewing. She concluded that

> the plan we have suggested of holding classes at home is by no means too difficult even for a lady who may feel that she is not proficient in any of the subjects we have

[97] Address on 5 April 1866, in Bethune Society, *Proceedings*, pp. 58-59. See also H. W. Schupf, "Single Women and Social Reform in Mid-nineteenth Century England: The Case of Mary Carpenter," *Victorian Studies*, 17, 3 (March 1974).

[98] "Sebikā bhaginī sampradāy," *Antahpur*, 2, 17-18 (May-June 1899). See also *BP*, 8:1, 493-494 (September-October 1905).

named. As for sewing, practice alone can fit any person to teach it to others and the best means therefore would be one which will be as useful to the teacher as to the subsequent pupils—we advise a strict overhauling, darning and patching of all household stores of linen and clothing. As to the other subjects for instruction, health and geography, there are several easy text books of both which the would-be teacher could first study and which will quite fit her to give the elementary instruction she is likely to need for her pupils. We know from experience that a lady who should thus simply and quietly try to help her less instructed neighbours will find much happiness in the work, and that if she lives in a dull and remote village she will look forward as to a pleasant entertainment to the assembling of her little class.[99]

During the famine of 1900, Hemantakumari Chaudhuri, then living in Sylhet, wrote an impassioned plea calling on educated women to use their knowledge in the service of society in the manner of Florence Nightingale or Sister Dora. Although she recognized that it would be impossible to attract many *bhadramahilā* to become involved to that degree, she thought that it would be easy to take in homeless girls and provide them with a useful education, training them to be *susrusākārinī*, or nurses.[100] As editor of *Antahpur*, she also added a postscript to a contribution to that journal in 1902 which called on women to provide more services for the poor. Hemantakumari, an extremely capable and far-sighted woman, commented that such service could not be provided without training. She said that there was a need for nursing colleges, although a start could be made by learning from the many books and journals available in Bengal. She recommended that some of these books be placed on school curricula.[101]

[99] *Brahmo Public Opinion*, 14 November 1878.
[100] Hemantakumari Chaudhuri, "Susrusā kārinī," *Antahpur*, 3, 8 (September 1900).
[101] "Sebābrata," *Antahpur*, 5, 2-3 (June-July 1902).

By 1905, similar articles on the need for women to participate in social work were appearing in the *Bāmābodhinī Patrikā*. It was said that

> at present there is no dearth of examples of this philan-
> thropy among European men and women. But as long
> as the good fortune and happiness of this country con-
> tinue, then we will be able to find women of good families
> among the women of this country with the same self-
> sacrificing spirit of service to others.[102]

A subsequent article suggested various courses of action for
Bengali women: they could form Mahila Samitis for the advancement of women; they could contribute to Bengali literature; they could set up schools for children based on the
model of English Sunday Schools; and they could help men
in public activities from behind the scenes. An example of the
latter was Sarala Debi's mobilization of a girls' choir to sing
a national song she had written at the Calcutta session of the
Indian National Congress in 1904.[103]

In England, by the turn of the century philanthropy had
progressed from being merely the province of the well-meaning untrained gentlewoman to include that of the trained social
worker. As early as 1857 the National Association for the
Promotion of Social Science had suggested that women be
educated for charity work.[104] This call was echoed with feeling
by Florence Nightingale in her tract "Cassandra":

> How different would be the heart for the work, and how
> different would be the success, if we learnt our work as
> a serious study, and followed it out steadily as a profes-
> sion!

[102] Amritalal Gupta, "Siksitā ramanīdiger kartabya," *BP*, 8:1, 490 (June
1904).

[103] Amritalal Gupta, "Siksitā ramanīdiger samājer prati kartabya," *BP*, 8:1,
493-494 (September-October 1904).

[104] S. Rowbotham, *Hidden from History*, 3rd ed. (Ringwood, Victoria,
1975), p. 49. On the question of training women for social work, see also
R. G. Walton, *Women in Social Work*.

Were the physician to set to work at *his* trade, as the philanthropist does at his, how many bodies would he not spoil before he cured one![105]

Although in England the professionalization of philanthropic work was far more advanced than in Bengal, there were many similarities in the situation of women philanthropists in the two areas. In both Britain and Bengal, philanthropy was thought to be suitable for women, even though it did allow them to come into contact with a less fortunate side of life than they had been used to. The womanliness of self-sacrifice was acknowledged in both cultures. The only experience women could bring to bear on their work was that of managing a household, which gave them a skill in managing people that could be utilized in social work. All formal procedural techniques were learned from men. In both England and Bengal, the success of any scheme run by women depended ultimately on male approval and patronage. Links with the public sector could only be maintained through males. Men also had greater economic power and were in a better position to arrange financial support. In England, women "depended on liberal-minded men for acceptance and the furthering of their ideals."[106] In Bengal the dependence was even greater, and the room for female initiative less. The situation envisaged by Mary Carpenter in 1857 was only beginning to come about in Bengal at the turn of the century:

Although women should be the managers of girls' schools, ... they may need to be sustained by the power and business habits of men, especially in the relation which these institutions bear to Government. The actual working which I have witnessed for a quarter of a century of a united committee of gentlemen and ladies, with a sub-committee of the former for business details, and one of

[105] Florence Nightingale, "Cassandra," in R. Strachey, *The Cause*, Appendix I, p. 405.
[106] R. G. Walton, *Women in Social Work*, p. 66.

the latter for domestic management, would lead me to advise it strongly.[107]

The rapid development of social work as a profession among women in Britain was fueled by the growing number of educated middle-class women, especially unmarried ones, looking for a satisfying career in harmony with social ideals of womanhood. In Bengal not only were there fewer educated women—among whom few were unmarried—but there was also some criticism of women's participation in organized charity work as being too westernized and alien to their own tradition. One critic, in reviewing a Bengali biography of Mary Carpenter for the *Calcutta Review*, firmly believed that philanthropists of her type were a product of English culture, energy, history, and social and political life:

> So what good purpose can be served by making Bengali girls read this, when Hindu society presents few opportunities and no machinery for that *kind* of philanthropy, which demands an energy and power of combining scattered materials which not even Hindu *males* possess.[108]

This criticism may have been applicable to the conduct of philanthropy in the nineteenth century, but by the twentieth century initial attempts to imitate English models of social work were adapted to harmonize with, and respond to, local needs and conditions.

Prostitution and welfare work

In nineteenth-century Bengal, in both women's organizations and philanthropic projects undertaken by women, there was a lack of engagement in social problems outside the realm of experience of the *bhadramahilā*. Reformers took the lead in

[107] Mary Carpenter, "Reformatories for Convicted Girls," in National Association for the Promotion of Social Science Transactions 1857, cited *ibid.*, p. 25.
[108] "Review of Kumāri Kārpentārer Jiban-charit. By Rajani Kanta Gupta. Calcutta 1882," in CR, 75, 150 (1882).

seeking to alter the fate of widows and *kulīn* brides, as the hardships of their lot were often evident within the extended families of the *bhadralok* themselves. Most of the preoccupation with social reform reflected a concern for the problems affecting their own community. Broader social problems among low-caste women such as poverty, destitution, poor working conditions, and prostitution received scant attention. Indifference to the lives of the *chotolok* was not confined to women, but was a shared characteristic of the *bhadralok* as a whole.

The problem of prostitution was an area in which one can observe the flow of influence from middle-class evangelicism in Britain to the Bengali Brahmo *bhadralok* reformers, an influence that did not carry through to the *bhadramahilā*. In England, the "reclamation" of prostitutes and concern for their welfare had been a major preoccupation of Evangelical reformers from the pre-Victorian era. By 1839, the Religious Tract Society had issued five million tracts directed at the rescue of "fallen women."[109] During the 1850s some High Church sisterhoods started houses of refuge for prostitutes, and Evangelical organizations founded the Rescue Society, the London Female Preventive and Reformatory Institute, and the Home of Hope. A series of similar organizations followed throughout the century.[110] From 1869 to 1883, the repeal of the Contagious Diseases Acts enforcing regular medical inspection of prostitutes for venereal disease was a major moral reform issue. The campaign against the acts was led by Josephine Butler, a strong feminist, and thus provided a focal point for the militancy and energies of women activists and gave them valuable experience in public political life. The main thrust of the campaign was an attack on double standards of morality.[111]

---

[109] E. Trudgill, *Madonnas and Magdalens*, p. 282.

[110] J. Laver, *The Age of Optimism* (London, 1966), pp. 105-107.

[111] S. Rowbotham, *Hidden from History*, pp. 52-53. The acts were introduced as a bill in 1864, and passed in 1869. The compulsory inspection system was abandoned in 1883 as a result of pressure from Josephine Butler's campaign.

In Bengal, prostitution was an accepted social institution. Certain classes of prostitutes had a recognized status in society as singers, actresses, and performers. Yet the demarcation between "good" and "bad" women was still very sharply drawn. An underlying reason for resistance to the liberalization of purdah could have been that many of the freedoms offered were already enjoyed by prostitutes. As in Victorian England, the spotless virtue of the "madonna" implied the existence of the "Magdalen," so the protection of women from exposure to male sexuality that was part of the purdah system relied on the existence of a substratum of prostitutes.[112] The distinction catered exclusively to male needs and appetites. Women were divided into two polarized categories in order that men could benefit from both.

Association with prostitutes seems to have been a regular feature of the *bhadralok* lifestyle. Only rich merchants and *zamindars* could afford to keep mistresses, but in all the towns and cities there was a large prostitutes' quarter, visited even by schoolboys.[113] In his autobiography, Krishna Kumar Mitra related how he was beaten with *lāthis* by some of his classmates in Mymensingh when he refused to join them in playing *holi* with prostitutes.[114] In central and north Calcutta the prostitutes' quarter was situated close to the main areas of schools and colleges.[115]

The Brahmo *bhadralok*, having imbibed the puritanical morality of the Evangelicals, were among the first to take an interest in the reclamation of prostitutes. In 1863 Keshub Chunder Sen wrote to Frances Power Cobbe that

[112] See E. Trudgill, *Madonnas and Magdalens*. For a discussion of this phenomenon in Australian history, see A. Summers, *Damned Whores and God's Police* (Ringwood, Victoria, 1975). H. Papanek makes this point with regard to India in her article "Purdah."

[113] See S. K. Mukherji, *Prostitution in India* (Calcutta, 1934), "Colonies of Prostitutes in Towns," pp. 235-244.

[114] Krishna Kumar Mitra, *Ātmacarit*, p. 40.

[115] S. K. Mukherji, *Prostitution in India*, pp. 235-240. There were continual complaints about this state of affairs in the vernacular press; see *RNNB* 1863-1905.

there is another department of female improvement to which our attention has been directed of late—how we may counteract the progress of prostitution and reclaim fallen women. I purpose to write to the Secretary of the London Female Preventive and Reformatory Institution by this mail, to give me information as to what amount of progress has been made in England in this matter.[116]

In fact the issue was pursued no further at the time. A few years later, sporadic attempts were made by individual Brahmos to control the problem of prostitution. They did not always direct their efforts toward reclamation. After Krishna Kumar Mitra became a Brahmo he tried to have the prostitutes banished from their quarter in his home town of Baghil, in Tangail district. He showed more concern for saving "ruined youths" than "fallen women," and he told the owners of the bazaars where the prostitutes lived that if their tenants were not turned out all the houses would be destroyed. Some prostitutes also lived in Binnaphoir bazaar, as tenants of *zamindar* Janhabi Chaudhurani. She did not agree to banishing them because she realized that there was nowhere else for them to go and that banishment was not a sensible solution to the problem.[117] Apart from this, their presence in the market was financially advantageous to her.

In the 1870s Nabakanta Chatterjee and a group of young Brahmos made a few attempts to rescue girls from prostitution, with varying degrees of success. One well-publicized case was that of Laksmimani. Her mother, a prostitute, was going to take her to a brothel, but she contacted some Brahmo friends to rescue her from that fate. They did, and won the legal battle that ensued. She was taken to Calcutta, where she lived in the home of Sibnath Sastri until her marriage to a schoolteacher from Jalpaiguri in 1877.[118] On another occasion

[116] Letter dated 22 March 1863, in Frances Power Cobbe, "Keshub Chunder Sen," *East and West*, 2, 23 (September 1903).

[117] Krishna Kumar Mitra, *Atmacarit*, pp. 68-69.

[118] Nalinikanta Cattopadhyay, *Nabakānta Cattopādhyāy*, pp. 104-106; Sibnath Sastri, *Atmacarit*, pp. 94-95.

Nabakanta rescued a *kulīn* girl from Bikrampur from prostitution, but the lack of any other viable means of support after the death of her mother forced her to take up that profession later. At the time there were no refuge organizations in Bengal.[119] Sibnath Sastri was once approached by a prostitute who told him her life story and begged him to take her child and give it a better life. As the child was still being breast-fed, Sibnath advised her to wait for a few months, but she never contacted him again.[120]

It was not until the end of the century that organized efforts were made not only to save women from prostitution but to provide them with alternatives. In 1896 Sasibhusan Mallik founded the Dacca Girls' Rescue Home. There was a school attached, and girls were also taught religion and sewing by *zenana* missionaries. In 1897 only three prostitutes had been "rescued," but their numbers gradually increased. The home relied on public donations.[121] A Protestant home for prostitutes had been set up by an Englishwoman before this, but it catered mainly to Europeans and Anglo-Indians.[122]

Even though a form of the Contagious Diseases Acts, known in Calcutta as Act XIV, had been introduced, there does not seem to have been a strong public outcry against it. The act apparently failed because prostitutes themselves objected to examination by male doctors, but there is no record that the *bhadralok* or *bhadramahila* supported their cause.[123] One women's paper concerned with public affairs and edited by a woman, the *Banga Mahila*, recorded that it deplored the acts because they violated the rights of the public in order to pro-

---

[119] Nalinikanta Cattopadhyay, *Nabakānta Cattopādhyāy*, pp. 107-108.

[120] Sibnath Sastri, *Ātmacarit*, pp. 104-105.

[121] *BP*, 6:1, 386 (March 1897); Nagendrabala Mallik, "Dāccā bālikār uddhārāsram," *Antahpur*, 4, 10 (October 1901).

[122] Amritalal Gupta, "Siksitā ramanīdiger samājer prati kartabya," *BP*, 493-494.

[123] S. K. Mukherji, *Prostitution in India*, pp. 413-414. The Contagious Diseases Acts were introduced in Calcutta in 1864 and repealed in 1888. They were replaced by the Cantonment Act in 1889. It was said in 1879 that on average twelve women were arrested daily under the acts; U. Chakraborty, *Condition of Bengali Women*, pp. 26-30.

tect soldiers.[124] In India the acts were enforced mainly in cantonment areas. In 1875 Keshub Chunder Sen accepted a request from Josephine Butler to become a member of the General Council of the Federation for the Abolition of Government Regulation of Prostitution, noting that he was glad that the federation would include India within the scope of its activities.[125] There is no other public record, however, of his having campaigned actively in support of the issue.

As most social reformers in nineteenth-century Bengal shied away from coming to terms with the full social and economic implications of prostitution, it is not surprising that the *bhadramahilā* were even less able to tackle it. Although Brahmo women often lent support to their husbands' rescue schemes, and looked after the girls they managed to save, there is little record of their active participation. Annapurna Cattopadhyay gave shelter to a few prostitutes, hoping to reform them, but the success of her efforts is not known.[126] Nagendrabala Mallik helped publicize the work of her husband's rescue home among women, and sought donations from them.[127]

This lack of evident interest by the *bhadramahilā* in an issue that concerned the status of women generally has to be accounted for. Women, in their domestic role, were still closely tied to the traditional social structure that did not encourage criticism and questioning of the status quo. In fact, they identified with the value of respectability that was the hallmark of their class. Psychologically, women's acceptance of purdah and its limitations on their own freedom depended on their being seen as virtuous. For them to minimize the polarity between "good" and "bad" women would have been to undermine the rationale for tolerating many of the restrictions of purdah. The *bhadramahilā* had less contact with evangelical and Victorian puritanism than their menfolk, and therefore

[124] *Banga Mahilā*, 31 August 1870 in *RNNB* 10 September 1870.
[125] International Abolitionist Federation, *The New Abolitionists* (London, 1876), pp. 193-194; letter dated 31 August 1875.
[126] Amritalal Gupta, *Punyabatī nārī*, p. 93.
[127] Nagendrabala Mallik, "Dāccā bālikār uddhārāsram," *Antahpur*, 4, 10.

lacked the kind of consciousness that believed in the possibility of "reclamation." In any case, the sheltered lives of purdah women would have given them little opportunity for the kind of reclamation work undertaken by middle-class women in England, which involved going out and confronting the actual conditions in which prostitutes lived. Even in England, the success of moral reform work with prostitutes was questionable. More attention was paid to moral salvation than to the crucial underlying economic and social causes of prostitution. The failure of the *bhadramahilā* to become involved in work of this kind should not be seen simply as a dismissal of the issue, but a reflection of their peripheral stature and powerlessness in the face of large-scale social problems.

It was only in the twentieth century, when an increasing number of educated women sought meaningful activity, that the *bhadramahilā* began to look beyond their own immediate areas of experience and to examine more serious social problems. The training in public life gained through membership of voluntary associations and participation in philanthropic activities gave them the skills needed for dealing with major social issues. The lack of awareness and detached attitude characteristic of many of the *bhadramahilā* in the nineteenth century were increasingly difficult to sustain in a time when women were beginning to enter the public worlds of paid employment and political activity.

✨ NINE ✨

The *Bhadramahilā* in Public Life:
Employment and Politics

There has recently been a lively debate among social scientists concerning the use of the domestic/public dichotomy in discussing the lives and status of women across cultures.[1] Some maintain that the two spheres are not distinct: in certain rural societies, the domestic world is the public world; elsewhere, the two constantly interact—domestic matters have important repercussions in the public world, and vice versa. The issue is certainly a complex one. However, in nineteenth-century Bengal the division between the female domestic world and the male public world was clearly defined in spatial as well as ideological terms. The domestic world of women and the family was physically delineated by the boundaries of the *antahpur*. In contrast, the exclusively male public world was spatially unlimited and concerned with broad matters, including the family. In this chapter, "public life" covers the involvement of women in activities or issues outside the traditional realm of the domestic world and the limits of the conventional female role, particularly in the areas of employment and political participation. Moves toward public life did not necessarily entail the expansion of physical horizons beyond the *antahpur*, but meant contact with and awareness of events taking place in the once exclusively male "outside" world dominated by the colonial administration and economy.

[1] M. Z. Rosaldo, "Woman, Culture, and Society: A Theoretical Overview"; S. C. Rogers, "Woman's Place"; L. Tilly, "The Social Sciences and the Study of Women . . ." in M. Z. Rosaldo and L. Lamphere, *Woman, Culture, and Society.*

Employment

In the Calcutta Census of 1901, 725 women registered themselves as employed in what could be termed "professional"
occupations. These included the categories of principals, professors and teachers (587), administrative and inspecting officials (6), qualified medical practitioners (124), photographers (4), and authors, editors, and journalists (4).[2] Even though
the number of *bhadramahilā* registered was minuscule in proportion to the number of employed *bhadralok*, it had in fact
doubled since the 1891 Census, and represented an extremely
significant trend.[3] Census figures on female employment can
only partially indicate the extent of employment among the
bhadramahilā. Many were engaged in part-time, semiformal,
or short-term work arrangements, and would not have been
registered as employed. Nor do the statistics give any information on the religious, caste, or marital background of
professional working women. One can only assume from other
available evidence that most would have been single or widowed Christian and Brahmo women.

For the first time, the *bhadramahilā* were brought into contact with the economic world of wage labor based on formal
contract. The phenomenon of independent earning power began to affect the lives of women by giving them a greater sense
of individuality. It also extended the boundaries of their experience by bringing them into contact with the realities of
the male world of colonial administration as it was experienced by the *bhadralok*.

The increase in employment among the *bhadramahilā* par-
alleled the growth in public institutions catering for women,
especially in the fields of health and education. In order that
more women could take advantage of the new services offered,
it was necessary to have females provide those services. While
the limits of the separate world of purdah were widening,

[2] *1901, Calcutta. Town and Suburbs Census.*
[3] Proportions of females to males in relation to the above categories are,
respectively, 10.3, 24.7, 9.6, 3.7, and 3.2

female officials were needed to act as mediators between it and the expanded world of males.

At the same time, the provision of education for women, and the continued expansion of the upper limits of female education, raised women's expectations for something additional to marriage. The admission of women to university degrees did not necessarily distract them from the traditionally expected role of wife and mother, but it did give women with higher qualifications cause to think that their lives should be different from those of their mothers and grandmothers, and that they should give others the benefit of their advancement through various forms of public service. A longer process of education and a rising age of marriage, especially in the Brahmo community, meant that some women entered the workforce for a short period before withdrawing from it on marriage. Indeed, a very small number of women did not marry but became independent career women.

The *bhadralok* had to come to terms with the increased number of educated and well-qualified *bhadramahilā*. Rather than let women follow their own course of development, which was immediately perceived as threatening, it was asserted that "it behoves the leaders to yield to the inevitable, and adopt means to regulate within proper bounds the legitimate aspirations of Indian women."[4] When the first two women graduated from Calcutta University, an editorial comment in the *New Dispensation* voiced similar words of caution:

> Whatever may be said against the university policy of admitting girls to the degree examinations, we are bound to accept facts, and the fact is that we have already a certain number of she-B.A.'s. What are we to do with them? If left to themselves and to their degrees, they will rot as teachers and will have nothing except their own conceit to feed upon. We do not know how far this policy of letting lady graduates alone will contribute to the mor-

[4] *Hindoo Patriot*, 1 February 1902 in *RNNB* 8 February 1902.

als of the community. The best principle would be to utilise them in the interests of the public.[5]

Prior to this explosion in education, the social reform movement had generated among the *bhadralok* a heightened awareness of the oppressive restrictions imposed on women. Some perceived that this handicap was often connected with women's total dependence on male support. The plight of widows was of particular concern. The inability of widows to maintain themselves after the loss of a male protector led the *Māsik Patrikā*, in 1854, to advocate vocational training for the *bhadramahilā*. This did not mean professional training, but skill in various forms of craft that could be sold commercially to bring in a small income. It was said in encouragement that middle-class women in England did embroidery and dressmaking for sale.[6] At a later date, a series of articles in the *Bāmābodhinī Patrikā* discussed various ways in which widows could earn their livelihood. As was often the case, many of the suggestions lacked thought as to their practicability in the Bengali context. The suggested range of occupations was diverse: wood engraving; embroidering insignia on soldiers' uniforms; operating a printing press; bookbinding; painting; *zenana* education or teaching in the *mofussil*; picklemaking; gardening; lacemaking; making fans; making dolls for sale at fairs; dressmaking; midwifery; and medicine. The estimated possible earnings from most of these occupations were very low, and would have been barely adequate to support a family. For instance, from making decorated fans by purchasing ordinary palm-leaf fans in the market and adorning them with fringes and ribbons, it was thought that a widow could earn herself five or six rupees a month.[7] By 1904, Lilabati Mitra was concerned that the kinds of traditional crafts widows practiced to eke out a living were no longer popular with

[5] *New Dispensation*, 8 July 1883.
[6] "Grihakathā," *Māsik Patrikā*, 3 (16 October 1854).
[7] "Bhārater bidhabā o anāthā strīlokdiger jībikā lābher kata prakār upāy hoite pāre?" prize essay, anonymous, *BP*, 4:2, 290 (March 1889); "Dukhinī bidhabā o anāthā diger jībikār upāy," *BP*, 4:2, 291 (April 1889).

consumers. She recommended the adoption of more commercially oriented enterprises catering for new tastes, such as the manufacture of stockings. A machine could be purchased from England for 200 rupees that would produce a pair of stockings every fifteen minutes. It could make half-stockings, full stockings, and thick Darjeeling stockings, all catering to the reformed dress of the "new woman." She calculated that the seller would earn twenty-five to thirty rupees per month. Other suggested occupations included typewriting, picture framing, making cardboard cartons, photography, basket weaving, applique work, crochet, woolwork, and the embroidering of mottos on cloth or card. All of these new occupations could conveniently be followed within the home, after some training from a skilled practitioner or male relative.[8]

A number of *bhadramahilā* were beginning to face the problem of finding ways to lessen the total dependence on men that left women helpless if they fell on hard times. A plea for equal vocational training for men and women was made on the grounds of the likelihood of having to cope with such an eventuality.[9] In an article in *Antahpur*, Prabodhini Ghose suggested that every woman should learn to weave her own cloth rather than be told by men to manufacture useless handicrafts or embroidery to sell for a pittance. She lauded as an example of self-sufficiency the Assamese custom of having a loom in every house to weave all cloth for domestic use. Although a woman would not actively earn money by this means, she could considerably reduce the size of the family budget and acquire a useful practical skill.[10]

There is no evidence that any of these vocational ideas were taken up, although none of them required high levels of ed-

[8] Lilabati Mitra, "Strīlokdiger arthakarī silpasiksā," *Antahpur*, 7, 3 (July 1904).
[9] Binodini Sengupta, "Asmadesīya bālikā-jīban," *Antahpur*, 3, 9 (October 1900).
[10] Prabodhini Ghose, "Bangamahilādiger arthakarī silpacarccā," *Antahpur*, 4, 1 (February 1900).

ucation, and most were easily adapted to the domestic situation. Women would not have been drawn into a much deeper understanding of the wider economic situation by such piecemeal genteel pursuits, where any commercial exchange would probably have been handled by an intermediary. Professional occupations were distinct from these vocational skills in that they required specialized training and relatively advanced educational qualifications. They also involved work outside the home, and brought the *bhadramahilā* into a direct economic relationship with the colonial administration. In all these ways professional employment extended the narrow limits of the world of the *bhadramahilā*, even while it depended on the existence of this separate world. Purdah meant that a field of employment was opened to women without necessitating competition or even contact with men. As a result, women could rise to high-status positions in the fields that were open to them, rather than accepting positions of subordinate status in the same occupations as males, as tended to happen in the west.[11]

Teaching was considered to be one of the most acceptable professions for women, and it employed the largest number of *bhadramahilā*. In the earliest days of female education the services of male teachers were used, but that was perceived as an obstacle to its wider social acceptance, and the expansion of female education created an urgent demand for women teachers. Some of the first generations of educated women decided to extend the benefits of their knowledge to others by taking up teaching as a vocation, at least for some time.

Training schemes for teachers were haphazard, and there was no uniformly accepted qualification during this period. Following suggestions made by Mary Carpenter on her visit in 1866,[12] proposals were presented in 1867 for a Government Female Normal School in Calcutta. Protracted negotiations never reached a satisfactory conclusion, however, and the

[11] H. Papanek, "Men, Women, and Work," p. 104; "Purdah," p. 311.
[12] Mary Carpenter, *Six Months*, pp. 123-124.

scheme was eventually discarded.[13] A Government Training College of a reasonable standard was not set up in Calcutta until 1906.[14] A Female Normal School was set up in Dacca in the 1860s with greater success. The main burden of teacher training in the nineteenth century was borne by Christians and Brahmos, with minimal government assistance. The flexibility of the situation probably provided more women with the opportunity to teach than if there had been greater stress on qualifications. Many women who felt that they had been reasonably well educated at home went on to open schools and to teach without specific training. The report of the Director of Public Instruction in 1904-1905 announced that of 80 women teaching in upper girls' schools, 12 were graduates, 28 had passed lower-level university examinations, and only 8 were trained teachers. In the middle schools, the respective figures were 2, 13, and 14 out of a total of 142. Of 466 upper primary teachers, 1 was a graduate, 8 had passed lower university examinations, and 53 were trained. For lower primary, out of 3,853 women the respective figures were 1 B.A., 1 F.A., 19 E.A., and 186 trained teachers.[15]

One of the first recorded instances of a *bhadramahilā* taking up teaching was that of Bamasoondoree Debee of Pabna. She had been educated at home by her husband; yet in 1863, at the age of twenty or twenty-one, she set up a female school in which she trained other girls to become *zenana* teachers. Whether the school was a financially profitable wage-paying enterprise or not is unknown.[16] Monorama Majumdar, the first woman preacher in the Brahmo Samaj, was also among

[13] Letter from the secretary of the Bamabodhini Sabha on "Siksayitrī bidyālay," *BP*, 3, 53 (January 1868); "Gabarnment siksayitrī bidyālay," *BP*, 6, 90 (February 1871); *GRPI 1869-70*, p. 42; U. Chakraborty, *Condition of Bengali Women*, p. 56.

[14] *Daily Hitavadi*, 24 March 1906, *Hindi Bangavasi*, 26 March 1906 in *RNNB* 31 March 1906; U. Chakraborty, *Condition of Bengali Women*, pp. 57-58.

[15] "Strīsiksā o gabarnment," *BP*, 8:2, 509 (January 1906).

[16] *Somprakās*, 14 December 1863 in *RNNB* 19 December 1863; *ibid.*, 9 May 1864 in *RNNB* 14 May 1864.

9. Poet Kamini Ray (1864-1933),
author of the collection "*Alo o chāyā*"
("Light and Shadow").

the first to take up teaching as a profession. She met with a
great deal of hostility when she began teaching in Barisal in
the 1860s, but she persisted.[17] In 1878 she was appointed
second mistress of the Dacca Government Adult Female School
on a salary of sixty rupees per month.[18]

Not all Bengali women were equally free to take up these
new opportunities. Although a number of women are iden-

---

[17] Interview with her great-granddaughter, Roma Chatterjee, Calcutta, 6
October 1977.
[18] *Brahmo Public Opinion*, 25 July 1878; *IMS*, 11 August 1878.

tifiable as Brahmos, there are many others whose background remains obscure. They were probably either Christians or Hindu widows. Christians were often from lower caste and class groups in which earning one's living was a necessity, and were unhindered by any ideological taboo; and some Hindu widows were also forced into employment by economic necessity. Until the turn of the century very few other Hindu *bhadramahilā* would have been able to overcome traditional prejudices against female employment outside the home.

The Dacca Female Normal School was supposed to cater to Hindu widows, but it is not clear how many of them took advantage of the opportunity this provided. The Report on Public Instruction for 1869-1870 classified the twenty students in this institution as including fifteen from the "lower ranks" and five from the "middle ranks." The school seemed to be fulfilling its aim of providing teachers. Past pupils were reported to be teaching in girls' schools in Rajganj and south Rangpur.[19] Radhamani Debi, a former pupil, was appointed as a teacher at Serpur Girls' School in 1866 on a salary of thirty rupees per month. She must have been one of the first graduates of the school, as the lieutenant-governor asked the commissioner of Dacca for a photograph of her to be sent to England. The impression of her erudition was enhanced by the observation that she wore glasses when reading.[20]

The Native Ladies' Normal School of the Indian Reform Association also produced some trained teachers. In 1874, Srimati Krisnakamini Debi, trained at the school, was appointed to teach at Ranaghat Girls' School. Another teacher from the school opened a girls' school in Harinabhi.[21] One of the most prominent graduates was Radharani Lahiri, who was appointed as second teacher at the Bethune School in 1880 on 60 rupees per month. In 1886 she was promoted to assistant superintendent on 100 rupees per month.[22] She was

[19] *GRPI 1869-70*, p. 222.
[20] *BP*, 2:1, 31 (March 1866).
[21] *BP*, 10, 130 (June 1874); *BP*, 10, 131 (July 1874).
[22] *BP*, 2:2, 188 (September 1880); *BP*, 3:3, 260 (September 1886).

one of the few Bengali *bhadramahilā* not to marry but to follow a career.

Candramukhi Basu, a Bengali Christian and the first woman M.A. from Calcutta University, was appointed assistant superintendent of the Bethune School in 1884 at 75 rupees per month.[23] In 1886 she replaced an Englishwoman as superintendent on a monthly salary of 150 rupees.[24] In general, there was a lack of suitable opportunities in the higher educational service for women graduates. Commenting on the information given in the Report on Public Instruction for 1904-1905 that a graduate was teaching lower primary, an article in *Bāmābodhinī Patrikā* expressed the view that although it was a pleasure to see that a graduate was attracted to teaching small children, she was probably being paid a very low wage and therefore would not remain in the position for long.[25]

Some women were prepared to venture far afield in pursuit of good teaching posts. In 1890 Miss Sarat Cakrabarti, B.A., went to teach at Alexandra Christian Girls' School at Amritsar.[26] Kamini Basu, sister of Candramukhi, was headmistress of Dehra Dun Girls' School.[27] In 1891, Aghorekamini Ray set off for Lucknow to train at the Isabella Thoburn Teachers' College. She spent fourteen hours a day in classes and study, for a period of nine months. On her return to Bankipur in February 1892 she set up her own school, putting into practice the methods she had learned.[28] In 1893, Kumudini Khastagir left her teaching position at Bethune School to teach at the Maharani Girls' School in Mysore.[29] Sarala Debi succeeded her in 1895-1896, taking some time off during that period to act as private secretary to the maharani on the princely salary

---

[23] *BP*, 3:2, 236 (September 1884).
[24] *BP*, 3:3, 260 (September 1886).
[25] "Strīsiksā o gabarnment," *BP*, 509.
[26] *BP*, 4:4, 310 (November 1890).
[27] "Derādun kanyā pāthsālā," *BP*, 8:1, 496-497 (December 1904-January 1905).
[28] Prakascandra Ray, *Aghor-prakās*, pp. 108, 111, 169.
[29] *BP*, 5:1, 339 (April 1893).

of 450 rupees per month.[30] The conservative nationalist news-paper *Bangabāsī* criticized her for aping the west by taking up a post far from home without any acceptable motivation, such as the need to earn a living. She acknowledged that there was some truth in the accusation, because although she believed in a woman's right to earn her living, her main reason for going had been an unmotivated whim. She decided to return to Calcutta.[31]

The development of female education created a demand for women in the educational bureaucracy. The most obvious need was for an inspectress for the girls' schools and *zenana* education schemes that were proliferating by the 1870s.[32] In 1876 Mrs. Monomohini Wheeler, daughter of the Reverend Krishna Mohan Banerjea and widow of an English missionary, was appointed inspectress for Calcutta, Twenty-Four Parganas, and Hughly districts on a monthly salary of 200 rupees with a traveling allowance of 30 rupees per month. In 1879 she was promoted to the Bengal Subordinate Educational Service.[33] A Bengali Christian, she was not restricted by traditional restraints on women's freedom of movement, and even traveled to England and Europe to observe methods of school inspection. She also went around the various outlying districts of Bengal on tours of inspection, braving public hostility.[34] Although Mrs. Wheeler had been publicly criticized in the *Somprakās* for mistakes she made because of an insufficient knowledge of Bengali,[35] the appointment of an Englishwoman as her successor caused much greater consternation. Many Bengali women in the Educational Service had

[30] *BP*, 5:4, 371 (December 1895); *BP*, 5:4, 374 (March 1896); Sarala Debi, *Jībaner jharāpātā*, pp. 106-108.

[31] Sarala Debi, *Jībaner jharāpātā*, pp. 123-124.

[32] *BP*, 7, 93 (May 1871); *BP*, 9, 119 (July 1873).

[33] M. F. Billington, *Woman in India* (London, 1895), pp. 33-34; U. Chakraborty, *Condition of Bengali Women*, pp. 92, 94; *GRPI 1875-76, 1877-78; The Quarterly Civil List for Bengal*, 47 (Calcutta, 1878).

[34] See, for instance, a news report of her tour of Dacca, Mymensingh, Barisal, and Tipperah in *IMS*, 6 January 1878.

[35] *Somprakās*, 24 August 1896 in *RNNB* 29 August 1896.

applied for the position and been turned down. As almost all of the girls' schools under inspection gave instruction in the vernacular, this decision lent weight to the accusation of racial discrimination leveled against the colonial government by liberal newspapers such as the *Sanjībanī*. The appointment was taken as a further indication that the Provincial Educational Service was espousing the same policies as the Indian Educational Service, which had long been closed to natives.[36] In another instance, the appointment of a woman to the educational bureaucracy was seen as a threat to male employment prospects. The Calcutta newspaper *Nabajug* objected to the appointment of Nirmalabala Shome, M.A., as examiner for English in the Entrance Examination. The appointment of a woman and a Christian was seen as "unnatural" when there were educated males who could have filled the position.[37]

Objections to the hiring of female teachers from England were being voiced from as early as 1886, when the post of lady superintendent of the Bethune School fell vacant. By then there were a number of qualified Bengali women who could have taken up the post at a lower salary.[38] Nationalist feeling was satisfied when Candramukhi Basu was appointed, but the controversy resumed when she resigned in 1901. The government wisely decided to appoint Bengali candidates in her place. Surabala Ghose, B.A., became lady superintendent, and Kumudini Das, B.A., the principal.[39] However, most mission schools continued to appoint senior staff from England, thus leaving few opportunities for advancement for the qualified *bhadramahilā*.

Medicine was another profession in which employment possibilities for educated women were enhanced by the operation

[36] *Sanjībanī*, 19 December 1901 in *RNNB* 28 December 1901; *Antahpur*, 4, 12 (December 1901).

[37] *Nabajug*, 16 March 1901 in *RNNB* 23 March 1901.

[38] *Sanjībanī*, 24 July 1886 in *RNNB* 31 July 1886; *Nava Medini*, 19 July 1886 in *RNNB* 7 August 1886.

[39] *Indian Mirror*, 28 September 1901 in *RNNB* 5 October 1901; *Hindoo Patriot*, 8 October 1901 in *RNNB* 19 October 1901; *Antahpur*, 4, 12 (December 1901); *Pratibāsī*, 10 March 1902 in *RNNB* 15 March 1902.

of the purdah system. The need for women doctors was not uniformly accepted. A conservative newspaper, the *Nababibhākar Sādhāranī*, maintained that

> women have not been dying hopelessly for want of female doctors. In most countries the female population exceeds the male population, and the female population is daily increasing. This would not have been the case if women had died largely for want of good medical treatment.[40]

Others held that in cases of serious illness there had never been any hesitation in admitting a male *vaidya* or doctor to the *zenana*.[41] In a contrary vein, those in favor of women doctors claimed that

> we know of several instances in orthodox Hindu families, where the female members suffer from the most complicated diseases, but yet would not allow male doctors to visit and treat them. The consequence is, they are treated second-hand through the assistance of uneducated quack native midwives, and in ninety-nine cases out of a hundred, they are never radically cured.[42]

The indirect method of treatment used by male doctors was described by Koilash Chunder Bose, assistant surgeon, during his testimony in the 1878 Bose versus Bose adultery case. He had been instructed by the accused that his niece had leukorrhea and needed treatment. When cross-examined, he said

> the custom for Hindu ladies is to instruct others [male members] about their ailments. The rule is to communicate through a maid servant, her mother, or guardian. It did not strike me at all strange that Upendro should instruct me. The disease is very common among women. . . . I never spoke to Khettermoney, about that sort of

---

[40] *Nababibhākar Sādhāranī*, 30 May 1887 in *RNNB* 4 June 1887.
[41] *Doinik-O-Samācār Candrikā*, 19 May 1896 in *RNNB* 23 May 1896; see the quotation from this source in Chapter Six; letter from Keshub Chunder Sen in *New Dispensation*, 9 December 1883.
[42] "Female Doctors in Bengal," *Brahmo Public Opinion*, 27 June 1878.

things. I did not treat her. I asked her about it through the maid servant and she denied.[43]

Despite the general acceptance of this situation, in a climate of growing nationalist fervor the absence of women doctors was a claim used to accuse the government of neglect. During the plague outbreak of 1897, vernacular newspapers were unanimous in condemning the government for subjecting women passengers on trains and steamers to inspection by male doctors.[44]

In England, women were allowed to take medical degrees from 1877.[45] In contrast with nursing, the medical profession was seen as eminently suitable for middle-class women.[46] In Bengal it was customary for low-caste women to practice midwifery and for a few others to become *kabirajes*, but women's right to medical education was not immediately accepted.[47]

Dr. Coates, the principal of the Calcutta Medical College, favored the admission of women to medical studies, observing that "if any gentlemen will endow the class and produce the ladies, we will do our best to aid such a good and useful work—one more needed in India than in any other country."[48] Protracted negotiations went on before the scheme was finally implemented. When his daughter passed her final examinations at Bethune College in 1882, Durga Mohan Das applied to the Department of Public Instruction for permission to enroll her in the Calcutta Medical College. The request was turned down, and she was forced to go to Madras to further

[43] Evidence of Koilash Chunder Bose, *Indian Mirror*, 13 August 1878.

[44] *Hitabādī*, 12 March 1897, *Bangabāsī*, 13 March 1897 in *RNNB* 20 March 1897.

[45] P. Thomson, *The Victorian Heroine. A Changing Ideal 1837-1873* (London, 1956), p. 71.

[46] Emily Davies, "Medicine as a Profession for Women" read at a meeting of the National Association for Promotion of Social Science, 1862, in *Thoughts*, p. 37.

[47] Fourteen women were listed as *kabirajes* in the 1891 *Calcutta Census*.

[48] "Female Doctors in Bengal," *Brahmo Public Opinion*, 27 June 1878.

her studies.[49] In 1883 the government passed a resolution admitting women to the college. The minimum admission requirement was a pass in the F.A., although many thought that this could be lowered to the E.A. without significantly lowering standards, and would guarantee quicker results.[50] The Campbell Medical School opened its doors to women in 1887. The standard of entry was lower than for the Calcutta Medical College, and the course lasted for three years.[51]

In 1884 the government announced scholarships of twenty rupees per month for female medical students, tenable for five years.[52] The press recommended the award of a scholarship to Kadambini Ganguly, Calcutta University's first woman graduate and the first female student to enroll in the Medical College.[53] Kadambini was awarded one in July 1884, with provision for retrospective entitlement from the time she commenced her studies in July 1883.[54] The study of medicine by women was further legitimized by a pamphlet issued by the "high priest" of the Baidyanath temple, proving that the study of medical science by women was not opposed to Hinduism.[55]

In the period up to 1905, the number of Bengali women coming forward to study medicine was still small. By 1907 it was estimated that about 17 of the 425 students at the Calcutta Medical College were female.[56] Women who became doctors were rewarded for their efforts by the possibility of earning a substantial independent livelihood. Kadambini Ganguly passed the L.M.S. successfully to become the first woman

[49] *Nababibhākar*, 28 August 1882 in *RNNB* 2 September 1882; *Bhārat Mihir*, 10 October 1882 in *RNNB* 14 October 1882. She passed her first round of examinations, but later gave up the course because of ill health. *BP*, 3:2, 247 (August 1885); Sarala Debi, *Jībaner jharāpātā*, p. 216.

[50] *Pratinidhi*, 5 July 1883 in *RNNB* 7 July 1883.

[51] J. C. Bagal, *Bethune School*, pp. 46-47.

[52] *Educational Gazette*, 16 May 1884, *Prabhābatī*, 17 May 1884, *Sanjībanī*, 17 May 1884 in *RNNB* 24 May 1884.

[53] *Samay*, 19 May 1884, *Prabhābatī*, 19 May 1884, *Nababibhākar*, 19 May 1884 in *RNNB* 24 May 1884.

[54] *Banga Bidyā Prakāsikā*, 10 July 1884 in *RNNB* 12 July 1884.

[55] *Surabhi and Pataka*, 18 February 1886 in *RNNB* 27 February 1886.

[56] H. Sharp, ed., *Progress*, pp. 151-152.

doctor in 1886, although she had failed by one subject in her first attempt.[57] In 1888, she was appointed as a doctor at the Lady Dufferin Women's Hospital on the ample salary of 300 rupees per month.[58] She also set up a flourishing private practice, and amassed considerable wealth by spending some time in the service of the maharaja of Nepal. In 1893 she left her husband and family behind and went to England, to further her studies.[59] She returned with qualifications from Edinburgh, Glasgow, and Dublin, and was appointed superintendent of the Dufferin Hospital. A year later she was made doctor in charge of outpatients of the Eden Female Hospital.[60] Jamini Sen, another prominent lady doctor, passed her L.M.S. in 1897, and went to work in Nepal in 1899. Later in her career she undertook further studies in Glasgow and England. She never married, but devoted all her energies to her career.[61]

The isolation connected with private medical practice, especially in the *mofussil*, made women doctors vulnerable to public criticism. They had to be constantly on guard against attacks on their reputation, as well as occasional physical assault. Charges of admitting female students of dubious background, thereby destroying the reputation of "respectable" students by association, were continually brought against medical college authorities. Most of these attacks were not mounted by conservatives but by Brahmos, who were eager to establish conclusively the respectability of the profession that many Brahmo girls were being encouraged to enter.[62] When Kadambini Ganguly began practicing medicine in Calcutta she was attacked crudely in an editorial in the *Bangabāsī*.

[57] *BP*, 3:3, 260 (September 1886).

[58] *BP*, 4:2, 283 (August 1888).

[59] See Punyalata Cakrabarti, *Chele belār din guli*, pp. 12-13, 21, 126-128 for personal reminiscences of her grandmother Kadambini.

[60] *BP*, 5:1, 339 (April 1893); *BP*, 5:3, 352 (May 1894); U. Chakraborty, *Condition of Bengali Women*, p. 54.

[61] Goutam Neogi, "Dr. Miss Jamini Sen (1871-1932)," *Indian Messenger*, 96, 1 (7 January 1978); *BP*, 6:1, 384 (January 1897).

[62] *Sanjībanī*, 1 September 1888 in *RNNB* 8 September 1888; *ibid.*, 13 October 1888 in *RNNB* 20 October 1888; *ibid.*, 24 November 1888 in *RNNB* 1 December 1888.

The editor was sued for libel, and sentenced to imprisonment in 1891.[63]

Many less prominent lady doctors took up practices in the *mofussil*.[64] They were often subjected to hostile and derisive reactions from the local male population. In 1901, Dr. Bidyulata Mallik was dismissed by the management committee of Rampur Boalia Charitable Dispensary. No charge was brought against her, nor was she given an opportunity to defend herself.[65] The "Malda Lady Doctor's Case" of 1902 was an extreme example of male contempt for women doctors. Pramilabala, a lady doctor of Malda, charged Madan Gopal Chaudhuri, *zamindar*, of abduction with evil intent, and "of having used criminal force with intent to outrage her modesty." She had been called out at night on the false pretext of attending Madan Gopal's wife, and been taken to his boat and assaulted. Newspaper reports expressed indignation at the light punishment imposed on the accused—a fine of 1,000 rupees, which was easily within his means.[66] This kind of hostility and occasional aggression made it extremely difficult for female doctors to carry out their professional duties.

In medicine, as in teaching, professional employment gave the *bhadramahilā* direct experience of frustration at the discriminatory policies of the colonial government. The vernacular press voiced strong objections to the amount of public revenue spent on hiring European lady doctors, who did not speak vernacular languages, when qualified Bengali lady doctors were available in increasing numbers. European lady doctors also charged high fees, which some native lady doctors felt bound to match, thereby putting their services above the means of those most in need. The charge was generally about ten rupees a visit, although one Eurasian lady doctor in Chit-

---

[63] U. Chakraborty, *Condition of Bengali Women*, p. 54.
[64] *BP*, 5:1, 339 (April 1893).
[65] *Hindu Ranjikā*, 22 June 1901 in *RNNB* 6 July 1901.
[66] *Sanjībanī*, 26 June 1902, *Dāccā Prakās*, 29 June 1902 in *RNNB* 5 July 1902; *Sanjībanī*, 3 July 1902 in *RNNB* 12 July 1902; *ibid.*, 10 July 1902 in *RNNB* 19 July 1902.

tagong charged eight for a town visit and thirty-two for the *mofussil*. Posts opened up by the Lady Dufferin Fund, which had been set up to bring medical treatment to the *zenana* women of India, were monopolized by Europeans and Eurasians. In 1905 there were complaints that the European lady superintendent of the Dufferin Hospital in Calcutta was dismissing native nurses in favor of Eurasian nurses from Bombay.[67]

There is ample evidence to sustain the genuineness of these complaints. In broad terms, initial sexual discrimination in England was being turned into racial discrimination in India. Discrimination against women doctors in England forced them to look to the colonies for employment. *Work and Leisure*, a journal devoted to discussion of female employment prospects, was of the opinion that

> the competition of a few hundred medical women can have but little, if any, effect upon the incomes of medical men in England, while thousands might be absorbed in Oriental countries without injury to any one. India alone affords a vast field to medical women, and we are glad to learn that many of the students at this school [London School of Medicine for Women] have become Medical Missionaries.[68]

In India, English women doctors were able to take advantage of the racial discrimination of the colonial power to monopolize all available positions, thereby hindering the advancement of Indian women doctors. The colonial mentality, and basic self-interest, prevented English lady doctors from perceiving any common elements in their experience of discrimination. Indian women doctors were left to labor under the oppressive effects of dual discrimination on grounds of both sex and race.

[67] There were constant complaints of this nature from the 1890s. See *RNNB* 1890-1905.

[68] *Work and Leisure, The Englishwoman's Advertiser, Reporter, and Gazette*, 6, 7 (July 1881).

Whereas medicine was a prestigious profession, for the lower ranks of the *bhadramahilā* on the margins of society, such as widows, midwifery was a more feasible career. Educational requirements were less exacting, the training period was shorter, and employment was easily obtainable. The opinion voiced by Keshub Chunder Sen in 1883 was shared by many:

> To us Indians, in the present state of Native Society, lady M.D.'s are an expensive luxury which may possibly be excluded from all serious consideration at least for some time to come, but competent midwives are to us a necessity which cannot be dispensed with. Indian women do not die because of the absence of female doctors possessed of high University honors, but deaths, miserable and horrible, have actually resulted from the want of good midwives. It is this great question, therefore, which, affecting, as it does, the lives of thousands of the middle classes of the Native population, must be faced and solved by all reformers and philanthropists as the most pressing question of the day in India.[69]

Midwifery courses were opened at Calcutta Medical College in 1870.[70] Initially, twelve women were enrolled for a one-year training course.[71] As usual, concern was expressed that all women selected for the course should be "respectable." Special purdah arrangements were considered necessary to attract such women, and extra vigilance was required to deter those of "bad repute."[72] In 1879 Srimati J. L. Ghosh and Srimati T. M. Ray, "midwives, holding diploma of the Calcutta Medical College Hospital," proudly advertised their practice at 103 College Street, Calcutta, in the pages of *Brahmo Public Opinion*.[73] By 1880 there were about half a dozen

[69] Letter from Keshub Chunder Sen, *New Dispensation*, 9 December 1883.
[70] *Somprakās*, 24 January 1870 in *RNNB* 29 January 1870.
[71] *Indian Mirror*, 10 December 1869 in *RNNB* 29 January 1870.
[72] *Ārjya Darpan*, 29 April 1881 in *RNNB* 30 April 1881; *Samay*, 14 July 1884 in *RNNB* 19 July 1884; *Sanjībanī*, 14 May 1887 in *RNNB* 21 May 1887.
[73] *Brahmo Public Opinion*, 7 August 1879.

trained midwives practicing in Calcutta. Their success was attracting others from the *mofussil*, and expansion of the training program was recommended because of the increasing supply of recruits. Many "Hindoo widows of respectable families" were prepared to take up midwifery.[74] Brahmos encouraged *bhadramahilā* who had to earn their living to train as midwives. Basantakumari Debi, widowed as a child, was attracted to Brahmoism when teaching at the girls' school in Mymensingh. Her family opposed her conversion, and to remove her from their efforts to reclaim her, the Mymensingh Brahmos sent her to Calcutta to study midwifery in the early 1890s. In 1896 she married a missionary of the Sadharan Brahmo Samaj. It is not known whether she continued to practice professionally after her marriage.[75]

Government employers often felt that it was more useful, and economical, to employ midwives instead of doctors. The Chittagong District Board, very dissatisfied with its European lady doctor, felt that it would be of more benefit to the local community to have a skilled midwife.[76] In 1898 the Tippera District Board considered opening a midwifery class to be taught by the lady doctor of the *zenana* hospital in Comilla, as her hospital workload was fairly light.[77] The District Board of Contai was advised to appoint a midwife who could also serve as teacher of the local girls' school, to save extra expenses.[78]

Other occupations gained a handful of adherents from among the *bhadramahilā*. Educated women who needed to support themselves could become governesses. Occasional advertisements asking for Bengali women to act as "governess and companion" appeared in the press.[79] Mohini Khastagir was appointed governess to the maharani of Cuch Behar in 1878 on a salary of fifty rupees per month.[80] Sarala Debi was ap-

---

[74] *Ibid.*, 22 July 1880.
[75] Srinath Canda, *Brāhmasamāje callis bathsar*, pp. 257-258.
[76] *Sangsodhinī*, 1 March 1895 in *RNNB* 16 March 1895.
[77] *Tripura Hitaishini*, December 1898 in *RNNB* 10 December 1898.
[78] *Nihar (Contai)*, 30 June 1903 in *RNNB* 4 July 1903.
[79] *IMS*, 18 May 1879; *ibid.*, 18 July 1880.
[80] *Brahmo Public Opinion*, 25 July 1878.

pointed librarian of the Calcutta Public Library in 1890, but did not take up the position because of public objections to a woman filling a post that involved constant direct dealing with men.[81] Female photographers advertised purdah studios, where women could have their photographs taken without any contact with men. If the women were still reluctant to leave their homes, female photographers would go to the *zenana* for the additional cost of two rupees carriage hire.[82]

The *bhadramahilā* were very slow to press for entry into the legal profession, which was the province of so many of their menfolk. Female *zamindars* were often involved in litigation over property, and there were also numerous criminal and assault cases involving lower-caste women in which women lawyers could have served a useful function. Men may have objected to female encroachment on their professional monopoly. One of the main obstacles, both in India and in England, was bureaucratic: although a woman could study law, she was not allowed to practice it. In 1897 Miss Matilda Cohen, M.A., applied to become an attorney of the Calcutta High Court, but was rejected.[83] Cornelia Sorabji, a Parsi law graduate of Bombay University, had been excluded from enrolling as a *vakil* in Bombay in 1897 because the judges felt that "it would be impertinent of an Indian High Court to admit women to the Rolls before England had given the lead."[84] In 1904 she was appointed by the Bengal government as legal adviser to *pardānasīn* in the Court of Wards. Despite her success in this capacity, she was not admitted to the Rolls until 1922.[85]

By the late nineteenth century, the field of clerical employment for women was expanding. In the early stages, the only

[81] Dr. Mahendra Lal Sircar objected, and was supported by the *Samay*. 8 August 1890 in *RNNB* 16 August 1890.

[82] See advertisement for the "Mahila Art Studio and Photographic Store" in the back of Durgadas De, *Encore! 999!!! or Srīmatī* (Calcutta, 1899). The 1901 *Calcutta Census* listed four female photographers.

[83] *BP*, 6:2, 392 (September 1897); *Sanjībanī*, 14 August 1897 in *RNNB* 21 August 1897.

[84] C. Sorabji, *India Calling*, pp. 100-102.

[85] *BP*, 8:1, 489 (May 1904); C. Sorabji, *India Calling*, p. 302.

women to take advantage of this were Eurasian or English. The surplus of women in England, and the social taboos on "respectable" women earning their own livelihood there, meant that many looked to the colonies for the possibility of earning an independent income without incurring social disapproval.[86] The colonial system in India provided many opportunities for these women, but not without provoking a hostile reaction from educated Indian men, who were themselves having difficulty in finding clerical positions. It was felt that English women were taking positions away from Indian men, thus contributing to unemployment among the *bhadralok*. Men did not resent the *bhadramahilā* taking up positions that served women living in purdah, because that did not substantially challenge their own chances of employment or their ideological perceptions of women's role. In general, employed *bhadramahilā* were not competing with men, and could therefore rise to positions of high status within their field. However, in unsegregated public employment, where Englishwomen were employed above them, the *bhadralok* felt themselves reduced to a humiliating position of subordination. Whereas in western industralized countries women would act as low-status assistants to men in any given field, in India the position was reversed and male graduates could find themselves working as subordinates of English women. The perceived emasculation of men under these conditions added to their feelings of frustration and humiliation at colonial rule.

In 1904 an advertisement appeared in the *Calcutta Gazette* for the post of registered apprentice in the Office of the Director of Public Instruction. The salary was only ten rupees a month, but the candidate was expected to have "a B.A. or F.A. with a knowledge of typewriting."[87] This was but one example of the tightness of the labor market and the paucity

[86] See A. J. Hammerton, *Emigrant Gentlewomen. Genteel Poverty and Female Emigration 1830-1914* (London, 1979).

[87] *Sri Sri Bisnu Priya-O-Ananda Bājār Patrikā*, 7 December 1904, *Hitabādī*, 9 December 1904, *Bangabāsī*, 10 December 1904 in *RNNB* 17 December 1904.

of jobs for graduates commensurate with their qualifications. It also showed the growing demand for secretarial skills, in which English women would be more likely to have training than most Bengali graduates.

In 1881 the government announced that women were to be employed in telegraph offices.[88] Eurasian women were the only group to respond, and were attacked by the vernacular press for depriving native males of employment.[89] One newspaper claimed that Englishmen "not content with plundering India themselves are asking their mothers and sisters to help them."[90] In some departments of the East Bengal State Railway Authorities there was also a tendency to employ Eurasian girls as typists rather than Bengali male clerks who could have been hired at much lower salaries.[91] The Postal Department was accused of the same bias.[92]

Bengali women's journals showed a markedly different response to the creation of new fields of employment for women. In 1899 the *Bāmābodhinī Patrikā* reported that in Hughly district the postmaster had been replaced by an Englishwoman on fifty rupees per month. The editorial comment was that any expansion of women's sphere of work was a good thing.[93] In 1905, the *Bāmābodhinī Patrikā* gave statistics for women employed as clerks in post and telegraph offices in Germany (200,042), Great Britain (100,084), Russia (60,000), Austria (50,000), and France (18,000). The article claimed that there were 60,000 female clerks in British India, all of whom were Europeans or Eurasians. The editorial called on educated native ladies to take an interest, with the reminder that Japan,

[88] *BP*, 2:3, 188 (July 1881). The editor commented that in England the employment of women in telegraph and post offices was common.
[89] *Pataka*, 4 September 1884 in *RNNB* 12 September 1884; *Bhārat Bāsī*, 12 October 1884, *Sādhāranī*, 12 October 1884 in *RNNB* 19 October 1884.
[90] *Bheri*, 27 November 1885 in *RNNB* 5 December 1885.
[91] *Sahacar*, 5 June 1895 in *RNNB* 15 June 1895.
[92] *Hitabādī*, 7 May 1897 in *RNNB* 15 May 1897; *Pratibāsī*, 15 July 1901 in *RNNB* 3 August 1901.
[93] *BP*, 6:4, 412 (May 1899).

another Asian nation, had about 60,000 female clerks.[94] From their inception, Bengali women's journals noted with approval the developments in the female workforce elsewhere, especially in Britain and the United States.[95] During the nineteenth century, however, the social disapproval of working conditions that entailed mixing with men as colleagues and clients effectively barred the *bhadramahilā*'s entry into the sphere of clerical work.[96]

In many respects male enthusiasm for female employment dwindled as the prospect became a reality. In 1857, Girish Chunder Ghose had written an editorial on "Female Labor" in the *Hindoo Patriot* which concluded with a glowing paean to the American woman:

> The American lady, as she may turn out if she has her right, is woman only in sex and amiability. Her mind is masculine, her occupations are masculine, her rights and privileges are on a broad equality with those of men. She is less a cormorant upon the purse of her husband than the London belle. She works for her bread. She carries the gentleness of her nature into the counting house. She imparts a gloss to the rough manner of trade, and a polish to the style of the press. As a doctor, she relieves her sex from otherwise unavoidable subjection to indelicacies against which disease leaves no help. She is fine in every department of business where the head works more than the hand, and civilization owes to her a lasting debt in America. We can only admire the destiny of the Western

[94] *BP,* 8:2, 505-506 (September-October 1905).
[95] See for instance *BP,* 3, 55 (March 1868), or "Strīlokdiger kārjyaksetra," *BP,* 3:2, 234 (July 1884).
[96] *Amrita Bazar Patrika,* 5 September 1901 in *RNNB* 7 September 1901 reported a charge of misconduct brought against a Muslim postal clerk by a Eurasian female clerk with the comment that so long as males and females were employed in the same office such scandals were inevitable. P. Kapur, *The Changing Status of the Working Woman in India* (Delhi, 1974) noted that the entry of middle-class women into clerical positions, and indeed into formerly male spheres of employment, was a post-Independence phenomenon (p. 45).

Hemisphere, for ages must roll away before we can attempt to realise it in our own country.[97]

This viewpoint was eclipsed as the century went on and the number of educated women increased. In 1896, the reactionary *Banganibāsī* proclaimed that "the earning of their own livelihood by women is a thing repugnant to the Hindu religion." It cautioned Brahmins and Kayasthas against sending their daughters to Bethune College because many Bengali ladies were earning their livelihood after finishing their education there.[98]

Despite the advances that had undoubtedly been made, the expansion in female employment in Bengal at the end of the nineteenth century was not nearly as rapid as it had been in England and the United States.[99] Obviously the purdah system was a major cause of the discrepancy, barring as it did women's entry into unsegregated occupations.[100] A book on female employment in India sponsored by the maharani of Baroda, published in 1911, illustrated this point well. Numerous occupations practiced by women in England—such as poultry keeping, horticulture, acting as estate agents or as domestic architects, hotel and restaurant management, factory inspection, and many others—were put forward as possibilities for women in India. In reality, most of these professions would have been rejected by the *bhadramahilā* as conflicting with purdah and home duties.[101]

---

[97] "Female Labor," *Hindoo Patriot*, 16 April 1857 in M. N. Ghosh, *The Life of Grish Chunder Ghose*, p. 252.

[98] *Banganibāsī*, 15 March 1896 in *RNNB* 21 March 1896.

[99] In America, the number of women in clerical positions increased from 5.3 percent to 25.6 percent of the non-agricultural female workforce between 1890 and 1920. A. Kessler-Harris, "Women, Work and the Social Order" in B. A. Carroll, ed., *Liberating Women's History. Theoretical and Critical Essays* (Urbana, Illinois, 1976), p. 337. In England, the percentage of women in "middle-class" or white-collar occupations increased from 12.6 percent in 1881 to 23.7 percent in 1911. L. Holcombe, *Victorian Ladies at Work* (Hamden, Connecticut, 1973), p. 216.

[100] H. Papanek, "Men, Women, and Work," p. 104; E. Boserup, *Woman's Role in Economic Development* (London, 1970), pp. 217-218.

[101] The Maharani of Baroda and S. M. Mitra, *The Position of Women in Indian Life*.

Women who entered white-collar occupations in England generally came from the "surplus" of unmarried women in the population. There was no corresponding group among the *bhadramahilā*. In Bengal, apart from a handful of women who never married, widows formed the closest approximation to a group of single women. Although traditionally they were provided for in the family, they were regarded as a burden. The opportunity to earn their own living should therefore have been welcome both to widows themselves and to those responsible for their support, but ideological proscriptions prevailed over economic realities, and widows were almost as restricted as other women by the limits of purdah.

For the few *bhadramahilā* who acquired an advanced education, marriage marked the end of any career aspirations they may have had. In some cases marriage even interrupted their educational progress. Sarala Das, along with Kadambini Basu, was coached by Dwarkanath Ganguly to be one of the first candidates to be admitted to the E.A. The university gave them permission to sit the examination in December 1878, but as Sarala was to be married to Dr. P. K. Ray before that date she did not sit. Later she started a girls' school in Dacca and taught there herself, but not in a salaried position.[102] Hemantakumari Chaudhuri did not sit for her E.A. because she was married before then, in 1885.[103] Sarala Sen graduated from Calcutta University in 1897. She married barrister Satisranjan Das, son of Durga Mohan Das, shortly thereafter. She had once thought of remaining single in order to carry out good works, but the happiness of her marriage persuaded her that this was enough in itself.[104]

A few *bhadramahilā* gained some work experience after completing their education, but did not continue to work after marriage. Sisir Kumari Bagchi graduated in 1898, aged twenty.

[102] Prabhatcandra Gangopadhyay, in Sarala Ray Centenary Committee, *Sarala Ray*, pp. 93-95.

[103] Interview with her daughter, Sailaja Chakravarty, Calcutta, 13 February 1978.

[104] Amritalal Gupta, *Punyabatī nārī*, pp. 8-11.

She taught briefly at the Brahmo Girls' School before her marriage.[105] Sibnath Sastri's daughter Hemlata was lady superintendent at the school for a period in the early 1890s, but gave up the position on her marriage in 1893. Although these interim positions did provide women with valuable work experience, they were "genteel" occupations in the sense that women were paid "pocket money" rather than a proper salary. Hemlata received twenty-five rupees per month as lady superintendent, and her successor Labanyaprabha Basu, a single woman, received thirty-five.[106] The feeling that a married woman should devote her time to home and family was reinforced by the prevalent middle-class ideology of Victorian England.[107]

The expansion of female employment in Bengal was a complex and gradual development. The purdah system proved both a boon and a bind to the educated *bhadramahila*. It restricted the range of occupations they could enter and inhibited their freedom of movement, but its very existence provided some of them with the opportunity to act as mediators with the outside world.[108] Men were excluded from this role, so women had an open field in which they could rise to the highest positions. During the period to 1905, most employed *bhadramahila* were engaged in providing services to the separate female world of purdah.

Economic necessity was not the main motivation in seeking employment for most educated *bhadramahila*. The most highly educated women, and those who were most likely to find professional employment, usually came from a financially prosperous elite. They sought employment in order to gain

---

[105] Interview with her son, Kalyan Dutt, Santiniketan, 16 November 1977.

[106] Gurucharan Mahalanabis, *Ātmakathā*, pp. 126-128.

[107] See quotation from Frances Power Cobbe in Chapter Eight, and a letter from an Englishwoman on "Women's Work" in *Paricārikā*, 1, 9 (February 1878).

[108] As E. Boserup, *Woman's Role*, noted: "The employment of a limited number of women in the professions makes it possible for the great majority of women to avoid exposure to contacts with male professional staff," p. 127.

work experience, to put their knowledge to a socially useful purpose, and for personal satisfaction. Yet the era also began to open up opportunities for *bhadramahilā* who needed to work for their living. Widows training to be midwives or teachers, for instance, sought employment because of financial necessity. For the married *bhadramahilā*, no matter what the financial position of her family, paid employment was not an option. She could economize within the household, but was not free to supplement the family income by working.

Although at this stage only a small number of women were employed, the pattern of their employment set trends for the future. The need for mediators between the *antahpur* and the ever-encroaching outside world was established, as was the precedent of salaried financial independence for women. Contact with the public world of the colonial administration gave the *bhadramahilā* direct experience of the racial discrimination and attendant frustration commonly felt by the *bhadralok*, and contributed to the development of a nationalist political consciousness.

Political awareness and participation

The growth of nationalist sentiment among the *bhadralok* from the late 1860s could not but have filtered through to the *antahpur*. The humiliating incidents of racial discrimination experienced by Bengalis in their dealings with the colonial rulers had such a deep impact that family life and personal relations were inevitably affected. In this way, women had vicarious experience of racial humiliation and the resultant dissatisfaction with colonial rule. However, the *bhadramahilā* were not directly involved with the workings of the colonial administration or economy, nor did they have any immediate access to information about how it operated. They had no intellectual understanding of the detrimental effects of colonialism. In the nineteenth century, most *bhadramahilā* could only respond to nationalism as a result of indirect personal experience.

The lack of direct contact with British administration meant that women were likely to have retained notions of the providentiality of British rule for longer than their menfolk. Major developments such as female education were seen as an outcome of enlightened British encouragement, and British attitudes toward women were commended as the expression of a superior civilization. Women had no direct acquaintance with the less benevolent aspects of colonial rule to counteract this impression.

Politics was not considered a suitable subject for women. The editorial in the first issue of a new journal for women started in 1875, the *Banga Mahilā*, stated that

> in this journal we will make special efforts to assemble as much as possible on current events. We will not discuss political events and controversies because politics would not be interesting or intelligible to women in this country at present. But we will not be adverse to describing them insofar as they touch on social customs and behavior.[109]

It was not until 1884 that *Bāmābodhinī Patrikā* introduced articles on political subjects, with the explanation that

> in Bengal the time to teach women about politics has not yet come. In a country where many well-educated youths are incapable of understanding politics it will be a long time before the way can be prepared for teaching politics to women. But whether our women understand politics or not, it is essential that they possess a general knowledge of the past and present state of the country.[110]

An article on the political history of ancient India was followed by two others continuing the saga up until the advent of British rule. This was described in the terms used by British historians, according to whom the British "delivered" India from tyranny and established the rule of law. In 1905, *Bāmā-*

[109] *Banga Mahilā*, 1, 1 (May 1875).
[110] "Āmāder deser tin abasthā," *BP*, 3:2, 237 (October 1884).

bodhinī Patrikā ran a series of informative articles on eco-
nomics, which took the form of dialogues between two women
on subjects such as the origin, division, and exchange of wealth,
and the difference between productive and unproductive capital investment.[111]

Not surprisingly, the combined effect of physical seclusion
and lack of information on political developments meant that
women's active participation in politics was minimal. As early
as 1871, *Bāmābodhinī Patrikā* recorded the presence of Hindu
women at a Town Hall meeting of students, but it was not
clear from this account who they were or why they were
there.[112] In 1882, the *New Dispensation* mentioned that some
zenana ladies came in carriages to cast their votes in the municipal elections in Burdwan.[113] However, these are very tenuous indications of the general level of political consciousness
among women.

Women were not drawn into political controversy until the
period of agitation over the Ilbert Bill, which allowed Indian
judges to try cases involving English women. Representatives
of the educated *bhadramahilā*—"Binodini, Sulochona, Cha-
pala, Bhabini, Manorama, Horosundari, Thakomoni, etc.
etc."—wrote to Lord Ripon calling for the bill to be passed,
on the grounds that native civilians who had been through
the rigors of training abroad were entirely competent as judges,
and that Indian women were not "ignorant and enslaved."
With some satisfaction, they pointed out that while many of
them were well-educated and some even had degrees, there
was not "a single graduate" among the English ladies who
were protesting against the bill.[114] A few months later the

[111] "Arthanīti," *BP*, 8:2, 502-503 (June-July 1905); *BP*, 8:2, 505-506 (September-October 1905); *BP*, 8:2, 508 (December 1905); *BP*, 8:2, 509 (January
1906).

[112] *BP*, 6, 92 (April 1871).

[113] *New Dispensation*, 21 May 1882.

[114] *New Dispensation*, 22 April 1883. The identity of the signatories is
difficult to establish with certainty because surnames and addresses were not
given. "Manorama" Majumdar of Barisal, and "Horosundari" Datta, both
educated Brahmo women, may have been among them. In 1883 the only
Bengali female graduate was Kadambini Ganguly.

New Dispensation referred derisively to the letter, calling it a "squib . . . in the shape of a memorial." "Contemporaries both in India and in England" were ridiculed for taking it to be "a serious piece of composition."[115] The disparaging of political awareness among the *bhadramahilā* seems gratuitous. Kamini Sen led a movement in favor of the bill among students at the Bethune School and College. Girls wore black ribbons on their sleeves when Surendranath Banerjea was jailed, just as their male counterparts did.[116]

Some sections of the community were opposed to the holding of political views by women. When Ramabai attacked the government for mismanagement in the Poona Plague Hospital in 1897, the *Bangabāsī* expressed the view that "this is no reason why a woman should write so strongly against the Government."[117] However, the Ilbert Bill agitation made some nationalist politicians aware of the political potential of women. At a meeting of the Indian Association in 1883, Surendranath Banerjea suggested that the services of Indian womanhood could be used "in the political elevation of the country." The idea came to him after receiving numerous "tokens of sympathy" from women during his time in prison. Characteristically, the *New Dispensation* had reservations as to the propriety of the proposal: "Every one knows the amount of abuse to which we are subjected in consequence of the Criminal Bill agitation; is it definitely proposed to carry harmless and helpless ladies through the dirt of all this Billingsgate?"[118] Nevertheless, by 1892 some unnamed candidates for the Calcutta Municipal elections were using "respectable native ladies" to canvass votes, despite conservative disapproval.[119]

Hindu nationalists used women as political symbols of national awakening. Many of the heroines of Bankim Chandra Chatterjee, for instance, were depicted as brave fighters in the service of their country. Through their heroism, they presented

---

[115] *New Dispensation*, 24 June 1883.
[116] Sarala Debi, *Jībaner jharāpātā*, pp. 28, 216.
[117] *Bangabāsī*, 18 September 1897 in *RNNB* 25 September 1897.
[118] *New Dispensation*, 22 July 1883.
[119] *Pratikar*, 5 February 1892 in *RNNB* 20 February 1892.

a challenge to Bengali males to assert their masculinity in defense of the country and in protection of their women, whose rightful place was ultimately in the home.[120] Bengal was identified with the Mother in the nationalist anthem "Bande Mataram." The symbolic force of the concept of Mother created a basis for acceptance of women's involvement in political activity.

The Mother-centered rhetoric of Hindu nationalism may help to explain how Sarala Debi gained recognition as a leader of militant nationalism in its early stages. She did not attempt to become involved in the formal political activity of male associations, but used the symbolic power of local history and legend to create political consciousness, and was one of the most energetic and imaginative proponents of Bengali nationalism. Her activities were varied: the creation of Pratapaditya as a Bengali hero of stature equal to that of Shivaji; publication of a series of children's books on the lives of Bengali heroes; composition of patriotic songs; and the organization of classes for increasing physical stamina by means of sword and *lāthi* play, boxing, and gymnastics.[121] All of these emphasized aggressively "masculine" qualities such as physical strength, bravery, and heroism. Her defiance of the conventional female role did not escape notice. The *Rangalay* felt "uneasy and suspicious":

> In Sanskrit literature and in Sanskrit *Puranas* and chronicles one comes across female characters who were wives and mothers of heroes, but under the influence of her English learning the Bengali girl of the day will be content with playing nothing short of the *role* of the hero herself.[122]

[120] For instance *Anandamāth* (1882) and *Debī Caudhurānī* (1884). See the review of *Debī Caudhurānī* in *New Dispensation*, 18 May 1884.

[121] *Sanjībanī*, 4 June 1903 in *RNNB* 13 June 1903; *Bangabāsī*, 23 May 1903 in *RNNB* 30 May 1903; *Jyoti* 15 October 1903, *Basumati* 17 October 1903 in *RNNB* 24 October 1903. See also her autobiography, Sarala Debi, *Jībaner jharāpātā*.

[122] *Rangalay*, 6 September 1903 in *RNNB* 12 September 1903.

A conjunction of favorable circumstances, including her financial and social position as a member of the Tagore family, her own strong personality, and the rhetorical thrust of Hindu nationalism, made it possible for her to participate actively in politics in a way that was open to very few women. The only woman in the pantheon of early nationalist heroes, she saw herself as a participant in a general political struggle rather than as a representative of women's interests. She did not attempt to mobilize women as a group at this stage. The freedom she experienced in the role of nationalist activist may have made her loath to stress her separate female identity with its associated restrictive code of behavior. Ultimately, Sarala Debi was such an outstanding and exceptional figure that her activities had few implications for the general political participation of women.

The formation of the Indian National Congress in 1885 marked the beginning of organized political activity at a national level. By 1889, a handful of women had been drawn into the annual Congress meeting. Owing to the efforts of Dwarkanath Ganguly, six women delegates were present at the 1889 Congress session in Bombay. The two from Bengal were Dwarkanath's wife Kadambini, and Swarnakumari Debi, wife of Janakinath Ghosal.[123] The presence of both women was closely connected with the extent of their husbands' links with Congress politics. Orthodox opinion objected even to this limited participation, and ridiculed Dwarkanath for insisting on the right of women to be represented in Congress to express their views, and on their right to be elected members of the Legislative Council. Ironically, the trump card of the conservatives was that "it must be too much to demand for them rights which have not yet been granted to their more

[123] Prabhatcandra Gangopadhyay, *Bānglār nārī-jāgaran*, p. 87; names of delegates were also listed in Chabi Ray, *Bānglār nārī āndolan*, p. 46; *BP*, 4:4, 304 (May 1890) mentioned that there were ten women at the Bombay session, including two Englishwomen, three Maharastrians, a Parsi, Ramabai, and three Bengalis.

advanced sisters in England and America."[124] The *Sangbād Prabhākar* was of the opinion that ladies should attend Congress as visitors, but not as delegates.[125]

At the sixth session, held in Calcutta the following year, Swarnakumari Debi was the only woman delegate.[126] Her presence was barely noticed. Kadambini Ganguly, who moved the vote of thanks to the chairman in English, was the center of attraction on that occasion. Annie Besant hailed Kadambini's participation as "a symbol that India's freedom would uplift India's Womanhood."[127] As the implications of nationalism for the position of women had barely been considered at this early stage, her enthusiastic statement presaged the rhetoric of a later generation. In the 1890s, the revivalist aspect of nationalist ideology invoked a restoration of the traditional social order that emphasized a passive domestic role for women. Women who were marginally involved with Congress affairs, such as Kadambini Ganguly or Swarnakumari Debi, were there primarily because of their husbands' activities rather than as representatives of any constituency in their own right. They put forward no demands and voiced no opinions; they were token representatives rather than full political participants.

Most *bhadramahilā* would not have been able to follow the Congress proceedings, which were conducted in English. The physical mobility, financial resources, and knowledge of English required for women to be able to attend Congress sessions in different parts of India excluded most middle-class women. Those who could participate formed a tiny elite of westernized Hindu and Brahmo women. A visitor to the Benares Congress in 1905, not herself a prominent figure, seemed impressed by the social standing of the other Bengali lady visitors, who included the women of R. C. Dutt's family, Lady Abala Bose,

[124] *Pratikar*, 3 January 1890 in *RNNB* 18 January 1890.
[125] *Sangbād Prabhākar*, 15 August 1890 in *RNNB* 30 August 1890.
[126] Brajendranath Bandopadhyay, *Swarnakumārī Debī*, p. 26.
[127] From A. Besant, *How India Wrought for Freedom,* quoted in Prabhatcandra Gangopadhyay, *Bānglār nārī-jāgaran*, p. 87.

and the former editor of *Antahpur*, Hemantakumari Chau-dhuri.[128] Like this observer, many women saw Congress sessions as social occasions and public spectacles rather than as serious political gatherings, because of their limited participation. In Calcutta in 1901, purdah women were present as observers for the first time, and about two hundred women from respectable Calcutta families attended.[129] Their presence reinforces the impression that most *bhadramahilā* were only able to attend Congress when it was in their home city, and that there was probably some social benefit to be gained from attendance at such an important event. Sarojini Ghose, a typically domestic *bhadramahilā*, attended one or two of the Calcutta Congress sessions to observe the variety in dress and customs of people from other parts of India.[130]

Surendranath Banerjea attempted to arouse women's enthusiasm for the Congress cause by lecturing on "Women's Duties towards Congress" to a gathering at the home of Dr. Mohini Mohan Bose in 1890.[131] In the same year, an article in *Bāmābodhinī Patrikā* suggested ways in which women could become involved with Congress: they could contribute donations, collect subscriptions, sell their own handiwork to raise funds, or publicize its activities through writing books and teaching their own children about it. Ardent nationalists tried to impress women with the urgent need for their participation by claiming that Congress could not function without their help.[132]

Women's interests were better served by the National Social Conference, created as an adjunct to the Indian National Congress in 1887 and held annually after the conclusion of the main Congress sessions. An anonymous account of the conference held in Lahore in December 1900 was enthusiastic

[128] Sri Sasimukhi Debi, Benares, "Benārās Kangreser āngsik citra," *BP*, 8:2, 509 (January 1906).
[129] Sri Tarulata Debi, "Jātiya mahāsamiti," *Antahpur*, 4, 12 (December 1901).
[130] Renuka Ghose, *Sarojinī-carit*, p. 46.
[131] *BP*, 4:4, 308 (September 1890).
[132] Sri Su-Singha, "Jātiya mahā samiti," *BP*, 4:4, 309 (October 1890).

about the way issues such as the extension of female education could be tackled on a national scale.[133] An article in *Antahpur* on the 1902 Congress session in Ahmedabad noted that at least thirty women were present. It was pointed out, however, that although women could not really advance equally with men in the political sphere, they could easily contribute along with men to the National Social Conference, especially in matters concerning women.[134] Even so, the Social Conference was a predominantly male concern, probably because of its importance as a "neutral" platform that enabled government servants to comment on public issues.[135] In 1902 there were fifty women and one thousand men present at the Conference.[136]

During the early years of Congress, the representation of women remained low. Only about twenty of the nine hundred delegates to the 1904 session were women.[137] At the Benares Congress in 1905, women took the initiative in holding their own session for the first time. Over six hundred women from all parts of India gathered. Most of the speeches were in Hindi, including those by Bengalis, although a few were in English. An article about the meeting in *Bāmābodhinī Patrikā* did not give details of the speeches, but most were on the subjects of patriotism and the duties of women, or female education. The main purpose of the meeting was the creation of female solidarity across India, and the mobilization of women's support for the nationalist movement.[138]

Unlike English women, the Bengali *bhadramahilā* were not politicized over the question of the franchise. Through the press, the Bengali *bhadralok* were aware of the parliamentary

---

[133] "Samājik samiti," *Antahpur*, 4, 1 (January 1901).
[134] "Jātiya mahāsamiti," *Antahpur*, 5, 10 (February 1903).
[135] C. H. Heimsath, *Indian Nationalism and Hindu Social Reform* (Princeton, 1964), p. 190. Heimsath's detailed account of the activities of the National Social Conference does not even mention the presence or participation of women.
[136] *BP*, 7:3, 473-474 (January-February 1903).
[137] *BP*, 8:1, 496-497 (December 1904-January 1905).
[138] Sri Ni- Debi, "Kāsite strī-sammilanī," *BP*, 8:2, 509 (January 1906).

campaigns of J. S. Mill and of the struggle for the vote for women going on in Britain. Progressive *bhadralok* supported the cause of female suffrage in Britain. A writer in the journal *Dāsī* noted with approval that through their own efforts women were gradually taking hold of their rights.[139] Brahmo leaders were in close contact with feminists such as Frances Power Cobbe, who was an active supporter of female suffrage. She put the case forcefully:

> In a government like ours, where the basis of representation is so immensely extensive, the whole business of legislation is carried on *by pressure,*—the pressure of each represented class and party to get its grievances redressed, to make its interests prevail. The non-represented classes necessarily go to the wall. . . . To be *one of a represented class* is a very much greater thing in England than merely to drop a paper into a ballot-box. It means to be able to *insist* upon attention to the wants of that class, and to all other matters of public importance which may be deemed deserving of attention.[140]

In India, her suffragist argument for the right to representation was seen as more relevant to the situation of the *bhadralok* than that of the *bhadramahilā*. It was the *bhadralok* who paid heed to the strategy and tactics of the English feminists in their struggle for the vote. An item in the *Brahmo Public Opinion* in 1880 noted that

> the women of England cry shame to us in point of organisation and agitation in matters affecting our rights and privileges. Profiting by the advent of the Liberal Ministry to power, the women are convening meetings after meetings to agitate the question of their suffrage to vote at Parliamentary elections.[141]

[139] Dwarkanath Sarkar, in an article on the Diamond Jubilee in *Dāsī*, 6, 3-4-5 (March-April-May 1897).
[140] F. P. Cobbe, *The Duties of Women*, pp. 181-182.
[141] *Brahmo Public Opinion*, 3 June 1880.

The same newspaper also drew a parallel between the discontent and restlessness among educated English girls and the frustration of educated Bengali youth:

> The difficulty now felt is due, we think, to the improved culture that the young women of England are now receiving. This seeming unrest is the natural result of the awakened appetites of the intellect—the demand of conscious power for a sphere of exercise and usefulness. This illustrates very clearly the nature of the discontent for which the educated youth of this country are every now [and] then taken to task. The cause appears to be the same in both cases.[142]

Presumably the author did not consider that the *bhadra-mahilā* had reached that stage of discontent. It would have been true that as a group their aspirations had not yet been raised to a point where they could not be satisfied by the traditional roles of wife and mother. Women in the home were remote from the formal political process, and so would not have understood suffrage as an issue that had any relevance for them. The question of female suffrage was not raised at all until 1909, when female members of the British Indian Association sought voting rights for elections of the Imperial Legislative Council.[143]

Whereas in England the catalyst in the politicization of women was the issue of female suffrage, in India it was the wider cause of nationalism. The gradual politicization of

[142] *Ibid.*, 9 January 1879.

[143] G. Pearson, "Women in Public Life in Bombay City with Special Reference to the Civil Disobedience Movement," Ph.D. dissertation, Jawaharlal Nehru University, 1979, p. 210. The Reforms Act of 1921 extended the franchise to women on the basis of selective property and educational qualifications. By 1926, women were enfranchised on the same terms as men in all provincial legislature elections. See National Committee on the Status of Women, *Status of Women in India* (New Delhi, 1975); A. Basu, "The Role of Women in the Indian Struggle for Freedom," in B. R. Nanda, ed., *Indian Women* (New Delhi, 1976); G. Forbes, "Votes for Women: The Demand for Women's Franchise in India 1917-1937," in V. Mazumdar, ed., *Symbols of Power. Studies on the Political Status of Women in India* (Bombay, 1979).

women's journals such as *Bāmābodhinī Patrikā* and *Antahpur*
over the period 1900-1905 is clear. The process would have
contributed to the political education of a large number of
women. An article in *Antahpur* about the 1901 Congress session, written by a woman, discussed the political content of
the session in a serious manner. The writer showed a keen
interest in the political function of Congress, and discussed
specific issues without resorting to the rhetoric of patriotism.[144] An article in the same journal in June 1902 on "Salt"
criticized the government for introducing the salt tax, which
had crippled India's own salt-making capacity and caused
great hardship to large sectors of the people.[145] The Russo-
Japanese war and the ensuing victory of the Japanese over a
major western power was given full coverage. Sarala Debi
started a Red Cross ambulance corps to assist wounded Japanese soldiers, and women raised funds to help the families
of the Japanese war dead.[146] Japan was hailed as an "ideal
nation," and *Antahpur* proudly published photographs of all
the Japanese generals involved in the war.[147]

Patriotism permeated the whole of life. Women became
uncharacteristically militant, inspired by nationalistic fervor.
Boldness, bravery, and physical fitness were accepted as female
virtues when they served a political purpose. Kumudini Mitra,
B.A., wrote *Sikher balidān*, a history of the sacrifices made
by the Sikhs in defense of their religion. A reviewer of the
book in *Bāmābodhinī Patrikā* drew the obvious conclusion
that if the Bengalis wanted to rise as a nation they should

[144] Tarulata Debi, "Jātiya Mahāsamiti," *Antahpur*, 4, 12.
[145] "Laban," *Antahpur*, 5, 2-3 (June-July 1902).
[146] Sarala Debi appealed for the services of four doctors and twenty-five youths to form the corps. The result of her endeavors was not recorded. *Antahpur*, 7, 2 (June 1904); Amritalal Gupta, "Mahilādiger sabhā samiti," *BP*, 8:1, 496-497 (December 1904-January 1905).
[147] "Rus-jāpāner sandhi," *BP*, 8:2, 505-506 (September-October 1905); see frontispieces of *Antahpur* for most of 1904. S. Sarkar also mentions the Japanese victory of 1904-1905 as contributing to the general mood of "self-reliance and confidence in the heritage of the East" which preceded the *swadeshi* movement. S. Sarkar, *The Swadeshi Movement in Bengal 1903-1908* (New Delhi, 1973), pp. 28-29.

emulate this kind of patriotic, self-sacrificing spirit.[148] In 1903, a lady correspondent in *Sanjībanī* called on Bengalis to undergo physical training in order to repel and prevent the insults and assaults heaped on Bengali women by Europeans.[149]

In terms of the mobilization of the *bhadramahilā*, the most significant political event was the partition of Bengal into the provinces of East (Muslim) and West (Hindu) in October 1905. The anti-Partition movement represented a change in political style, away from the formal politics of statutory bodies and voluntary associations centered in Calcutta, to informal *mofussil* politics that used techniques of popular agitation in an attempt by the *bhadralok* to establish solidarity with the rural peasantry in opposition to British rule.[150] Unfortunately, most historians have tended to overlook both the part played by women in the *swadeshi* movement to boycott foreign imports in favor of local products, and the effect it had on them.[151]

Women's political consciousness had been developing gradually before October 1905. There had been a cumulative increase in political awareness, expressed through the pages of the main women's journals. The emphasis on using *swadeshi* goods, even prior to Partition, had helped make politics directly meaningful to women as consumers. The renewed admiration for indigenous handicrafts accorded recognition to an area in which women's special skills and talents were prominent. A comprehensive exhibition of *swadeshi* goods was held at the 1901 Congress session in Calcutta. Among the categories that were relevant to women were *swadeshi* textiles; household goods such as carpets, mosquito nets, bamboo ware, brass and metal utensils, soap, perfume, and ornaments; food-

[148] "Pusthakādi samālocanā, Srīmatī Kumudinī Mitra, Bi E, *Sikher bali-dān*," *BP*, 8:1, 498 (February 1905).

[149] *Sanjībanī*, 4 June 1903 in *RNNB* 13 June 1903.

[150] See J. R. McLane, "Calcutta and the Mofussilization of Bengali Politics," in R. L. Park, ed., *Urban Bengal* (Ann Arbor, 1969).

[151] Sumit Sarkar's otherwise excellent work on the *swadeshi* movement in Bengal, *The Swadeshi Movement*, devotes barely a page to women's activities, thereby relegating them to insignificance: pp. 287-288.

stuffs; medicines; books and stationery; and items of home decoration such as lithographs, photographs, and frames. Women exhibited their work, and many won medals or certificates of merit. One of the main aims of the organizers of the exhibition was to persuade women to wear *swadeshi* saris, in order to revive the cloth industries that were dying out through lack of patronage in centers such as Dacca, Santipur, Murshidabad, and Tripura.[152] Sarojini Ghose was one *bhadramahilā* who realized after attending the exhibition that it was not right to continue using foreign goods.[153] In 1903, Sarala Debi helped encourage the use of *swadeshi* goods by opening the Laksmir Bhandar in Cornwallis Street. The shop sold consumer goods from all parts of Bengal, to women only. A Brahmo widow was hired to take charge of sales.[154]

From the beginning of 1905, *Antahpur* reported on rumors of plans for Partition and the agitation that had already begun against it.[155] In August, *Bāmābodhinī Patrikā* announced details of the final plan, ending with a rousing call to "brothers and sisters of divided Bengal! Uniting in the strength of the mother-tongue on this sad day, let us succeed in this test of loyalty with tear-soaked eyes in a blood-smeared body."[156] In November, an item in the occasional English supplement in the same journal reported a "people's proclamation" that "we hereby pledge and proclaim that we as a people shall do everything in our power to counteract the evil effects of the dismemberment of our Province and to maintain the integrity of our race."[157] In October, *Bāmābodhinī Patrikā* had published a satirical drama about Partition. The characters included Bengal, the Minister, the Lieutenant-Governor, and the Governor-General. The "Governor-General" expressed the view that the "real" people of Bengal, the cultivators, regarded the

---

[152] "Jātiya silpa o bhārat mahilā samāj," *Antahpur*, 4, 12 (December 1901).
[153] Renuka Ghose, *Sarojinī-carit*, p. 46.
[154] Sarala Debi, *Jībaner jharāpātā*, p. 152; S. Sarkar, *The Swadeshi Movement*, p. 116.
[155] *Antahpur*, 7, 9 (January 1905).
[156] *BP*, 8:2, 504 (August 1905).
[157] *BP*, 8:2, 508 (December 1905).

English as their *mā bāp*, and that the anti-Partition agitation was the negligible product of a few obstreperous England-returned Bengalis. The "Governor-General" was best qualified to know the needs of the people of Bengal:

> Look, we were not born in Bengal, we have not learned Bengali, we do not practice Bengali traditions or customs, we will not settle down or establish landed property in Bengal; but still we understand what is good for them better than they can themselves. Their lack of understanding is the cause of our sorrow.[158]

This dramatic piece put forward all the arguments against Partition, and showed the way in which the government had responded to each of them, with a considerable degree of sophistication. Women readers, whose backgrounds ranged over a wide span of progressive and orthodox families, undoubtedly were familiar with the issues debated and had a clear understanding of the political situation.

A new development in women's affairs at this time was that they were organizing themselves into political action. An article in *Bāmābodhinī Patrikā* in November 1905 noted that male efforts to arouse female opinion were no longer needed. Women had advanced to the extent of calling their own public meetings to galvanize men into action, and in the home they used their influence to mobilize husbands, sons, and brothers. On 16 October 1905, nearly five hundred women had gathered to watch the laying of the foundation stone of the new Federation Hall, to protest against Partition.[159]

The cooperation of women was an essential factor in the success of the boycott movement. In Mymensingh in August 1905, Bengali ladies resolved to give up all English-made articles. Some female *zamindars* exhorted their tenants and sub-

[158] "Bangabibhāg nātaker ek angka," *BP*, 8:2, 505-506 (September-October 1905).

[159] "Swades-pujār bangamahilā," *BP*, 8:2, 507 (November 1905); see Punyalata Cakrabarti, *Chele belār din guli*, pp. 138-139, for an eyewitness account.

ordinates to use only *swadeshi* goods.[160] Bengali Christian teachers in mission schools stopped wearing shoes and stockings as a protest against Partition.[161] Meetings of women in support of *swadeshi* were reported in Dacca, Barisal, and elsewhere.[162]

Women played a strong propagandist role during the *swadeshi* movement. *Antahpur* and *Bāmābodhinī Patrikā* often published patriotic poems by women.[163] Women also published poems and letters in the general press,[164] and prominent female writers lent their skills to publicizing the *swadeshi* cause.[165]

Women demonstrated their commitment to the boycott movement by various patriotic sacrifices. In Bankipore, they gave up foreign bangles for ones made of conch shell.[166] They took up spinning on the *carkā*, more a symbolic gesture than a practical one, although it was said that they could produce textiles to rival those of Santipur.[167] Those who took the vow to spin were expected to do a little every day in order to have enough yarn to make into a sari at the following *pūjā*.[168] Many women stopped wearing foreign cloth altogether, even to fes-

---

[160] *Daily Hitavadi*, 22 August 1905 in *RNNB* 26 August 1905; *Sanjībanī*, 24 August 1905 in *RNNB* 2 September 1905.

[161] *Daily Hitavadi*, 13 September 1905 in *RNNB* 16 September 1905.

[162] *Sanjībanī*, 31 August 1905 in *RNNB* 9 September 1905; *Kasīpur Nibāsī (Barisāl)*, 13 September 1905 in *RNNB* 23 September 1905.

[163] See, for instance, poems by Ambujasundari Dasgupta, Sri Ni-, and Saratkumari Debi of Dacca in *BP*, 8:2, 507 (November 1905), or the poem by ten-year-old Asalata Sen in *Antahpur*, referred to in Kamala Dasgupta, *Swādhīnatā-sangrāme bānglār nārī* (Calcutta, 1963), p. 25.

[164] *Sanjībanī*, 31 August 1905 in *RNNB* 9 September 1905; *Sandhyā*, 13 September 1905 in *RNNB* 16 September 1905; *Basumatī*, 16 September 1905 in *RNNB* 23 September 1905; *Sanjībanī*, 12 October 1905 in *RNNB* 21 October 1905; *Sri Sri Bisnu Priya-O-Ananda Bājār Patrikā*, 21 September 1905 in *RNNB* 30 September 1905.

[165] J. C. Bagal, *Jātiya āndolane banganārī* (Calcutta, 1954), p. 10.

[166] *Bihar Bandhu (Bankipore)*, 15 September 1905 in *RNNB* 30 September 1905.

[167] *Indian Mirror*, 28 January 1906 in *RNNB* 3 February 1906; *ibid.*, 23 March 1906 in *RNNB* 24 March 1906.

[168] See article by Hiranmayi Debi, daughter of Swarnakumari Debi, in *Bhāratī*, December 1905, quoted in J. C. Bagal, *Jātiya āndolane*, p. 8.

tive celebrations.[169] Hemantakumari Chaudhuri took up weaving, and made clothes for her large family out of the coarse cloth. Her husband even used to wear it to the office.[170]

For items that could not be replaced by *swadeshi* substitutes, such as knitting machines, women turned to the industrial products of Japan instead of Europe.[171] More than five hundred women in Mymensingh gathered at the home of leading *swadeshi* activist Ramendrasunder Trivedi to listen to his composition "Banga Laksmir Brata Katha," and then took a vow not to light the cooking fires for that day.[172] Pupils at the Bethune School refused to welcome the Princess of Wales.[173] Women's magazines carried advertisements for *swadeshi* goods. An advertisement for *swadeshi* soap made by the Bengal Soap Factory claimed that it was equal in quality to English soap, and used political persuasion to sell the product by saying that a drain of *lakhs* of rupees abroad every year would be stopped if everyone vowed to purchase only *swadeshi* soap.[174] Hemantakumari Chaudhuri toured houses in Sylhet collecting subscriptions to send to Surendranath Banerjea to help the anti-Partition campaign. The district commissioner received a complaint against her husband because of this, but he responded by protesting that although he was a government servant, his wife was not and was therefore free to serve her country as she wished.[175]

The heightened fervor of political feeling during Partition could not be disregarded. Those who attempted to do so were ostracized and even physically threatened. Srinath Canda met with violent hostility for cordially receiving Sir Andrew Fuller, the first governor of East Bengal, at his girls' school in My-

---

[169] Krishna Kumar Mitra, *Ātmacarit*, p. 201.
[170] Hemantakumari Chaudhuri, unpublished *srādh* memoir of her husband.
[171] *Indian Mirror*, 28 January 1906 in *RNNB* 3 February 1906.
[172] J. C. Bagal, *Jātiya āndolane*, p. 7.
[173] It was probably this incident that prompted the Hon. Mr. Richards to describe the girls as "real swadeshi goods" on the occasion of the prize distribution. *Sandhyā*, 22 February 1906 in *RNNB* 3 March 1906.
[174] *Antahpur*, 8, 1 (May 1905).
[175] Hemantakumari Chaudhuri, *srādh* memoir.

mensingh.[176] Girish Chandra Sen, editor of the women's journal *Mahilā*, was threatened and abused for having published an article expressing the opinion that it was unnatural for women to join political movements.[177]

Naturally, women's views were not homogeneous. One Manisa Debi gave a talk to the Mahila Samiti in October 1905 in which she criticized some aspects of *swadeshi*. She ridiculed those *bābus* who drove around in rubber-tired landaus but lectured against the use of *bilātī* or English goods in the home. In her opinion, it was counterproductive to give up kerosine lanterns and electric lights for earthenware lamps, electric fans for hand-held ones, or matches for flint. She favored the renunciation of all intoxicants, rather than simply changing from foreign to local liquor and from cigarettes to native *biris*. She advocated taking what was best from everywhere, in a spirit of cooperation rather than hate.[178] There is no evidence, however, to suggest that there were any major divisions of opinion among women, although some were obviously more active and committed than others. Surendranath Banerjea mentioned the case of a "fashionable Bengallee lady" who was implored by students to give up foreign goods as she was coming out of Whiteaway and Laidlaw's stores. On the other hand, he also applauded the fortitude of three hundred ladies who were present as visitors at the Provincial Conference in Barisal in April 1906. When police dispersed the conference, the ladies chose to walk home in the burning sun as a protest rather than to wait all day in the *pandal* for their carriages.[179] On the same occasion, Srimati Sarojini Basu took all the gold bangles off her right arm and sent them to leading anti-Partition fighter Aswini Kumar Dutt, vowing that she would not wear gold bangles again until the ban on the singing

---

[176] Srinath Canda, *Brāhma samāje callis bathsar*, pp. 319-320.

[177] Girish Chandra Sen, *Ātma-jīban* (Calcutta, 1906), p. 145.

[178] Manisa Debi, "Swadeser unnatikalpe mahilādiger kartabya," *Punya*, 5 (October-November 1905).

[179] S. N. Banerjea, *A Nation in Making*, pp. 204, 226.

of "Bande Mataram" was lifted.[180] Lilabati Mitra gave refuge in her home to young men who had been expelled from *mofussil* colleges for singing "Bande Mataram."[181] Aurobindo's sister, Sarojini Ghose, launched an appeal for him after his arrest, and raised 15,000 rupees in a few days.[182]

The shift from formal politics of theoretical debate to a new style of informal, active politics opened up opportunities for women to take part in political activity. They gained an understanding of nationalism through the experiences of their daily lives. Giving up foreign cloth and using only *swadeshi* goods were methods of involvement that were intrinsically connected with their domestic role. Unfortunately, as the raising of women's political consciousness was a result, rather than an aim, of the *swadeshi* movement, it was neglected after it had served its immediate purpose. When the new techniques of popular agitation adopted by the *bhadralok* failed to mobilize the peasantry in support of *swadeshi*, they were abandoned. The alternatives resorted to were either a return to formal politics or militant terrorism, both of which tended to exclude all but exceptional women.

The limits of female participation in *swadeshi* have been defined as the lack of female leaders, with the possible exception of Sarala Debi; the absence of girls in *samitis* or volunteer movements; and the orthodox ideology of the *swadeshi* age.[183] Though true in part, this underrates and even ignores the ways in which women did participate. Sarala Debi may have been the only woman to have attained public prominence as a leader of men, but women leaders of their own sex were not scarce. Hemantakumari Chaudhuri and Lilabati and Kumudini Mitra are just a few of the best known.[184] Enough women

[180] Krishna Kumar Mitra, *Ātmacarit*, p. 221; J. C. Bagal, *Jātiya āndolane*, p. 9.
[181] *Līlābatī Mitra* (Calcutta, 1924), p. 31.
[182] Krishna Kumar Mitra, *Ātmacarit*, p. 239.
[183] S. Sarkar, *The Swadeshi Movement*, p. 288.
[184] See the poem by Sarala Debi paying tribute to Hemantakumari Chaudhuri: Sarala Datta, "Srīmatī Hemantakumārī Caudhurīr prati," *BP*, 8:2, 510-511 (February-March 1906).

had been trained in the "politics" of female voluntary associations and philanthropic organizations to lead and organize other women in a political manner. Women formed their own *samitis*, and took *swadeshi* vows—activities not inferior to joining the volunteer movements, and ones that may have had a stronger impact. It was widely believed in official circles at the time that women were the bastion of conservatism. This made their participation all the more effective, as their political activities could not be dismissed as the antics of westernized *bābus*. Revivalist ideology was ambivalent on the question of women's political role. The rhetoric was certainly not "conducive to the equality of the sexes," but it did see the need for women to be involved in politics, as much because of their influence over their menfolk and the home lifestyle as for any altruistic concern for women's own personal growth and stimulation. Some contemporary observers argued that the *swadeshi* movement would not have succeeded at all without the aid of women, and that their part in its success had, in fact, led men to realize the value of female education and independence for the good of the nation.[185] Sibnath Sastri related that at the time of Partition he was in Darjeeling. When he returned to Calcutta in November 1905, many women told him that *swadeshi* had changed their attitudes. Before, if they had been seen at a meeting by outsiders, they would have turned away and giggled, but now they would look squarely at them.[186]

Some writers have maintained that during the *swadeshi* movement, and indeed in most public political movements, the *bhadramahilā* played a nurturing and supportive role to their more active menfolk.[187] While that is undoubtedly true, the positive contribution of women should not be overlooked. Contemporary evidence shows that women played a strong

[185] Amritalal Gupta, "Swadeśī āndolan o ramanīr kartabya," *BP*, 8:2, 512 (April 1906).
[186] Quoting from a sermon by Sibnath Sastri to the Sadharan Brahmo Samaj, *ibid*.
[187] J. C. Bagal, *Jātiya āndolane*, p. 8.

role in the anti-Partition and *swadeshi* movements. They have only been relegated to a "feminine" nurturing role by later historians. Many women who were later to become active in nationalist politics, particularly in the Gandhian era, gained their initial political awareness and experience during the *swadeshi* period.[188] Although women in the rest of India may not have been widely involved in political activity before the advent of Gandhi, the political perceptions of the Bengali *bhadramahilā* were shaped by *swadeshi*.[189]

Emergence into public life, both through employment and through political participation, extended the role of the *bhadramahilā* beyond the domestic world. This development was a direct result of the social changes taking place under colonial rule in the nineteenth century, particularly the new phenomenon of women's education. A range of hitherto unavailable options were extended to women, enabling them to participate in the outside world. Paradoxically, the move away from the *antahpur* may also have reinforced the secondary status of women. The *bhadramahilā* moving into previously male worlds had to contend not only with social opposition, but also with the disadvantage of their own inexperience in an unfamiliar setting. Later historians have certainly neglected and even ignored the participation of women in public affairs because they were overshadowed by more prominent and numerous men. However, the *bhadramahilā* of the time were not conscious of discrimination or exclusion. To them, in 1905, there was a sense of excitement at having broken the barriers of the *antahpur*, and of exhilaration at the promise of continued expansion of opportunity in the future.

[188] See Kamala Dasgupta, *Swadhīnatā-sangrāme*, for biographical details of women nationalists that show this.

[189] G. Pearson, "Women in Public Life." Women in Bombay did not become involved in political action until Gandhi and the non-cooperation movement.

Conclusion

By the end of the nineteenth century, the *bhadramahilā* of this story—the Svarnalatas, Mahamayas, Usabalas, and Rassundaris—had achieved remarkable breakthroughs in a number of areas. Literacy was no longer denied them, and through the printed word women could broaden their knowledge of their own society and the world around them. Ways to lessen the horrors of childbirth were being explored, purdah rules were relaxed to allow for movement beyond the confines of the house, and the citadel of professional employment had been breached. Women enthusiastically absorbed new ideas on diverse topics, from a cure for malaria or a recipe for guava jelly, to methods of child rearing that stressed the importance of a regular routine and direct maternal care, and words of advice on how to please an educated husband.

The English-educated *bhadralok* under British rule shared a common and distinctive lifestyle. Women's understanding of the new status indicators was crucial to the establishment and consolidation of *bhadralok* identity. Moreover, their lives were vitally affected by utilitarian, "modern" adaptations of customary domestic practices, and they eagerly accepted and experimented with new methods of medical treatment, postnatal care, cooking, budgeting, and home decoration. In all of this they encountered little opposition from orthodox sectors of the community who were against any departure from traditional ideals of womanhood, even though such practical changes often carried ideological implications and resulted in far greater transformations than those brought about by the conscious proclamation of new ideals.

The introduction of female education illustrates the interdependence between practical and ideological change. The acquisition of the practical skill of literacy had enormous significance for women. They learned about the world beyond the *antahpur*, and in turn used literacy as a channel for ex-

357

pressing their thoughts and feelings to a wider audience than the immediate circle of kin. Over time, it led to unforseen consequences, such as a gradual rise in the age of marriage; the transference of the responsibility for training young girls from home to school, with a corresponding decline in their familiarity with traditional household skills; and the beginning of white-collar female employment. In the realm of ideology, new perceptions of the functions of wife and mother provided models that stressed each woman's individual responsibility for the maintenance and transmission of the new *bhadralok* identity. A self-consciousness and enhanced importance were imparted to traditional roles, as befitted the rising expectations of the educated women who had to fill them. They willingly accepted the burdens and responsibilities inherent in reshaping familiar roles in their gladness at being released from many of the restraints that they considered oppressive or harmful. In some instances, however, ideas and expectations were ahead of social practice. Women were avid consumers of modern fiction, which gave currency to the romantic notion of marriage for love, whereas the chances of fulfilling these romantic yearnings were almost nonexistent at that time.

The need for a new ideal of womanhood suited to the requirements of the *bhadralok* under colonial rule gradually gave rise to the stereotype of the *bhadramahilā*. The *bhadramahilā* represented the new Bengali woman of the later nineteenth century. The set of values she represented were those of cleanliness, orderliness, thrift, responsibility, intelligence, and a moderate interest in and knowledge of the public world of men. These were added to, rather than substituted for, the traditional virtues of self-sacrifice, benevolence, devotion to the husband, respect for elders, and household competence. She was also expected to have certain practical skills, including literacy, accounting, and the ability to rear children and manage the household with some observance of precise routine and organization; to mix socially with friends, colleagues, and superiors of her husband, and occasionally to act as hostess at official functions; and to be involved with other women of her position in organized groups or associations for self-improvement or charitable purposes.

The model of the *bhadramahilā* was strongly influenced by the Victorian ideal of womanhood, transmitted through the colonial connection and adapted to suit the social conditions of Bengal. The extension of female education and literacy through the later nineteenth century brought greater numbers of women under the influence of the ruling culture. *Bhadralok* men encouraged women to conform to the Victorianized ideal of the *bhadramahilā*, so as not to be found lacking when judged by British standards of "civilization." By the turn of the nineteenth century, the *bhadramahilā* ideal was widely emulated, and was fast becoming the dominant model of social behavior.

Although the limitations of the role of wife and mother restricted the extent to which women could control their lives, they were able to influence the direction of change and the development of the *bhadramahilā* stereotype. They implicitly resisted simple westernization, and attempted to harmonize what they valued in traditional society with what they saw as worthy of imitation in the ways of Victorian women. For instance, the *bhadramahilā* were far more ready to embrace and master new techniques of homeopathic and allopathic medicine, which could be put to direct use, than to play the decorative role of social hostess. They pursued education with enthusiasm and used it to follow up their own interests, which ranged from the reading of the Hindu scriptures in order to acquire spiritual knowledge to the writing of manuals against the injustices and superstitions of traditional society.

In the final analysis, however, the *bhadramahilā* were not in a position to transform their lives according to their own needs and wishes. They accepted the value system of the dominant male group. They were far more hesitant than men were in recording their experiences and impressions. Consequently, there were no major initiatives taken by women as a group to assert their interests in the face of male opposition. Despite close links with British women, there was no equivalent among the Bengali *bhadramahilā* to the activities of the English suffragettes and campaigners for women's rights. Important changes in the condition of Bengali women in the nineteenth century, often made in the face of orthodox disapproval, did not lead to the development of a women's movement or a feminist consciousness. The *bhadramahilā* perceived that women were subject to social oppression, but they did not react to this awareness by what we would now describe as group militancy.

As conditions at the time seemed to warrant some sort of group action, it is instructive to look at the reasons why it did not happen. There are a number: cultural stereotypes of womanly behavior did not encourage expressions of militancy or aggression; the household atmosphere was not conducive to the creation of a group consciousness such as could be generated in public forums; and the economically dependent position of women inhibited any rebellion against those responsible for their support. The fundamental factor, however, was that the *bhadramahilā* saw themselves as representatives of "modernity" in opposition to "tradition" rather than as women opposed to men. Although by the late nineteenth century women were for the first time conscious of themselves as a group with a special identity and social mission, their initial battles against the conservative forces of orthodox society had been fought with the active support and encouragement of the progressive *bhadralok*. The right to acquire education, or to discard purdah, had been denied them by representatives of conservative orthodoxy, female as well as male, not by men as a group.

The capacity of the *bhadramahilā* to affect wide-ranging changes in social relationships was limited by the narrowness of class interest. They interpreted their own disadvantages as resulting from repressive orthodox customs, but did not extend their analysis to the relations of men and women of the *chotolok* to arrive at a more generalized feminist perspective. To have done so would have shown an awareness well in advance of the historical period. At that stage, they were intent on reforming traditional customs that adversely affected women of their own class, but were not particularly concerned with improving the overall condition of women. From their perspective, the dichotomy between tradition and modernity seemed to be of much greater importance than that between men and women. Their primary identification was with members of the *bhadralok* class rather than with women as a category. Class was a more significant means of self-definition than sex.

By the turn of the century, growing nationalist sentiment among the *bhadralok* meant that race, as a category, overshadowed women's possible identification as a separate group on the basis of sex. In a situation where the *bhadralok* saw themselves as battling against a position of dependence and subordination, the *bhadramahilā* came to share their view of the oppressiveness of colonial rule. The sense of common purpose seen in their joint agitation against the partition of Bengal helps explain the lack of a feminist consciousness. The struggle against a common oppressor effectively diverted attention from other potential conflicts within the social system.

The *bhadramahilā* began to take an interest in the hitherto male world of nationalist politics. The process by which women had defined their identity as *bhadramahilā* had involved hardship and opposition. As a result, they had been drawn into the network of institutions that constituted the "modern" world of British India. They were literate, and had their own channels of communication with the colonial state through the operation of the legal and educational systems. A few of them functioned directly under the British administrative bureaucracy as employees. They consolidated their new identity through societies and journals meant exclusively for women, showing a self-conscious awareness of themselves as a group.

At the same time, the *bhadramahilā* was created as a new stereotype of ideal womanhood to suit the social conditions of late nineteenth-century Bengal, and differed from the traditional definition of the ideal Hindu woman more in style than in substance. Women were not in a position to perceive that much of their new-found freedom was superficial. Greater mutuality in marital relations gave men more control over domestic concerns without providing women with opportunities to influence public life in return. Access to nondomestic employment did not admit women to the male world of civic affairs but to a separate domain that serviced the needs of women. They were still excluded from policymaking on broad issues that affected both men and women.

If we judge them by their own aims and standards, however, the *bhadramahilā* did make enormous advances. Changes in the minutiae of daily life, as well as in the abstract areas of beliefs and values, had brought them into the frustrating yet challenging world of colonial India. The ideal of womanhood that they had helped to shape was to gain wide acceptance in the twentieth century, and behavior once considered exceptional was to become commonplace. The present Bengali *bhadramahilā* are probably unaware that a vast number of freedoms which they now take for granted were only made possible by the pioneering efforts of their nineteenth-century sisters.

Biographical Notes

The following pages give brief biographical notes on some of the women who figure in this story. It must be stressed that the list is not comprehensive, but merely a representative selection of the various types of women who participated in the changes that took place in the period described. Their individual qualities and achievements take on a deeper meaning when seen in the wider context of women's responses to changes in the social, economic, and political environment of colonial Bengal. These notes sketch the barest outline of their lives.

Aghorekamini Ray

Born in 1854, she was married at age ten to Prakascandra Ray. They had five children. She was initiated into Brahmoism at twenty-nine. Pursuing her interest in education, at the age of thirty-five she went to Lucknow for six months of training at a missionary college in order to run her own girl's school in Bankipore. She died in 1896.

Annada Gupta

Annada was born in 1835 in a village in Dacca district and married nineteen-year-old Brahmo Kalinarayan Gupta at the age of eight. Her first child was born in 1847, but died in infancy. She gave birth to sixteen children, six of whom died in infancy. Her husband persuaded her to become a Brahmo, gave her a basic education, and helped her to become a "perfect wife."

Annapurna Cattopadhyay

She was born in 1857 in Bikrampur district, and convinced her father, a Brahmin, to educate her. At the age of twelve

her cousin arranged for her to marry Srimanta Cattopadhyay, a medical student. He later became a Brahmo, as did
she. He set up a medical practice in Bogura. Encouraged by
her husband to be independent, she read, studied, and became
a skilled midwife. She had six children of her own, not including those who died in infancy.

Bala Shoondaree Tagore

Born in 1833 in Jessore, she was married at the age of ten to
the son of Brahmo Prasanna Kumar Tagore. He arranged for
her to be educated by a pandit, and for a time by an English
governess. He also directed her attention toward Christianity.
Not long after they had decided to seek baptism, in 1851, she
died of consumption.

Bamasundari Debi (a)

Bamasundari, a Hindu, was born in Mulghur in 1839. She
was educated in secret and married at nine to a famous legal
practitioner, or *vakil*. She had seven children, whom she helped
educate. Her biography describes her as a "great housewife"
and "ideal woman." She died of diabetes in 1887.

Bamasundari Debi (b)

She was born in Bikrampur subdistrict in 1837, married at
the age of ten, and widowed two years later. A pious Hindu,
she went to live in Dacca with her brother, who was a Brahmo.
He gave her some education, and she eventually joined the
Brahmo Samaj, giving up most of the vows of the Hindu
widow. She traveled to Calcutta to hear Keshub Chunder Sen
preach in 1879, and also saw Ramakrishna. In 1892 she returned to her home village, where she died of cholera.

Bamasundari Canda

Born in 1858, she was married and widowed at an early age. Brahmo relatives arranged for her to escape to Mymensingh for her education. In 1876 she married Brahmo Srinath Canda, a teacher, in the first widow marriage to be celebrated in Mymensingh. The crowd of onlookers was over one thousand, and people even climbed trees to see the event. She had nine children, and was an active leader of women's activities in the Mymensingh Brahmo Samaj. Her five daughters were well educated, and one of them, Labanyalata, was involved in the nationalist movement. Bamasundari died in 1940.

Brahmamayi Das

Brahmamayi was born in Bikrampur subdistrict in 1846, and married to nine-year-old Durga Mohan Das at the age of four. He gave her a basic education. They became Brahmos during his service with the High Court in Barisal, where she persuaded him to buy land and set up a "Brahmo quarter." She was well loved for her generosity in caring for homeless widows who sought refuge. In 1876, at the age of thirty-one, she died three days after giving birth to a premature and still-born-child—her seventh.

Candramukhi Basu

A Bengali Christian, she was one of the first women to pursue higher education. She sat for the equivalent of the Entrance Arts in 1877, before women were permitted to sit for that examination. She became one of the first female graduates of Calcutta University in 1883, and passed her M.A. with honors in 1884. That same year she was appointed assistant lady superintendent of Bethune College, on a salary of seventy-five rupees per month. She became the first Bengali lady superintendent of the college in 1886. Later she married a Kashmiri and went to live in Dehra Dun.

Dayamayi Sen

Born in 1855 in Sylhet district, she was given a basic education at home. At ten she was married to a deputy inspector of schools, Nabakisor Sen. They lived away from the extended family, and she initially experienced some difficulty in learning traditional domestic skills. In 1891 she died of asthma. She had ten children, but only three survived her.

Harasundari Datta

Born in 1858, she was married to fourteen-year-old Srinath Datta at the age of seven. He became a Brahmo in 1869 and arranged for her escape from his father's home in 1870, taking her to Calcutta for her education. He left for England in 1871. In 1873 she became a boarder at the Hindu Mahila Bidyalaya. Miss Akroyd, the principal, commented on her loneliness at being cut off from her family and parted from her husband. He returned in 1875. For most of their later married life his job as estate manager took him to a series of remote places, but his wife and family of eight children accompanied him. She developed considerable skills in household management to meet the challenge. Their marriage was exceptionally close.

Hemantakumari Chaudhuri

Hemantakumari was born in 1868, in Lahore, the daughter of Brahmo social reformer and educationalist Nabin Chandra Ray. She was educated in Hindi, Bengali, Sanskrit, and English, but instead of taking her Entrance Arts examination, she was married at the age of seventeen. Her husband was a gazetted officer in Shillong, where she founded a girls' school and a female education association. She had eleven children. She edited the Hindi journal *Sugrihini* for six years from 1888, then became editor of *Antahpur* from 1901 to 1904. For fifteen years after her husband's retirement she was headmistress of a school in the Punjab. She was also an active Gandhian and Congress nationalist, and a municipal commissioner in Dehra Dun.

Jaganmohini (Sen)

Born in 1847, she was married at age nine to eighteen-year-old Keshub Chunder Sen, later to become the dynamic leader of the Brahmo Samaj reform movement in Bengal. After an initial rejection of her, he became reconciled to marriage and attempted to educate her. She found herself torn between what he expected of her and the cultural environment she had been brought up in. She had ten children.

Jnanadanandini Debi

Born in 1852, she married Satyendranath, son of the Brahmo philosopher Debendranath Tagore, at the age of seven. Her husband went to England shortly thereafter. In 1864 he became the first Indian member of the Indian Civil Service, and took his wife to live with him in various towns in western India. She was required to support her husband in his career, as a hostess and helpmeet. In 1877 she went to England alone for a visit, with her children. She was also an innovator in dress reform. She had two children. She died in 1941.

Jogamaya (Goswami)

Jogamaya was born in 1853 in Nadia district, and was married at six to eighteen-year-old Bijoy Krishna Goswami. He became a Brahmo missionary and spent a lot of time away from his family. Often they were very short of money, although they were supported by the Brahmo Samaj. She had five children. Later in life, when her husband left her to become a Hindu ascetic, she followed him. When he tried to leave her once again, to become a full *sannyasi*, she attempted to drown herself, but was rescued. They continued to live together as a family until her death from cholera in 1884.

Kadambini Ganguly

Born in 1861, she earned great distinction as a pioneer in women's education. The first woman to pass the Entrance Arts examination, in 1878, she was awarded a government scholarship to continue her studies, and became one of the first female graduates in 1883. From there she entered medical college, becoming the first female medical student. She emerged as the first female doctor in Bengal in 1886, and pursued a successful career as a government servant and in private practice. She went to Britain for over a year of further training in 1893. Earlier, she had married the Brahmo reformer Dwarkanath Ganguly. Through her husband she was involved in Congress politics.

Kamini (Sen) Ray

Kamini was born in 1864 in Backerganj. The daughter of a Brahmo, she was well educated and graduated with second-class honors in Sanskrit in 1885. She became a teacher at the Bethune College in 1884. At the age of twenty-five she published a volume of poems entitled "Alo o chaya" (Light and Shade), which brought her fame as a poet. She married at the age of thirty, and continued to write poetry up until her death in 1933. (See her picture in Plate 9.)

Koilasbasini Debi

She was probably born in 1837, but very little is known about this remarkable woman, although she was one of the very first Hindu women to write and publish. Her husband educated her from the age of twelve. After working in the house and looking after her children during the day, she studied at night. Her book on the condition of Hindu women, published in 1863, was said to have been written in a week.

Kumudini Mitra

Kumudini was born in 1882, the daughter of reforming Brahmos Krishna Kumar and Lilabati Mitra. After her graduation as a B.A. in 1903, she became active in the anti-Partition and nationalist movements, especially as a writer. She married in 1914, and had two children.

Kumudini Sinha

Born in 1855 into a well-respected Hindu family in Calcutta, she was married at ten. Her husband took up a position in the Commissariat Office in Lahore. At twelve she went to join him there, with her mother and younger sister. They became Brahmos. Her first child was born when she was sixteen. A year later they returned to Calcutta, where she had six more children. Four of these died in infancy or early childhood. She died in 1890, of bronchitis and other complications.

Labanyaprabha Datta

She was born in 1888 in Berhampur, the daughter of a *zamindar*. At nine she was married to Jatindranath Datta, who was in the legal profession in Calcutta. During the *swadeshi* movement she was very active, helping with funds and the use of *swadeshi* goods. She also converted her husband to the *swadeshi* cause. She became a Hindu devotee for a time after her husband's death in 1911, but was politically involved again after 1929.

Lilabati Mitra

Born in Midnapore in 1864, she was the daughter of Brahmo Rajnarain Bose. She was educated at the Bethune School in Calcutta until the age of fifteen. At seventeen she married Brahmo Krishna Kumar Mitra, and they had three children.

Up until her death in 1924 she was active in various women's associations, and in the *swadeshi* and nationalist movements.

Mankumari Basu

Born in Jessore in 1863, she was the niece of the famous Bengali Christian poet Michael Madhusudan Dutt. Like him, she was a well-known poet. She was a frequent contributor to the women's journal *Bāmābodhinī Patrikā*. At an early age she was widowed, and she died in 1943.

Monomohini Wheeler

Monomohini was the daughter of one of the most famous Bengali Christian converts, Reverend Krishna Mohan Banerjea. She married an English chaplain, and had two children. After his death she accepted the position of inspectress of schools, in 1875, overseeing *zenana* and purdah education in Bengal. She traveled to Europe twice on study trips, and her work involved frequent touring in the districts of Bengal. She retired in 1901.

Muktakesi Debi

She was born in Tripura in 1872. Her father was a schoolteacher, and had her educated in Sanskrit and Bengali. At the age of twelve she was married. She had seen photographs of her husband, and they had exchanged letters for a year before marriage. After her husband had completed his studies he took her to Puthia, where he was head teacher. She had one child, who died shortly after birth. A pious Hindu and devoted wife, she managed to continue with advanced study even after marriage, until her death from cholera at the age of seventeen, in 1888.

Nagendrabala Mustaphi

Born in 1878 in Hughly, she married at ten. Her husband became a devout Vaishnava. Educated through her own efforts, she became a very well-known and successful poet. Her poems were printed frequently in the main women's magazines and literary journals. She wrote twelve complete collections of verse, many of which were published prior to her death in 1906.

Radharani Lahiri

Although she was very prominent in Brahmo women's associations in the late 1870s, we have few details of her personal life. In 1878 she declined to accept a teaching position at the Native Ladies' Normal School on sixty rupees a month, but was appointed assistant to the lady superintendent of the Bethune School in 1880. She wrote and edited a collection of writings by women and a book of moral essays for children. As secretary of the Banga Mahila Samaj in 1880, she ran a competition for a prize essay on the "model housewife."

Rassundari Debi

An exceptional Hindu woman, born in 1810, she was the first to write her autobiography. In it she describes her marriage at the age of twelve, the way she taught herself to read, and the domestic details of her life. She had twelve children.

Sarala (Sen) Das

Born in 1878, she spent much of her life in Rangoon, where her father was a barrister. She was very Anglicized when she came to study at Bethune College at the age of eleven. She graduated as a B.A. from Calcutta University, and after a period of uncertainty as to how best to use her life to serve her country, she married a barrister and devoted herself to him. She died at the age of twenty-three.

Sarala Debi

Sarala was born in 1872, into the privileged and talented Tagore family. Well educated, her background enabled her to pursue an unorthodox course. She was an active and influential figure in the early nationalist movement, especially over the partition of Bengal in 1905. Her particular contribution was in the encouragement of a martial, heroic culture in Bengal that would serve the nationalist cause. She married a Panjabi nationalist figure at the age of thirty-three, and had one son. She died in 1945.

Sarojini Ghose

Born in 1874, she married at the age of eleven. A Hindu, she introduced a number of practical innovations into her life—in health care, house arrangement, and social behavior—to suit the new lifestyle observed by her husband, a jute merchant. She had four children and died in 1932.

Saudamini Ray

Born in Barisal in 1850, she was married at the age of eight to the son of a *zamindari* family. With her strength of character she pushed her more hesitant husband along a path of firm commitment to social reform. They became Brahmos, and she left purdah and appeared at social occasions. She had four children, the first three of whom died in early childhood and infancy. At the age of twenty-four she died shortly after giving birth to twins.

Subodhbala Debi

She was born in 1884, in Calcutta, in a Brahmo family, and was well educated. Her particular talent was in writing poetry, although she wrote very little after her marriage in 1902. She had one son, who died not long before she did in 1913.

Sudha Mazumdar

Sudha was born in 1899, into a Hindu *zamindari* family, and educated in both Bengali and English. In 1912 she was married to Satish Chandra Mazumdar. From then she accompanied him on his tours of duty as an Indian Civil Service Officer in rural Bengal. Away from her family, she directed her energies to active involvement in rural social work among women. A devout woman, she regarded social service as a form of dedication to religion.

Suniti Mallik

The only information available on Suniti is the short biography written by her husband in a published collection of her works printed around 1896. She was born in Calcutta, a Hindu. An old pandit gave her an advanced education in Bengali. Most of her poetry was written before the age of fourteen—possibly the date of her marriage—and she died an untimely death at sixteen.

Swarnakumari Debi

Born in 1855, Swarnakumari was one of the daughters of Debendranath Tagore. She was educated, and married at the age of twelve. In her time she achieved fame as a writer, and for over fifteen years she was editor of the monthly *Bharatī*, giving it up on the death of her husband in 1913. She wrote numerous novels, plays, and short stories, some of which were translated into English, and is considered a pioneer of the historical and romantic novel genre. She died in 1932.

Maharani Swarnamayi

Although she was renowned as one of the most powerful and benevolent *zamindars* of nineteenth-century Bengal, little is known about her personal life. She observed strict purdah, managing her estates through agents as intermediaries. Funds for the encouragement of female education, training in midwifery, and other schemes benefiting women were included in the scope of her charitable activities. The British awarded her the Order of the Crown of India in 1878. She died in 1897.

Swarnaprabha Bose

Swarnaprabha was born in Bikrampur. Her father was a supporter of female education, and sent her to school in Calcutta. She married the leading Brahmo reformer Ananda Mohan Bose, and was one of the first women to become actively involved in women's associations. She was the representative for Bengal on the general committee of the Sadharan Brahmo Samaj.

Bibliography

PRIMARY SOURCES

Women's journals

Abalābāndhab, 1878/79
Antahpur, 1898-1906
Bāmābodhinī Patrikā, 1863-1906
Banga Mahilā, 1875/76
Gārhasthya, 1884

Mahilā, 1897/98
Mahilā-Bāndhab, 1887
Māsik Patrikā, 1854/55
Pāk-Pranālī, 1883-1886, 1903
Paricārikā, 1878/79

Newspapers and journals

BENGALI

Bhāratī, 1877/78
Dāsī, 1897

Punya, 1897-1898, 1905
Sulabh Samācār, 1875

ENGLISH

Brahmo Public Opinion, 1878-1880
Brahmo Year Book, 1876-1882
Calcutta Review, 1855-1904
Indian Mirror, 1878
Indian Mirror, Sunday Edition, 1878-1881

Liberal and New Dispensation, 1882-1884
Modern Review, 1907-1910
New Dispensation, 1881-1883
Theistic Quarterly Review, 1879-1881
Yearly Theistic Record, 1881

Biographies and autobiographies

BENGALI

Bāmā-carit (Sradheyā Bāmāsundarīr jībancarit). Dacca, 1893.
Bandopadhyay, Brajendranath. Catuspāthīr juge bidusī bangama-hilā: Hatī Bidyālangkār, Hatu Bidyālangkār, Drabamayī. Sahitya-sadhak-caritamala series, no. 89. 2nd ed. Calcutta, 1964 (1952).

Bandopadhyay, Brajendranath. *Swarnakumārī Debī.* Sahitya-sad-hak-caritamala series, no. 28. 6th ed. Calcutta, 1965.

Bandopadhyay, Candicaran. "Janani Sonāmani Debī" (1913). In U. C. Banerjee (comp.), *Reminiscences, Speeches and Writings of Sir Gooroo Dass Banerjee Kt.* Calcutta, 1927.

Bandopadhyay, Muralidhar. *Srīmatī Saraswatī Sener sangksipta jī-banī. Racanā o patra.* Calcutta, 1930.

Bandopadhyay, Rebatikanta. *Snehalatā.* 2nd ed. Calcutta, 1914.

Basu, Prabhat. *Mahārānī Sucāru Debīr jīban-kāhinī.* Calcutta, 1962.

Bhattacarjya, Prasannakumar. *Swargīyā Debī Muktakesīr caritām-rita.* Calcutta, 1891.

Bose, Rajnarain. *Ātmacarit.* 4th ed. Calcutta, 1961 (1909).

Cakrabarti, Punyalata. *Chele belār din guli.* Calcutta, 1975 (1958).

Canda, Srinath. *Brāhmasamāje callis bathsar.* Calcutta, 1969 (1913).

Cattopadhyay, Nalinikanta. *Nabakānta Cattopādhyāy (jībanī o bangsa brittānta).* Calcutta, 1922.

Cattopadhyay, Srimanta. *Annapūrnācarit.* Calcutta, 1893.

Caudhurani, Indira Debi, ed. *Purātanī.* Calcutta, 1957.

Dāktār Prānkrisna Ācārja—jībanprasanga o upadesābalī. 2nd ed. Calcutta, 1973 (1936).

Datta, Harasundari. *Swargīya Srīnath Datter jīban-kathā.* Calcutta, 1922.

Datta, Kusummala. *Swargīya Ānandamohan Barddhan Mahāsayer jībaner katipoi smriti.* Tippera, 1927.

Datta, Saraccandra. *Dayāmayī Sener sangksipta jīban carit.* Sylhet, 1890.

De, Rajanikanta. *Caritamādhurī (chayjan brāhmikā sādhbīr jīban-ābhās).* Calcutta, 1919.

Deb, Saratkumari. *Āmār sangsār.* Calcutta, 1942.

[Ganguly, Dwarkanath]. *Jībanālekhya.* 2nd ed. Calcutta, 1879 (1876).

Ghose, Renuka. *Sarojinī-carit.* Calcutta, 1936.

Gupta, Amritalal. *Punyabatī nārī.* Giridi, 1923.

Haldar, Satakari. *Pūrbba smriti.* Calcutta, 1898.

Indira Debi. *Mahātmā Priyanāth Sāstrī Mahāsayer jīban-carit.* Cal-cutta, 1913.

Kabibar Madanmohan Tarkālangkārer jībancarit o tadgrantha sa-mālocanā. Calcutta, 1871.

Kar, Bangkabihari. *Bhakta Kālīnārāyan Gupter jīban-brittānta.* Cal-cutta, 1924.

Kumudinī-caritra, A Brief Sketch of the Life of Srimati Kumudinee the wife of R. C. Sinha of the New Dispensation Brahma Somaj of India. Cooch Behar, 1890.

Līlābatī Mitra. Calcutta, 1924.

Mahalanabis, Gurucharan. *Ātmakathā.* Calcutta, 1974.

Mahalanabis, Manika. *Brahmānanda Srīkesabcandrer patrābalī.* Calcutta, 1941.

Majumdar, Bhabaranjan. *Ācārja Giriscandra Majumdār.* Calcutta, 1913.

Mallik, Kuladaprasad. *Brahmarsir jībane bhagabāner kripār jay.* Calcutta, 1918.

[Mallik, Priyanath]. *Brahma-nandinī satī Jaganmohinī Debī.* Howrah, 1914.

Mallik, Suniti. *Akāl-kusum (kono swargagatā bangabālā biracit).* 2nd ed. Calcutta, 1896.

Mitra, Krishna Kumar. *Ātmacarit.* 2nd ed. Calcutta, 1974 (1936).

Mustaphi, Nagendrabala. *Amiya gāthā.* Calcutta, 1901.

Niyogi, Niranjan. *Sādhan o sebā. Nababidhān pracārak sradheya bhai Brajagopāl Niyogī Mahāsayer jībanālekhya.* Calcutta, 1963.

Prabhabati Debi. *Amal-prasūn bā prabhābatī-kabitābalī.* Jessore, 1900.

Rassundari Debi. *Āmār jīban.* Calcutta, 1898? (1877).

Ray, Prakascandra. *Aghor-prakās.* 2nd ed. Calcutta, 1958 (Bankipur, 1923).

[Ray, Rakhal Chandra]. *Jīban bindu (Srījukta Rākhālcandra Rāyer paralokgatā sahadharmminī Soudāminīr sangksep jīban brittānta).* Calcutta, 1880.

Roy, Gour Gobinda. *Ācārjya Kesabcandra.* "Middle, part 6," Calcutta, 1897; "End, part 1," Calcutta, 1900; "End, part 2," Calcutta, 1901.

Rudra, Subrata. *Kādambarī Debī.* Calcutta, 1977.

Sarala Debi, *Jībaner jharāpātā.* Calcutta, 1975.

Sarala Ray Centenary Committee. *Sarala Ray Centenary Volume.* Calcutta, 1961.

Sen, Candrakanta. *Bāmāsundarī bā ādarsa-nārī.* Calcutta, 1909.

Sen, Girish Chandra. *Ātma-jīban. Arthāth bhāi Giriscandra Sen karttrik bibrita ātmajībanbrittānta.* Calcutta, 1906.

———. *Brahmamayī-carit.* Calcutta, 1869.

Sen, Sudaksina. *Jīban smriti.* Calcutta, 1933.

Sengupta, Amritalal. *Jogamāyā Thākurānī, arthāth srīmadācārjya prabhupāda Bijaykrisna Goswāmī mahodayer sahadharmminī Srīsrīmatī Jogamāyā Debīr jīban carit.* Madaripur, 1916.

Short life of Dr Nishi Kanta Chattopadhyay, Ph.D. Dacca, 1902.
Srīksetramohan Datter jībanī. Calcutta, 1919.
Subodhbala Debi. *Nīrab sādhanā.* Calcutta, 1913.
Swarger phul. Calcutta, 1892.
Swarnalata Debi. *Mātri-tarpan.* Calcutta, 1914.

ENGLISH

Banerjea, S. N. *A Nation in Making. Being the Reminiscences of Fifty Years of Public Life.* Madras, 1925.
Banerji, A. *An Indian Pathfinder. Memoirs of Sevabrata Sasipada Banerji.* New ed. Calcutta, 1971.
Basu, P. S. *Life and Works of Brahmananda Keshav.* 2nd ed. Calcutta, 1940 (1938).
Beveridge, W. H. *India Called Them.* London, 1947.
Chapman, E. F. *Sketches of Some Distinguished Indian Women.* London and Calcutta, 1891.
Das, H. *Life and Letters of Toru Dutt.* Oxford, 1921.
Dutt, G. S. *A Woman of India—Being the Life of Saroj Nalini (Founder of the Women's Institute Movement in India) by Her Husband.* 2nd ed. London, 1929 (Bengali original 1926).
Gangooly, J. C. *Life and Religion of the Hindoos, with a Sketch of My Life and Experience.* London, 1860.
Ghosh, M. N., ed. *The Life of Grish Chunder Ghose, the Founder and First Editor of the 'The Hindoo Patriot' and 'The Bengalee' by One Who Knew Him.* Calcutta, 1911.
————. *Memoirs of Kali Prosunno Singh.* Calcutta, 1920.
Gupta, J. N. *Life and Work of Romesh Chunder Dutt.* London, 1911.
Mazumdar, S. *A Pattern of Life. The Memoirs of an Indian Woman.* Edited by G. Forbes. New Delhi, 1977.
Mukherjee, N. *A Bengal Zamindar: Jaykrishna Mukherjee of Uttarpara and His Times 1808-1888.* Calcutta, 1975.
Ray, P. C. *Life and Experiences of a Bengali Chemist.* Calcutta, 1932.
Roy, M. *My Life's Partner.* Translated by D. S. Mahalanobis. Calcutta, 1945 (1936).
Sarkar, H. C. *Ananda Mohan Bose.* Calcutta, 1929.
Sen, S. *Memoirs of an Octogenarian.* Simla, 1971.
Sorabji, C. *India Calling.* 2nd ed. London, 1935 (1934).
Storrow, E. *The Eastern Lily Gathered: A Memoir of Bala Shoon-*

daree Tagore with Observations on the Position and Prospects of Hindu Female Society. London, 1852.

Sunity Devee, Maharani of Cooch Behar. *The Autobiography of an Indian Princess.* London, 1921.

Tagore, Rabindranath. *Reminiscences.* Madras, 1971 (1917).

Tattvabhushan, S. *Autobiography.* Calcutta, no date.

Other contemporary works

BENGALI

Acarjya, Carucandra. *Sabhyatā-sangkat.* Calcutta, 1900.

Bamabodhini Sabha. *Bāmāracanābalī; pratham bhāg; The Hare Prize Fund Essay.* Calcutta, 1872.

Bandopadhyay, Bharatcandra. *Susrusā pranālī.* Calcutta, 1896.

Bandopadhyay, Candicaran. *Mā o chele.* Calcutta, 1887.

Bandopadhyay, Candranath. *Bīrānganā upākhyān.* Bhowanipore, 1871.

Basu, Amritalal. *Tājjab byāpār.* Calcutta, 1890.

Basu, Candranath. *Gārhasthyapāth.* 2nd ed. Calcutta, 1887 (1885).

Basu, Jogendracandra. *Jogendracandra Basu racanābalī (pratham khanda).* Edited by Nirmal Das. Calcutta, 1976.

———. *Model bhaginī.* 12th ed. Calcutta, 1905 (1886).

Basu, Mankumari. "Nabyagrihinī." *Bāmābodhinī Patrikā,* 4:2 (December 1888), 287.

Basu, Nandakrisna. *Bāmābodh.* Calcutta, 1879.

Bhattacarjya, Rakhaldas. *Swādhīn jenānā (Female Emancipation).* 2nd ed. Calcutta, 1886.

Biswas, Tarakanath. *Bangīya-mahilā. Arthāth nārījātir siksā bisayak prastāb.* Calcutta, 1886.

Bose, Rajnarain. *Se kāl ār e kāl.* Calcutta, 1976 (1874).

Chatterjee, Bankim Chandra. *Bangkim racanābalī,* Part Two. Edited by J. C. Bagal. 5th ed. Calcutta, 1973 (1954).

———. *Bankim Rachanavali (English Works).* Edited by J. C. Bagal. Calcutta, 1969.

———. *Bibidha prabandha (pratham o dwitīya bhāg).* Calcutta, 1964 (1939).

Chaudhuri, Hemantakumari. "Susrusā kārinī." *Antahpur,* 3 (September 1900), 8.

Dasgupta, Ambujasundari. "Kalikātār Gangāsnān." *Bāmābodhinī Patrikā,* 8:1 (November 1904), 495.

Dasgupta, Ambujasundari. "Kāsībāsinī." *Bāmābodhinī Patrikā*, 8:2 (June-July 1905), 502-503.

De, Durgadas. *Encore! 99!!!* or *Srīmatī*. Calcutta, 1899.

———. *Mis Bino Bibi Bi E (onār in e kors)*. Barisal, 1898.

Deb, Shib Chunder. *Sisupālan*. Part 1, Serampore, 1857; part 2, Calcutta, 1862.

Dutt, Gopal Chunder. *Sulochona or the Examplary Wife (A Story of Bengal Domestic Life); Sulocanā athabā ādarsa bhāsyā (bangabāsīdiger sangsārik byabahārābalambit upanyās)*. Calcutta, 1882.

Dutt, Michael Madhusudan. *Madhusudan racanābalī*. Edited by Brajendranath Bandopadhyay. Calcutta, 1965.

Ghose, Benoy. *Sāmayikpatre Bānglār samājcitra 1840-1905*. Part 1, Calcutta, 1962; part 2, Calcutta, 1963; part 3, Calcutta, 1964; part 4, Calcutta, 1966.

Ghose, Surjanarayan. *Boijnānik dāmpatya-pranālī arthāth bibāha, indriyaseban o santān uthpādan bisaye boijnānerbidhi ebang aboidha indriyasebaner pratiphal o pratikār, indriya sangjaman nārījātir janendriyer byādhi ityādir bibaran sangraha*. Dacca, 1884.

Gupta, Amritalal. "Mahilādiger sabhā samiti." *Bāmābodhinī Patrikā*, 8:1 (December 1904-January 1905), 496-497.

———. "Siksitā ramanīdiger kartabya." *Bāmābodhinī Patrikā*, 8:1 (June 1904), 490.

———. "Siksitā ramanīdiger samājer prati kartabya." *Bāmābodhinī Patrikā*, 8:1 (September-October 1904), 493-494.

———. "Swadesī āndolan o ramanīr kartabya." *Bāmābodhinī Patrikā*, 8:2 (April 1906), 512.

Gupta, Mohendracandra. *Strībodh*. Dacca, 1862.

Gupta, Purnacandra. *Bāngālī bou, or the Instructive Lessons on the Career of Life of the Native Females*. Calcutta, 1885.

Gupta, Ramtanu. *Strī-siksā pratham bhāg*. Calcutta, 1861.

Gupta, Swarnamayi. *Ūsā-cintā. Arthāth ādhunik ārjya mahilāganer abasthā samandhe kayekti kathā*. Calcutta, 1888.

Haldar, Radhabinod. *Pāskarā māg*. Calcutta, 1888.

Kavyabisharad, Kaliprasanna. *The Hitabadi Defamation Case. Rucibikār*. 3rd ed. Calcutta, 1899 (1897).

Khastagir, Annada Charan. *A Treatise on the Science and Practice of Midwifery with Diseases of Children and Women*. Mānab-

janmatattwa, dhātrī bidyā, nabaprasūt sisu o strījātir byādhi-sangraha. 2nd ed. Calcutta, 1878 (1868).

Koilasbasini Debi. *Hindu Female Education and Its Progress. Hindu abalākuler bidyābhās o tāhār sammunnati*. Calcutta, 1865.

———. *Hindumahilāganer hīnābasthā*. Calcutta, 1863.

Kundamala Debi. "Bidyā sikhile ki grihakarmma karite nāi?" *Bāmābodhinī Patrikā*, 6 (October 1870), 86.

Lahiri, Durgadas. *Dvādas nārī bā ārjya-mahilā*. Calcutta, 1884.

Lahiri, Radharani, ed. *Prabandha-latikā*. Calcutta, 1880.

Mahiladiger Tattwajnan Sabha. *Uddesya o niyamābalī*. Calcutta, 1882.

Mem sāheb (Byāngopanyās). Calcutta, 1886.

Meyekartrik likhit (pseudonym). *Āin! Āin!! Āin!!! Bhayānak bipad! Sarbbanāser kathā!! Kamalkāminī o Sureshbhāminīr kathopkathan*. Dacca, 1890.

Mitra, Lilabati. "Grihaswāsthye ramanīr dristi." *Antahpur*, 7 (January 1905), 9.

———. "Oalteyār." *Antahpur*, 7 (October 1904), 6.

———. "Strīlokdiger arthakarī silpasiksā." *Antahpur*, 7 (July 1904), 3.

Mitra, Peary Chand. *Pyārīcād racanābalī*. Edited by Asitkumar Bandopadhyay. Calcutta, 1971.

Mozoomdar, P. C. *Strīcaritra*. 3rd ed. Calcutta, 1936 (1890).

Mukhopadhyay, Bipradas. *Soukhin-khādya-pāk. Arthāth khecarānna, palānna, kāliyā, kormmā, sik, kābāb, kopta, katlet, cap, ityādi randhaner niyam*. Part one, Calcutta, 1889.

Mukhopadhyay, Jogendranath. *Jībanraksā*. Calcutta, 1887.

Nabin-Kali Dasi. *Kumārī siksā*. Calcutta, 1883.

Nagendrabala Mustaphi. "Prayojanīya prārthanā." *Bāmābodhinī Patrikā*, 5:3 (October 1894), 357.

———. "Samājonnatite nārījāti." *Bāmābodhinī Patrikā*, 8:1 (February 1905), 498.

Prasannamayi Dasi. *Bibhutiprabhā nātak*. Faridpur, 1905.

Ray, Jogendranarayan. *Banga-mahilā*. Chinsurah, 1881.

Ray, Kumudini. "Hindu nārīr gārhasthya dharmma." *Bāmābodhinī Patrikā*, 5:3 (December 1884), 359.

Ray, Siddheswar. *Boubābu*. Calcutta, 1889.

[Sadharan Brahmo Samaj]. *Sangīt-mukul (Brāhma bālak bālikādiger janya rabibāsarik noitik bidyālay kartrik pracārita)*. Calcutta, 1886.

Sanyal, Pulin. *Saral sisupālan. A Manual on the Management and Medical Treatment of Native Children.* Calcutta, 1885.

Sanyal, Trailokyanath. *Kesab carit.* 3rd ed. Calcutta, 1931 (1884). He uses the pseudonym Ciranjib Sarma.

Sarkar, Kedarnath. *Ritu-raksā.* Calcutta, 1891.

Sarkar, Pyaridas. *Strīsiksā pratham khanta.* Calcutta, 1876.

Sarma, Tarasankar. *Bhārat barsīya strīganer bidyā siksā. A Prize Essay on Hindu Female Education. The Zenana Opened, or a Brahmin Advocating Female Emancipation.* 2nd ed. Calcutta, 1851.

Sastri, Sibnath. *Sibnāth racanāsangraha.* Calcutta, 1975.

Sen, Candrakisor. *Rogi-carjyā.* Calcutta, 1895.

Sen, Keshub Chunder. *Bidhān bhagnī sanggha.* New ed. Calcutta, 1932.

Sen, Nabincandra. *Prabāser patra. Bhārater bhraman-brittānta.* Calcutta, 1892.

Soi (Kārjyakarī strī-siksā-sahacarī). Calcutta, 1890.

[Swarnakumari Debi]. *Sakhi samiti.* Calcutta, 1886.

———. *Srīmatīswarnakumārīgranthābalī.* Calcutta, 1916.

Uma Sundari Dasi. *Nārīracit-kābya.* Calcutta, 1879. She uses the pseudonym "Kono hindu kulanārī."

[Vidyalankar, Gourmohan]. *Strī siksā bidhāyak. Arthāth purātan o idānīntan o bidesīya strī loker siksār dristānta. The Importance of Female Education; or Evidence in Favour of the Education of Hindoo Females, from the Examples of Illustrious Women, Both Ancient and Modern.* Calcutta, 1822.

ENGLISH

Adam, W. *Reports on the State of Education in Bengal (1835 and 1838).* Edited by A. M. Basu. Calcutta, 1941.

[Ashmore, H.] *Narrative of a Three Months' March in India; and a Residence in the Doab, by the Wife of an Officer in the 16th Foot,* London, 1841.

Banerjea, K. M. *Native Female Education.* 2nd ed. Calcutta, 1858 (1841).

———. "Reform, Civil and Social." In G. Chattopadhyay, ed., *Awakening in Bengal in Early Nineteenth Century.* Calcutta, 1965, pp. 182-198.

Barnes, I. H. *Behind the Pardah. The Story of C.E.Z.M.S. Work in India.* 5th ed. London, 1902 (1897).

Bethune Society. *The Proceedings and Transactions of the Bethune Society from November 10th 1859 to April 20th 1869*. Calcutta, 1870.

Billington, M. F. *Woman in India*. London, 1895.

Bose, S. C. *The Hindoos as They Are. A Description of the Manners, Customs and Inner Life of Hindoo Society in Bengal*. Calcutta, 1881.

Carpenter, M. *Six Months in India*. 2 vols. London, 1868.

Chapman, P. *Hindoo Female Education*. London, 1839.

Chatterjee, Bankim Chandra. *Durgesa Nandini or the Chieftain's Daughter, A Bengali Romance*. Translated by Charu Chandra Mookerjee. 2nd ed. Calcutta, 1903 (Bengali original 1865).

————. *Krishnakanta's Will*. Translated by J. C. Ghosh. New York, 1962 (Bengali original 1878).

Chattopadhyay, G., ed. *Awakening in Bengal in Early Nineteenth Century (Selected Documents)*. Vol. I. Calcutta, 1965.

Chavasse, P. H. *Counsel to a Mother. On the Management of Her Children Being a Continuation and the Completion of "Advice to a Mother."* London, 1869.

Chunder, B. *The Travels of a Hindoo to Various Parts of Bengal and Upper India*. 2 vols. London, 1869.

Cobbe, F. P. *The Duties of Women. A Course of Lectures*. 2nd ed. London, 1882.

————. "Keshub Chunder Sen." *East & West*, 2 (September 1903), 23.

Collet, S. D. *Brahmo Marriages: Their Past History and Present Position*. London, 1871.

Cooper, E. *The Harim and the Purdah. Studies of Oriental Women*. New York, 1915.

Das, D. N. *Sketches of Hindoo Life*. London, 1887.

Davies, E. *Thoughts on Some Questions Relating to Women*. New York, 1971 (Cambridge, 1910).

Diver, M. *The Englishwoman in India*. London, 1909.

Dutt, R. C. *The Lake of Palms. A Story of Indian Domestic Life*. Translated by R. C. Dutt. London, 1902. Translated from *Sangsār*, 1885.

————. *Three Years in Europe 1868 to 1871 with an Account of Subsequent Visits to Europe in 1886 and 1893*. 4th ed. Calcutta, 1896 (1872).

Dutt, S. C. *India, Past and Present; With Minor Essays on Cognate Subjects.* London, 1880.

Dutt Gupta, B. *Sociology in India: An Enquiry into Sociological Thinking and Empirical Social Research in the Nineteenth Century—with Special Reference to Bengal.* Calcutta, 1972.

Ellis, E. *The Daughters of England, Their Position in Society, Character & Responsibilities.* London, 1842.

Fuller, M. B. *The Wrongs of Indian Womanhood.* New York, 1900.

Ganguli, T. N. *Svarnalata or Scenes from Hindu Village Life in Bengal.* Translation, 2nd ed. Calcutta, 1906 (Bengali original 1874).

Ghose, Girish Chunder. "Female Occupations in Bengal." Address to the Bengal Social Science Association. In B. Dutt Gupta, *Sociology in India.* Calcutta, 1972, Appendix V.

Ghose, Monomohan. "The Effects of English Education upon Bengali Society." In Bethune Society, *The Proceedings and Transactions of the Bethune Society. . . .* Calcutta, 1870.

Ghosh, M. N., ed. *Selections from the Writings of Grish Chunder Ghose: The Founder and First Editor of "The Hindoo Patriot" and "The Bengalee."* Calcutta, 1912.

Halsted, C. A. *The Obligations of Literature to the Mothers of England.* London, 1840.

Hamilton, W. *A Geographical, Statistical, and Historical Description of Hindoostan and the Adjacent Countries.* Vol. I. London, 1820.

Heber, R. *Narrative of a Journey through the Upper Provinces of India, from Calcutta to Bombay, 1824-25 (with notes upon Ceylon).* 2 vols. New ed. London, 1861.

Humphrey, E. J. *Gems of India; or, Sketches of Distinguished Hindoo and Mahomedan Women.* New York, 1875.

International Abolitionist Federation. *The New Abolitionists. A Narrative of a Year's Work. Being an Account of the Mission Undertaken to the Continent of Europe by Mrs. Josephine E. Butler and of the Events Subsequent Thereupon.* London, 1876.

Johnson, G. W. *The Stranger in India; or, Three Years in Calcutta.* London, 1843.

Kerr, J. *The Domestic Life, Character, and Customs of the Natives of India.* London, 1865.

Mackenzie, C. *Life in the Mission, the Camp, and the Zenáná; or, Six Years in India.* 2 vols. 2nd ed. London, 1854.

Mill, J. *The History of British India*. Vol. I. 4th ed. London, 1840 (1818).

Mitra, Peary Chand. "A Few Desultory Remarks on the 'Cursory Review of the Institutions of Hindooism Affecting the Interest of the Female Sex,' Contained in the Reverend K. M. Banerjia's Prize Essay on Native Female Education." In G. Chattopadhyay, ed., *Awakening in Bengal in Early Nineteenth Century*. Calcutta, 1965, pp. 273-297.

Mittra, B. M. "The Native Theatre." *Nineteenth Century Studies*, Calcutta, 6 (1974), 190-196.

Mozoomdar, P. C. "The Emancipation of Women in Bengal." *Calcutta Review*, 118 (April 1904), 125-131.

———. *Heart-Beats*. Calcutta, 1935 (1894).

———. "Hindu Women." *Theistic Quarterly Review*, 3 (October 1879).

Nightingale, Florence, "Cassandra" (1859). In R. Strachey, *The Cause: A Short History of the Women's Movement in Great Britain*. London, 1928, pp. 395-418.

Pal, D. N. *The Hindu Wife. A Few Sketches from Her Life*. 2nd ed. Calcutta, 1911 (1888).

Parkes, F. *Wanderings of a Pilgrim in Search of the Picturesque, during Four-and-Twenty Years in the East; with Revelations of Life in the Zenana*. Vol. I. London, 1850.

Roy, Raja Rammohun. *The English Works of Raja Rammohun Roy*. Edited by J. C. Ghose. Vol. II. Calcutta, 1901.

Ruskin, J. *Sesame and Lilies, Unto This Last, The Political Economy of Art*. New ed. London, 1907.

Sastri, Sibnath. *History of the Brahmo Samaj*. 2nd ed. Calcutta, 1974 (1911-1912).

———. *A History of the Renaissance in Bengal. Ramtanu Lahiri: Brahman and Reformer*. Translated by R. Lethbridge, 1907. 3rd English ed. Calcutta, 1972 (Bengali original 1904).

Sen, Keshub Chunder. "The Improvement of Indian Women." Address to the Bengal Social Science Association. In B. Dutt Gupta, *Sociology in India*. Calcutta, 1972, Appendix V.

Staley, M. E. *Handbook for Wives & Mothers in India*. Calcutta, 1908.

Sunity Devee, Maharani of Cooch Behar. *Nine Ideal Indian Women*. Calcutta, 1919.

[Swarnakumari Debi] Mrs. Ghosal. *An Unfinished Song*. London, 1913. Translated from *Kāhāke*, 1898.

Tattvabhushan, S. *The Philosophy of Brahmaism Expounded with Reference to Its History*. Madras, 1909.

University of Calcutta. *Convocation Addresses*. Vol. I, 1858-79; Vol. II, 1880-98. Calcutta, 1914.

Weitbrecht, Mrs. *The Women of India, and Christian Work in the Zenana*. Translated from the German. London, 1875.

Wollstonecraft, M. *Vindication of the Rights of Women*. Edited by M. Kraminck. London, 1975 (1792).

Government publications

Bengal Census, 1872
Bengal Census, 1881
Bengal Census, 1901
Bengal Library Catalogue of Books. Quarterly Appendix to the Calcutta Gazette, 1867-1889
Calcutta Census, 1872
Calcutta City Census, 1876
Calcutta. Town and Suburbs Census, 1881
Calcutta. Town and Suburbs Census, 1891
Calcutta. Town and Suburbs Census, 1901
First Annual Report of the Sanitary Commissioner for Bengal, 1868, Calcutta, 1869
General Report on Public Instruction in the Lower Provinces of the Bengal Presidency for 1846-47. Calcutta, 1847
———— *for 1847-48*. Calcutta, 1848
———— *from 1st May 1848 to 1st October 1849*. Calcutta, 1850
———— *from 1st October 1849 to 30th September 1850*. Calcutta, 1851
———— *from 1st October 1850 to 30th September 1851*. Calcutta, 1852
———— *for 1860-61*. Calcutta, 1862
———— *for 1869-70*. Calcutta, 1870
General Report on Public Instruction in Bengal for 1875-76. Calcutta, 1876
———— *for 1877-78*. Calcutta, 1878
The Quarterly Civil List for Bengal, 47. Calcutta, 1878

Report of the Sanitary Commissioner for Bengal for the Year 1876. Calcutta, 1877

Report on Native Newspapers, Bengal. 1863-1906

Reports of Publications Issued and Registered in the Several Provinces of British India. Bengal, 1881-1890, 1892, 1894-1898

Richey, J. A. *Selections from Educational Records. Part II.* New Delhi, 1965 (Calcutta, 1922)

Selections from Educational Records of the Government of India, v. I. *Educational Reports, 1859-71, Being Two "Notes on the State of Education in India" Compiled by A. M. Monteath in 1862 and 1867 and Part Two of "Education in British India prior to 1854 and in 1870-71" by A. P. Howell.* Delhi, 1960

Sharp, H. *Progress of Education in India 1907-1912. Sixth Quinquennial Review.* Vol. I. Calcutta, 1914

Private papers and miscellaneous items

Akroyd-Beveridge Papers. India Office Library. Akroyd, A.
    1. Governess Certificate 1872
    2. Pocket diary 1873
    3. Pocket diary 1874
    4. Pocket diary 1875
    5. Diary and Notebook in India 1872-1878
    6. List of donors—Hindu Mahila Bidayalaya
    7. Letters to Fanny Mowatt 1873, 1874
    8. Letters from D. N. Ganguly 1874
    9. Letter to S. D. Collet 1873

Akroyd-Beveridge Papers. India Office Library. Beveridge, W. H.
    1. Letters to Annette Akroyd 1875
    2. Letters 1875

Sisir Kumari Bagchi (privately held)
    Two books given to her as wedding presents in 1898

Indira Debi Caudhurani. (Rabindra Bhavan Library, Visvabharati University, Santiniketan.) Scrapbook

Hemantakumari Chaudhuri (privately held)
    1. *Srādh* memoir of her husband
    2. Letters to her daughter Santa

S. D. Collet Collection. Sadharan Brahmo Samaj Library
    1. Notes on Brahmo Marriages, 1871 (manuscript)
    2. Brahmo Marriage Records, I, July 1861—December 1875

3. Scrapbooks of newspaper cuttings 1862-1875
Sarajubala Dasgupta (privately held)
  1. Memoir (manuscript)
  2. Letters to her daughter Manashi
Hemanta Kumari Misra (privately held)
  Songbook, from 1892

Interviews

J. Bose, Calcutta, 10 March 1978
Sita Chakrabarti, Calcutta, 29 November 1977
Sailaja Chakravarty, Calcutta, 13 February 1978
Roma Chatterjee, Calcutta, 6 October 1977
Manashi Dasgupta, Santiniketan, 15 November 1977; Calcutta, 9
    December 1977
Santa Deb, Calcutta, 1 March 1978; 19 March 1978
Kalyan Dutt, Santiniketan, 16 November 1977
Hemlata Gupta, Santiniketan, 15 November 1977
Usha Haldar, Calcutta, 13 March 1978
Subala Lal, Calcutta, 29 November 1977
Lila Majumdar, Santiniketan, 15 November 1977
Sudhamayi Mukhopadhyay, Santiniketan, 16 November 1977
Manika Ray, Calcutta, 14 February 1978
Uma Ray, Calcutta, 29 November 1977
Santi Roy, Calcutta, 3 March 1978
Reba Sarkar, Calcutta, 28 September 1977
Amita Sen, Calcutta, 25 November 1977

SELECTED SECONDARY SOURCES

BENGALI

Bagal, J. C. *Jātīya āndolane banganārī.* Calcutta, 1954.
Bandopadhyay, Brajendranath. *Sāmayikpatra-sampādane banga-
    nārī.* Calcutta, 1950.
Basu, Ramdulal. *Bankimcandrer samkālīn goun oupanyāsikbrinda.*
    Calcutta, 1974.
Dasgupta, Kamala. *Swādhīnatā-sangrāme bānglār nārī.* Calcutta, 1963.
Gangopadhyay, Prabhatcandra. *Bānglār nārī-jāgaran.* Calcutta, 1945.
Mitra, Rhadaraman. "Gangār ghāt." *Oitihāsik,* 4 (January 1977).

Ray, Chabi. *Bānglār nārī āndolan—sangrāmī bhūmikāy dersa' bachar.* Calcutta, 1955.

Victoria Institution. *Bhiktoriyā institiusan satabarsa smaranikā 1277-1377.* Calcutta, 1971.

ENGLISH

Allen, M., and Mukherjee, S. N., eds. *Women in India and Nepal.* Canberra, 1982.

Bagal, J. C. "History of the Bethune School and College," Appendix I. In K. Nag, ed., *Bethune School and College Centenary Volume 1849-1949.* Calcutta, 1949.

———. *Women's Education in Eastern India—The First Phase (Mainly Based on Contemporary Records).* Calcutta, 1956.

Baroda, Maharani of, and Mitra, S. M. *The Position of Women in Indian Life.* London, 1911.

Borthwick, M. *Keshub Chunder Sen. A Search for Cultural Synthesis.* Calcutta, 1977.

———. "Young Bengal and the Waning of Its Radical Impact in the 1830s and 1840s." BA Honours thesis, Department of Indian Studies, University of Melbourne, 1972.

Boserup, E. *Woman's Role in Economic Development.* London, 1970.

Branca, P. *Silent Sisterhood: Middle-Class Women in the Victorian Home.* 2nd ed. London, 1977 (1975).

Broomfield, J. H. *Elite Conflict in a Plural Society: Twentieth-Century Bengal.* Berkeley and Los Angeles, 1968.

Cattell, M. *Behind the Purdah or The Lives and Legends of Our Hindu Sisters.* Calcutta, 1916.

Chakraborty, U. *Condition of Bengali Women around the 2nd Half of the 19th Century.* Calcutta, 1963.

Chatterji, B. "Gooroodass Banerjee and His Times. An Enquiry into the Socio-Political Conditions in Bengal, Late 19th and Early 20th Centuries." Calcutta, 1976 (unpublished).

Cowan, M. G. *The Education of the Women of India.* Edinburgh, 1912.

Davidoff, L. *The Best Circles. Society, Etiquette and the Season.* London, 1973.

Delamont, S., and Duffin, L., eds. *The Nineteenth-Century Woman. Her Cultural and Physical World.* London, 1978.

De Mause, L., ed. *The History of Childhood.* New York, 1974.

Ehrenreich, B., and English, D. *Complaints and Disorders. The Sexual Politics of Sickness.* London, 1976 (New York, 1973).

Forbes, G. H. "Votes for Women: The Demand for Women's Franchise in India 1917-1937." In V. Mazumdar, ed., *Symbols of Power. Studies on the Political Status of Women in India.* Bombay, 1979.

Ghose, L. "Social and Educational Movements for and by Women." In K. Nag, ed., *Bethune School and College Centenary Volume 1849-1949.* Calcutta, 1949.

Haller, J. S., and Haller, R. M. *The Physician and Sexuality in Victorian America.* Urbana, Illinois, 1974.

Hartman, M., and Banner, L. W., eds. *Clio's Consciousness Raised. New Perspectives on the History of Women.* New York, 1974.

Jeffery, P. *Frogs in a Well. Indian Women in Purdah.* London, 1979.

Kamm, J. *How Different From Us. A Biography of Miss Buss and Miss Beale.* London, 1958.

Kopf, D. *The Brahmo Samaj and the Shaping of the Modern Indian Mind.* Princeton, 1979.

———. *British Orientalism and the Bengal Renaissance. The Dynamics of Indian Modernization 1773-1835.* Berkeley and Los Angeles, 1969.

Laird, M. A. *Missionaries and Education in Bengal 1793-1837.* London, 1972.

McBride, T. M. *The Domestic Revolution. The Modernisation of Household Service in England and France 1820-1920.* New York, 1976.

McLane, J. R. "Calcutta and the Mofussilization of Bengali Politics." In R. L. Park, ed., *Urban Bengal.* Ann Arbor, 1969, pp. 63-85.

McLaren, A. *Birth Control in Nineteenth-Century England.* London, 1978.

McGuire, J. *The Making of a Colonial Mind: A Quantitative Study of the Bhadralok in Calcutta, 1857-1885.* Canberra, 1982.

Miller, J. H. " 'Temple and Sewer': Childbirth, Prudery, and Victoria Regina." In A. S. Wohl, ed., *The Victorian Family. Structure and Stresses.* London, 1978, pp. 23-43.

Mukherjee, S. N. "Bhadralok in Bengali Language and Literature: An Essay on the Language of Class and Status." *Bengal Past and Present,* 95:2:181 (July-December 1976), 225-237.

———. *Calcutta: Myths and History,* Calcutta, 1977.

———. "The Social Implications of the Political Thought of Raja

Rammohun Roy." In R. S. Sharma and V. Jha, eds., *Indian Society: Historical Probings. In Memory of D. D. Kosambi.* New Delhi, 1974, pp. 356-389.

Mukherji, S. K. *Prostitution in India.* Calcutta, 1934.

Nag, K., ed. *Bethune School and College Centenary Volume 1849-1949.* Calcutta, 1949.

Papanek, H. "Men, Women, and Work: Reflections on the Two-Person Career." In J. Huber, ed., *Changing Women in a Changing Society.* Chicago, 1973, pp. 90-110.

————. "Purdah: Separate Worlds and Symbolic Shelter." *Comparative Studies in Society and History*, 15 (1973), 289-325.

————, and Minault, G., eds. *Separate Worlds: Studies of Purdah in South Asia.* Delhi, 1982.

Pastner, C. McC. "Accommodations to Purdah: The Female Perspective." *Journal of Marriage and the Family*, 36:2 (May 1974), 408-414.

Pearson, G. *Women in Public Life in Bombay City with Special Reference to the Civil Disobedience Movement.* Ph.D. dissertation, Jawaharlal Nehru University, 1979.

Pinkham, M. W. *Woman in the Sacred Scriptures of Hinduism.* New York, 1967 (1941).

Raychaudhuri, T. *Bengal under Akbar and Jahangir. An Introductory Study in Social History.* 2nd ed. Delhi, 1969 (1953).

Rogers, S. C. "Woman's Place: A Critical Review of Anthropological Theory." *Comparative Studies in Society and History*, 20:1 (January 1978), 123-162.

Rosaldo, M. Z., and Lamphere, L. *Woman, Culture, and Society.* Stanford, 1978 (1974).

Rowbotham, S. *Hidden from History. 300 Years of Women's Oppression and the Fight against It.* 3rd ed. Ringwood, Victoria, 1975 (London, 1973).

Roy, M. *Bengali Women.* Chicago, 1975.

Sarkar, S. *The Swadeshi Movement in Bengal 1903-1908.* New Delhi, 1973.

Sen, A. *Iswar Chandra Vidyasagar and His Elusive Milestones.* Calcutta, 1977.

Sen, P. K. *Biography of a New Faith.* 2 vols. Calcutta, 1950-1954.

Tilly, L. A. "The Social Sciences and the Study of Women: A Review Article." *Comparative Studies in Society and History*, 20:1 (January 1978), 163-173.

Trudgill, E. *Madonnas and Magdalens. The Origins and Development of Victorian Sexual Attitudes.* London, 1976.

Urquhart, M. M. *Women of Bengal. A Study of the Hindu Pardanasins of Calcutta.* 3rd ed. Calcutta, 1927 (1925).

Vicinus, M., ed. *Suffer and Be Still—Women in the Victorian Age.* Bloomington, Indiana, 1972.

——, ed. *A Widening Sphere. Changing Roles of Victorian Women.* Bloomington, Indiana, 1977.

Walton, R. G. *Women in Social Work.* London, 1975.

Index

393

Library of Congress Cataloging in Publication Data

Borthwick, Meredith.
The changing role of women in Bengal, 1849-1905.

Bibliography: p.   Includes index.
1. Women—India—Bengal—History—19th century.
2. Bengal (India)—Social conditions. I. Title.
HQ1744.B4B67   1984   305.4′2′095414   83-43061
ISBN 0-691-05409-6 (alk. paper)